Under the Whole Language Umbrella

Under the Whole Language Umbrella

Many Cultures, Many Voices

Edited by

Alan D. Flurkey
Kyrene Elementary School District, Tempe, Arizona, and
University of Arizona

Richard J. Meyer
University of Nebraska–Lincoln

National Council of Teachers of English
1111 W. Kenyon Road, Urbana, Illinois 61801-1096

Whole Language Umbrella
P.O. Box 2029
Bloomington, Indiana 47402-2029

Grateful acknowledgment is made for permission to reprint the following: Two illustrations from WE LOOK AND SEE by William S. Gray, Dorothy Baruch, and Elizabeth Rider Montgomery, illustrated by Eleanor Campbell. Copyright 1946 by Scott, Foresman and Company. Reprinted by permission. One chart, reprinted by permission of Mark Collis and Joan Dalton: BECOMING RESPONSIBLE LEARNERS: STRATEGIES FOR POSITIVE CLASSROOM MANAGEMENT (Heinemann, A Division of Reed Elsevier Inc., Portsmouth, NH, 1991).

Manuscript Editor: Jane M. Curran

Production Editor: David Hamburg

Cover Design: Carlton Bruett; cover illustration by Blake Williamson

Interior Book Design: Doug Burnett

NCTE Stock Number: 30518-3050

The Whole Language Umbrella sees Whole Language as a dynamic philosophy of education. A confederation of Whole Language support groups and individuals, WLU serves Whole Language learning by promoting research, publications, and collaboration among educators.

Library of Congress Cataloging-in-Publication Data

Under the whole language umbrella : many cultures, many voices /
   edited by Alan D. Flurkey, Richard J. Meyer.
      p.   cm.
   Includes bibliographical references.
   ISBN 0-8141-3051-8
   1. Language experience approach in education. 2. Language arts
(Elementary) 3. Multicultural education. 4. Literacy.
I. Flurkey, Alan D., 1955–   . II. Meyer, Richard J., 1949–
LB1576.U52 1994
372.6—dc20   94–17030
                                                                  CIP

For Jane, who got so much started—A.D.F.

For Pat, Sadie, and Zoe—R.J.M.

Contents

Preface

The field of education is changing. This is evident from a variety of perspectives. There are sweeping panoramic views from which we can look at the competition between theories of language and learning and how they play out against each other in research and practice. We can look at literacy processes when multiple cultures and languages come together in a particular setting. We can inspect the ways that politics and education influence each other by looking at changes in law and policy. Or we can scale down even further to see how an individual learns the conventions of language; a young writer demonstrates sufficient control over genre and letter-sound relationships to achieve her goals by writing a personal correspondence; a young reader comes to know the world through literature. As professional educators, we can even turn our sights on ourselves by asking how we can best come to know the breadth of issues in this field and how we can advocate for our students and best support their learning.

To find where the most dramatic changes in educational practice are occurring, we need to look no further than those who are involved with whole language. Within the past twenty-five years, modern theories of literacy processes and language learning have brought astonishing change to the field of education with their implications for child-centered, meaning-centered practice. As an educational philosophy, whole language brings to the field a depth that can only come from powerful explanations for the processes of reading and writing, how people use literacy in their daily lives, how to meet the special needs of learners, how to construct a meaningful curriculum, and how we can move forward as professionals. These are the topics addressed by the chapters in this book. The contributors are among the most respected writers, researchers, teachers, and teacher educators in the field, and the reader will notice that the timbre of each voice is pronounced—enhanced. This is because the chapters draw their inspiration from presentations at "Many Cultures, Many Voices," the second annual Whole Language Umbrella Conference in Phoenix, Arizona. Read on, and you will find that these writers describe perspectives and practices which are bold and innovative.

Simple summations or characterizations cannot capture the essence of something as complex as an educational movement. Yet when we watch our students at play and note that their use of language mirrors the forms and functions of language used outside school; when we visit whole language classrooms and marvel at the control that their members exercise over the creation of curriculum; when the meanings that we ascribe to what we see are changed by the thoughtful writings of other teachers and researchers—then the metaphor of renaissance seems so apt. A whole language classroom where learners are invited to share in the creation of knowledge stands in stark contrast to the case of teaching as handing out programmed materials and grading worksheets. Indeed, Ken Goodman (in press) has regarded his psycho-sociolinguistic transactional model of reading, a concept crucial to understanding how whole language works, in terms of the Copernican revolution of thought about the universe, a scientific milestone of the Renaissance. Just as Copernicus provided medieval astronomers with an entirely new understanding of the heavens, the theories of language and learning associated with whole language have provided educators with a new way to think about learning, curriculum, and pedagogy.

With its powerful explanations, whole language has implications for the professionalization of teachers; whole language represents a revolution in thought that liberates teachers to be professionals. Teachers who subscribe to holistic theories of language learning no longer need to rely upon programmed materials, criterion-referenced test profiles, or administrative edicts to tell them how to teach their students. Instead, their curricular decisions are guided by what they know about learning and the knowledge of the literacy lives of the individuals in their classrooms. For whole language teachers who have been invigorated by coming to know the world through and with their students, for those who have undergone their own personal revolution of thought, this, indeed, is a bright time.

Reference

Goodman, K. In press. Reading, writing and written texts: A transactional, sociopsycholinguistic view. In *Theoretical models and processes of reading*, 4th ed., ed. Robert B. Ruddell, M. R. Ruddell, and H. Singer. Newark, Del.: International Reading Association.

Acknowledgments

We have had much help and support in bringing together the diverse voices in this volume. We wish to thank Dorothy Watson, who, as president of the Whole Language Umbrella, suggested that we draw together presentations from the second Whole Language Umbrella Conference in book form. Thanks also to Jerome Harste for his guidance in this effort, and to Yetta Goodman, who titled the conference and this selection of essays. We also wish to thank each of the contributors for their patience with the editing process.

We would like to acknowledge Michael Spooner, Jane Curran, and David Hamburg of NCTE for their guidance and thoughtful feedback throughout this process.

And as always in a work of this nature, we wish to thank our families for providing the support, patience, and time required to devote to this project.

Introduction: Three Themes

Richard J. Meyer
University of Nebraska–Lincoln

Alan D. Flurkey
Kyrene Elementary School District, Tempe, Arizona,
and University of Arizona

Teachers, teacher educators, educational researchers, and others involved with the school lives of children confront their own professional identity each day. We respond to the many complexities of our situations daily as we face children, other teachers, researchers, and various other colleagues. In doing this, we continually present who we are by acting on our knowledge base, our beliefs, and our understanding of the social setting in which we practice. Whole language educators are reflective about professional identity, and we work to be informed about research which, in turn, has an impact upon our practice. We listen to the many voices around us and learn from the diversity of cultures in which we live. These three themes—*identity, responsibility,* and *practice*—are at the heart of this book.

Identity and responsibility are not typically distinguished, and although we separate them in this book, they most certainly overflow into one another. Identity for whole language educators means understanding who we are as professionals, being aware of the community of educators to which we belong, and being aware of the issues which affect our practice. Responsibility refers to acting upon our identity. This includes being informed, being responsive, and being consciously and personally accountable for what we do. We work to keep ourselves informed of the research, politics, and other facets of education which might affect us. We also act upon the research and politics in order to advocate for those with whom we teach and do research. Such action includes advocacy, change in practice, reflection, consideration, and movement. As whole language educators, we are not comfortable accepting an identity from the situation in which we find ourselves. Rather, we form our own identities by taking responsibility for growing and learning as professionals.

Practice is the easiest theme to separate from the other two. Practice is tangible. Though there is not any single model of a whole language teacher's practice, there are many rich descriptions in the literature (see, for example, Wortman 1991 for the primary grades; Atwell 1987 for middle school; Newman 1991 for a description of her work with teachers). Practice is visible and operational—it is the day-to-day activity within the classroom which is informed by identity and responsibility. Practice, then, is informed and guided by responsibility and identity; identity is defined by practice and responsibility; and responsibility implies action with an impact on identity and practice.

Finally, we recognize that these three themes are woven together by the thread of reflection (Schon 1987; Newman 1991). As teachers, we are occasionally asked to support procedures or practices to which we do not subscribe philosophically. We may find ourselves confronted with pressures to have our students participate in "test wiseness" programs, or to compete for a "quietest line-up award." But instead of impulsively yielding to these pressures, it is the reflective quality that prompts whole language teachers to ask themselves difficult questions on a daily basis—questions like, "What will these children remember about this experience years from now?" or "What is the most important thing this student needs today?" or simply, "What is most important?" Indeed, we believe that the thoughtful, reflective stance that whole language teachers bring to their work best distinguishes them as professionals.

Identity

As whole language educators, we are part of a professional community which supports and helps us explore our individual understandings of reading, writing, speaking, and listening. Recently, influential writers have argued for restructuring preservice and in-service teacher education programs in our country as a solution to problems in the educational system (e.g., Goodlad 1990). Further, some have even called for the establishment of a national curriculum (Smith, O'Day, and Cohen 1990). There are many complex issues involved in the professionalization of teaching, but it seems to us that programs which target an entire system or span the country are flawed at their core. Broad programs like these tend to lose focus on professional choices that teachers make as individuals, and such programs are out of touch with issues at the very heart of the nature of teaching and learning. We argue that national programs which prescribe curricular goals without examining critical assumptions about the nature of literacy have the opposite effect on professionalization since they restrict the number and type of choices that teachers can make.

Rather than submit to pressures for change which come from the top down, we whole language teachers are taking control of much of the change that is expected of us. It is a trend which has its roots in more than twenty years of literacy research and which grows stronger and more noticeable with each year. We control change by seeking others who hold similar assumptions, thereby creating our own community of learners. And most importantly, we actively seek ways to improve our understanding of the processes of literacy, literacy instruction, research, and the ways in which they overlap.

Literacy Residence

The importance of the linguistic richness that children bring to school cannot be overstated. We need to begin with a respect for their knowledge of language and to build upon it in a way that enhances what they know. Our choice of what to do in the classroom will make the difference between experiences that students understand as assigned "work" and those that they see as authentic activity in an empowering setting (Cummins 1991). These decisions affect and are affected by our students' literacy residences.

We have created the term *literacy residence* to refer, metaphorically, to where an individual "lives" in terms of his or her literacy. It includes the oral language life of the individual and the impact of that oracy on learning to read and write as well as the functions of reading and writing in the person's life. It is extensive in that it includes all aspects of the oral and written language(s) in which a person communicates, including the rich social and cultural dimensions. We know that residence in a language is part of residence in culture and community. To understand literacy residence is to recognize the complexities of language. For example, in bilingual classrooms where language use is valued and unrestricted, close observation has revealed that very young bilingual children know to respond in different languages and tones based on their understanding of the linguistic competence of the receiver of their messages. They take into account a number of factors—the listener's age, social background, and competence in either language—so they can use language most effectively to meet their needs. This enables bilingual students to write to one student in their native language and speak to another in their second language—all with the appropriate formality and tone (Whitmore 1992).

A literacy residence, then, is a personal construction which is built within and across the many settings in an individual's life. There are cultural, economic, social, ethnic, gender, and political facets of literacy residence. In other words, literacy residence is that aspect of a person's identity which is related to literacy and language use. We have windows into each person's literacy residence when we listen to them speak, hear them read, and read their writing. In everyday dealings, our response to what a person shows us will affect what that person is willing to present in future encounters. When the setting is a classroom, the way in which students go about revealing their identities will be influenced by their perceptions of the teacher's identity—they wonder, "What is the teacher's expectation?" "Will my contribution to a discussion or my piece of writing be warmly received?" As such, literacy residence is an issue of identity for the educator, as well as for the students—the tone of a classroom relies on the teacher's expression of his or her identity as well as issues related to the students' expression of their identities. Caring, sensitive educators who understand and value the many, complex aspects of language use know this: the depths and complexities of an individual's literacy residence can probably never be known, but a search for insights into its many issues can become an exciting point of departure for language and literacy study with learners of all ages.

We understand that children must be allowed to write, read, speak, and listen in order to come to terms with the language system in which they have literacy residence. Just as children learn to speak by learning language, learning about language, and learning through language (Halliday 1988), they learn to read and write in a parallel way. A child's first language is cultivated in the home (the residence), as are almost all of the tacit attitudes and beliefs about language which the child brings to school. Like learning oral language, developing control over reading and writing processes begins before a child comes to school and will continue in school under conditions supported by a responsible teacher. Indeed, once a child enters school, his or her literacy residence can be saturated by the literacy priorities in school. Depending on these priorities, a child's literacy residence is accepted and built upon or is ignored. It may be devalued or even targeted for reconstruction—usually at the discretion of a teacher. In *Learning Denied*, Denny Taylor (1991) juxtaposes the richly literate home life with the school experiences of a child whose literacy residence is devalued or completely denied—Taylor chronicles what amounts to a proclamation of failure based upon a teacher's and school system's criteria for linguistic and academic competence. We believe that a teacher's stance—the way in which a teacher presents his or her identity to students—will either broaden the avenues of literacy development or drive that development to take place elsewhere.

Literacy residence is a *possibility,* and "[w]hen we are cut off or barred by others or by circumstances from the *possibility* of worth and meaning in our lives, we reap the pain of frustration, disappointment, hurt, and smoldering anger" associated with that denial (Carini 1987, 5). However, educators who cultivate their identities with a sophisticated awareness of literacy and language use appreciate the culture and language of individuals with whom they teach and learn. Intimidation and linguistic hegemony give way to academic democracy and opportunities for learning and teaching by all present.

Identity as a Condition for Teaching and Learning

Classrooms are not separate cultures unto themselves; however, depending on the teacher's identity, a classroom can be either open to the experiences of the world or closed-off and isolated. On the one hand, teachers and children may create a mutually constructed and negotiated setting which actively seeks to draw from the personal, social, and cultural experiences of all members; on the other hand, students may be relegated to the role of "recipient" in a completely teacher-dominated setting. But far from being truly passive recipients, students in either setting are aware of the parameters of the school setting. An example of the struggle some individuals face in dealing with restraints is found in Byrd Baylor's *Yes Is Better than No* as two Native Americans discuss ways of thinking:

> "But of course here in town with the Anglos you have to think in a different way. In their way."
> "Maria is trying to do that now . . . to think in their way. But I still got me an Indian mind," she says. "It won't think White. It thinks Indian."
> "Mine too," Rose says. "That's our *trouble.*" (1991, 123)

The "trouble" is not with Native Americans—or African Americans, or Hmong, or any other group—as much as it is with those people with whom these groups must interact in settings where the valued literacy residences are not their own.

Again, we want to stress that this is an area where teachers can make a direct and important difference. In the classroom, the circumstances of learning and teaching follow the contours of a teacher's identity. In this way, educators with a well-formed sense of identity can help others in the development of their own. As Jerome Harste and Carolyn Burke point out, the careful, thoughtful construction of the "instructional environment" (1979, 33) is the teacher's responsibility, and they urge teachers to understand the impact that it makes upon the children as learners.

Language and Culture

Literacy is a social and cultural activity in that reading, writing, speaking, and listening all have intended audiences and are purposeful activities. In any classroom, languages and cultures either collide or are woven together.

> The bonds of family, neighbourhood, class, occupation, country, and religion are knit by speech and language. We take eagerly to the magic of language because only by apprenticeship to it can we be admitted to association, fellowship and community in our social organisation which ministers to our needs and gives us what we want or what we deserve. The emphasis is on society and fellowship, in which a man [or a woman] may find his [or her] personality. (Firth 1950, 11)

But to successfully weave language and culture together, educators must give thought to how literacy works. Frank Smith (1986) offers one perspective in his development of the notion of a "literacy club," where prospective members learn to control written language as they become inducted into a "club" that they want to join. Hopeful initiates pursue membership because the activities that membership affords are useful, interesting, and enjoyable. And they like the people. They are shepherded by proficient mentors with whom they want to associate in much the same fashion that members are inducted into clubs like chess clubs or sports teams. The responsible educator, acting on behalf of children, understands the nature of clubs. Through his or her understanding of the club dynamic, the teacher works to assure that all students may join.

In the classroom, the teacher creates the context for the social activity, which can be more learner-centered and "clublike" in tone or, conversely, more teacher-controlled.

> Because the teacher has the power to define the context of the reading event, it is the teacher's definition of sense that becomes the criterion through which success is measured in that event. The student's failure to read the passage in a manner consistent with the teacher's definition of the context of the event may reflect the limited extent to which the teacher and student shared a definition of the event. (Bloome 1983, 171)

In describing the nature of literacy and language learning in school, Bloome and Green illuminate literacy's complex and interdependent variables by viewing setting as composed of concentric rings. Language and individual expectations are at the center, and the rings move outward to include instructional setting, institutional setting, community setting, societal setting, and cultural setting (1982, 310–11). Classrooms, being embedded in culture and constructed of individuals, consist of slices of all of these rings. In any act of teaching and learning there is a complex interplay of personal, social, and cultural variables that are unique to any group of students. Teachers who recognize this are better able to nurture literacy and language learning. In collaboration with their students, such teachers become community builders—experts at arranging conditions which allow literacy to flourish (Cairney and Langbien 1989; Hansen 1987, chapter 7).

Responsibility

As teachers, we assume professional responsibility when we choose to gain an understanding of current research and reported practices and to incorporate those understandings into individual practice. We also exercise professional responsibility by contributing to the field's knowledge base as we report to our colleagues what we have learned about what takes place in our own classrooms. Ferreiro (1991) discusses a teacher's intellectual growth as "pedagogic consequences" of professional responsibility; these are the decisions which the teacher brings to the classroom, tacitly or explicitly. Whole language educators are actively involved in understanding the learning that takes place in the classroom and seek to make explicit, articulated, well-informed decisions.

John Dewey knew the importance of teacher responsibility and saw some of the roadblocks to it. His sentiments, poignant and fresh after ninety years, could have been written yesterday:

> The tendency of educational development to proceed by reaction from one thing to another, to adopt for one year, or for a term of seven years, this or that new study or method of teaching, and then as abruptly to swing over to some new education gospel, is a result which would be impossible if teachers were adequately moved by their own independent intelligence. The willingness of teachers, especially of those occupying administrative positions, to become submerged in the routine detail of their callings, to expend the bulk of their energy upon forms and rules and regulations, and reports and percentages,

is another evidence of the absence of intellectual vitality. If teachers were possessed by the spirit of an abiding student of education, this spirit would find some way of breaking through the mesh and coil of circumstance and would find expression for itself. (1904, 16)

Linguistic Diversity

We have found that responsible teachers examine the source of their attitudes about the way children use language in the classroom, and beyond the classroom as well. The notion that certain dialects carry with them a certain degree of prestige (Hymes 1967) is a reality in our society, but the responsible teacher looks beyond that limited view. In pointing out that all languages are composed of dialects, Ken Goodman (1969) shows us that we need to accept the legitimacy of language variation. It is parochial to think that the dialects spoken by residents in eastern U.S. inner cities, the piedmont of North Carolina, or Latino communities of the American Southwest are "incorrect" or poorly learned versions of some "standard" form. Rather, all variants of a language are equal dialects in the sense that they provide efficient service to their users. As responsible teachers inform themselves of the realities of language and education, they realize that apparent inequalities among dialects reflect the deeper structure of ethnic, racial, and political forces.

We understand that language variation has been used as a "tag" to denote which children shall succeed and which shall not. In accord with local educational policy, it is true that children have been placed into categories in kindergarten and targeted for intervention. Those children appear locked in place from the first two months of their school careers (Rist 1970); however, responsible teachers are aware of these biases and act as advocates for children by teaching in ways that celebrate individuals and their literacy residences. Responsible educators permit, accept, study, and rejoice in the language varieties that they encounter. The writings of kindergarten teacher Vivian Paley provide a marvelous example of what can happen when a teacher who is sensitive to language diversity works with children to create a setting in which the contributions of all children are valued. About her contract with her students, she writes: "[If] you will keep trying to explain yourselves I will keep showing you how to think about the problems you need to solve" (1981, 223).

We are learning about the influence of language upon schooling as we engage in studies of language in school and at home. Shirley Brice Heath (1983) and Susan Philips (1971) offer particular insights into the literacy residences of children as they document patterns of language use in the home and community. By understanding the cultural differences in how users of particular dialects use language to relate to each other in nonschool settings, we may better understand the qualities of the linguistic diversity that different children bring to the classroom.

Responsibility often leads to consciousness raising. In his description of the lives of "Burghersiders," John Ogbu (1974) describes members of various groups with lower socioeconomic status, finding some being treated as immigrants and others like members of a lower caste. Those treated as immigrants have a greater chance of achieving the American ideal of success, while those treated as a caste are members of that caste for life. Although speaking and listening in school are but one facet of this study, the issues of language are expanded as they stretch into the sociopolitical realities of our country. Ogbu (1981) stresses the importance of focusing beyond the classroom as we consider the state of schooling. Mehan encourages us to gain a more complete understanding of "the role of language in education . . . [as it] contribute[s] to an understanding of the role of schooling in social stratification" (1984, 180). The classroom is but one part of a larger ecological view that encompasses issues such as corporate economy and stratification. When we make the commitment to examine language, we are also making a commitment to understanding the complex social and political web into which schools are woven.

Politics and Cultural Diversity

Teachers who seek to exercise their autonomy and professional judgment often face unexpected pressures resulting from broad-based political and economic forces that influence the field of education:

> To impositions from above is opposed expression and cultivation of individuality; to external discipline is opposed free activity; to learning from texts and teachers, learning from experience; to acquisition of isolated skills and techniques by drill, is opposed acquisition of them as means of attaining ends which make direct vital appeal; to preparation for a more or less remote future is opposed making the most of the opportunities of present life; to static aims and materials is opposed acquaintance with a changing world. (Dewey 1938, 19–20)

As we grow in our understanding of the important connections between language, culture, and text, it becomes impossible to discuss one without the other. We are also very much aware of the ethnocentric nature of some professed understandings of culture (Hirsch 1987; Ravitch and Finn 1987). These narrow views portray culture merely as a list of accomplishments; a list which largely fails to recognize the contributions of all the cultural groups of our society. Even so, there are still teachers and teacher educators who would have us believe *cultural deprivation* is a valid construct. We are a country of rich diversity, yet when one group assumes great amounts of power and wealth, some would have us believe that the only group worth belonging to is the one in power.

It is our responsibility to honor and validate the cultural diversity within our classrooms. And one area needing critical examination is the traditional practice of grouping:

> One index of the persistent refusal of schools to develop a means to empower minority and disadvantaged groups is the widespread practice of tracking students into ability groups. Tracking assumes that schools play a part in the meritocratic selection and allocation based on ability. In fact, however, tracking fosters the *illusion* of meritocratic competitions while in reality functioning as a "ranking" system that legitimates differences based on race, gender, and social power and locks students into positions of limited opportunity. (McLaren 1988, 49)

Professional responsibility requires the cultivation of a social and political conscience (Giroux and Simon 1988). As critics of our own teaching, we can develop our sense of personal, social, and political barriers that block the paths to literacy. In this way we can act as advocates for children and take an active hand in keeping the paths clear.

Historical Perspectives

We cannot overstate the importance of understanding the history of education—especially history which acknowledges the cultural, social, and political activities of various time periods—for the consequences of these activities can be seen in our classrooms today. Just as we are trying to understand our present culture, we are seeking our historical roots so that we might have a sense of grounded philosophical, theoretical, and practical traditions as educators. Yetta Goodman (1989) traces the roots of the whole language movement, showing the rich tradition of evidence and justification in support of whole language. Such evidence and justification are often absent from dry histories of education. A mere time-line approach is insufficient because it lacks a sense of the direction and rootedness of the powerful movements in education. We need histories that offer a commitment with which we can dialogue and debate as professionals. Few historians would value a history of the Civil War which listed names, dates, and places as the essence of that war. Language arts educators can settle for no less. Patrick Shannon (1990), for example, offers a history which educators may discuss and research further since it originates from a specific point of view: a social and political account of one hundred years of reading instruction in the United States. His text affords us an opportunity to transact with a history of education.

The social, political, and historical realities within the classroom are undeniably present. Responsible teachers willingly entertain diverse historical, social, and cultural perspectives on the world because such invitations provide opportunity for challenge and understanding by teachers and students alike.

Practice

Practice puts identity and responsibility into action. It expresses the teacher's beliefs and ideas (Wertsch 1991) as he or she transacts with the minds and literacy residences of others. Because whole language practice welcomes the contributions of all the minds at a particular setting, it provides for a collective zone of proximal development for teachers and learners (Vygotsky 1978; Moll 1990). Whole language also allows for flexibility in the roles of teacher and learner as these roles become less attached to age or time in a particular setting and more attached to authentic expertise.

Whole language teachers give children permission to value their own literacy. We know that language is relationship. Through language we cultivate and continue relationships using written and oral systems. The nature of the relationship is critical to language—and literacy—development on personal and interpersonal levels across the many functions of language.

Permission and Relationships

As teachers learn more about language and literacy, they begin to view their classrooms as language laboratories. It can be no other way because we cannot fashion a meaningful curriculum until we have explored our students' literacy residences, which requires permission. For us, permission means allowing children to freely express those ideas closest to their hearts and minds, to explore and cultivate their self-expression. Permission also means granting ourselves the opportunity to invest the time and energy required to really know and enjoy our students in the face of traditional approaches to teaching, severe time constraints, and attitudes of colleagues which might dissuade us. It means giving ourselves permission to reallocate our time to simply watch kids work and play so that we may better know what language learning looks like. And beyond student and teacher, permission means opening up the door of the classroom to parents who want to help, to classroom aides, and to the involved principal. It means that teachers and children have license to break with a curriculum which has no relevance, to break longstanding codes of behavior which are based on outdated assumptions from a time gone by ("children should be seen and not heard"); it means that children will have a safe place to explore reading and writing and speaking and listening and the latitude to construct their own community of learners as they see fit.

Finally, teachers who are sensitive to the concept of permission are builders of relationships. Ken Goodman (1986) said that whole language teachers have been accused of "loving their students into learning." That is an apparent reality. In truth, teachers who understand the nature of language learning and who are confident in their identities as professionals know that the dynamics of the classroom are deeply social. They are unafraid to cultivate rich, balanced, nurturing, and long-lasting relationships with students, parents, and colleagues. They realize that, above all, effective education is a human thing.

Research and Practice

Of course, not all teachers and researchers are convinced of the democratic and humanistic trends supported by assumptions inherent in a meaning-centered view of learning. Carole Edelsky, a whole language researcher and advocate, was told that she "thrives in the midst of this intellectually foundationless struggle [whole language], which is the chief source of her smoke and mirrors" (McKenna, Robinson, and Miller 1990). This is the voice of fear; it reflects a lack of understanding of both the paradigmatic differences represented by whole language and of the power of responsible, informed practice.

The "great debate" fostered by Jeanne Chall (1966) almost thirty years ago seems to persist today as Marilyn Adams (1991) seeks to reduce our understandings of human learning to a simple machine-like technology. But Adams is being met with strong resistance as informed advocates like Murphy point out that Adams "pays little more than lip service to the theoretical and pedagogical implications of the vastly growing literature on emergent literacy . . . [and the] significant demonstrations that reading is much more than the text-bound perception of words" (1991, 203). Proponents of a mechanistic view of learning and literacy seem to ignore the rich and complex variables that are at play in any classroom. However, Denny Taylor's work aspires to reveal such complexities; she offers sound ethnographic research documenting classrooms in which "teachers and children work together, becoming co-informants, as the reading and writing strategies of the one inform those of the other" (1989, 190).

Research which supports meaning-centered practices offers insights that fly in the face of conventional wisdom, and brings serious implications for changing traditional classroom practices. Even so, some educational materials and the policies that guide their use encourage teachers to relinquish professional responsibilities and deny students permission to explore their own literacy residences.

The use of basal reading systems in our classrooms amounts to an economic and political scandal (K. Goodman et al. 1988; Shannon 1989a) as large publishing companies exert de facto control over educating children in the language arts. Patrick Shannon finds that

> basals contribute to a hierarchical, class-based distribution of literacy among the student population. . . . The illusion of scientific validity of basals maintains the myths among poor and minority students that they are solely responsible for their difficulty in learning to be literate and among middle and upper class students that they are literate simply because they can pass basal tests and other standardized tests. (1989b, 631)

Dolores Durkin's (1981) study of five basal reader series revealed that little time during basal reading instruction is actually spent on teaching strategies of comprehension. The series she investigated focused on evaluating mastery of skills or recall of facts and sequences that children could recall from stories they had read; far from being meaning-centered, this reflects a "skills evaluation" point of view.

Appearing to be scientific in nature, basal companies offer us "cures" for our low-performing readers. They assume that we have no understanding of the reading process or reading instruction and offer us word-by-word instructions for children during reading instruction. Ken Goodman calls the basal companies "unseen authorities" (1989, 304) who seek to run our programs of literacy instruction. We have blindly relinquished our power over text, and

> [t]hings have gotten so out of whack that our review of how to teach reading comprehension shows that almost anything teachers do beyond a basal reading program significantly improves reading comprehension. (Harste 1989, 266)

Reflecting a recent trend, some reading series have made an effort to include "real literature" in their anthologies. However, Ken Goodman (1988) points out that these works of literature are often severely changed to the point of not being recognizable in order to control the vocabulary or balance ethnicity within the story. Yvonne Freeman (1989) presents evidence that state-mandated policies can change literature programs from meaning-based to skills-based, undermining the very heart of literature. The teachers in Barr and Sadow's (1989) study felt compelled to teach reading as specific skills and, therefore, spent less time reading textbook selections. Those teachers relied upon the skills segments of the reading series and were reluctant to use the many additional activities which are language-rich.

Barr and Sadow did not investigate whole language classrooms that were not using basals. If they had, we believe that they would have found that whole language educators are actively incorporating cutting-edge research into their daily practice and pursuing their own research agendas in their classrooms.

Written Language Processes and Instruction

Frank Smith (1992) explains that if we truly have faith in children as natural learners of oral language, then we ought to extend that faith to the written word as well and commit ourselves to the naturalness of learning to read. Reading is a process of making meaning that involves the reader and the author in a unique relationship (Rosenblatt 1978). In transacting with the author through the printed text, the reader constructs his or her own singular meaning.

In our daily practice we understand reading to be more than the "successive accurate identification of words in text" (K. Goodman 1991). Meaning construction is at the core of a complex process described by language systems and strategies. As readers, we use cueing systems to construct meaning: the letter/sound (graphophonic), the syntactic (grammatic), and the semantic (meaning) systems (Harste and Mikulecky 1984; K. Goodman 1984). As these systems work together, we use strategies to direct the construction of meaning: initiation, sampling of available cues, prediction, confirming and disconfirming, correction, and termination (K. Goodman 1984, 104–7).

There are narrower views of the reading process which stress sound/symbol relationships and that cast reading as mere word identification, but these perspectives lack a focus on meaning (Harste and

Burke 1979; Y. Goodman, Watson, and Burke 1987). Ken Goodman makes clear what reading is by addressing the notion of "decoding":

> The concept that underlies the use of the term "decoding" has become so distorted that we need to re-examine it carefully. . . . Both oral language and written language are [complementary] codes. . . . But if you look carefully at the term "decode," it implies that one is going from code to something other than code. If, in decoding, we go from code to something else, what else is that something else? An immediate answer is that if the reader moves from code to code, no decoding has taken place. If he moves from written language to oral language in some form, however distorted or complete, he has not decoded anything. In a similar manner the army signal corps operator receives a coded message that comes to him as a dot-dash signal over a radio. He then transcribes that into letter sequences. But he can't take that piece of paper with the letter sequences and say "Here, I've decoded the message." In fact, he has to get a code book out and somehow reconstruct the message which has been carefully obscured through several different encodings in order to keep other people from getting the message. It isn't until he gets the message that any decoding has taken place. Anything short of meaning, anything that doesn't, in fact, go from code to meaning is not decoding. (1982, 53)

Teachers must cultivate an understanding of the reading process in order to take ownership of reading instruction, transforming their experiences into very real practice which can be shared with principals, parents, researchers, and other teachers. Nancie Atwell (1987) does this effectively as she affords her middle school students the time and ownership of learning that they require in order to create a classroom where students can transact with texts to achieve a significant depth of response. She points out that the reading experiences of her students, closely linked to writing experiences, vary across many fiction and nonfiction genres. She makes discoveries about the students' reading, adjusts her program to meet individuals' needs, and then reports her practices, which are well grounded in a meaning-centered theory of reading and writing research. Atwell's sense of identity and responsibility provide the framework for her practice.

Literacy research has shown us that even children as young as kindergartners can be active participants in the literacy environment of their classroom by approximating reading and retelling or constructing stories with a text in hand. Elizabeth Sulzby contends that "[t]his indicates that, prior to formal instruction, important development is going on" (1985, 479). When children are given permission to read and transact with whole texts, they engage in authentic reading experiences, and as teachers, we have enhanced their understanding of reading as a sense-making process.

Not all young children are so fortunate in their school experiences. Recently, as Meyer (1992) sat in a kindergarten classroom, the teacher sat the children on the rug in a circle so that each child could see as the teacher read from a Big Book and used a pointer to show the children where she was reading. It was a familiar story to most of the children. The Little Red Hen had found a grain of wheat and could find no help from three other animals in the planting, harvesting, hauling, grinding, kneading, or baking of her bread. Finally, the hen asks who will help her eat the bread, and she suddenly has many offers for help—all of which she turns down. Ms. K, the teacher, closed the book and smiled at the children. Allison and Kenny raised their hands at the same time:

> *Allison:* That's not right.
>
> *Kenny:* No, she should have shared.
>
> *Ms. K:* But . . .
>
> *Allison:* We're supposed to share with each other.
>
> *Kenny:* Yes, we are and . . .
>
> *Ms. K:* But look. Look at the book. The duck and the cat and the pig . . . see them here. They are lazy. They are not helping. [*Ms. K turns to each page where the three animals are not helping the hen.*] They don't deserve any bread!

The discussion ends in silence as Ms. K puts the book away and dismisses the children to line up for recess.

The teacher had not permitted the children to own and express their responses. Nor had she allowed time for discussion so that children could do the things necessary for the negotiation of meaning: share their transactions with each other, and perhaps adjust what they thought originally, or defend it; or cultivate new thoughts collaboratively. She denied the literacy residences of the two children involved in the discussion and set an example for the other children about how meaning was made in the classroom; meaning was teacher-dependent.

The point we wish to make here is that reading involves a relationship between the reader, an author, and a text. As teachers, we need to help children cultivate that relationship by encouraging them to take as much ownership as possible when they are reading. In the classroom, reading must be a social activity which encourages and capitalizes on the relationships between the readers as they negotiate the meaning of a text with each other. When a teacher seeks to control these relationships rather than nurture and guide them, or when a teacher relinquishes control to a reading program, their very nature is changed, resulting in strange occurrences, such as children hating to read or considering the "school work" type of "reading" as something entirely different from reading outside of school.

Given the chance, young children come to know and understand intentionality in print—the meaning function inherent in print. When allowed to experience a variety of printed materials (magazines, cereal boxes, books, cassette tapes, newspapers), and by being read to and by watching others read, children explore the functions of print just as they explore them in oral language development. Meyer (1992) describes a writer far exceeding the expectations imposed by the traditional definition of writing in school. In home settings, he observed an emerging writer create checks to purchase items while playing store, design game boards, post signs for roads and buildings made out of blocks, print play money, fill out deposit slips, compose tickets to events, and make shopping lists.

While children are likely to have these experiences at home, they might not have them at school. Language theorists are aware of the shortcomings of traditional written language instruction:

> Until now, writing has occupied too narrow a place in school practice as compared to the enormous role that it plays in children's cultural development. The teaching of writing has been conceived in narrowly practical terms. Children are taught to trace out letters and make words out of them but they are not taught written language. The mechanics of reading what is written are so emphasized that they overshadow written language as such. (Vygotsky 1987, 105)

> Writing serves many functions in our culture, and those functions are likely to interact in complex ways with the nature of school learning. Until we understand those interactions better, simple suggestions for educational change are unlikely to lead to major changes in the success of our schools. (Applebee 1984, 592)

But whole language educators *do* understand the complex ways that functions of written language interact with schooling. JoBeth Allen and her colleagues investigated seven kindergarten classrooms and concluded that "the majority of their students will make progress in writing without required handwriting exercises, or other tasks of dubious value. . . . the children provide their own practice" (Allen et al. 1989, 146). Ken Goodman writes: "Perhaps the most significant insight from this writer's research is that children can literally teach themselves to recognize unfamiliar words as they read. They do this by regressing, by going back and gathering more information when they have made an error so that they can correct it" (1967, 5). One way to characterize whole language practice is through its pronouncement of faith in the linguistic brilliance of children. Whole language educators, through their awareness of how to support children's explorations of the functions of print, are the vanguard of change.

Classroom Research

The face of research is changing as the line between formal and informal research dissolves. This change is driven by shifting views of learning; no longer do we accept definitions of learning as the acquisition of skills. We now know literacy-learning to be the pursuit of control over oral and written systems as learners seek to understand the world. It is a pursuit which is developmental and which has individual, social, and cultural aspects. Accompanied by this changing view of learning are changing criteria for what counts as legitimate research data. Paper and pencil tests are yielding way to rich anecdotal accounts of the learning process which inform practice and point the way to further theory development and research. And this research is no longer generated and handed down from "the ivory tower."

Instead, teachers are assuming increased importance as they demand a voice in the "why and how" of research that affects their classrooms. For example, Sondra Perl (1983) reports on a school district initiating the process approach to writing, which involved teachers as collaborators in research. The teachers were involved as writers in writing workshops for the purpose of gaining an understanding of the writing process, the variety of genres, a sense of audience, and other aspects of authorship. Like Atwell, mentioned earlier, many of the teachers have published their results, thereby adding their voices to the research literature on writing.

Cochran-Smith and Lytle are university faculty who include preservice and inservice teachers in research projects. Individuals decide upon a problem, define it, and approach it with sensitivity to cultural, socioeconomic, gender, and ethnic issues. Cochran-Smith and Lytle see teacher research as a vehicle for staff development and remind readers that:

> The cultural diversity of U.S. schools and schoolchildren demands that every teacher, whether new or experienced,

thoughtfully examine the local meanings of disparities between home and school, community and school system, and teacher and student and then take responsible action to improve the educational choices and life changes of their own students. (1992, 113)

To fully understand literacy processes, teachers of reading and writing must be readers and writers themselves, sharing in the process with children and colleagues. This close-up research where teachers see firsthand how literacy processes unfold is the most important because it has direct and immediate consequences for changes in practice. Teachers who engage in this type of classroom research also know that they have a right to be critical of the research and literature presented to them in various journals and books. As they sharpen their "kidwatching" (Y. Goodman 1985) skills, they come to trust their own informed choices as creators of curriculum. This is how the historical boundaries which separate the territories of consumers and producers of understanding are becoming "fuzzy" (Lampert 1991). These research experiences enable teacher-researchers to conclude "that many of the instructional assumptions currently made are faulty at best and debilitating at worst" (Harste and Burke 1979, 177).

Closing Thoughts

Whole language educators take responsibility for understanding the complex nature of literacy and are among the most responsible professionals in the field. They do not dismiss the importance of advocacy for children in their pursuit of learning. And they understand that teaching is more than filling an eight-hour day with activities to occupy children—they know that on every side, teaching faces multiple political, social, economic, and cultural issues.

In her chapter in the first section of this book, Dorothy Watson describes whole language educators as "uppity." We concur, and it is high time! As teachers, we are working in an era in which, for the first time, it is possible to reinvent our profession, construct our own identities, and become leaders of change in education. We are committed to greeting the new century with identity, responsibility, and well-articulated practice.

Notice that each writer in this book has a distinctive voice—a personal expression, a unique story to tell. These are the concepts that we want to resonate throughout *Under the Whole Language Umbrella: Many Cultures, Many Voices*. Read with these in mind.

References

Adams, M. 1991. A talk with Marilyn Adams. *Language Arts* 68:206–12.

Allen, J., W. Clark, M. Cook, P. Crane, I. Fallon, L. Hoffman, K. Jennings, and M. Sours. 1989. Reading and writing development in whole language kindergartens. In *Reading and Writing Connections*, ed. J. Mason. Needham Heights, Mass.: Allyn and Bacon.

Applebee, A. 1984. Writing and reasoning. *Review of Educational Research* 54 (4): 577–96.

Atwell, N. 1987. In the middle: Writing, reading, and learning with adolescents. Upper Montclair, N.J.: Boynton/Cook.

Barr, R., and M. Sadow. 1989. Influence of basal programs on fourth-grade reading instruction. *Reading Research Quarterly* 24 (1): 44–71.

Baylor, B. 1991. *Yes is better than no.* Tucson: Treasure Chest Publications.

Bloome, D. 1983. Reading as a social process. *Advances in Reading/Language Research* 2:165–95.

Bloome, D., and J. Green. 1982. The social contexts of reading: A multidisciplinary perspective. *Advances in Reading/Language Research* 1: 309–38.

Cairney, T., and S. Langbien. 1989. Building communities of readers and writers. *Reading Teacher* 42 (8): 560–67.

Carini, P. F. 1987. Another way of looking: Views on evaluation and education. Address for the Cambridge School Conference, Cambridge School, Weston, Mass.

Chall, J. 1966. Learning to read. New York: McGraw-Hill.

Cochran-Smith, M., and S. Lytle. 1992. Interrogating cultural diversity: Inquiry and action. *Journal of Teacher Education* 43 (2): 104–15.

Cummins, J. 1991. Presentation at the American Indian Language Development Institute, Tucson, June.

Dewey, J. 1904. The relation of theory to practice in education. In *The third yearbook of the National Society for the Scientific Study of Education. Part 1: The relation of theory to practice in the education of teachers.* Chicago: Chicago University Press.

———. 1938. *Experience and education.* New York: Macmillan.

Durkin, D. 1981. Reading comprehension instruction in five basal reader series. *Reading Research Quarterly* 16 (4): 515–44.

Ferreiro, E. 1991. Keynote address at IMPACT: Diversity in Action Conference, sponsored by the Division of Language, Reading and Culture, Project IMPACT, the extended university, and the University of Arizona, Tucson, April.

Firth, J. R. 1950. Personality and language in society. *The Sociological Review* 42:37–52.

Freeman, Y. 1989. Literature-based or literature: Where do we stand? *Teacher Networking,* Summer, 13–15.

Giroux, H., and R. Simon. 1988. Schooling, popular culture, and a pedagogy of possibility. *Journal of Education* 170 (1): 9–26.

Goodlad, J. 1990. Better teachers for our nation's schools. *Phi Delta Kappan,* November, 185–94.

Goodman, K. 1967. Word perceptions: Linguistic bases. *Education* 87 (9): 539–43. Reprint, Indianapolis: Bobbs-Merrill.

——. 1969. Let's dump the uptight model in English. *Elementary School Journal* 70 (1): 1–13.

——. 1982. Decoding: From code to what? In *Language and Literacy,* vol. 1, ed. F. Gollasch. Boston and London: Routledge and Kegan Paul.

——. 1984. Unity in reading. In *Becoming readers in a complex society: 83rd yearbook of the National Society for the Study of Education,* part 1, ed. A. Purves. Chicago: University of Chicago Press.

——. 1986. *What's whole in whole language?* Portsmouth, N.H.: Heinemann.

——. 1988. Look what they've done to Judy Blume! The "basalization" of children's literature. *The New Advocate* 1 (1): 29–44.

——. 1989. Access to literacy: Basals and other barriers. *Theory into Practice* 28 (4): 300–306.

——. 1991. Reading: The psycholinguistic guessing game. In *The whole language catalog,* ed. K. Goodman, L. Bird, and Y. Goodman. Santa Rosa, Calif.: American School Publishers.

Goodman, K., P. Shannon, Y. Freeman, and S. Murphy. 1988. *Report card on basal readers.* Katonah, N.Y.: Richard C. Owen.

Goodman, Y. 1985. Kidwatching: Observing children in the classroom. In *Observing the language learner,* ed. A. Jagger and M. Smith-Burke. Newark, Del.: International Reading Association.

——. 1989. Roots of the whole-language movement. *Elementary School Journal* 90 (2): 113–27.

Goodman, Y., D. Watson, and C. Burke. 1987. *Reading miscue inventory: Alternative procedures.* Katonah, N.Y.: Richard C. Owen.

Halliday, M. A. K. 1988. There's still a long way to go . . . : An interview with emeritus professor Michael Halliday. *Journal of the Australian Advisory Council on Languages and Multicultural Education* 1:35–39.

Hansen, J. 1987. *When writers read.* Portsmouth, N.H.: Heinemann.

Harste, J. 1989. The basalization of American reading instruction: One researcher responds. *Theory into Practice* 28:265–73.

Harste, J., and C. Burke. 1979. Examining instructional assumptions: The child as informant. *Theory into Practice* 19 (3): 170–78.

Harste, J., and L. Mikulecky. 1984. The context of literacy in our society. In *Becoming readers in a complex society: 83rd yearbook of the National Soci-*

ety for the Study of Education, part 1, ed. A. Purves. Chicago: University of Chicago Press.

Heath, S. B. 1983. *Ways with words: Language, life, and work in communities and classrooms.* Cambridge: Cambridge University Press.

Hirsch, E. D. 1987. *Cultural literacy: What every American needs to know.* Boston: Houghton Mifflin.

Hymes, D. 1967. Models of the interaction of language and social setting. *Journal of Social Issues* 23 (2): 8–28.

Lampert, M. 1991. Looking at restructuring from within a restructured role. *Phi Delta Kappan* 72 (9): 670–74.

McKenna, M., R. Robinson, and J. Miller. 1990. Whole language and the need for open inquiry: A rejoinder to Edelsky. *Educational Researcher* 19 (8): 12–13.

McLaren, P. 1988. Broken dreams, false promises, and the decline of public schooling. *Journal of Education* 170 (1): 41–65.

Mehan, H. 1984. Language and schooling. *Sociology of Education* 57:174–83.

Meyer, R. 1992. A young writer at home and in school. Ph.D. diss., University of Arizona, Tucson.

Moll, L. 1990. Introduction. In *Vygotsky and education: Instructional implications and applications of sociohistorical psychology,* ed. L. Moll. Cambridge: Cambridge University Press.

Murphy, S. 1991. The code, connectionism, and basals. *Language Arts* 68: 199–205.

Newman, J. 1991. *Interwoven conversations.* Portsmouth, N.H.: Heinemann.

Ogbu, J. 1974. *The next generation: An ethnography of education in an urban neighborhood.* New York: Academic Press.

———. 1981. School ethnography: A multilevel approach. *Anthropology and Education Quarterly* 21 (1): 3–29.

Paley, V. 1981. *Wally's stories: Conversations in the kindergarten.* Cambridge, Mass.: Harvard University Press.

Perl, S. 1983. How teachers teach the writing process: Overview of an ethnographic research project. *Elementary School Journal* 84 (1): 19–24.

Philips, S. 1971. Participant structures and communicative competence: Warm Springs children in community and classroom. In *Functions of language in the classroom,* ed. C. B. Cazden, V. P. John, and D. Hymes. New York: Teachers College Press.

Ravitch, D., and C. Finn. 1987. *What do our 17-year-olds know?* New York: Harper and Row.

Rist, R. 1970. Student social class and teacher expectations: The self-fulfilling prophecy in ghetto education. *Harvard Educational Review* 40: 411–51.

Rosenblatt, L. 1978. *The reader, the text, the poem: The transactional theory of the literary work.* Carbondale: Southern Illinois University Press.

Schon, D. 1987. *The reflective practitioner.* New York: Basic Books.

Shannon, P. 1989a. *Broken promises: Reading instruction in twentieth-century America.* Granby, Mass.: Bergin and Garvey.

——. 1989b. The struggle for control of literacy lessons. *Language Arts* 66 (6): 625–34.

——. 1990. *The struggle to continue: Progressive reading instruction in the United States.* Portsmouth, N.H.: Heinemann.

Smith, F. 1986. *Insult to intelligence: The bureaucratic invasion of our classrooms.* Portsmouth, N.H.: Heinemann.

Smith, M., J. O'Day, and D. Cohen. 1990. National curriculum American style. *American Educator,* Winter, 10–17, 40–46.

Sulzby, E. 1985. Children's emergent reading of favorite storybooks: A developmental study. *Reading Research Quarterly* 20 (4): 458–81.

Taylor, D. 1989. Toward a unified theory of literary learning and instructional practices. *Phi Delta Kappan,* November, 185–93.

——. 1991. *Learning denied.* Portsmouth, N.J.: Heinemann.

Vygotsky, L. S. 1978. *Mind in society: The development of higher psychological processes.* Ed. M. Cole. Cambridge, Mass.: Harvard University Press.

——. 1987. *The collected words of L. S. Vygotsky.* Vol. 1: *Problems of general psychology,* ed. R. Rieber and A. Carton. New York: Plenum.

Wertsch, J. 1991. *Voices of the mind: A sociocultural approach to mediated action.* Cambridge, Mass.: Harvard University Press.

Whitmore, K. 1992. Inventing a classroom: An ethnographic study of a 3rd grade bilingual learning community. Ph.D. diss., University of Arizona, Tucson.

Wortman, R. 1991. Authenticity. Ph.D. diss., University of Arizona, Tucson.

I Identity

Voice, culture, and story are key concepts in whole language. As metaphors, each can be explored in many different ways to help us comprehend what whole language is all about. We come to recognize the value of each individual's contribution in our classrooms by listening closely to what he or she has to say. Our goal is to have our students realize the value of their own voices and use their voices to make contributions to their own communities. And we realize that we come to know the world through the stories that we are told, the stories that we share, and the stories that we tell to ourselves.

But how do we flesh out the meaning of whole language and our identities as whole language educators? In this section readers will find that each writer has a different approach to this subject. In her address to the second annual Whole Language Umbrella Conference, reprinted here with minor revision, keynote speaker Dorothy Watson suggests that we come to know who we are by sharing the stories of authors, theorists, researchers, and learners. She points out that "we have defined whole language linguistically, historically, pedagogically, curricularly, and politically. Whole language has got to be the most defined and redefined concept in education today." Carole Edelsky includes the concept of story when she focuses on the ways in which research helps to determine what is involved in being whole language educators. Norma Mickelson discusses how we can go about telling others who we are. Judith Wells Lindfors, Patrick Shannon, and Adrian Peetoom explore the relationship between the individual and the community, each from a different vantage point. Lindfors reflects on the relationship of the individual to the community and how community evolves in an elementary classroom. Shannon further illuminates the concept of the rights of the individual learner by relating these rights to the U.S. Constitution's Bill of Rights. And Peetoom discusses what happens when the rights of the individual and the community come into conflict.

1 Many Cultures, Many Voices

Dorothy Watson
University of Missouri–Columbia

When I was asked to address the opening session of the second Whole Language Umbrella Conference, I was pleased but nervous about the responsibility. At one point worry took over, and my solitary attempts to write stopped dead in their tracks. It was time to practice my unwavering belief in collaboration. I needed friends. My first call for help was to Ken Goodman. I chatted with Ken about his presentation at our first WLU Conference. I suggested that because it was such a moving speech and because there were a lot of people who had not heard it, it deserved repetition. And, I said with hesitation, would he mind if I just read it again at the Phoenix conference? After what seemed to be an unnecessarily long silence, Ken replied, "No, Dorothy, that would be a sin." I controlled my disappointment but could not resist telling Ken that as far as his work was concerned, a lot of us had sinned.

I was dismayed that Ken was not demonstrating the whole language spirit of sharing, but, undaunted, I sidled up to another friend. Years of experience have taught me that if I sounded pitiful enough, Rudine Sims Bishop would always come to my rescue. I reminded Rudine of a perfect talk that she had given several years ago—a presentation that we always referred to as "the vitamin speech." "How about it, Rudine, that talk is just right for 'Many Cultures, Many Voices' . . . for old time's sake?" After what seemed to be another unnecessarily long silence, she caved in. But I could tell (I am sensitive to these things) that she really did not think it was a good idea. Something in her voice made me reconsider the value, no matter what the struggle, of raising my own voice.

Under the Umbrella—Together

Whole language: What is this force? What is this collection of thought and action that has brought us together from classrooms around the world? What is the substance and essence of this philosophy of learning and teaching that has inspired educators from diverse societies and cultures to raise their voices—to tell their *stories?* Perhaps whole language cannot be described or defined any better than to say, *it is our stories:*

- Stories that have their roots in the works and messages of countless researchers and theorists who help us see that children, when given a chance, are smart, and that teachers are the professionals who can best tap children's intelligence, energy, and imagination

- Stories that are written by a community of teachers who, with the help of their students, have dared to create new classrooms and important curricula

- Stories that are told through the work of a growing number of educators who are represented by us—teachers, administrators, librarians, authors, publishers, and parents gathered under the umbrella tonight

- Stories—often including pesky ones that keep getting us into trouble as we create their plots and themes—that reside so deep within us that they capture our learning, our teaching, and our imagination; and once we have those pesky stories in our heads, it seems that nothing can shake them out of us— and no one can scare them out of us

Welcome

Welcome to the second Whole Language Umbrella Conference. Welcome to a festival of learners and of language. Welcome to a celebration in which we can experience the beauty and achievements of many cultures, where we can listen to the stories told and songs sung by many voices, and perhaps, to use Paulo Freire's term, where we can create a culture circle of our own, one in which no voice is lost.

To Jane and Alan Flurkey and all those who have artfully designed this conference with such great dedication, we are indebted for helping us take another step along the whole language path. To reach our greatest potential and to distinguish our support groups from all the other organizations available to us, we know that we must do more than recognize cultures other than our own; we must give voice to those whose lives place them on the fringes of society and schooling. Thanks, Alan and Jane, for this invitation to become more sensitive and more caring and for helping us find the courage to pull down the barriers that wall out knowledge and understanding.

What can we expect of this conference? Last year, after our first WLU Conference, Grace Vento-Zogby took all the evaluation forms back to Utica, where she spent days reading and digesting those thoughtful comments. Of all our fine experiences in St. Louis, Grace found that the experience that remained with everyone was the opportunity for *talk*—talk with other professionals who shared our interests and concerns. Through our talk we sorted things out so that we could inquire more deeply into our important questions and concerns, and through our talk we could more fully celebrate our successes. This year the conversations will continue—again there will be talk, inquiry, and celebrations.

And if, through our talk, our beliefs are confirmed by a teacher's practices or if a teacher nods in agreement with our ideas (and even takes notes on a suggestion that we make), we can expect to feel gratified that the work in our classrooms, in our schools, and in our libraries is confirmed and valued by people whom we trust. But in addition to the confirmation of our familiar practices, through our talk we can expect to experience the unfamiliar—a tentative theory with which someone is wrestling, a classroom strategy, a poem, a picture— an idea that makes our pulses beat faster and that causes us to draw fourth-grade stars and exclamation marks in the margins of our notebooks to remind us, when we return home, to reflect on these important ideas.

We can also expect to have our blind spots revealed, to be nudged into that discomfort zone of whole language where we must make our intentions as teachers much clearer, and our agendas as educators more explicit. At this conference we may make some tough decisions—maybe some that we have been putting off—decisions about how our students are evaluated or what materials are allowed in our classrooms; we may make decisions about what really should take up our students' and our own time and energy—what is so right and good that it can be called our curriculum; and we may make decisions about those students who are overtly or covertly denied because they bring their nonstandardized minds, bodies, ages, interests, and needs to a standardized classroom and curriculum.

During this conference, we, as individuals and as groups, may make some "policy decisions"—decisions that require all our political wisdom in order to conduct ourselves productively with both those who support us and those who do not—colleagues, parents, administrators, publishers, and people who write about us in newspapers, magazines, and professional journals. No one at this conference will presume to make decisions for us, but here we can decide to do more than just wring our hands over thorny problems—whether those problems involve mandated tests that mask our students' abilities and worth, or how to exist ulcer-free with the skills-based eclectic next door who fills the curricular cauldron halfway with obligatory texts and tests, adds a numbing amount of workbooks and worksheets, stirs in large quantities of direct "banking model" instruction, and, just to add a bit of flavor to this tasteless ferment, sprinkles some whole language on top. And if that teacher does not understand whole language practices and principles, just put anything in and *call* it whole language.

At this conference, we are educators doing our homework. Here we will talk about, study, mull over, reason with, reflect on, and reject some of what we see and hear. But here is our chance to become *enabled*, which in turn gives us the anchor needed for becoming *empowered*.

At this conference, we will be doing what we invite our students to do. We will take ownership of our own professionalism by making choices and taking risks. Choices and risks. If we have chosen whole language, it necessarily involves both. I am reminded of the message that Beverly Greeson wrote on the board one evening in our graduate class called Whole Language Curriculum. The message was advice from that wise philosopher Bert to his friend Ernie: "If you want to learn to play the saxophone, you've got to lay down the ducky and pick up the saxophone." Choices and risks. If we have chosen to play the saxophone, at this conference we will get to talk about how rewarding and how scary it is to let go of the ducky. Here we can experience with friends the theory and practice of playing the saxophone, as well as the rewards and frustrations of learning to do so.

At this conference, we, as educators and as members of our support groups, can expect to plan our next steps, even if they are shaky and tentative ones. As members of an umbrella organization, we must decide where we will place our next efforts as leaders in the whole language movement. WLU is organized with an enthusiastic advisory board. Our network of active interest groups has grown stronger, but we need to move ahead in our responsibility to our profession and to our membership. This is a working conference. We can expect to get very tired this week, but we will not get sick and tired. *For this is our work, and it ignites us rather than burns us out.*

Our Stories

This week we will hear voices of those to whom we eagerly listen—authors, theorists, and learners—all emerging from a kaleidoscope of societies, ages, genders, experiences, politics, and cultures—and resulting in the heartbeat of the whole language movement, the heartbeat that gives life and meaning to our whole language culture circle. But first we must recognize our own worth, reflect on our own history, and realize our own strength that rises from the bedrock of our own culture.

To help us with our inquiry, I am going to take the liberty of defining *culture* as a powerful collective of all the qualities that define us as human beings. Some of those qualities are expressed in the art of Diego Rivera, R. C. Gorman, or Norman Rockwell; the music of Mozart, Mariachi, or The Grateful Dead; the dance of Maria Tallchief, Gregory Hines, or Mikhail Baryshnikov; the architecture of the Navajo hogan, the high-rise apartment, or the row house; the poetry of Nikki Giovanni, Lucy Tapahonso, or Langston Hughes; the literature of Isaac Bashevis Singer, Margaret Laurence, or Toni Morrison.

Culture is the nuances, the looks, the sayings, the lessons, the jokes, the quirkiness, the rituals, the rules, the connectors, the contexts, the designs of our lives that we as members of groups have in some way allowed to emerge, not only from our past but from what is being created right here and now in the circles of our families, our classrooms, our support groups—our lives.

In order to respect the lives of those outside our own groups, we first need to understand the qualities within ourselves that have contributed to the sum total of who we are and what we consider of value and importance. Even though we may have consciously or unconsciously rejected some attributes, we are inextricably shaped by people, language, and experiences that were, or are, so pervasive and powerful that they help identify us as human beings, just as they help identify our culture circle: I know that I am FDR, the New Deal, and Bible stories for Presbyterian boys and girls; I am Saturday matinees, Shirley Temple, and Gary Cooper; I am also Woody Guthrie, Patsy Cline, and Station KVOO in Tulsa. I am all those side-splitting wisecracks from family and friends, stories that I absorbed while sitting on the fender of our old Ford V-8 as it moved around the town square on magical Saturday nights. I am "Idle hands are the devil's workshop" and "Fish or cut bait" (I rejected "Pretty is as pretty does"). I am friendship rings and Girl Scout camp songs. I am a lot of penny candy, home-canned peaches, and Chubbet dresses.

We are *all* so many precious things of quality that we could make E. D. Hirsch look culturally deprived. Through our cultures we make sense of our lives. But through *culture shared,* we are informed and enabled; through culture shared, we make sense of the world.

And now let's practice our own beliefs. I invite you to share a bit of yourself, and in doing so begin the renewal of your own culture and the search for other cultures, other voices. Would you, in your note-books or the margins of your programs, write down some things out of your past or present lives that are so pervasive and powerful that they could be thought of as part of your culture, things that in some way help define you as you—the person, the teacher, the human being that you are? Now I invite you to spot someone whom you do not know, to introduce yourself, to talk for a while, and to share something from your culture specific list. Finally, I invite you to reflect on, perhaps even write about, this experience and about your new acquaintances.

We know that lasting and deep appreciation of diversity is not gained by shaking hands and talking with someone at a conference for a few minutes. It is also not gained through the February Brotherhood Assembly and the Ethnic Food Festival. We cannot even be sure that it will be achieved when learners of diverse backgrounds come together in a classroom. These "tokens," however, should not be belittled; rather, they should be assessed for what they are—beginnings, or perhaps even better, little celebrations along the way toward more genuine recognition of the richness of many cultures and the beauty of many voices.

Authors' Stories

Whole language educators know that literature shared can be an invitation to culture shared, and we depend upon authors to let us see and feel the lives and hear the voices of others. I have chosen one author as a representative of all those writers who have spoken so eloquently to our students and to us.

Perhaps all of Katherine Paterson's books are celebrations of people and their relationships with others, but in her book *Gates of Excellence: On Reading and Writing Books for Children* (1981) Paterson directly shares her life with us. In the following passage she makes us feel the helplessness of not being seen or heard for who we are. As you experience Paterson's story, I invite you to think about those students whose lives are shaped by rich traditions and language that clash with or in some way are not comfortably and conveniently matched with the larger society, which includes organized schooling:

I can remember clearly how it feels not to have any words. In those months after I went to Japan in 1957, I would often find myself being taken somewhere by Japanese friends, not knowing where I was going or whom I was going to see. When I got to wherever I had been taken, I would find myself surrounded by people who were talking and laughing away, but because I did not know their words, I was totally shut out. As I began to learn a few words, people would try with infinite, exaggerated patience to talk with me. And because my speech was so halting and miserable, they would try to help me, try to put words into my mouth, try to guess what on earth it was I was trying to convey. When I was finally able to get out a sentence near enough to Japanese so that my listeners could grasp what I was driving at, they felt sure I'd appreciate knowing how I *should* have expressed that particular thought, and they would gently, firmly, and ever so politely, take my pitiful little sentence apart and correct it for me.

I'm sorry to report that I was not grateful. I wanted to yell, cry, throw a tantrum. *I am not a fool!* I wanted to scream. If only you could know me in *English,* you would see at once what a clever, delightful person I am. But, of course, I didn't say it. I couldn't say it. I didn't have the minimum daily requirement in either vocabulary or syntax. The first time I saw the play "The Miracle Worker," I knew what had been happening to me in those days. It was the rage of those starving for words.

In 1961, after four years in Japan, I boarded a jet in Tokyo and landed about twenty hours later in Baltimore. I was met by my parents and one of my sisters and taken home to Virginia. Every night for many weeks I would get out of the soft bed, which was killing my back, and lie sleepless on the floor. I was utterly miserable. "These people," I would say to myself, meaning my own family, "these people don't even know me." The reason I thought my family didn't know me was that they didn't know me in Japanese. (Paterson 1981, 7–8)

Real appreciation of someone else's identity comes from long-term experiences in which all the learners can, as Katherine Paterson put it, see themselves and others in their own language, in their own achievements and successes, displaying their own trophies.

But if learners cannot come together face to face over time, we must seek out the literature, explore the accomplishments, and build communities in which respect for wide ranges of cultural diversity becomes a way of life. And that way of life has no room for a killer culture in which those in power have an inflated sense of their own language and traditions.

Researchers' and Theorists' Stories

As whole language educators, we listen to the voices of researchers
and theorists whom we trust. I am convinced that never has a group
of educators taken their profession so seriously, felt so responsible, or
studied so hard. Witness a TAWL (Teachers Applying Whole Language) meeting where teachers are critically investigating the theories
and research of another educator, asking what all this has to do with
them and their students and how the assumptions and suggestions
stack up with what they know to be true about learners and learning.

Of all the researchers and theorists to whom we have attended
in understanding whole language principles and practices, I have
done the ridiculous—I have selected one to represent them all. I have
chosen Paulo Freire because of his influence on the lives of three
friends—teachers who have experienced such hurtful and shabby
treatment from colleagues that one of them seriously considered re-
signing from a successful ten-year teaching career, three teachers who
have virtually withdrawn to the saneness of their classrooms and
closed their doors. These teachers come together in an attempt to cope
with some of the torment that they have faced for almost two years. I
would like to read an excerpt from Shor and Freire's *A Pedagogy for
Liberation* (1987) that touched them, and then tell you the reactions of
the teachers.

> This is a great discovery, education is politics! When a teacher
> discovers that he or she is a politician, too, the teacher has to
> ask, "What kind of politics am I doing in the classroom? That is,
> in favor of whom am I being a teacher?" The teacher works in
> favor of something and against something. Because of that he
> or she will have another great question, "How to be consistent
> in my teaching practice with my political choice? I cannot pro-
> claim my liberating dream and in the next day be authoritarian
> in my relationship with the students."

Freire's words gave these teachers courage and perspective.
They had learned some hard lessons from the almost daily gut-
wrenching experiences that included being denied and ignored by
former colleagues. After a great deal of sorting out and struggling with
Freire's words, they came to a *realization* and a *question*. They realized
that when they made the decision to live a whole language curriculum,
they had engaged in a political act. They did not set out to do so, but
it happened. This was scary, but the realization and the fear it brought
gave them an opportunity to be courageous. And their thoughtful

question: "While we're proclaiming *our* need for freedom and liberation, are we hearing all the voices within our own classroom? Are some
students' beliefs, traditions, efforts, and abilities valued over others,
just as others' opinions and practices are prioritized over ours?" As the
teachers asked liberating questions about the unquestioned obedience
that was expected of them, they began to investigate choice and voice
and ownership in their own classrooms. This is grass-roots whole
language politicalization.

These teachers began to heal and to become enabled when they
realized that Freire was right: education *is* politics (at least for them it
was), and they had to move politically both outside and inside the
classroom. But curiously, it was primarily their actions *within* the classroom that enabled and empowered them. As one of the teachers said,
"I'm not so scared now, because I'm a teacher again, and one of the
things I am teaching my students is how to be heard."

Learners' Stories

And it is time that we heard from students. While listening to authors,
to theorists, and to ourselves, we urge learners to raise their inquiring
voices. I have chosen three examples of students' voices to share with
you. I have selected these examples because they are quiet but powerful examples of kids becoming informed, speaking up for themselves,
and speaking out for beliefs that are worthy of their time and energy.

In a collaborative study, Kittye Copeland and Kathryn Mitchell
Pierce invited Copeland's students to reflect on their science experience. William's learning log entry is typical of the children's reflections: "Science. We went outside. I picked a group of onions. I learned
that an onion has a bud inside of it that makes it grow." (See Figure
1.1.) Classmate Chip knew that his teacher encourages and expects
children to be candid about their learning and that they are not expected to play at schooling, so he was forthright in his comments: "I
like science. I picked a whole onion. It was neat. I did not learn
anything." (See Figure 1.2.)

Grace T was told that school board members would be visiting
her classroom because there had been a complaint about, among other
things, her lack of textbook use. The principal was supportive of
Grace's curriculum and suggested that she tell her students that they
would be having visitors and that they might want to welcome the
visitors and to explain what went on in the classroom. Grace told her
fifth graders about the visitors, and the kids talked about how they

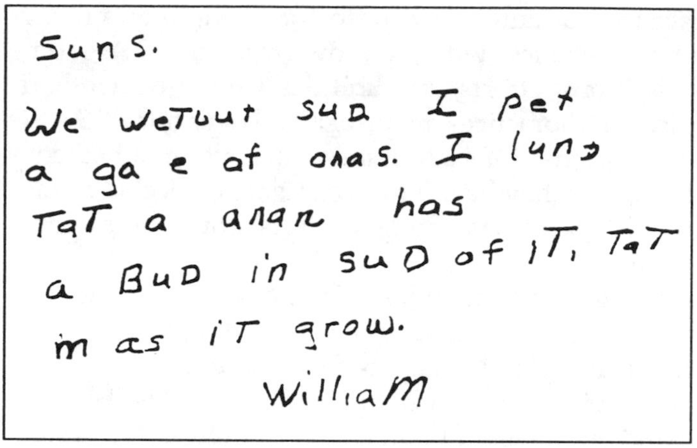

Suns.

We weTout sua I pet a gae af onas. I lun TaT a anan has a BuD in suD of iT, TaT m as iT grow.
                                   William

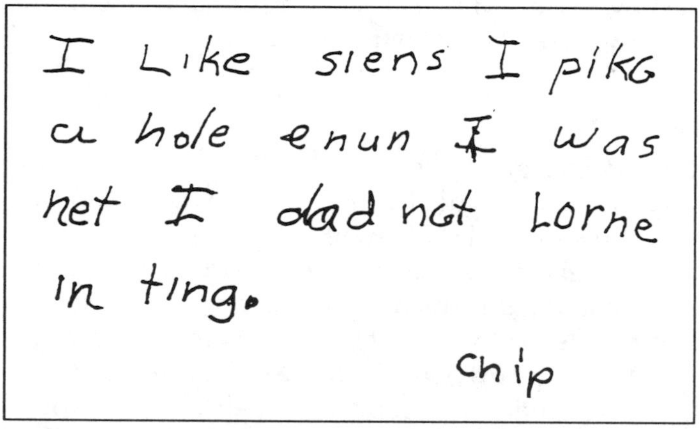

I Like siens I pikG a hole enun I was net I dad nat Lorne in ting.
                                   Chip

Figure 1.1. A science entry in William's learning log.

Figure 1.2. A science entry in Chip's learning log.

could make their visitors welcome. Then one of the students suggested that guests to the classroom could not possibly understand, based on one visit, everything going on there. On the student's suggestion, a committee of five children worked hard for a week making a guest book and composing the following letter to be given to everyone who visited their room:

Dear Visitor,

Thank you for coming to our classroom. We think you will understand us better if we tell you a bit about our room and offer a few suggestions.

First of all, please take a walk around the room. Although we try to run a tidy ship, this is a working classroom, so you will find unfinished projects, work in progress, and OUR STUFF. WE do the bulletin boards (not Mrs. T by herself), we write our assignments on the board, we arrange the books and try to keep the files orderly. We *live* here.

We also have a say in what we want to study through our special expert projects, and we choose our own books to read. We would be glad to answer your questions about any of the 50 topics we have learned about this year.

Please read some of our completed stories. If you want to talk to an author or if you want our autograph, just ask. If you look at some of our unfinished stories or research reports you might find different spelling or funny grammar. We call this our rough draft spelling and writing. Don't worry, we get better as we go along. No, we don't have spelling tests and grammar sheets. We just write stories, poems, do research and draw pictures to illustrate our work.

We also talk a lot to each other. If you think we are wasting time, just listen in. But we can be quiet, too. If we are having silent reading time, please join us by getting a book. You might want to read some we've written.

Since we write a lot in this room, we hope you will, too. Please sign our guest book. You'll notice that there is lots of room in the book to write your comments and questions. If there is something you like about us, please say so. If there is something you think we should be doing differently, we are all ears.

> Sincerely yours,
>
> Grade Five and Mrs. T

Yeh, Yeh, Yeh

In a second-grade classroom at Columbia Catholic Elementary School, Gary Shaw encouraged his students to speak up for themselves and for others when they felt the cause was a worthy one. When Kristen and Alexis noticed that only the boys got to be servers during the communion services, they felt slighted and decided to talk with their teacher. Shaw explained that he thought the priest chose boys as servers in order to get to know and to bond with them; letting them participate in the services might result in their growing up to become priests.

The two girls did not buy the argument, so their teacher suggested that they write to Father (see Figure 1.3). Kristen and Alexis did not sign their letter initially, but then Shaw reminded them that the priest would not retaliate, and that when people feel strongly about an

Dear Father Flanagian,
     the girls in out class say
it's not far that the boys are
the only ones that get
to be the severs
I bet that if you ask
half a million of the
servers if ther doing
it to be a Preast when
thay growup thale say
no. I do hope that
you can do somthing about
this if you can't
pleas send the popes
adres

Alexis
tall singed Alexis, Kristen

Kristen
Meedey

P.S. Please write
back

Figure 1.3. Alexis and Kristen's letter of complaint that girls were not chosen as servers during the communion services.

issue they usually strengthen their position by signing their names. Not only did the girls sign their names, but they drew pictures of themselves and provided a little description (Alexis is tall, Kristen medium).

Our Colleagues' Voices

We respond to *all* our colleagues' voices, not just the select group of teachers who are as informed as we are. We encourage dialogue with those who, in our eyes, are making a muddle of whole language principles and practices, those who are "doing" whole language and manipulating the "stuff" of whole language. We also listen carefully and are sensitive to the hopes and potential of the enthusiastic but scared whole language novices. We remember that perhaps the reason we know better than they or that we are more successful in our practices is that we started before these teachers did; we have had a chance to get it wrong and then get it right; we self-correct; we have colleagues and students to help us grow. And now it is up to us to issue the invitation that moves less informed learners from simply talking the talk and walking the walk of whole language to singing the songs and dancing the dances of whole language—that is, to practicing whole language principles not as a mimic, but as an artist, as a teacher. It is easy to fall into a "stage theory" of whole language when we are working with less experienced educators. When this happens, we expect all teachers to walk the same thorny path that we walked and to have the same conversations that we had. We think that if they read the right books and if they attend the right meetings they will "develop" into us. Educators with fewer experiences in whole language are not automatically or necessarily less capable than we are. Some of their experiences will be similar to ours, but they and their students will also have unique and extraordinary experiences, some that will be richer and more informative than ours, and some that will be tenuous and confusing. Nevertheless, their voices must be heard.

We must hear the voices of the cautious skeptics and must attempt to understand and respond thoughtfully to reasoned questions. We must never avoid the questions of the skeptics just to keep an uneasy peace. Such discussions can help us grow in our own understanding and will lead us to important inquiry.

We also must hear the voices of the dissenters—those who ask us questions and then will not listen to our answers or do not like the answers that we give. They dismiss us by saying that we are not responsive or intellectual enough to talk with them. They are the ones who say, "Those teachers can't even define whole language." We need to point out to these detractors that we have defined whole language linguistically, historically, pedagogically, curricularly, and politically. Whole language has got to be the most defined and redefined concept in education today. We invite them to listen. I believe, however, that there comes a time when we need to let the detractors, those who would minimize our efforts and our answers, know that we have had enough. We can find ourselves emotionally and physically drained from the struggle of defending our principles and practices. Our time, energy, and hope must be available to those who will enter into a real dialogue.

Sometimes people ask me if I believe whole language is for all learners. I have no trouble answering that one. "Yes, all learners." I am also asked, "Is whole language for all educators?" My answer to that one is, "Maybe not." If that educator is not a learner, our efforts to inform may be futile, and we may want to direct our efforts toward those who are learners. Depending on how much energy, patience, and time we have, we can continue to invite, to highlight articles and put them in mailboxes, even to get resisters to attend conferences and classes, but we cannot feel responsible or guilty or even angry when the invitations are ignored and our messages fall on closed minds.

The Whole Language Umbrella

The Whole Language Umbrella is a network of whole language teachers, an umbrella under which we can invite all educators, researchers, theorists, parents, publishers, and learners to gather. Under the umbrella we can sing the songs and dance the dances of all cultures. We can search out the very best in us all, and we can create our own culture circle.

Under the umbrella and in our TAWL groups, there is even room for some whom we might never have expected to find there. A miracle sometimes happens. One did in our area when a parent complained to the school board about a teacher practicing whole language. This parent caused a great deal of pain and undermined two years of building a whole language curriculum. The miracle is that eleven years later that parent called a local tutorial service to ask about having her second child tutored—in whole language. Miracle or hard work?

I suppose that we have to let it rest for some. There are those Dicks and Janes who are always going to think that we are strange. But don't underestimate the funny Baby Sallys of this world—Sally just might join us under the umbrella. (See Figure 1.4.)

Look, Dick.

Look, Jane.

See Sally.

Sally

Figure 1.4. Sally and her umbrella, from W. S. Gray, D. Baruch, and E. R. Montgomery, *We Look and See* (Glenview, Ill.: Scott, Foresman, 1946).

References

Paterson, K. 1981. *Gates of excellence: On reading and writing books for children.* New York: Elsevier/Nelson Books.

Shor, I., and P. Freire. 1987. *A pedagogy for liberation: Dialogues on transforming education.* Westport, Conn.: Greenwood Press.

2 I Hear Voices

Judith Wells Lindfors
University of Texas at Austin

I Hear Voices." I smiled to myself as I wrote this title, remembering an orientation program in which I had participated many years ago. It was 1961, and I was preparing (along with 149 others) to go to East Africa to teach English in a secondary school for two years. At one point during our orientation program we were given a test that was apparently designed to weed out those among us who were psychologically or emotionally unfit for the experience of living and working in an African setting—in a culture vastly different from our own. The test was composed of a set of statements to which we simply had to respond "yes" or "no." One item on this test that struck me as being especially unsubtle was this: "I hear voices that nobody else hears." And so I smiled as I wrote my chapter title and remembered this test item, but also as I realized how different are the voices to which I refer in my title from those of my long-ago psychological test. *Those* voices were unreal and unheard (at least by most of us). In striking contrast, the voices to which I now refer are both *real* and *heard.* They are the nineteen voices in the kindergarten community in which my story takes place. They are children's voices—voices not in the sense of disturbances of air waves and vibrations that impinge on ear drums—but rather, voices in the sense of self and (distinctive) expression of self, what Mikhail Bakhtin might call "the speaking personality" (Wertsch 1991) or what in writing Don Graves calls "the person in the print." This is the voice I mean: *self*-expression.

I describe the story of these voices and my discovery of the children's awareness of them for several reasons. First, I tell the story as a way of validating—legitimizing—classroom exploration. Not research. That notion no longer needs help. By exploration I mean wandering and wondering and noticing and reflecting and interacting—and wandering and wondering some more. Second, I relate the story as a way of thinking about classroom communities, especially the balance of individuals and groups within them. And finally, it may simply be of interest to readers to know what an outsider saw in a classroom that could belong to a reader. Ways of life in a classroom tend to be taken for granted by those within it, a case of the fish being the last to discover water. And so the look and sound of a classroom to an outsider might be of some interest to readers.

Messing About

My story begins with my coming to Marion Coffee's kindergarten classroom. I had come because, to state it most simply, I needed to be in an excellent classroom for a time. I had for too long been supervising student teachers in typical Texas classrooms. I had for too long been frustrated by the task of trying to help my undergraduate students imagine classrooms they had never seen, for their life experience of education has been played out totally within Texas in its test-driven era. I needed, in short, to have my vision and sense of possibility restored. I needed to renew my belief that even in my test-driven state of Texas, wonderful interactions among children and teachers can, and do, still occur. As test mania has increasingly taken over in Texas, classrooms with such interactions at their core are ever harder to find. But I knew that Marion's kindergarten was one. Test mania may come and test mania may go, but Marion's classroom will always be *that* kind of classroom.

We go back a long way, Marion and I, at least to 1970 when we were fellow students in a graduate class at the University of Texas. We continued over the years to be aware of each other, with our kids in the same school and same grade levels, with my son in the Cub Scout troop that Marion's husband led, and with Marion often having U.T. student teachers in her classroom and me on the U.T. faculty, often in the role of student-teaching supervisor. But our connectedness has increased during the past few years as we have interacted more and more about, and have shared materials relating to, the inservice workshops and short intensive courses that Marion has increasingly been called upon to give. It was in the context of one of our professionally focused conversations that I proposed that we do some sort of research together in her classroom. Marion eagerly agreed.

The science educator David Hawkins is the one I have to thank for giving a name ("messing about") and dignity to the activity that Marion and I engaged in that semester. In his article titled "Messing About in Science," Hawkins takes Water Rat from Kenneth Grahame's *Wind in the Willows* as his starting point: " 'Nice? It's the *only* thing,' said the Water Rat solemnly, as he leant forward for his stroke. 'Believe me, my young friend, there is *nothing*—absolutely nothing—half so much worth doing as simply messing about in boats. Simply messing,'

he went on dreamily: 'messing—about—in—boats—messing—' "
(Grahame 1908 [1933], 12). Hawkins asserts that children's classroom
learning in science should engage them in three phases, the most
neglected of which—"honoring the philosophy of the Water Rat"—he
calls "Messing About," a time "devoted to free and unguided exploratory work." He ends his article by returning to the Water Rat—the
ultimate educational philosopher, it would seem. Says Hawkins,

> there . . . are three major phases of good science teaching . . . and
> . . . the one most neglected is that which made the Water Rat go
> dreamy with joy when he talked about it. At a time when the
> pressures of prestige education are likely to push children to
> work like hungry laboratory rats in a maze, it is good to remem-
> ber that their wild, watery cousin, reminiscing about the joys of
> his life, uttered a profound truth about education. (Hawkins
> 1982)

Now if the importance of messing about is "a profound truth"
for children learning in school, I take it to be no less "a profound truth"
for teachers learning in school. So to say that Marion and I were not
engaged in formal research, which begins with an explicit research
question and systematically gathers and analyzes data related to it,
this is not to trivialize our undertaking, but only to say that it was
different, "the charm of it" (again in the words of the Water Rat) being
that "whether you arrive at your destination or whether you reach
somewhere else, or whether you never get anywhere at all, you're
always busy" (Grahame 1908 [1933], 13).

Busy we were, Marion and I. We had our river—our place to do
our messing about (Marion's classroom). We also had our "boat"—our
means of exploring. Two mornings a week I came to Marion's room
and observed during Centers Time and Whole Group Study Time, the
time when the whole class sat in a circle on the rug and Marion focused
on a particular concept. I would drift from center to center or, during
Study Time, would sit on the floor immediately behind the circle of
children. Notebook in hand, I would write furiously whatever I was
seeing and hearing that was interesting or intriguing—bits of conversation, descriptions of activities, and interactions. No taping. Besides
the fact that, initially, I was not looking for or at anything in particular
and wanted to be completely free to drift, tape-recording the class
would have made this kind of exploration experience impossible.
Audiotaping in the classroom would have required a formal research
proposal, submitted to the Austin Independent School District a year
in advance, with subsequent approval granted by everyone from the

superintendent on down. But simply "observing" in Marion's class-room—wandering around and writing—required approval only from Marion and her principal.

After Study Time the children would go off to P.E., and Marion and I would sit and talk about what had been interesting that morning, and Marion would tell me about some of the other happenings that had occurred when I was not there.

This went on for several weeks. I began to feel uncomfortable, and I think Marion did, too. We had a boat and a river for our explor-ing, but we had no topic or focus. You see, we were not pure Water Rats, only modified Water Rats—Water Rats who had been to college. I was waiting for a topic to emerge, and this was not happening. I felt that Marion was waiting for me to suggest a topic, that she expected the usual situation in which a university professor comes into a teacher's classroom as "Primary Investigator" to carry out some re-search project and engages the teacher as a partner, more or less, but never as one who jointly *owns* the research. And this Primary Investi-gator role was one that I had every conscious intention of avoiding. So Marion was waiting for me to suggest a direction, and I was waiting for her—for some indication of an area of her interest. And we sat. And we talked. And we felt uncomfortable.

Focusing

At last it happened. During our conversation one morning while the children were at P.E., I happened to remark, "I noticed today that these kids seem to have such a sense of community." Marion said, "Commu-nity! Now *that's* something I've always been interested in!" She went on to talk with real feeling about how she has always attempted to foster a strong sense of community in her classroom. She told me of the frequent comments that visitors to her classroom had made about this. And so we decided to look at it and for it: the children's talk (and other behavior) as it fostered and as it reflected their sense of commu-nity. My notes and noticings became a bit more focused, and Marion began writing down anecdotes that related to her interest in commu-nity. Our stories accumulated; our talk continued.

I am glad now that we did not begin by defining *community*, for as we went along, it became increasingly apparent that our notions of community—though largely similar—were also interestingly and val-idly different. I came from the outside and focused in, whereas Marion, coming from the inside, focused *out*. I saw this classroom as an intact, self-contained unit, an entity whose workings I could examine, a microcosm. My focus was entirely within the classroom walls. But Marion's orientation was outward, beyond the classroom. She was keenly aware of this classroom as but one society within a larger one. Her interest in classroom community was driven by her goal that her children would increasingly move out into and make a difference in that larger community, taking their classroom community notions with them. And so, in our conversations, Marion would tell me about an incident that she had observed involving young adult men playing baseball at a nearby park, or she would bring an article from the newspaper telling of a public lecture being given about "community." And I would think, "Interesting, but what does this have to do with what we're focusing on?" In time, I came to understand the connection. But if we had begun with a definition of *community*—necessarily a compromise, consensus definition—this difference in our perspectives could not have flourished, and we could not have learned from it.

After the children's expression of community became our focus, I began to see and hear what I expected—which of course says more about my limited ability to see and hear at that point than it says about the children. One of the most obvious indications of the children's awareness of "our group" was the shared procedures that they carried out and talked about, sometimes in ways that would make little sense to an outsider, but that were perfectly understood by the children. Here's an example from my notes:

> It's Centers Time and Maria and some other children are playing in Big Blocks. They have constructed a platform, their "ice skating rink," and they are "skating" on it in stocking feet. Juan, a monolingual Spanish speaker newly arrived from Central America, comes to the edge of the group. He takes off one shoe. Maria calls out, "Mrs. Coffee! Mrs. Coffee! Juan is seven." The classroom rule is "Only six in Big Blocks at a time." It's a rule that David shows he knows when, on another morning, he stands at the edge of Big Blocks and—with head nods—silently counts the children already there. Six head nods. He turns and walks away to another center.

We might expect members of a community to know not only what the expected procedures are for its functioning, but also when and how those guidelines can be suspended, those rules bent. One demonstration of this knowledge came on a day when the children in Big Blocks had made a wonderful long train. Tammy, one of the official six in Big Blocks, tells Samantha (an outsider) that she can come for a ride on the train. This will, she acknowledges, make more than six in

Big Blocks, but Samantha will leave as soon as she finishes her train ride. The Big Blocks group accepts this as a legitimate bending of the "Only six in Big Blocks" rule.

One expected procedure was for the children to first help clean up the centers in which they played and then help in any other centers where help was needed. Cleanup time reverberated with comments like, "Lindsay, you have to clean up with us" (because she had been playing in that center but was not helping to clean up), or Marion's comments to children not engaged in helping at other centers after their own was clean:

> "Which center would y'all like to help in?"
> "Big Blocks."
> "Good idea—they look like they can use some help," or, "OK, girls, we have lots of other places to help."

This is not to say that the cleanup rule was always complied with; but its existence was not challenged, as shown by this example from my notes:

> Edward has been sitting alone at the book center, very intently copying the name of a book into his pocket spiral notebook. The cleanup bell rings. He continues his copying, his concentration undiminished. Janice, indicating the small blocks center in which Edward had been playing earlier, says, "Edward, you're supposed to help." Edward replies, "I'm not in that center anymore." Janice says, "You're still supposed to help." She walks away. Edward continues with his copying.

Edward, like his classmates, knew the way it was "supposed" to be. He shared with them an understanding and acceptance of "We do it this way."

Recognition of procedures—ways of doing things—was not all these children shared, of course. Evident to me from the outset was their shared understanding that this was a place where helping each other was valued. And expected. I have not yet figured out how this was so well understood so early in the year, but it was. Examples in my notes are abundant. I choose just two, both from Study Time.

> The children are studying five. On the floor in front of each child is a piece of paper with five lima beans on it. Marion has told the children to turn their beans so that they are all on the white side. Tammy, sitting beside Juan, sees that he has not done this. She knows, of course, that he has not understood Marion's instruction, given in English. She reaches over, turns his five beans to the white side, then turns back to her own.

The topic is rhyming words. Marion asks Jamie for a word that
rhymes with "goat." Jamie is stuck. He can't think of any.

> *David:* You know it, Jamie. It's something you wear.
> *Marion:* That's a good clue.
> *David:* It's not a shirt.
> *Jamie:* Coat.

These five year olds constantly played out their understanding that
they were responsible for others in the group. Helping someone function successfully was another aspect of shared understanding of how
we do things in this place.

A third area that I expected to find expressed as part of these
children's sense of community was their common history, their shared
experiences. I knew these to be rich and abundant—going fishing in
the nearby creek and then setting up aquariums in the room, making
pumpkin pie, going to the observatory, and so on. I expected lots of
talk about "Remember the time we . . . ?" And there *was* a lot of such
talk, talk that fostered and reflected the *we* notion that pervaded this
classroom. But I had not expected that it would sometimes involve
what, to an adult, would seem like such inconsequential events.

> Standing in line, waiting to leave the room for P.E. one morning,
> David says to Lindsay, "Remember how we went to the water
> fountain and drinked? Remember how we went to the water
> fountain and went around in a circle?"

Nor had I expected to find it so casually woven into conversation—just
a passing comment that *we* understand, as when Marion comments
that Juan's drawing "looks like Saturn that we saw in the telescope
when we went to the observatory." Sometimes it was a markedly
in-group remark, a comment whose significance an outsider would
not grasp. For example, one day in December Marion and a small
group of children were sitting at the art table, glittering their Christmas ornaments. The talk was relaxed and warm. Suddenly Janice said,
"Mrs. Coffee, what if we painted your porch?" Marion laughed and
said, "Well, it better wash off, that's all I got to say." The group—the
in-group—laughed. They knew the reference was to Nicole's show-
and-tell story earlier that day, of going to her friend's house and
painting the friend's porch.

Shared procedures, shared expectations of helping one another
and being responsible for one another's welfare, shared history—now
that sounds like an *adult's* notion of community. And our interest was
in the *children's* notion. How could we get them to "define" *community*
for us, to tell us what it meant to them? It was easy enough to see

reflections of our notion. But what was their notion? We decided to have Marion interview the children individually to see if we could get at this. This turned out to be a disaster—for two reasons.

First, the questions were wrong. In an attempt to be open and not impose our categories on the children, we had come up with questions that were meaningless and incomprehensible to them, questions to which they just could not respond:

- How would you know this was your class?
- If something was going wrong, what could you do to help?
- When you're in another group, does it seem different from ours? How?

We wanted them to come up with the categories, but what they came up with was puzzlement, a look that was the visual equivalent of "Huh?"

Early in the interviews, Marion identified the second major problem: interviewing children individually, instead of in small groups. She was well aware of how individual children were better able to understand a task by observing other children at the task. She knew, too, how often these children picked up on and extended one another's ideas.

We tried again. This time Marion carried out group interviews—focused discussions—with four children at a time. The focusing question was this: "Suppose a new child came to our class. What would you tell the child about our class?" If this proved too "open" for a particular group, Marion would get more specific: "What would you tell the child about how we do things here?" She also would ask some version of the question "We've done a lot of special things that the new boy or girl would have missed. What are some of the special things we've done that you'd like to tell the new girl or boy about?"

Given the shaping of the questions—the focus here on procedures and shared experiences—it is not surprising that these are what the children provided. These may not have been the categories the children would have come up with on their own, but at least the categories were not alien to the children, and they were able to elaborate on the categories by providing a rich array of specific examples.

And now came Marion's crisis, the crisis which engendered her major discovery. It had to do with rules. Marion audiotaped the group interviews, and I transcribed them. Examining the transcripts, Marion felt inundated with the children's listing of rules, many of the "Don't do . . . " variety, and many of them completely new to her—rules that she had never heard before, much less initiated. This was very upsetting. Marion fostered a free and responsible environment, and here these children seemed obsessed with don'ts. And where did rules like "Don't swing the mouse by the tail" even come from?

It took an educational anthropology doctoral student, Sarah Burkhalter, to help. When Marion told Sarah about this upsetting turn of events, Sarah laughed and said, "Of course! That's how a group defines itself. This is the children's attempt to help the newcomer join the group. 'Here's how we do things. Now you can be one of us. Now you can belong.' " Looking at the children's responses again, from this new perspective, Marion breathed easier. Now the child's "Don't swing the mouse by the tail" seemed to be her specific, personally meaningful rendering of "Be gentle with the animals," a rule shared by all.

The Outsider's View

My discovery was quite different from Marion's. I relate it with some embarrassment. Sometimes we make what seems to be an important discovery, but when we stand back and look at it, it suddenly seems trivial and obvious—even silly—and we say to ourselves, "Well, anybody would know that. What made me think it was such a big deal?" My discovery was that kind. I suspect that it was not a discovery for Marion because she knew it all along. And it may not be a discovery for other teachers, who live in the classroom and who may know it, too. But I was the outsider here and did not know it. So, embarrassed or not, I relate my discovery, hoping that it may interest teachers to know an outsider's perspective. My observations may make opaque an aspect of the classroom that may, to teachers, be transparent.

I carried with me a deep-seated (though unconscious) notion that *individual* and *group* represented two opposite values, and that the extent to which one was valued and fostered was the extent to which the other was diminished. I imagined some total amount that was distributed on the two sides of a balance scale. More on one side meant less on the other; one side down, the other up. Now this was a very simplistic view, and I suspect my notion came from a variety of sources:

- from my acquaintance with anthropologically oriented literature such as Susan Philips's Warm Springs Indian Reservation research (1972, 1982) or Kathryn Au's work with Hawaiian children (1980)

- from my reading of the competition-vs.-cooperation debate that has pervaded the educational literature for many years now

- from my reading of feminist literature such as Carol Gilligan's *In a Different Voice: Psychological Theory and Women's Development* (1982) or sociolinguist Deborah Tannen's *You Just Don't Understand: Women and Men in Conversation* (1990)—research and writing that suggest males value and voice toward being independent and individual, whereas females value and voice toward connecting, affiliating, nurturing, supporting

But whatever the sources, this polarity notion was mine: The more you value and foster group cohesion, the less you value and foster individuality. The more you attend to the chorus, the less you attend to the individual voice. It took a class of nineteen five-year-old children to show me *that,* and *how,* I was wrong. I had been listening for, and thus hearing, a group *we:*

> *We* do it this way.
>
> *We* help each other.
>
> *We* share a history.

But I began to notice that the *we* that shared procedures, expectations, and a history was not a faceless, voiceless mass *we*—not a pack, not a herd—but a *we* of quite distinct individuals, recognized by the children as distinct. Theirs was a *we* of Tammy and David, Molly and Samantha, Jonathan and Jamie. Even in the first month of school, before the children knew everyone's name, they noticed and commented on *individuals*—their particular characteristics, preferences, clothing, activities, abilities, habits. What strikes me now as so remarkable is that it occurred in such an unremarkable way, in unremarkable incidents like these, as recorded in my notes:

> It's September 26. The children are seated in a circle on the rug playing a game in which one child is blindfolded, another child greets him or her, and the first child must guess which child spoke. After one child has correctly guessed that it was Samantha who was the speaker, Janice comments, "Samantha has a deep voice; that's how she knew." And now it is Samantha's turn to be "it." She listens to the speaker (David) and says, "I don't know the name." Marion says, "Then describe the person. Tell what the person looks like." Samantha says, "He has a shirt that's blue and has stars on it." (He does.)

> I enter the room during Centers Time and to my astonishment find no one in Big Blocks. Kim sees my surprise. "What?!" I say to her. "There's no one in Big Blocks today."

> *Kim:* That's because someone isn't here today.
> *Me:* Who's that?
> *Kim:* Orlando. He loves Big Blocks.

Samantha often comes late. One day she is absent and Trisha, noticing her absence, tells Marion, "Samantha is *really* late to-day."

It is Centers Time and Samantha and I are sitting at the art table. Samantha tells me, "Trisha knows a bunch of Banish." (In fact, Trisha knows no Spanish at all, but regularly pretends she does, bending over Juan and emitting long strings of nonsense.) Marion and four children (including Juan) are sitting at the art table. The children are glittering their Christmas ornaments. Each child has three colors of glitter and is supposed to keep the three separate. Juan has mixed his together.

> *Trisha:* Uh-oh, Mrs. Coffee.
> *Nicole:* Juan did three colors.
> *Marion:* That's OK. He didn't understand.
> *Tammy:* Cause he speaks Spanish. But he's learning En-
> glish.

All unremarkable. Which may be why it took awhile for me to hear them.

I also became increasingly aware of the children's expression of appreciation for individual expertise or accomplishment. Again, the examples from my notes tend to be casual, easy, unremarkable. The following all happened to occur in mid-October and all involve Jamie (a child who was repeating kindergarten):

> Jamie is at the computer. He has created a wonderful picture—a variety of patterns and colors—and it is starting to print. Edward is watching as Jamie's picture is progressively revealed. He says, with unmistakable appreciation, "Oh, those are pretty. How did ya make that?!"

> Now Molly is at the computer with Jonathan. She tells him, "I want Jamie to show me how to do it." She calls to Jamie across the room: "Jamie!"

> It's Centers Time and Jamie and Trisha are at the art table. Jamie looks at Trisha's drawing and says, "Gosh, that's a neat one!"

> It's Whole Group Study Time. The focus is patterns. Marion has lined up several children in a row a couple times, to demon-strate different patterns (e.g., alternating children with different colored clothing). Now the pattern is boy–girl–boy–girl–boy–girl. No one can guess what the pattern is. They try color of

clothing (red–blue), height (tall–short), shoe fastenings (tie–velcro), hair length (long–short), but no one can guess. Marion is about to tell what the pattern is when Jamie mutters that he thinks it's boy–girl. Marion says enthusiastically, "That's right, Jamie. Jamie got it!" The children burst into spontaneous applause. Jamie smiles.

Individuals within a Group

How does this happen? I asked myself so many times that semester, and ask myself still. How can we have not individual *or* group, but rather individual *within* group: group enhancing individual and individual enhancing group? I don't know the answer, but I do know that it did not occur by accident in Marion's classroom. No coincidence here. Rather, a teacher deeply committed to a community of individuals, each contributing in unique ways to "groupness"—community. It was inevitable that Marion would play this out in countless demonstrations (to use Frank Smith's term), demonstrations both intentional and inadvertent. I expected to see her play out the "groupness" of *we*. What I had not expected was the "individualness" comprising that *we*.

First, the room itself—the physical environment—demonstrated a *we* of nineteen individuals:

- Nineteen small labeled containers in a group on the window sill, each containing a seed that an individual child had planted
- Nineteen leaves gathered on a recent walk, grouped on a bulletin board, each labeled with name of leaf and child who had found it
- Nineteen alien pictures—or Halloween pictures with dictated stories—in a cluster on the bulletin board, each with artist's/author's name
- The "With a Friend" book the children had made, a book Marion kept on the chalk tray where the children had easy and constant access to it, one page of the book written and illustrated by each child
- The "What's in Space?" mural covering one wall—a mural with nineteen labeled sections
- Two large graphs on the wall, one of nineteen pairs of shoes, the other of nineteen pets (actual or hoped for)
- Above the computer, a large sheet of paper listing things you can do with computers, each suggestion provided by a child and written down by Marion, along with the name of the child whose suggestion it was

Everywhere I looked I saw—literally *saw*—the message: we are a group of nineteen individuals and every one (note: every *one*) of us contributes. It was a powerful visual message.

Second, there were Marion's frequent demonstrations of appreciation for an individual child's contribution to the group. Sometimes these were explicit, as in the pencil-sharpening incident:

> It's Whole Group Study Time and Marion begins by saying, "I wanna say some special things to some special people who did some special things." She write-talks "Th-a-n-k y-ooo-u" on the chalkboard beside the rug where the children are seated in a circle. "This was all started by Charles," she tells them. "Charles noticed that the pencils needed to be sharpened. I started sharpening them, but it took too long. Charles started sharpening the pencils and then others joined in. So the first one I want to say thank you to is Charles." She writes his name under the "thank you." Several children say, "I helped," and Marion writes these names in the thank-you list. She concludes, "These people really helped us and really worked hard, and these pencils will last the whole year."

Often the demonstrations of appreciation were implicit—Marion reading the children's individually authored storybooks aloud at the start of Whole Group Study Time or using two patterned easel paintings done during Centers Time when the focus of Study Time is patterns, or making a center using the tongue-twister game that Jonathan has brought from home. But whether explicit or implicit, the message of appreciation for individual contributions to the group was evident.

Third, Marion frequently followed a child's suggestion. The following examples from Whole Group Study Time are typical:

> The children, as a group, are dictating text for a picture story about a girl getting lost from her mother in a grocery store. Nicole suggests, "Ms. Coffee, why don't we name the story?" Marion says, "OK. Let's name the story." After they discuss and finally agree on a title, a child suggests "She is lost" as the first sentence, a sentence the other children accept. But Charles asks, "Doesn't *lost* mean that she's in the store and her mother is someplace else?" Marion replies, "That's a good point." The children change their opening sentence to "She is lost from her mother in the store."

> The focus of Group Study Time is rhyming words. Marion uses a thumbs up/thumbs down activity: if Marion gives a pair of words that rhyme, the children put their thumbs up; if the words don't rhyme, they put thumbs down. After providing several word pairs herself, Marion begins to call on individual

children to give the word pairs. She continues to put her thumbs up or down, along with the children. Edward says to her, "I think everyone's got it." Marion, recognizing this as a tactful suggestion answers, "Oh, you mean I shouldn't do it?" Edward says, "Yes." Marion does not do it on the next round, and, indeed, everyone gets it. She says, "I think that was a good suggestion of Edward's." Again the message is clear: Individuals influence what we do here. Individuals' ideas are important.

But not only their ideas. The individuals themselves are important. This was demonstrated most dramatically on those occasions when the special situation of an individual child became the deliberate focus of group concern. I give but two examples, both from the first month of school. I include them in their entirety because they are so powerful.

It's Whole Group Study Time. Marion begins by telling the children, "Samantha is sad today." The children look for Samantha in their circle and see that indeed she is sad. Samantha could best be described as a downward droop occupying rug space. Head, eyes, shoulders all *down.* Marion continues, "She's sad because she wanted to play in Big Blocks, but there were already six people so she couldn't. What could we say to Samantha to make her feel better?" Hands go up. Marion calls on a child who says, "Samantha, you can play in Big Blocks tomorrow." Samantha continues to droop.

> *Marion:* She's still sad. What else can we tell her?
> *Another child:* Samantha, you can play in Big Blocks *first thing* when you come in tomorrow morning.

Still Samantha droops.

> *Marion:* What could we do to be sure that Samantha gets to play in Big Blocks tomorrow?

Several children suggest, "Write it down."

> *Marion:* OK. I'll write it right up here on the chalkboard. "S-a-man-tha. B-ii-g Bl-o-ck-s."

And Samantha? As soon as she hears Marion begin to write, her whole body lifts toward the chalkboard. Eyes, head, shoulders up now, her whole body a unit focused intently on Marion's act of writing.

You see, Samantha knows that if you *say* something it could be just a windy promise; but if you *write* it, it's a contract. The children become concerned that the writing might be erased. Perhaps Marion should write it higher. But even if she did, one points out, someone could still climb on a chair and erase it. Marion says, "Well, you know what I'll do? I'm going to do something I used to do last year and it worked. I'll write right here 'Do not e-ra-se.' "

The second example also occurred in Whole Group Study Time:

> Marion plays a professional tape as she shows an accompany-
> ing book about words you can use to make people feel better.
> Then she tells the children that this book and tape are special,
> different from the ones the children are used to, because this
> book and tape include a Spanish version. She reminds them that
> Juan doesn't speak English, so often he doesn't know what the
> children are saying or what the stories are about. She tells them,
> "So today, we're going to make Juan feel better by playing the
> tape in Spanish. So everybody needs to be quiet so Juan can
> hear. You'll see what it's like for him every day." She turns her
> chair so that it directly faces Juan. As the tape begins, Juan—
> who until that moment has been idly looking around—sud-
> denly stops, then turns toward her. The direction of her chair,
> the inclination of her body, the position of the book, her eye
> contact, her smiles, the language in the event—all these clearly
> just for him.

The message? It *matters* if Samantha is sad. It *matters* if Juan can't
understand the stories we read in English. Why? Because each is
important to us; each is *one* of *us*. Those three words say it all for me:
one of *us*, the *one* and the *us* both important and mutually enhancing.
This is what I found to be the essence of this kindergarten community.
Each one a distinctive, recognized, and valued *one* of *us*. The one not
sacrificed for the us, nor the us sacrificed for the one. Each voice heard,
recognized, valued—making us the *we* that *we* are.

Whole Language and Community

I believe that whole language has everything to do with community,
for it is within communities that language development and use necessarily occur. It makes sense to me that whole language classrooms
should be each-one-one-of-us communities for the following reasons:

1. I *know* language to be at one and the same time unique and
universal. Each child creates and uses a language which—in its
specifics—is distinct from everyone else's. And yet the general
pattern of its development and the purposes for which each
child uses it are common to us all: human ways and purposes.
Unique—the *one*. And universal—the *us*. Give me, then, a classroom community that recognizes and values both the *one* and
the *us*.

2. I *know* language and self to be inextricably and wonderfully
entwined. Deborah Tannen, writing of individual conversa-

tional style, reminds us that the style—the way of expressing—*is* the person, the person *is* the style. Exuberant, reserved, empathetic—each is both the self and the expression of self, Bakhtin's "speaking personality" again. Give me, then, a classroom community where individual voice—self and expression of self—is valued.

3. I *know* language to be inextricably entwined with community—developing and existing within it, and through it, and because of it. Give me, then, a classroom community where the group is cohesive, supportive of the individual voices within it.

4. I *know* language to be inextricably entwined with thought and its development. Vygotsky (1978) tells me that the many voices of the child's social experience become what James Wertsch calls, in the title of his recent book, *Voices of the Mind* (1991). Give me, then, a classroom community where children's distinct, individual voices can contribute to the development of one another's minds.

We have chosen for ourselves the label *whole language*. If language in its wholeness—social, intellectual, personal—is what we seek to help children develop, then each-one-one-of-us classroom communities are, I believe, good places to do it.

And I think of the Texas skills-and-drills classrooms from which I was fleeing when I came to Marion's kindergarten, and I feel sorry for the limited opportunities that the children in those classrooms have to come to know one another's voices and to forge cohesive communities out of them. And then I think, in contrast, of the accumulating descriptions that whole language teachers are providing of life in their classrooms—the portraits we find in Mills and Clyde's *Portraits of Whole Language Classrooms: Learning for All Ages* (1990), and in Edelsky, Altwerger, and Flores's *Whole Language: What's the Difference?* (1990). Classrooms like Karen Smith's and Carol Avery's and Nancie Atwell's. As I read these descriptions, in my mind's eye and ear I see and hear each-one-one-of-us classroom communities—classroom communities like Marion's. It is to her classroom that I turn for my closing example.

It concerns an event that occurred in September, during one of my early visits. It was a quite unremarkable event at the time. Yet in my subsequent reflections on that kindergarten community, this mundane event has taken on special significance, coming to stand as a kind of symbol of what I learned in that classroom, among those children who knew, and valued, the distinctive voices that comprised their community.

> The children were sitting in a circle on the rug, playing the familiar game in which one child is blindfolded and tries to identify the child who speaks to him or her. It was Edward's turn to be "it." He walked to the one small chair in the circle and sat down. Marion blindfolded him. The other children's hands went up, each child wanting to be chosen to be the speaker. Marion chose Molly. In a voice that was her own—not disguised—Molly said, "Hello, Edward." A great grin enveloped Edward's face. "Oh, that's Molly," he said confidently. "I know that voice." And so he did. In more ways than he ever dreamed.

References

Au, K. H. 1980. Participation structures in a reading lesson with Hawaiian children: Analysis of a culturally appropriate instructional event. *Anthropology and Education Quarterly* 11 (2): 240–52.

Edelsky, C., B. Altwerger, and B. Flores. 1990. *Whole language: What's the difference?* Portsmouth, N.H.: Heinemann.

Gilligan, C. 1982. *In a different voice: Psychological theory and women's development.* Cambridge, Mass.: Harvard University Press.

Grahame, K. 1908 [1935]. *The wind in the willows.* New York: Charles Scribner's Sons.

Hawkins, D. 1982. Messing about in science. In *A report of research on critical barriers to the learning and understanding of elementary science.* Boulder: University of Colorado. (ED 225 812)

Mills, H., and J. A. Clyde. 1990. *Portraits of whole language classrooms: Learning for all ages.* Portsmouth, N.H.: Heinemann.

Philips, S. U. 1972. Participant structures and communicative competence: Warm Springs children in community and classroom. In *Functions of language in the classroom,* ed. C. B. Cazden, V. P. John, and D. Hymes, 370–94. New York: Teachers College Press.

———. 1982. *The invisible culture: Communication in classroom and community on the Warm Springs Indian Reservation.* New York: Longman.

Tannen, D. 1990. *You just don't understand: Women and men in conversation.* Ed. M. Guarnaschelli. New York: William Morrow.

Vygotsky. L. S. 1978. *Mind in society: The development of higher psychological processes.* Ed. M. Cole, V. John-Steiner, S. Scribner, and E. Sonberman. Cambridge, Mass.: Harvard University Press.

Wertsch, J. 1991. *Voices of the mind: A sociocultural approach to mediated action.* Cambridge, Mass.: Harvard University Press.

3 Whole Language Assessment and Evaluation: Connecting with Parents

Norma Mickelson
University of Victoria, Victoria, British Columbia

In considering assessment and evaluation in whole language, before we ever consider connecting with parents, there are certain principles about which we must be clear. These are briefly outlined below.

Our evaluations must be:

1. centered in the classroom
2. consistent with our overall goals
3. consistent with what we know about language processes
4. comprehensive and balanced

Our evaluation procedures need to be:

1. numerous, leading to profiles over time
2. multifaceted
3. qualitative as well as quantitative
4. based on what we know about the constructive nature of learning
5. focused on the professional judgment of those closest to the learner
6. positive
7. noncompetitive
8. helpful in leading to growth for the learner
9. adaptive
10. negotiated

It is also important, of course, to examine our own understanding of assessment and evaluation and to realize that we may be carrying around some unjustified assumptions—beliefs which I call *misconceptions*. Among these misconceptions are the following:

1. Evaluation is separate from instruction.
2. Language is learned hierarchically; therefore, it should be tested sequentially.
3. Evaluation is testing.
4. Tests tell us what children know.
5. Readability formulas are reliable and valid indicators of difficulty levels.
6. Grade-equivalent scores tell us at what grade level a child should be reading.
7. Standardized tests are "objective" measures of performance.
8. The "omniscient outsider" (Smith 1986) knows better than we do.
9. Teacher observations are neither valid nor reliable.
10. Tests determine appropriate grade levels for students.

It is critically important, before any assessment (gathering of data) is made or any evaluation (value judgment) is carried out, that we as educators know what we are trying to do. Our aims, goals, curriculum, methods, materials, and assessment and evaluation procedures must be coherent. If they are not, the validity of our educational endeavors is in serious doubt.

One of the basic issues in educational assessment and evaluation is that there are many voices which must be heard—voices which are legitimate and which pose different questions. These include the voices of students, teachers, parents, school administrators, district personnel, local school boards, and ministry or state officials. Students, parents, and teachers are concerned with individual children. Teachers and school administrators need to know if programs are working. District personnel, school board members, and ministry or state officials are concerned with systems analysis. Unfortunately, many at all levels of the educational spectrum believe that methods of assessment and evaluation are the same for each of these "voices"; of course, they are not. Systems analysis is not concerned with individuals and can be legitimately conducted through appropriate sampling procedures. The assessment and evaluation of individual children is best carried out through performative procedures, one of which is portfolio assessment.

Because educational curricula, methods, materials, and assessment and evaluation programs are changing, it is essential not only that parents be informed but that they also be involved. Some of the ways in which this can be accomplished are as follows:

1. home visits or information letters
2. orientation meetings
3. professional libraries
4. newsletters
5. information booklets
6. parent-teacher-child conferences
7. triangulated observations (those made by more than one person)
8. classroom visits
9. parent helpers
10. parent advisory groups
11. parent-teacher or home-school groups
12. work samples with informational notes included
13. letters to "incoming" parents
14. encouraging parents to become writers and readers themselves

Many of our teachers have now moved to parent-teacher-child conferences where the children are responsible for planning, managing, and conducting the conference. This involves several important steps:

1. discussing with the students the possibility of a student-led conference
2. planning the conference
3. informing the parents
4. having individual students role-play the conference with a fellow student
5. organizing the conference day: welcoming parents, making appropriate room arrangements, deciding on time allocations, providing refreshments, obtaining parent feedback

An important aspect of assessing student progress involves getting information *from* parents. This can range from asking parents what they would like to know about their children to having parents provide information about their children's home activities. Forms used for this information gathering are available in *Evaluation of Literacy: A Perspective for Change* (Anthony et al. 1991).

After the conferences have been completed, "reports" go home summarizing the students' progress as outlined in the conferences and indicating areas of mutual concern or plans agreed upon for future focus. This is a marked change from sending home "reports" which the teacher has written (or tabulated!) and about which the children know little or nothing. Some sample "reports" written after parent-teacher-child conferences are given below:

Dear Mr. and Mrs. ——

It was a pleasure to meet with both of you together with Jennifer to discuss her progress. I am pleased that you were satisfied with her achievement to date and am grateful that you are willing to assist us in having her make independent choices and assume responsibility for those choices in out-of-school activities.

Dear Mr. and Mrs. ——

Our conference with Adam was most productive. I was pleased that you felt his portfolio indicated areas in need of attention and that you are willing to provide extra assistance in arithmetic and spelling at home. Adam seems most enthusiastic about our cooperative plans, and this points to success in the future.

Dear Mr. and Mrs. ——

Brittany enjoyed organizing and preparing her materials for our conference. I was pleased that she was able to demonstrate for you her high degree of independence and analytical skills. Also, she is looking forward to your providing her with more reading experiences and seems particularly happy about joining the library and having her own personal library card.

Dear Mr. and Mrs. ——

Thank you for a most reassuring conference on Craig's progress. I was pleased that he recognized his difficulty in concentrating on the task at hand and that he agreed to have you provide him with opportunities to undertake and complete tasks at home. It should also help him to work cooperatively with others if you arrange more opportunities for him to mix with other children.

Dear Mr. and Mrs. ——

Your comments during our conference were most helpful. It was gratifying to note your recognition of Julia's outstanding ability in art and also your willingness to help her develop her reading to a higher level of achievement. Providing her with opportunities to read interesting books should certainly help her fluency; also, joining the public library would greatly benefit her.

It should be noted, of course, that information about specific curricular areas has been provided during the parent-teacher-child conference. The written report sent home simply confirms what was communicated and agreed upon in the conference.

Parents are partners in the education of their children. If they are fully informed and involved in the school's curricular and evaluation program, they will become not only strong advocates but also "whole language parents."

References

Anthony, R., T. Johnson, N. Mickelson, and A. Preece. 1991. *Evaluating literacy: A perspective for change.* Portsmouth, N.H.: Heinemann.

Smith, F. 1986. *Insult to intelligence: The bureaucratic invasion of our classrooms.* New York: Arbor House.

4 Research about Whole Language; Research *for* Whole Language

Carole Edelsky
Arizona State University

There's research . . . and then there's research. My guess is that any educational professional has a way of distinguishing between the two, a way of putting certain research into the category called "research" and relegating the rest to the less desirable category of—well—"research." I realize that all those educational professionals would have different meanings for those categories, that they would have different bases for distinguishing, that they might divide up the research world differently depending on why they were doing the dividing up. The differences are not my concern here; it is simply the division itself to which I want to call attention. The following discussion is about one way that I divide research and one purpose for which I divide it: to strengthen the whole language movement. My categories are "research *about* whole language" and "research that is about and also *for* whole language."

Before I explain those categories, some general comments about research are in order. First, it gets harder and harder to define research in order to separate it from other creative endeavors, and, according to some discussions, to separate research from life, since learning, talking, and thinking are creative endeavors. I do not find it helpful, however, to think of everything as everything. We do not live that way, treating things, people, and experience as though they were the same; we do not analyze and critique, as though there were no conceptual boundaries. We may find our categories to be overly simple and our definitions to be inadequate. So much the better. We *should* keep learning and changing how we divide up experience and on what bases. But it does not help us to come to grips with complexity if we refuse to articulate the present bases for our ever-evolving categories.

In any case, it used to be pretty safe to claim the following characteristics that distinguished research from other activity: research was systematic, intentional inquiry (Cochran-Smith and Lytle 1990). But now, the times are marked by "blurred genres" (Geertz 1983)—ethnographies with fictionalized vignettes (as in Meredith Cherland's 1990 study of girls' reading), short stories as research (such as David Schaafsma's 1990 story of relating to someone labeled as mad), cartoons as full-length novels (such as Art Spiegelman's 1973 novel, *Maus*, about survivors of the Holocaust). As research genres change, systematicity may not be a defining attribute after all.

The second general point is that research cannot get outside of itself. It always "proves" its premises. Research premises are built into the design of research; the most a research study can do is provide some details about those premises. If the researcher's premise is that language is a resource for making meaning, the research will show *in what ways* language is a resource for making meaning, or *how* people learn that language is a resource for making meaning. It will not show that language is *not* a resource for making meaning. Embedded in every research question and in every plan for answering the question are one or more basic premises. Premises in research about whole language will relate in some way to the premises of whole language itself. That is why research that pits whole language with *its* basic premises against skills education with *its* basic premises cannot ever answer whatever question that the research asks in some unbiased way—that is, in a way free of *any* premises. Lynn Rhodes and Nancy Shanklin discuss this issue at some length in the introduction to their 1989 bibliography on research bases of whole language.

If the activity of research of whatever stripe cannot break loose from its own premises, it is also unlikely that educational research, especially mainstream educational research, will blaze new trails or seriously challenge prevailing practice. In a stunning analysis of the relationship between U.S. social policies, educational policies, and educational research, House (1991) argues that the last decade of educational research has followed rather than led governmental action. Whether mainstream educational research fine-tunes, refutes, or corroborates current practices, it legitimizes what is already going on by taking current practice and policy as its research topic. An interesting example of this legitimizing—with an added twist—can be seen in a recent review of research on reading-comprehension instruction (Dole et al. 1991). Dole and her colleagues aim to "inform instructional practice" by discussing how reading is not a large set of separate skills but a small set of strategies—as though this idea were new, as though it had not already made its way into even such conservative documents as state department frameworks on reading and language arts. The interesting twist is that not only do Dole and her colleagues report research that has to run to catch up to the practice it is trying to inform, but they fail to cite *any* (and thus they marginalize *all*) of the nonmainstream research that did indeed lead practice in this area: for example, the research by Ken Goodman (1969), Louise Rosenblatt (1938, 1978), and Jerry Harste and Carolyn Burke (1977).

The research on which I want to focus in thinking about "research about" and "research for" whole language, however, is not that early research that led practice, nor is it the research that whole language educators use as a base for their theory—the research of Goodman, Piaget, and Vygotsky, some of the research on language acquisition, or research from the field of sociolinguistics (see bibliographies compiled by Rhodes and Shanklin 1989, and by Diane Stephens 1991). Leaving this research out of the present discussion has nothing to do with wanting to marginalize it. To the contrary. People interested in whole language must come to realize that whole language is a perspective more infused with research and theory than other educational perspectives which rest more heavily on tradition, conventional wisdom, and principles of scientific management (K. Goodman 1989). Knowing some of the early research that provides foundational support for whole language is crucial. For example, thinking that "miscues" is simply another word for errors—not understanding the revolutionary premises about reading that are embedded in Ken Goodman's early (1969) miscue research—means not understanding key elements of a whole language framework.[1]

Research *about* but Not *for* Whole Language

Instead of that foundational whole language research, the present discussion focuses on those categories mentioned above ("research about," "research for") and uses examples from recent research. Research done about whole language by people who are not whole language educators or researchers is usually "horse-race research": which "approach" gets there faster/better? The recent meta-analysis by Stahl and Miller (1989), pitting whole language and the Language Experience Approach against basal reading approaches, is an example. In that meta-analysis, Stahl and Miller wrongly describe whole language as though it were based on a "getting-the-words" view of reading, lump whole language together with the Language Experience

Approach, and "discover" that this mixed-bag "approach" was better for teaching print concepts, while a basal approach was better at teaching "the word recognition skills prerequisite to effective comprehension" (as measured by tests, of course). Another example is the research agenda to investigate whole language in comparison to traditional methods for teaching language arts proposed by McKenna, Robinson, and Miller (1990). They suggest that the main goal of a whole language research agenda should be to evaluate its effectiveness, primarily, though not entirely, on the basis of (improved) tests.

Not all of the research on whole language by non–whole language researchers is a horse race, however. Some of the research in this category asks questions like what features characterize classrooms where minority children succeed, and it chooses whole language as well as other classrooms as sites to investigate. A research assistant in one of those studies, wearing her skills lenses as she observed, indicated in her field notes that an exceptional whole language teacher did not interact with children any differently than do teachers in skills classrooms (Smith 1991).

Another piece of research in this category (Bergeron 1990) attempted to derive a single definition of whole language from the various writings about whole language, including writings by critics and skills-framework researchers. That is, the views of those who understand whole language from the inside as well as those who (mis)understand it from the outside and are hostile to it are combined (and confused) to derive this "definition" of whole language. (The obvious question to ask of this—or any—definition should be, who says so, and why?!)

While research about whole language by non–whole language researchers offers minor advantages (e.g., it publicizes whole language), in general, this research is a liability to the whole language community and also to the general community. Horse-race research is usually based on test scores. Most tests of language are based on two decidedly *non*–whole language ideas: (1) language can be separated into component parts; and (2) how one deals with the component parts on a test is how one deals with those parts when they are integrated into an instance of language-in-use. Research that relies on tests legitimizes these erroneous but widespread assumptions. Because they are about parts, tests are also about doing exercises—exercises in reading or spelling or adding or using a map. Research based on tests further validates exercise doing and makes it that much harder to reduce the preponderance of exercises in school curricula. Tests also reflect almost nothing of what whole language teachers do. They not only shrink whole language beyond recognition; they similarly shrink human beings. No one is a 73 or a 4.6. But even worse, test-based research legitimizes the ways in which tests are used, the prime way being to sort and rank students. Such sorting and ranking in school contributes to sorting and ranking people out of school, perpetuating a stratified society. Thus, even when it puts whole language in the limelight, research that augments and does nothing to diminish the existing power of the preponderant uses of tests undermines important ideas and goals of whole language.

Even when horse-race research on whole language done by non–whole language researchers is not test-based, it damages whole language. It uses supposedly neutral yet actually skills-based units to compare whole language to something else. Skills-based units like "lessons" and "time on task" are not appropriate units for looking at whole language classrooms (Goodman 1989).

The most immediate danger from research on whole language by non–whole language researchers, however, is that it pretends to be about whole language but really is not. Because these researchers do not understand what whole language is about—a theoretical framework, not an instructional approach or a set of methods—they misrepresent it. They classify non–whole language classrooms as whole language. They look at whole language classrooms through a skills lens for evidence of "whole-language-ness" and thus fail to see any. They downplay and distort key whole language concepts. And because their own unacknowledged theoretical biases teach them that education is about methods rather than theoretical views, they refuse to accept whole language's claim to having a theoretical view.

Research *about* and *for* Whole Language

Research about whole language done by whole language educators does not leave out that theoretical view. Indeed, foregrounding a whole language theoretical framework—and getting it right—is an absolutely necessary feature of research *about* whole language that is also *for* whole language. Accounting for the theoretical framework means to consciously and deliberately think about a whole language perspective on language and language learning throughout the breadth of the research process: planning the study, formulating the questions, analyzing the data, and writing the report. Research that is *for* whole language serves the interests of the whole language community; therefore, it also serves the interests of high-quality education in a more democratic and more just society.

Purposes of Research

Most immediately, research *for* whole language is conducted for the purpose of helping whole language educators learn more about what happens in whole language classrooms, what happens in communities where there are whole language classrooms, what happens to other teachers who are colleagues of whole language teachers, or what happens within school districts when teachers get together to try to create a whole language school. The purpose of research *for* whole language is not to win adherents to whole language. (Whole language wins adherents through example, through grass-roots organizing, through print and visual media.) One main purpose of research *for* whole language is to help us learn more about ourselves and this complex enterprise in which we are engaged.

A more long-range purpose is that research *for* whole language aims to be transformative. Like action research as described by Dixie Goswami (1991), whole language research *for* whole language has an agenda for change—not only to change the status quo of a basal-reader technology, but to change the status quo of a society stratified by gender, class, race, and a variety of other divisions. Obviously, research alone cannot undo what is oppressive about an oppressive society. *Transformative,* applied to research, does not mean research has to accomplish transformation by itself. Transformative research is that which, along with many other favorable conditions, at least has transforming potential. Some research *for* whole language aims to "take on" oppressive aspects of social categories like gender, class, or race (e.g., Solsken, in press). Some aims to transform relationships within classrooms with the intent of transforming conditions for teaching and learning, including conditions of belief. In some of this research, the classroom or district in which the research takes place is what is to be transformed; in other research, the goal is for the readers of the research report to learn something that will help them transform their own practices at some future time. It is important to keep in mind that the transformation intended by research *for* whole language is not just any change; it is change geared to increased democracy and reduced stratification, change geared to end terrible social imbalances in power, privilege, and lived biographies. Research *for* whole language is part of envisioning and sometimes enacting a more equitable, emancipated world.

Margie Siegel and her colleagues (Gitlin, Siegel, and Boru 1989) describe some possibilities for such research; for example, researcher and teacher collaborating to develop a curriculum that critiques as well as empowers. And Jo Beth Allen, Barbara Michalove, Betty Shockley, and Marsha West (1991) conducted such research, with the deliberate intent of transforming the viewpoint of the teachers, the conditions of schooling for the children, and the attitudes of professionals who would read their report—attitudes that blame families and home cultures for school failure.

It is noteworthy that research aiming directly at social inequities associated with race, gender, and class—research that ends up being *for* whole language because it is so congruent with whole language positions and because it is so useful to whole language educators—is often done by researchers who do not foreground a whole language theoretical frame. Denny Taylor's work comes immediately to mind. Her case studies, written with Catherine Dorsey-Gaines (Taylor and Dorsey-Gaines 1988), of the considerable literacy in black families—literacy that cannot overcome the desperate, societally constructed conditions against which they have to struggle—expose the myth that these families' struggles are of their own making and that improved literacy would lift them out of the morass. Taylor's lengthy case studies of academically failing children (1988, 1991) provide overwhelming evidence that it is a failure of educational and institutional practice that is the problem, not a failure of the child's intellect. Pam Clark, a committed whole language principal, says that her school psychologist read Taylor's *Learning Denied* (1991), and though the psychologist has made no overnight, dramatic turnarounds, she now stumbles over the diagnoses she used to make with ease, and she seems uncertain of her own recommendations for more testing. Clark thinks this Taylor-induced cognitive dissonance is finally going to cause the psychologist to shift her premises and her practice in a way that will benefit all the academically troubled children in her school.

Issues

Criteria

If research *about* and *for* whole language has unique goals, it also wrestles with unique issues—or with ordinary issues in unique ways. As an example of the latter, researchers in general (mainstream and not-so-mainstream; qualitative and quantitative) are concerned with criteria for the quality of research. Though the proposed criteria from these different perspectives and power positions are different from each other, a concern with criteria is common. Research *for* whole language is concerned with criteria, too, but the criteria themselves may be unique.

Dixie Goswami (1991) discusses an interesting set of criteria for research that she calls *action research.* First, like research *for* whole language, action research should be transformative. Not potentially—*actually.* Something should change. What is changing is studied as it changes. Second, action research is ethical (and non-exploitative). Third, the research is made meaningful to all participants. Then, too, it is generative (i.e., it energizes participants for years to come).[2]

It would seem that the category I have labeled *research for whole language* could use these same criteria. But they do not all work, as can be seen from the following examples of action research criteria and research *for* whole language that do not—and should not have to—meet these criteria.

1. Causing immediate change. Some research *for* whole language does, in fact, provoke and study an immediate change. For example, Cousins's (1988) study in collaboration with a special education teacher focused on both changing the curriculum and investigating the role of language in learning with the new curriculum. Cousins concluded that a curriculum rich in choice and opportunities for reflection prompted children to use language for expanding ideas and trying out different roles, and gave students a chance to look and be proficient. In a traditional special education curriculum, however, students' language use was simplistic and minimal, and students acted out the stereotypes of special-education students (off-task, uninvolved).

But not all research *for* whole language promotes immediate change. Karen Smith's study (1993) of the bases for her students' and her own responses in a literature study, tape-recorded as it took place several years ago, aims to change practice for others, elsewhere, but it is not creating classroom change at the moment. That study reveals what goes into responses in a literature study: the teacher's knowledge about literature, about learning, about students' interests; the teacher's familiarity with students' life histories in and out of school; the teacher's concerns for the power relationships in and therefore the "feel" of the interaction; the teacher's caring (caring about the students, caring about the story world); students' concerns about constructing a story world; students' worries and reflections about reading strategies; and students' caring for each other as readers and as friends.

2. *Making the research meaningful to all participants.* My research (in progress) on conversational structures during literature studies in Karen Smith's classroom from 1985 through 1990 was not made meaningful to the students who appear on the videotapes that I am transcribing. Now, as a researcher, I am trying to understand what conversational moves inside what conversational structures allow Karen Smith and the students to make each other look so good. At the time of taping, though, no one (least of all me) knew the videotapes would be used for studying classroom interaction; those sessions were taped for use in an undergraduate teacher preparation program.

3. *Energizing the participants.* It is not at all clear that it is the research describing how writing or science or anything else operates in a whole language classroom that is what energizes people for years to come. If anything, it is the writing, the science, or the educational activity itself.

The criteria for research *for* whole language are both positive and negative. The positive criteria simply repeat the distinguishing characteristics. That is, research *for* whole language foregrounds a whole language theoretical framework and serves the goals of the whole language community. The first negative criterion is that the research does not violate basic ideas within a whole language theoretical framework (e.g., it does not treat practice as methods by investigating typical whole language events like literature sessions, writing conferences, or theme cycle discussions without tying them to the theoretical, philosophical, or political premises that breathe life and meaning into them). The second negative criterion is that research *for* whole language is non-exploitative. It may evolve into shared authorship and shared presenting at conferences. If it does more than observe what is going on (i.e., if it takes students' and teachers' time), it gives back more than it takes—for example, in new curriculum plans and new learning for all involved in the project.

Other Concerns of Researchers

Some other issues for people doing research *for* whole language concern audience, researcher, research genres, and power. Whole language researchers do more than think about these issues. Based on certain premises in their framework, they act in new ways in regard to audience research, genres, and power. In so doing, they help extend concepts and practices of educational research.

Audience. As Elizabeth Long noted for ethnographies (1991), it is highly unusual when the audience for research consists of the participants or informants in the research. Researchers most often study "down" (those less privileged and of lower status than themselves), sometimes "up," but in any case, almost always "different." When researchers study "same," this is not only unusual; it is also problematic for the researcher. When the researched are also the readers of the research, the researchers can be "found out"—for violating a voice, for misrepresenting a scene, for deconstructing a myth. There are subtle differences and rhetoric for conveying the more familiar persona of trusted, empathetic outsider, the passionately indignant outsider, the pained but still objective outsider—and for conveying the far less familiar and even more sympathetic or indignant or pained persona of the true insider. The question follows: Can a researcher remain "inside" to the same extent if the other insiders are displeased with the report?

Researcher. Issues connected to researchers are being resolved with fewer potential shadows. Instead of staying in the hands of university and research development office researchers, research *for* whole language is the province of many people: classroom teachers, principals, teachers with students, teachers and university researchers, state department administrators with teachers, student teachers and classroom teachers and university researchers, and other combinations. Whole language research, therefore, is contributing part of the new answer to the question: Who has the right to do research, to produce knowledge, to define a reality? (See Cochran-Smith and Lytle 1990 for a lengthy discussion related to this question.) Practitioners who create theory in reports of their research give new meaning to a whole language faith in praxis.

Genre. Research *for* whole language comes in a variety of genres. Much of this variety is related to the above issue of researchers; that is, when teachers are doing the researching, types of research include not only university styles of research but also journals, stories, essays, and accounts of oral inquiry processes (Cochran-Smith and Lytle 1990). Another source of new genres is the university. Some of the newer research *for* whole language is novelistic—unabashedly fictional. Barone (1987) has argued that since all texts are fiction or "fashioned" through human agency, and since it is only the modes of fiction employed in the "fashioning" that distinguish one genre from another, there is no reason to claim a distinction between admittedly and un-wittingly fictionalized accounts. Researchers' lack of awareness of their own fictionalizing is no warrant for privileging their work, for calling it "research" while relegating deliberate fictionalizing to the realm of fiction. Barone does, however, distinguish between his own genre (educational criticism) and the genre of novels. Novels, accord-ing to Barone, focus more on characterization (appealing to life histo-ries and psychodynamics); Barone's novelistic educational criticism focuses more on action or a portrayal of events. Schaafsma's novelistic research (1990), however, does emphasize character. Unlike most short stories, though, Schaafsma's story of Lillie, a mentally disturbed young woman, is framed in a prologue and epilogue defending story as a mode of inquiry, explaining the inquiry focus (madness embedded in a conservative religious community), and discussing the conse-quences of the research for the researcher (Schaafsma was informed yet thrown off balance by a story that harbored more complexity and uncertainty than even he, its creator, knew).

It is easy to see the connections from research as something fashioned to research as something fictionalized to research as fiction to research as story. It is also easy to see the appeal of thinking of research as stories. Such a metaphor fits the whole language theoreti-cal stance on created or fashioned and "fictionalized" knowledge. It makes it easier to foreground storytellers, storyteller rights, told sto-ries, and untold stories (Bloome 1991). Moreover, it fits a general bias in scholarship about children's literacy—a bias in favor of narrative (Pappas 1990). But like any bias, this one blocks out other possibilities. Christine Pappas argues that literacy researchers' and educators' ten-dency to make story primary prevents them from giving sufficient attention to the information about nonstory genres that children ac-quire and the nonstory genres that children write. A preference for metaphors highlighting story may or may not reflect a species prefer-ence for story (Bruner 1986) but, according to Pappas, the educational preference (including the research preference) for story also contrib-utes to the loss of children's early facility with nonfiction genres by the time they reach middle childhood. Still, seeing a tie between story and research has certainly expanded the range of types of research *for* whole language as well as types of educational research in general.

Power. Whole language theory recognizes that knowledge is socially constructed, that power arrangements enter into social con-structions, that the perspective of the powerful is reflected in what counts as both legitimate, "official culture" knowledge and everyday taken-for-granted knowledge. Thus, "everyone knows" (or at least they knew it until women began to organize and to struggle together about power distributed according to gender) that women are more emotional and less logical than men. And everyone knows (or they knew it until whole language educators began to offer competing knowledge and to reclaim their rightful power as professionals) that people learn to read by learning to match sounds and letters first. Research is always political in the sense that research is about knowledge construction, knowledge construction is always tied to perspectives, and perspectives always have some relationship to power.

Not all researchers understand that. Indeed, many positivists maintain that it is possible to be above it all, removed, neutral, not linked to any perspective and therefore neither supporting nor opposing existing power arrangements. Whole language researchers know that just as there is no unbiased perspective, no truth devoid of context, so there is no disinterested search for truths. Researchers, like everyone else, have meta-narratives about what education and literacy should be for (Luke, in press). A meta-narrative embedded in the discourse of whole language researchers is that education and literacy are ultimately for empowerment and equity.

Major Research Activities

Some research that I am calling *research for* may seem wrongly categorized. But since research is an interested (i.e., political) activity, the political context for a particular study must be considered. I am thinking here of a study by Carole Stice and Nancy Bertrand (1989) that pitted whole language against traditional classrooms in a contest for test scores. This seems to contradict the purpose of research *for* whole language. That purpose is not to prove whole language is better, but to improve the whole language community and help it reach its goals. Most of the time, that improvement comes from providing more information on questions in which whole language is interested. But sometimes, for local political reasons, the whole language community needs horse-race research. It was just such local reasons—a Tennessee legislature that demanded test-score data as a price for granting permission to "do" whole language—that prompted the research by Stice and Bertrand. Their research showed that children in the "pilot" whole language classrooms did as well as or better on tests than children in the traditional classrooms. Not surprisingly, given their whole language perspective, Stice and Bertrand did not stop with analyzing test scores. They also provided comparative qualitative data on children's perceptions of themselves as readers (children in whole language classrooms were more confident readers) and their strategies for solving literacy problems (children in whole language classrooms talked about and used a much greater variety of strategies when they had problems reading; children in traditional classrooms could "sound it out" and ask the teacher, but after that, they were stuck). This research and a few other test-score contests analyzed by whole language researchers *for* whole language may not be the preferred genre, but they have been politically necessary. Until the movement for authentic assessment becomes more widespread at the grass-roots level, such research will continue to be useful for instrumental purposes.

Other research that compares whole language and non–whole language classrooms does not offer a test-based finish line. For example, Karin Dahl, Penny Freppon, and their colleagues have studied primary children in inner-city whole language classrooms and traditional skills-based classrooms in order to understand what literacy learning demands are made on the children in each setting, what they learn, and what social relations and conditions provide the medium for the learning (Freppon and Dahl 1991; Dahl, Purcell-Gates, and McIntyre 1989). In general, learners reflected the curriculum that they were experiencing: If the focus was letters, children learned letters. If the focus was making sense, they learned to use print to make sense. Traditional curricula promoted intellectual dependency; whole language curricula promoted independence.

Another important research activity compares whole language classrooms and whole-language-in-name-only classrooms. For example, Glenellen Pace (1991) describes actual classroom events from classrooms labeled "whole language" and carefully analyzes just why it is that certain activities tied to a piece of literature did not reflect a whole language framework, regardless of the label. And Jerry Harste's (1989) critique shows how three teachers with seemingly different programs actually looked at reading comprehension in the same non–whole language way: they equated it with the ability to answer literal, text-driven questions. This research, called "gatekeeping" by some, is clearly unsettling. Nevertheless, it is important work. When Pace and Harste critique practice against principle, they provide a much-needed service to the whole language community. They foreground whole language's theoretical perspective in a way that cannot be ignored (putting it "in your face"). When so much in education (tracts, published materials, teacher education, state department agency mandates, district assessment programs) denies the existence of the very thing that distinguishes whole language from other movements and from prevailing educational ideology—that is, its theoretical framework— even solid whole language educators need occasional reminders of the theory-practice fit that whole language is about. Rather than functioning as a gatekeeper, it is more accurate to say this research functions to maintain the integrity of whole language and to ward off its cooptation—not by teachers trying to learn a new way of thinking and practicing but by entrepreneurs who use the whole language label opportunistically for their own gain. This research also helps whole language change by providing updated versions of new classroom instantiations of theory and of new meanings for theory based on the ever-changing practice of whole language teachers.

Most of the research *for* whole language does not seek to make comparisons, however. It looks in depth at one or a few classrooms, teachers, or children in order to better understand aspects of whole language education or phenomena spotlighted by a whole language framework. A few of the questions such research has asked follow:

1. How do teachers reduce academic risk through their literacy curricula? The answer of JoBeth Allen and her colleagues (1991) was that teachers in one school encouraged genuine engagement, used whole texts, provided adult models who loved to read, gave children real reasons for reading and writing and plenty of time to do so, and supported risk taking.

2. How do children come to learn to "do school" in a whole language classroom? My collaborative study with Draper and Smith (1983) proposed that children in one classroom started the year with their antennae out. When the teacher held coherent values, maintained a few ambiguous rules like "use your head," and offered a curriculum "deal" that consistently required meaningful work, children jumped at the "deal."

3. How do children learn about various sign systems in the social world of their classrooms? Rowe (1987) described two kinds of intertextual connections important to literacy learning: connections between children's existing knowledge and that demonstrated by other authors; and connections between their current texts and various aspects of their own past experiences.

Most phenomena held up for close investigation have concerned literacy. Not all of these investigations, however, have taken place in whole language settings. For example, in taking the whole language premise that literacy is grounded in culture, Meredith Cherland (1990) showed how cultural themes of time, individualism, and gender were reflected in girls' reading in a small northern town. Margaret Phinney (1991) investigated literacy as a medium for creating and displaying identity, concluding that from moment to moment, two six-year-old girls struggled with both separateness and connectedness to each other as they talked and read and wrote together. Studying writing as a thoroughly socially embedded activity, Anne Dyson (1987) helped whole language educators by conceptualizing the writing that she was seeing in a primary classroom in an urban magnet school as becoming not less context-dependent as children's writing abilities grew, but more socially embedded, more entangled in a web of social relationships. The whole language premise that assessment of literacy is tied to theories of literacy was the anchor to a project conducted at adult literacy centers in Philadelphia, using the assessment protocols developed by Lytle, Marmor, and Penner (1986). When adult clients were asked to pick what they could read from pieces of community print (actual menus, TV listings, bus schedules, and so on), they favorably impressed both their tutors and themselves, engendering higher expectations for the subsequent tutoring sessions.

Questions That Need Investigation

Usually, research *for* whole language does not ask the question: Which works better? That question is incomplete. It requires an addition: Better for what? As Smith and Heshusius (1986) taught, "what works" depends on what work one wants done, and that in turn depends on through what lens one is looking. Some far more interesting questions that have barely begun to be addressed follow:

1. What makes people become whole language teachers? Since teachers today did not themselves go to whole language elementary schools, and since we supposedly teach as we were taught, what accounts for teachers who abandon how they were taught and create their teaching from scratch? Life history interview research (Casey 1989) would be helpful here, as would life histories of whole language programs (e.g., Bird 1989).

2. What content is learned in whole language classrooms? Do children's conceptions and misconceptions about science and social

studies in whole language theme cycles look different from those that have been described in other classrooms (Guzzetti and Snyder 1991)? How are the ways and relationships through which children learn content in whole language classrooms reflected in what they learn?

3. How can people work with critique in whole language classrooms? What happens when teachers themselves try to learn and get children to learn how to question authors' premises, how to critique discourse for the positions it creates for readers? What can be done to help students critique the racism and sexism in their daily lives yet at the same time refrain from promoting alienation?

4. Are whole language classrooms similar "culturally"? That is, is there a general "whole language culture" that crosses settings, with common norms of interaction, common roles, common means of organizing relationships, common narratives? If so, how does that culture accommodate and conflict with other cultures with which it comes in contact in the classroom? What meanings are given to these accommodations and conflicts by teachers? students? administrators? parents? other community members?

5. What are the long-term consequences for children in whole language classrooms for several consecutive years? What happens to children as they leave a whole language elementary school and enter junior high or, later on, high school? Are they different from children who did not have a whole language education? In retrospect, as they reflect on their lives thus far, what did their whole language years mean to them?

6. What is the impact on the community of a schoolwide whole language program? At Machan School in Phoenix, parents have begun to take a more obviously active part in their children's education by requesting teachers or attempting to stay within the school neighborhood boundaries despite many household moves (Draper 1991). In the neighborhood of another whole language school in Phoenix, sales of children's literature increased at a local bookstore as did use of the public library (by parents as well as children). In other words, what is the "whole language fallout" in students' homes? on the street? in other institutions?

7. Are there unwanted meanings that underlie such key whole language narratives as "the child is an active learner" or "whole language classrooms nurture all learners" or "reading is a process"? Valerie Walkerdine (1990, 1991) urges us to look at the "mythical

status" of these and any bedrock narratives and to ask: What do they normalize? What do they pathologize? What do they blind us to? For instance, for a long time, Solsken's belief in whole language as an "equal opportunity" educational movement prevented her from seeing the ways that gender arrangements at home and in the community were being played out in whole language classrooms (Solsken, in press). Sumara and Walker (1991) have begun to answer this question by examining the actualities and limits behind a rhetoric of child-centeredness and empowerment. Those notions not only have limits; according to Walkerdine, they also have unacknowledged undersides. Feminist, poststructuralist critique (e.g., Gilbert 1991; Lather 1991) could suggest some possible directions to take. As with all research *for* whole language, the value to the whole language community of these efforts at deconstruction would be to help us better understand the complexities of our work and adjust theory and practice in line with those understandings.

Conclusion

As the whole language movement gains visibility, research about whole language is becoming a more frequent topic. Those of us interested in strengthening whole language as a *perspective* (and therefore ensuring that the movement has substance and not just numbers) know that there is research about whole language . . . and then there is research about whole language. It is the research about whole language that is also *for* whole language that interests us. It is that research that strengthens and enriches and promotes the evolution of whole language as a perspective.

Notes

1. On the other hand, every researcher whose early work is used by whole language educators to support their theoretical perspective is not necessarily a supporter of whole language. Charles Read, the phonologist whose research on invented spelling informs a whole language view of what children learn about written language, may be an example here. In a paper prepared for the Orton Dyslexia Society ridiculing whole language (Liberman and Liberman 1989), Read is presented as being in agreement with the authors: he supplied them with some material and apparently pointed out its ridiculous nature. What was the material held up for ridicule? It was whole language advice about encouraging children to focus on sense rather than sound when they come to unfamiliar words.

2. Dixie Goswami made a "generative" point herself when discussing generativity. She distinguished between thinking about transformative, action research as giving people skills and thinking about it as giving people tools. She much prefers the latter metaphor. Skills are not so obviously cultural as tools are (tools are considered cultural artifacts and are displayed as such in museums). Tools are more clearly part of our material cultural reality. Thinking in terms of tools makes it harder for us to hide from the fact that our research, our literacy, our schooling, our living, is cultural and historical, not natural or universal. Tools, if useful, get used; skills may or may not be used. Goswami used the example of Charlene Thomas to illustrate the point. Thomas, a poor Black parent who had dropped out of school herself and who had difficulty reading to her children when she began working with researcher Amanada Branscombe, learned to use research tools during the research. She found those useful enough to continue to use them to study her own children. Other poor parents also used the research tools to study alimony payments and public housing activity—and to get action. Thinking of people having skills often converts to thinking of them as having (or lacking) traits (e.g., "literate," "good speller," "mediocre writer"). Thinking of people as using tools directs us to think of people as actors in events, as engaging in cultural practices.

References

Allen, J., B. Michalove, B. Shockley, and M. West. 1991. "I'm really worried about Joseph": Reducing the risks of literacy learning. *Reading Teacher* 44 (7): 458–72.

Barone, T. 1987. Research out of the shadows: A reply to Rist. *Curriculum Inquiry* 17:453–63.

Bergeron, B. 1990. What does the term whole language mean? Constructing a definition from the literature. *Journal of Reading Behavior* 22: 301–29.

Bird, L. 1989. *Becoming a whole language school: The Fair Oaks story.* Katonah, N.Y.: Richard C. Owen.

Bloome, D. 1991. Response to Gilbert and Walkerdine. Paper presented at CELT Rejuvenation Conference, Mt. Holyoke, Mass., June.

Bruner, J. 1986. *Actual minds, possible worlds.* Cambridge, Mass.: Harvard University Press.

Casey, K. 1989. Teacher as author: Life history narratives of contemporary women teachers working for social change. Ph.D. diss., University of Wisconsin, Madison.

Cherland, M. 1990. Girls reading: Children, literacy and culture. Ph.D. diss., Arizona State University, Tempe.

Cochran-Smith, M., and S. Lytle. 1990. Research on teaching and teacher research: The issues that divide. *Educational Researcher* 19:2–11.

Cousins, P. 1988. The social construction of learning problems: Language use in a special education classroom. Ph.D. diss., Indiana University, Bloomington.

Dahl, K., V. Purcell-Gates, and E. McIntyre. 1989. *An investigation of the ways low-SES learners make sense of instruction in reading and writing in the early grades.* Final Report to the U.S. Department of Education, Office in Educational Research and Information (Grant N. G008720229).

Dole, J., G. Duffy, L. Roehler, and P. D. Pearson. 1991. Moving from the old to the new: Research on reading comprehension instruction. *Review of Educational Research* 61:239–64.

Draper, K. 1991. Personal communication with author.

Dyson, A. 1987. *Multiple worlds of child writers.* New York: Teachers College Press.

Edelsky, C., K. Draper, and K. Smith. 1983. Hookin' 'em in at the start of school in a "whole language" classroom. *Anthropology and Education Quarterly* 14:257–81.

Freppon, P., and K. Dahl. 1991. Learning about phonics in a whole language classroom. *Language Arts* 68:190–97.

Geertz, C. 1983. *Local knowledge: Further essays in interpretive anthropology.* New York: Basic Books.

Gilbert, P. 1991. The story so far: Gender, literacy, and social regulation. Keynote address, CELT Rejuvenation Conference, Mt. Holyoke, Mass., June.

Gitlin, A., M. Siegel, and K. Boru. 1989. The politics of method: From leftist ethnography to educative research. *Qualitative Studies in Education* 2:237–53.

Goodman, K. 1969. Analysis of oral reading miscues: Applied psycholinguistics. *Reading Research Quarterly* 5:9–30.

———. 1989. Whole-language research: Foundations and development. *Elementary School Journal* 90:207–21.

Goswami, D. 1991. Featured address at the Conference on Ethnographic and Qualitative Research in Education, University of Massachusetts, Amherst, June.

Guzzetti, B., and T. Snyder. 1991. Meta-analysis of instructional interventions to overcome misconceptions in science. Paper presented at the annual meeting of the International Reading Association, Las Vegas.

Harste, J. 1989. The basalization of American reading instruction: One researcher responds. *Theory into Practice* 28:265–73.

Harste, J., and C. Burke. 1977. A new hypothesis for reading teacher research: Both teaching and learning of reading are theoretically based. In *Reading: Theory, research, and practice; 26th Yearbook of the National Reading Conference,* ed. P. D. Pearson, 32–40. St. Paul, Minn.: Mason.

House, E. 1991. Big policy, little policy. *Educational Researcher* 20 (5): 21–26.

Lather, P. 1991. *Getting smart: Feminist research and pedagogy in postmodernism.* New York: Routledge, Chapman and Hall.

Liberman, I., and A. Liberman. 1989. Whole language vs. code emphasis: Underlying assumptions and their implications for reading instruction. Paper presented to the Orton Dyslexia Society, Dallas.

Long, E. 1991. Keynote address at the Conference on Ethnographic and Qualitative Research in Education, University of Massachusetts, Amherst, June.

Luke, A. In press. From psychology to linguistics in the production of the literate: Meta-narrative and the politics of schooling. In *Literacy in social processes,* ed. F. Christie. Woodanga, New South Wales, Australia: Literary Technologies.

Lytle, S., T. Marmor, and F. Penner. 1986. Literacy theory in practice: Assessing reading and writing of low-literate adults. Paper presented at the annual meeting of the American Educational Research Association, San Francisco.

McKenna, M., R. Robinson, and J. Miller. 1990. Whole language: A research agenda for the nineties. *Educational Researcher* 19 (8): 3–6.

Pace, G. 1991. When teachers use literature for literacy instruction: Ways that constrain, ways that free. *Language Arts* 68:12–25.

Pappas, C. 1990. Is narrative "primary"? Some insights from kindergartners' pretend readings of stories and information books. Paper presented at the National Reading Conference, Miami.

Phinney, M. 1991. The relationship between school writing and student identity. Paper presented at the Conference on Ethnographic and Qualitative Research in Education, University of Massachusetts, Amherst, June.

Rhodes, L., and N. Shanklin. 1989. *A research base for whole language.* Denver: LINK.

Rosenblatt, L. 1938. *Literature as exploration.* New York: Appleton-Century.

———. 1978. *The reader, the text, the poem: The transactional theory of the literary work.* Carbondale: Southern Illinois University Press.

Rowe, D. 1987. Literacy learning as an intertextual process. In *Research in literacy: Merging perspectives; 36th yearbook of the National Reading Conference,* ed. J. Readance and R. Baldwin. Rochester, N.Y.: National Reading Conference.

Schaafsma, D. 1990. Lillie dancing. *Language Arts* 67:116–27.

Smith, J., and L. Heshusius. 1986. Closing down the conversation: The end of the quantitative-qualitative debate among educational researchers. *Educational Researcher* 15:4–12.

Smith, K. 1993. Responses in literature study sessions. Ph.D. diss., Arizona State University, Tempe.

Smith, K. 1991. Personal communication with author.

Solsken, J. In press. *Literacy, gender, and work in families and in school*. Norwood, N.J.: Ablex.

Spiegelman, A. 1973. *Maus: A survivor's tale*. New York: Pantheon Books.

Stahl, S., and P. Miller. 1989. Whole language and Language Experience approaches for beginning reading: A quantitative research synthesis. *Review of Educational Research* 59:87–116.

Stephens, D. 1991. *Toward an understanding of whole language*. Technical Report no. 524. Champaign, Ill.: Center for the Study of Reading, University of Illinois at Urbana-Champaign.

Stice, C., and N. Bertrand. 1989. The texts and textures of literacy learning in whole language versus traditional/skills classrooms. In *Thirty-eighth yearbook of the National Reading Conference*, ed. S. McCormick and J. Zutell. Rochester, N.Y.: National Reading Conference.

Sumara, D., and L. Walker. 1991. The teacher's role in whole language. *Language Arts* 68:276–85.

Taylor, D. 1988. Ethnographic educational evaluation for children, families, and schools. *Theory into Practice* 27:67–76.

——. 1991. *Learning denied*. Portsmouth, N.H.: Heinemann.

Taylor, D., and C. Dorsey-Gaines. 1988. *Growing up literate: Learning from inner-city families*. Portsmouth, N.H.: Heinemann.

Walkerdine, V. 1990. *Schoolgirl fictions*. New York: Verso.

——. 1991. Keynote address, CELT Rejuvenation Conference, Mt. Holyoke, Mass., June.

5 Patriotic Literacy: The Intersection of Whole Language Philosophy and the Bill of Rights

Patrick Shannon
Pennsylvania State University

I am a patriot. That is, I am personally committed to making the United States honest and just in all its acts—just as I am committed to making my acts with others honest and just. As a patriot, I am vigorous in celebrating the good qualities and deeds of Americans and our culture as we seek peace, freedom, and self-determined social justice. As Americans, we are at our best when we act unselfconsciously moral toward others, sharing what we enjoy with others simply because they too are human beings who—if you make a semantic substitution in our most valued text—are all equal with certain inalienable rights.

As a patriot, I am just as vigorous in criticizing and urging corrections of my country's failures, omissions, and wrongs—and, as such, I expect others to criticize me for the same. I act on these celebrations and criticisms with my pen, with my time and strength, and with my possessions. I actively struggle for a government and a set of institutions which increase the possibility of our realizing peace, freedom, and justice. This struggle for better government is the patriotic thing to do because patriots, just like me, have made a difference in how Americans live today.

The Struggle to Continue

You must remember that when this country started, people of African descent were considered only $\frac{3}{5}$ human, that women had few rights of property and no right to vote, and that Native Americans had no right to live. Slavery was an accepted practice, supported by the government, defended by the army, and at the center of the political spectrum. Denial of women's right to vote was accepted, supported, defended, and at the political center. Leaving workers without pensions, medical care, or the right to organize was accepted, supported, defended, and at the political center. Unchecked monopolies, exploitation of the environment, and apartheid in schools and public life were at the political center. All of these failures, omissions, and wrongs were addressed only by patriots seeking peace, freedom, and justice for all human beings.

Of course, these words and facts can be distorted so that peace becomes the justification for the massacre of nonwhite male civilians, women, and children in Grenada, Panama, and Iraq; freedom becomes the right to go without needed health care or to own a handgun; justice is something that can be purchased; and patriotism is something you can tie up in a yellow ribbon. These distortions of truth show us that language is political and at the essence of politics.

But I am a patriot who will not let government and its institutions nor business or science take language or the right to use it patriotically away from me or you or our students. In schools, this struggle began at least one hundred years ago in this country. For example, in 1884 Francis Parker wrote the following as a rationale for what he called the "New Education":

> The methods of the few, in their control of the many, still govern our public schools and to a great degree determine their management. The problem for these few is how to give the people education and keep them from exercising the divine gift of choice; to make them believe that they were educated and at the same time to prevent free action of mind. The problem was solved by quantity teaching. However, the new education is the one central means by which the great problems of human liberty are to be worked out. (436)

This is our struggle to continue. It is a struggle which finds some of its expression in the mass of principles which are associated with whole language philosophy. Through their concerns about the politics of process and content in literacy programs and all of schooling, whole language advocates join Francis Parker in this century-long struggle against quantity education—that is, schooling based on measurement, on numbing drill and practice sheets, all for the glory of high test scores so that politicians, state officials, administrators, and the public will not have to think about schooling beyond this bottom line.

However, the stakes of literacy education and schooling are higher than test scores. Parker declares the stakes to be the divine gift of choice and human liberty—and when anyone speaks of human liberty and literacy, the text that quickly comes to mind is the United States Bill of Rights.

We have recently observed the 200th anniversary of the ratification of this country's most important set of ideas. In celebration of these ideas, consider the following: governmental violation of the Bill of Rights is a primary area of patriotic criticism, and schools' failure to prepare children to exercise those rights is cause for great concern. In this chapter, I situate whole language philosophy and its use in classrooms in a larger social context and discuss how whole language philosophy supports the Bill of Rights and prepares students to weather the storm of the systematic attack on civil liberties sure to come with a conservative Supreme Court.

Rights and Responsibilities

You may remember from high school civics that the Bill of Rights was written to limit the powers of government to infringe on the lives and choices of individuals. The document was written because the framers of the Constitution did not trust governments. That is, they did not trust the individuals and groups who would run government to act morally, ethically, and justly toward its citizens. Right from the start, questioning and criticizing of government were built into celebrations of a government that would recognize the rights of individuals.

For educators, then, the question becomes, "How do we learn to use in a responsible fashion the freedom that these rights acknowledge?" The glib commentators who distort this question to, "How do we keep kids from unlearning their natural inclination toward choice and active use of mind?" are actually perpetrating a romantic myth about a child's mind. Yes, children are active, creative, and lovely in their thought and deed, but they also are often reckless, rude, and parochial. Most whole language advocates are not interested in offering students license to do as they please, as opponents often claim. Rather, whole language advocates are interested in giving students freedom to develop in ways that enhance the development of all other students; a freedom in which the individual finds his or her greatest expression within a group. Therefore, any question of rights is also a question about the individual's *responsibility* to other people.

Again we can look to the "New Education" for direction. In 1897, John Dewey offered this explanation for how schools can help to prepare students to be patriotic:

> To do this means to make each one of our schools an embryonic
> community, active with types of occupations that reflect the life
> of the larger society, and permeated throughout with the spirit
> of art, history, and science. When the school introduces and
> trains each child of society into membership within such a little
> community, saturating him with the spirit of service, and pro-
> viding him with the instruments of effective self-direction, we
> shall have the deepest and best guarantee of a larger society
> which is worthy, lovely and harmonious.

In other words, in order for citizens to act out the ideal of patriotism,
they must actually experience this patriotism at some more basic,
simplified level. Because traditional society and family have not prepared citizens to exercise their rights in responsible ways, schools
must be reorganized along the lines that Dewey mentions. In this way,
students become citizens of the school community—citizens who have
the rights afforded all other citizens. Here the habits of service, caring,
choice, and independence prepare students to be American patriots.
Dewey reiterates Thomas Jefferson's belief that our system would
eventually decline unless invigorated regularly. Dewey stated that
"democracy has to be born anew every generation and education is the
midwife."

For us, Dewey sets forth an august task. We must organize our
lives at school in order to allow students to act democratically in a
protected environment. With this type of schooling, citizens are protected from students' immature responses, and students are protected
from the cynicism which surrounds and invades many adult civic acts.
It is my belief that a democratic classroom can be found at the intersection of the Bill of Rights and whole language philosophy. Let's
examine the first ten amendments to the Constitution from a whole
language perspective.

Article I

*Congress shall make no law respecting an establishment of religion, or pro-
hibiting the free exercise thereof; or abridging the freedom of speech, or of the
press; or the right of the people peaceably to assemble, and to petition the
Government for a redress of grievances.*

Although James Madison would not have known it at the time
he wrote the First Amendment, this could be called the whole language amendment. That is, the amendment implies voice, ownership,
response, choice, and many more axioms of whole language. But just
as with whole language, there is much more to the First Amendment
than slogans. There are issues of process and content to consider.

The Constitution suggests that the state cannot favor one religion over another. As a result, the traditional public school practice of celebrating holidays during the entire month preceding them has fallen into disrepute of late. This seems a bit odd to me since the teachers in my area celebrate Halloween (pagan ritual), Christmas (Christian holiday), Valentine's Day (pantheistic celebration), Arbor Day (arguably a Druid ritual), and St. Patrick's Day (often a celebration of beer in this country). Of course, religion was not the real intent of any of these holiday celebrations at school, although traditionally school prayer, Bible reading, and pro-Christian history were intended to help us all go to a Christian heaven.

Today, however, this fear of established state religion has frightened teachers away from the study of religion as schools of thought and as an important part of history. You cannot understand several aspects of contemporary history—the English in Ireland, Israel's West Bank, India's north-south conflict, the conflict between the Native Americans and the national governments in upstate New York and southern Ontario—unless you have some sense of Protestantism, Catholicism, Judaism, Islam, Hinduism, Buddhism, and Spiritualism. And perhaps we should know something about Shintoism as well, so that we might better understand the Japanese. Unless religions are part of the curriculum, we cannot hope to foster our students' appreciation for informed responsible free speech about our world. With the study of religions in the curriculum, we can expect tolerance, if not appreciation and acceptance, of religious beliefs. For many of us, religion in the curriculum means we have homework to do. Perhaps the current push to raise student knowledge of geography affords us the opportunity to study religions actively. In turn, this opens up productive contextualized discussions of morals, science, and women's rights.

In whole language classrooms, freedom of speech means much more than the right to talk to your neighbor during class. Speech in the classroom can be interpreted as broadly as has been done by the U.S. Supreme Court—dance, music, art, and symbols, as well as talk, are included in the consideration of freedom of speech. Recently the Supreme Court considered a case which challenged Indiana's law prohibiting nude dancing in public and private places as a violation of First Amendment rights. Before making a snap judgment on this issue, consider that the nudity was part of dance—and dance after all is protected, as speech and whole language advocates often include dance with props as a means of response to literature and creative expression. The question becomes, What's the difference between nude dancing and dancing the hokey-pokey with a hat on? Life ain't easy with whole language *or* the Bill of Rights!

In such legal cases, the argument in favor of censorship typically seeks to prohibit acts of obscenity, incitement to deprive others of their rights, and the pronouncement of known falsehoods—all are to be prohibited from public communication. However, it seems to me that this is where the ideas of responsible speech (of all types) must begin. At times, popular culture pushes the limits of all three of these reasons to censor. And MTV films and tabloid headlines bring much of this into our homes. Madonna's "Truth or Dare" masturbation video, NWA's lyrics about Vietnamese and Iranian shopkeepers, Spike Lee's movie *Do the Right Thing* concerning Italian American and African American relations, Andrew Dice Clay's or Henny Youngman's monologues about women, minorities, and the disabled all tempt the censor in us. And again, these may seem to be easy cultural artifacts to dismiss. However, how do you separate them from (and I date myself with the first example) Peggy Lee singing "Fever," Stephen Foster's "Old Uncle Ned," Shakespeare's *Merchant of Venice*, Bob Fosse's choreography for *Cabaret*, or John Ford's version of Native Americans—all of which were popular culture in their day?

The lesson for and from whole language classrooms, of course, is not to regulate or to censor, but to allow freedom, to provide a wide variety of opinions, to declare your own opinions, and to challenge the assumptions upon which statements from pop culture and student remarks are based. And we have precedence from the past again. Here are Leila Patridge's field notes from 1885—shortly after Little Big Horn and just before Wounded Knee:

> "We have still a few minutes left, let us talk more about the people whom we are going to study. Who are they, Henrietta?"
>
> "The Indians."
>
> "How long had they been in this country when the Puritans came?"
>
> "I don't know; I guess they always lived here."
>
> "Perhaps they did. No one knows certainly. When these white men landed in the Indian country, how did the Indians treat them?"
>
> "Kindly. They were good to them, is the unanimous opinion."
>
> "The children of the Puritans live here now; where are the children of the Indians?"
>
> "They've gone West! They've moved away!" are the vigorous answers; but the omnipresent slow boy, who sometimes says the right thing at the right time, takes his turn now and

remarks in the most moderate and matter of fact fashion—
"Those that they didn't kill, the white men drove away."

"To whom did all this land belong before the white men came?"

"To the Indians," assent the entire class unhesitatingly.

"How did the Indians get their living?"

"By hunting and fishing!" is the general belief.

"Yes, where did they hunt?"

"In the woods," is the ready reply.

"Children, the white men came here to the Indian's country; settled on his land, without paying him anything for it or even asking if they might have it; cut down his forests to build their houses and keep their fields; shot the wild animals that lived in these woods, and often killed the Indians themselves. What do you think of that?"

This is such a sudden sally, coming from within their own gates too, that the young women and men look for a moment as if they were indeed involved in thought. But presently, Douglas finds an excuse and puts it thus: "Well, the Indians killed the white men" concluding triumphantly, "and took their scalps, too."

"That is true," grants the teacher, "but was it strange when the white men took everything away from the Indians and left them not even their land?"

"But this was a beautiful country and the white men wanted to come here to live," reasons a small sophist eagerly.

"So because they did, and because they knew more, and because there were more of them, and because they had guns, it was right for them to do it, was it?" [The lesson continues until the students and teacher agree that they should study Indians and their culture carefully.] (Patridge 1885, 452–53)

Such open discussion will work toward responsible opinion. With a regular diet of this sort, responsible opinion will be defined not simply as personal beliefs but as socially examined, justified speech. And it's not just the explicit content that becomes problematic and subject to student comment.

When my daughter, Laura, started kindergarten, she entered a classroom in which the teacher thought that children had to be controlled in order to be good and that they had to be drilled on rules in order to learn proper procedures. By the way, the district called this a whole language school. This meant that music classes taught bus safety by singing an adapted version of "Wheels on the Bus," gym classes taught bus safety by learning how to line up and sit quietly, and art classes taught bus safety by putting the precut forms of people and buses into preoutlined patterns on a different sheet of paper. This was called an integrated curriculum. After a month, my wife and I attempted to switch Laura from one school to another rather than endure this logic any further. After a one-hour visit to the Friend's School in our town, Laura pulled me aside during our observation to tell me that she wanted to attend this school because there were, and I quote her, "no rules for art projects." Freedom of speech to control art, music, writing—broadly defined—is important to even the youngest of our students.

Whole language teachers further students' understanding of the First Amendment when they negotiate directions for the product and the process of speech and when they find countertexts—movies, songs, plays, and so on—to balance what appears to be the sexist, racist, classist, and materialist values of popular culture across time.

Whole language advocates speak and write often about providing students with opportunities to write in different styles for various purposes and audiences. At times, this means classroom or school newspapers. The Supreme Court has not been kind to student newspapers, affording administrators the right to censor *any* article without notification or public rationale. I admit that a headline like "Shannon Sucks" would not be pleasant to read. But it seems to me that whole language advocates cannot make use of this right of censorship if they wish to remain true to their convictions of ownership and their beliefs about preparing students to be patriotic citizens. As a whole language educator, I want to know if the article "Shannon Sucks" is responsible journalism. If they've got the goods—let 'em print it, eh? My belief is that after a brief flurry of "Shannon Sucks" articles, the tide will turn to remarkable news reporting and editorials. And I speak from experience.

For example, at a local school close to where I live, a student free press recently printed its third issue. The first issue had articles about skateboarding (outlawed on public streets in my town) and seven about teachers and love affairs among preadolescents (tabloid-style stuff). Issue three, with no interference from teachers or parents, has only one juicy article on what happens in the parking lot at the local high school during lunch, and a series of articles on why a nearby town must boil its water to drink and what the recent opening of a Wal-Mart has meant to our town. Neither of these topics was addressed seriously by the local daily newspapers, and the students wanted other students to know about them. I believe in freedom of the press, even at school.

The right . . . to petition . . . for redress of grievances is, I think, the most important form of civic writing. And here again whole language recognizes that writing is not limited to the use of the alphabet—it includes posters, buttons, songs, T-shirts, cartoons, and marches, as well as letters to the editors, petitions, and declarations of independence. The above phrase was included in the Bill of Rights in order to assure citizens of the rule of reason and reasonableness. Likewise, students also need to know the reasons for authority, rules, and actions. I am not talking about the authoritarianism of Lee Cantor's Assertive Discipline. I mean reasons behind the laws of the school and classroom. If teachers and administrators cannot provide a rationale for a rule that others will find in the public interest, perhaps they ought to reconsider the rule and accept students' right to assemble peaceably in order to redress the grievance.

With the sit-up-straight, no-talking, follow-the-rules, listen-to-Christian pieties of traditional schooling, student participation in controlled newspapers cannot help the participants or the paper's readership to understand the rights and responsibilities granted and assigned to every citizen by the First Amendment. In fact, to be patriotic, students will have to unlearn all those school lessons. Yet, whole language philosophy and practice encourage students' freedom of justified beliefs, responsible freedom of speech and press, and active peaceful assembly for the interrogation of governing rules and actions. That is, whole language advocates support and promote the First Amendment.

Articles II and III

A well regulated Militia, being necessary to the security of a free State, the right of the people to keep and bear Arms, shall not be infringed.

No Soldier shall, in time of peace be quartered in any house, without the consent of the Owner, nor in time of war, but in a manner to be prescribed by law.

The Second and Third Amendments are not necessarily language related, and I will not address them here (although much could be learned from studying the rhetoric on both sides of the gun laws).

Article IV

The right of the people to be secure in their persons, houses, papers, and effects, against unreasonable searches and seizures, shall not be violated, and no Warrants shall issue, but upon probable cause, supported by Oath or affirmation, and particularly describing the place to be searched, and the persons or things to be seized.

The obvious point here is that whole language schools and teachers cannot accept the recent Supreme Court ruling that warrants are not necessary for search, if probable cause is strong. In other words, if you expect trust to be established, you cannot violate students' right to security in their belongings—desks, lockers, cubbies—without an impartial third party agreeing that a search is warranted. Fear of drugs has pushed people to the point of violating citizens' Fourth Amendment rights. Fear is leading us to lawlessness against the lawless. In this way, we live a contradiction that will work against our public good in the long run. For at some point you must ask *whose* individual probable cause will rule the day.

A less obvious but just as important point is a person's right to be psychologically secure in his or her person and home. This is a whole language issue because it strikes at the heart of risk taking, which allows students to outgrow themselves by trying and testing new ideas and actions. Students will not become patriotic if they feel insecure about their safety. Perhaps two examples from my daughter's first month at school will help make my point clearer.

Laura went to kindergarten believing that she could read and write—and she could. Her first encounter with her teacher was as follows—I quote from an audiotape that my wife, Kathleen, took as data for a book she is writing on home-school connections.

> *Mrs. L:* Can you write your name? Will you write your name for Mrs. L?
>
> *Laura:* Yes, L-A-U-R-A.
>
> *Mrs. L:* Yes, but that's not how we write it at school. We write L-a-u-r-a.
>
> *Laura:* Those are hard.
>
> *Mrs. L:* Can you write it this way?
>
> *Laura:* Those are hard. I write L-A-U-R-A.
>
> *Mrs. L:* Would you like to practice writing your name? Write *a* for Mrs. L.

Laura, who had been waiting "all her life" to go to school, stopped reading and writing at home after the first day of school. She even stopped signing her name, and she started yelling at her brother to follow the rules and stop being bad.

What had happened here was a violation of Laura's self-security. A signature is a very personal possession, and Mrs. L had taken it away from Laura, leaving her feeling insecure in her person. In the same way, I should think that a teacher's commentary on the contents of journals, on vocabulary, on dialect, or on mannerisms could do the very same thing.

Dismissal of home, history, or capability also seems to be an act of violence—an act which violates the Fourth Amendment rights of students. In my second example, Laura was plugging along during the fourth week of school. She did not like school and said so often. But she saw some light at the end of the tunnel because Mrs. L was about to open the art center after the rules of conduct and use were taught for each article in the center. Laura painted her first picture and placed it on the drying rack. Just before cleanup for dismissal, Mrs. L held up Laura's painting and asked, "What's wrong with this painting?" According to the accounts of two students and a parent in the classroom at the time, Laura claimed her painting. Still holding the painting high, Mrs. L disclosed that, against the rules, the painting did not have a name on it, and she threw it into the wastebasket in front of the class. As you recall, Laura stopped signing her name after the first day. Laura would not talk about school when she got off the bus that day. She told her mother, "don't ask about school," and went up to sit in her room. Our next-door neighbor told us what was wrong because her son was crying at lunch about the incident. The mother in the classroom that day confirmed our neighbor's story. Laura thought that she had been bad at school and that we would be angry with her for breaking school rules. When we told her we thought that everyone makes mistakes and that we thought throwing someone else's work away was a questionable practice, Laura responded that she had a plan and that we should not worry. All the same, we made an appointment with Mrs. L the next day.

Laura got off the bus the next noon, displaying a new painting with only her name painted in foot-high letters—and they were all in capitals. (You can see the intersection of the ideas behind the first and fourth amendments in Laura's response.) When we met with Mrs. L later in the day, she told us that obviously the painting experience had been good for Laura because that day she had signed her name to the painting. Mrs. L missed the point that "L-A-U-R-A" was all Laura painted and that it was all capitals. Laura never returned to the school.

In whole language classrooms, students must learn to be secure in their person and papers so that they can get on with the business of learning. Moreover, they begin to expect to be secure unless they behave in an unreasonable or unlawful manner.

Articles V, VI, VII, and VIII

No person shall be held to answer for a capital, or otherwise infamous crime, unless on a presentment or indictment of a Grand Jury, except in cases arising in the land or naval forces, or in the Militia, when in actual service in time of War or public danger; nor shall any person be subject for the same offence to be twice put in jeopardy of life or limb; nor shall be compelled in any criminal case to be a witness against himself, nor be deprived of life, liberty, or property, without due process of law; nor shall private property be taken for public use, without just compensation.

In all criminal prosecutions, the accused shall enjoy the right to a speedy and public trial, by an impartial jury of the State and district wherein the crime shall have been committed, which district shall have been previously ascertained by law, and to be informed of the nature and cause of the accusation; to be confronted with the witnesses against him; to have compulsory process for obtaining witnesses in his favor, and to have the Assistance of Counsel for his defence.

In suits at common law, where the value in controversy shall exceed twenty dollars, the right of trial by a jury shall be preserved, and no fact tried by jury shall be otherwise re-examined in any Court of the United States, than according to the rules of the common law.

Excessive bail shall not be required, nor excessive fines imposed, nor cruel and unusual punishments inflicted.

These are the law-and-order amendments which are completely consonant with whole language philosophy and practice. They ask us to consider student deportment in a manner similar to the way in which whole language educators handle students' writing. In whole language classrooms, when students seek help with writing, they ask for it, but they do not have to disclose all the problems that they are having. They expect a reasonably timely response from their peers and their teacher, and then they have a chance to ask these helpers what is meant by the offered advice. Finally, they never expect to see papers as we saw them when we went to school—dripping blood as a morally superior teacher taught us our sins of inattention, lack of logic, and poor small-muscle coordination.

In other words, during writing workshops students have the right not to testify against themselves, to a speedy trial from their peers, to confront accusers, and not to receive excessive punishment. I am not making light of these rights. I am suggesting that the management system of writers' workshops—which is deeply embedded in whole language philosophy and practice—can be a metaphor for a classroom management system. And as such it will teach students their rights and responsibilities as citizens so that they can be patriotic in, and later out of, school.

How does this work in classrooms? John Schmidt, third-grade teacher at MacArthur Elementary in Duluth, Minnesota, starts with a community of learners week in which he negotiates with his class a student bill of rights, a procedure for identifying an accused transgressor of those rights, a procedure for jury selection and for advocacy, and a mechanism for conduction of this type of classroom business. His students' bill of rights for last year included the following:

> We, the citizens of 201 have the right to be safe, to be treated fairly, to study and learn, to hear, to get help, to give help, to a quiet work space, to use school equipment, to be respected, to tell how we feel, to have fun, and to tell what we think.

Laws (rules) were proposed to realize these rights, and all citizens of 201 are responsible to one another to preserve those rights. All must fill the roles of court recorder, court clerk, jury member, advocate, prosecutor. But the accused has the right to pick his or her advocate from anyone in the class. Tuesday and Thursday from 2:00–3:15 the court can be in session, with John Schmidt as judge and the students doing the rest.

Although time-consuming to accomplish, developing the law-and-order rights as the basis for a classroom or school management program pays literacy and citizenship dividends. That is, classroom management becomes part of the curriculum. Moreover, it allows students a stake in the conduct of schooling, which cut Schmidt's discipline problems in half. Again whole language principles of choice, voice, and responsibility seem tailor-made to help students understand, use, and expect the Fifth, Sixth, Seventh, and Eighth Amendments to be used.

Article IX

The enumeration in the Constitution, of certain rights, shall not be construed to deny or disparage others retained by the people.

The Ninth Amendment is ambiguous, and constitutional scholars have argued over it for two centuries. According to constitutional historians, James Madison offered the amendment in response to a congressional complaint that the Bill of Rights could never be comprehensive in the protection of human dignity. The Ninth Amendment was supposed to cover issues not mentioned in the other amendments. It has been called "the implicit amendment" because it supposedly allowed judges to combine the implicit meaning of other amendments in order to articulate new rights. For example, the right to privacy (not mentioned in the Constitution) was construed from the implied understanding of the First and Fourth amendments. If you have freedom of expression and the right to feel secure, then logically the Ninth Amendment guarantees you the right of privacy from government intrusion. Whole language practices of personal journals and optional sharing of all student compositions can help students understand how the Ninth Amendment could be used in privacy matters.

The First and Fourth Amendments might also be combined to argue for an individual's right to his or her culture. Culture is not mentioned in the Constitution, nor has it been named in a court case defining free speech. Yet Americans are beginning to acknowledge America's multicultural history and the multiracial and multicultural composition of its population. With its philosophical acknowledgment of the multiple meanings of text, of the roles of context in meaning making, and of the role of culture in that context, whole language promotes the right of individuals to their own culture. The fact that whole language advocates utilize multicultural literature in classrooms expands the definition of voice and security so that our students can acknowledge the rights of individuals and groups of Americans to be and remain different from one another. This acceptance of difference is a major shift from traditional schooling which, through standardized tests, standardized curriculum, and standardized classroom management schemes, attempts to homogenize students into something called American culture. In the whole language classroom, we can organize our language arts, social studies, sciences, and arts programs as part of a process of identifying our cultural differences, locating those differences in relation to one another, and finding ways in which we can live and work together with those differences. Cultural differences are a fact of life in school and a right guaranteed by whole language and Ninth Amendment.

Article X

The powers not delegated to the United States by the Constitution, nor prohibited by it to the States, are reserved to the States respectively, or to the people.

Education is a state's right which is slowly being swallowed by the federal government—which by the way, is decidedly anti-whole language. Apparently, federal employees believe the federal government would run more smoothly if there were not so many patriots working hard for peace, freedom, and justice. *Becoming a Nation of Readers* (Anderson 1985), *What Works: Research about Teaching and Learning* (1986), and *Beginning to Read: Thinking and Learning about Print* (Adams 1990) and its summary are among several government-endorsed documents which declare whole language to be "indifferent," "unnecessary," "unpractical," "educational malpractice," and something that must be stopped dead in its tracks. Each document was offered at the same time the federal government was cutting its financial commitment to education—preschool through postsecondary.

Most recently, conservative interests have called for national tests in all subjects and in reading and math at set intervals. If implemented, this program of national tests would affect the literacy curriculum in every school in the country. The defenders of this policy who suggest that these national assessments might include portfolio principles are naive. The federal government seeks state-by-state comparisons, but educators cannot compare student portfolios without making them into test substitutes. I doubt that any educational lobby which regularly consults the pro-phonics Reading Reform Foundation on literacy matters is going to produce a test which is good for education, for students, for teachers, or for the Bill of Rights.

Blatant attempts to force a national curriculum through testing seem unconstitutional to me. Perhaps, during whole language writing workshops, students, parents, teachers, and administrators should let our government know our constitutional concern immediately. We should let all politicians know that we want a real education president and Congress, which will not tread on the rights of teachers and students.

There are only ten amendments in the Bill of Rights—some important amendments came later: the end of slavery, equal treatment under the law, women's right to vote. However, the Bill of Rights is worthy of celebration by itself for the rights it grants:

Whole Language Amendment (First)

Risk-Taking and Support Amendment (Fourth)

Ethical Community Amendments (Fifth through Eighth)

Culture Amendment (Ninth)

Local Control Amendment (Tenth)

These are rights for whole language educators to celebrate, use, and promote among their students. Despite what the federal government declares, whole language advocates can be among the most patriotic of educators.

Conclusion

Whole language advocates should engage the Bill of Rights in their classrooms, but not because these amendments will single-handedly eliminate the failures, omissions, and wrongs of our country once and for all times. The pessimists and cynics speak about the impossibility of singular acts of patriotism to change our way of life in the face of overwhelming human suffering caused by greed, racism, and sexism. Teachers promoting the Bill of Rights cannot change it all at once. This cynicism has caused the middle class to retreat from public life and public caring—what I am calling patriotism—because in the competitive ethos of the United States they see no reason to act unless they can win it all. And teaching is a middle-class occupation.

However, advocacy of whole language works against this unpatriotic pessimism—at least it does pedagogically. Most advocates started individually to challenge literacy programs which their peers and most educators considered to be unchangeable. That is, these advocates began to act, often alone, because they sought a better life for their students and themselves in their classroom. They took pedagogical risks, they resisted pressures to conform in an unquestioning manner to tradition, and they now persist because they believe that they can make a difference in the literacy development of the individual children in their classrooms. Of course, it would be easier for them to become cynical because their acts do not change literacy education for the nation. But now with the support of others who think and feel as they do, whole language advocates work confidently with individuals to make a difference.

In the same way that whole language has helped individuals pedagogically, the celebration, promotion, and use of the Bill of Rights within classrooms can help individuals politically. That is, it can help all Americans—people of color, women, the poor, and the middle class—to wake up and reengage in public life as patriots who seek peace, freedom, and justice.

References

Adams, M. 1990. *Beginning to read: Thinking and learning about print.* Cambridge, Mass.: MIT Press.

Anderson, R., E. Hiebert, J. Scott, and I. Wilkinson. 1985. *Becoming a nation of readers.* Washington, D.C.: National Academy of Education, Commission on Reading.

Dewey, J. 1897. The university elementary school: Studies and methods. *University Record* 1:42–47.

Parker, F. 1884 [1937]. *Talks on pedagogics: An outline of the theory of concentration.* New York: Kellog. Reprint edited by E. A. Wygant. New York: John Day.

Patridge, L. 1885. *The "Quincy Methods" illustrated.* New York: Kellog.

What works: Research about teaching and learning. (1986). Washington, D.C.: U.S. Department of Education, Office of Educational Research and Improvement.

6 The Bible and Whole Language

Adrian Peetoom
Scholastic Canada, Chatham, Ontario

Ardent advocates of the Right have targeted whole language teachers for attacks. There is more to that ultra-conservatism than fundamentalist, Bible-believing, and born-again Christian impulses, of course, but those components play an important role in that movement. Advocates of the Right do not like what some teachers are doing with their kids and want those teachers to stop their practices. They say they base their claims on what the Bible teaches them. My question is, Should these teachers stop? My answer is, Sometimes they should, sometimes they should not.

Not all whole language teachers will agree about the "sometimes." Here is the opening paragraph of an article by Lillian Hentel in *Centerspace,* the newsletter of the Center for Establishing Dialogue in Teaching and Learning:

> A little first grade boy came up to me recently to tell me that when Halloween comes, he is not going to celebrate it, because it is the birthday of the devil. This little boy's right, and his parents' right to do so or not is protected by the US Constitution, under freedom of religion. But, if his parents were to come to me as a teacher, and say that they did not want any of the students in his class, or in the school, or in the district, to celebrate Halloween, this would be censorship, and this form of censorship is creeping into the school systems more and more. (Hentel 1991, 8)

My response is that this particular teacher might easily have stopped Halloween celebrations in her classroom. I have a hard time

With great pleasure I express my profound gratitude to the following four friends who read earlier drafts and who, each in their own way, had a direct hand in helping me shape this work: Jane Baskwill, Henk Bruinsma, Fran Buncombe, and Connie Weaver. My thanks also to Dr. Paul Marshall for freely sharing some of his thoughts on tolerance and toleration, which shaped my own version. Of course, I remain completely responsible for the content of this chapter.

seeing the presence of a Halloween celebration as a benchmark case. I know a good many teachers who are getting sick of Halloween and its substantial chunk of time and attention in many primary classrooms each October. Teachers complain to me about having to build other themes and more long-term curricular enterprises around Halloween or other holidays. They are frustrated with an "events-driven curriculum." Could Halloween be reserved for life outside the school walls, without damage to any tender psyches, child's or teacher's, and without seeing it as a crucial civil rights case? The Hentel article implies that to let go of Halloween might put "our educational system at risk." That is silly.

Let's be serious. A number of years ago I first heard about innovative teachers pejoratively being singled out as "liberal humanists" and being maligned by fundamentalist Christians in Alberta, Nova Scotia, and Ontario. Some time ago, a Reverend Ken Campbell orchestrated tense public meetings in places like Peterborough, Ontario, around novels by Margaret Laurence and other Canadian authors and accused some literature teachers of reprehensible long-term objectives.

In both Nova Scotia and Alberta, Concerned Parents organizations have circulated newsletters that rail against teachers who supposedly weaken our national destiny by refusing to teach phonics, spelling, and grammar. These phenomena are not unknown in the United States. In fact, the two national experiences mix. Not long ago in the sleepy town of Bowmanville, Ontario, at a parents' meeting called to crucify the *Impressions* basal series (Holt Canada), the guest speaker came from Florida.

I also need to point out that censorship and the casting of suspicion on teachers and school librarians is not limited to religious types. The secular concept of "political correctness," which originates as far out on the Left as the concerns that I first mentioned originate on the Far Right, also demonstrates a penchant for intolerance toward books and people. For example, a 1991 *Toronto Globe and Mail* story of "the twisted trail of a book unfairly maligned" describes the unofficial disappearance from Toronto school bookshelves of Ian Wallace's beautiful picture book *Chin Chiang and the Dragon's Dance* (Margaret K. McElderry/Douglas and McIntyre, 1984), winner of Canada's 1985 Amelia Frances Howard-Gibbon Illustrator's Award. Apparently there was an unconfirmed and undocumented rumor that the ethnic Chinese community might be offended by presumed slight inaccuracies in some of the illustrations. In fact, the article implied that no one from the Toronto Chinese community actually objected, but that some from outside the community decided that they ought to have objected. The final paragraph of the article states:

> "Chin Chiang" may not actually have been ordered off the shelf. There has been no public statement criticizing it. Yet everyone I spoke to knew it was "problematic." There was no genuine review process. This is how a good book becomes tainted, and it shouldn't have happened. (MacCallum 1991)

But back to Halloween. However that event may look to some of us, to the parents of the boy mentioned previously it looks serious enough that they do not want their child exposed to it. Let's try to walk in their shoes for a bit to understand how they might see Halloween today, and why they would like teachers not to "celebrate" it in their son's classroom.

First, their tradition has taught them to take the Bible seriously as their book of faith, a book to be interpreted literally and as written for all ages. References to the Devil, Satan, and an assortment of demons are sprinkled throughout it. The reality of those creatures is clear to them, as it has been to the long church tradition that nurtured those parents. Halloween rose out of the Middle Ages, a time so full of health and safety hazards that it was a miracle that anyone ever reached old age. Those hazards were understood to be caused by ever-present evil forces all around, demons and devils ruled by Satan. A reasonable theory for its time, I would suggest.

However, Halloween was but a prelude to a more important day, All Saints' Day, usually November 1, the celebration of all those who figured strongly in the stories of the church. These stories bound church people together in a tight community, which set them apart from those who did not belong. Typically the Christian church, if not its leadership then certainly its people, would juxtapose evil and good, sin and grace, Satan and God, and do it with a fervor typical for the times (see Huizinga 1924 [1969]). How much better to celebrate All Saints' Day if the night before you ridiculed their former tormentors, the Devil and his demon helpers, with masks, songs, revelry, and, above all, lights that would make them flee, for they shun the light and seek the darkness. It is serious business, and risky too, but in a few hours the combined power of the saints will protect and shield, and after the threats of the previous night, the honor and power of those saints can be appreciated so much more.

Not everywhere in Europe did the same specifics reign, but the pattern was common: sheets, masks, candles or torches, knocking on doors, special songs and chants just for this occasion. As Protestantism gained influence, the de-emphasis on the array of Catholic saints made November 1 disappear from public view, observed only inside some church walls. But Halloween remained public, turned into an incidental evening of revelry for the young. In fact, it was supposed to be for the very young only, not for crafty ten year olds who would milk each house for the maximum amount of loot. School paid no attention to it, for it was a home-and-street ritual only.

Over the last thirty years Halloween seems to have become a more present and important event. For instance, in what has become an October industry, school book-club publishers make sure that at least one book related to Halloween is included, likely one of the high sellers on the list.

For Christians who are still convinced that the Devil and demons are real, the disappearance of childlike innocence is accompanied with what to them looks like sinister adult stuff. The media and pop-rock music seem full of evidence of Devil worship, Satan worship, demon possession, witchcraft, and communication with the dead, as presumed legitimate alternatives to the Christian faith. Astrologers, soothsayers, palm readers, witches, séancers, and various strands of New Agers have widespread fingers in our cultural pie these days.

As the Christian church is shrinking, and it is, so the un-Christian church is gaining ground, or so it seems to many Christians. Halloween, always under some suspicion by Christian parents but tolerated as long as it was a childhood ritual with definite borders, seems now to have become a focused *celebration* of precisely those dark forces that the original Halloween was supposed to *unmask*.

The parents of the little boy described by Hentel (1991) are beginning to fear that an elaborate and pedagogically controlled Halloween looks like the essential school step into a world that no one should take lightly and that all should fear. Their response is, "Not for my son, please, and not for my neighbor's children, if we can help it."

Do teachers really want to say to such a parent: "It is my individual right as teacher to insist that Halloween become part of my classroom's curriculum"? Do they insist that the boy, shielded at home, become unshielded at school? Is it not against whole language views to presume that the student can divide himself in two? And is excusing him from the classroom for the time of Halloween a solution . . . or a punishment?

I want to ask teachers: Why Halloween? Can't we let go? Can't we substitute something else not likely to hang out the same heavy signals? If the whole thing is light and innocent to us, why not drop it and let students celebrate outside of school? But perhaps Halloween is not innocent to you? What if inside your own soul lurks a need for Halloween? And what if some parents insist on Halloween in your classroom, for it is not innocent inside their souls either?

Battle lines are seldom clear and unequivocal. In fact, whenever I study histories of human conflicts I end up smitten. So seldom do I find the real conflict in the official records. So often the conflict is represented by minor issues and symbols—a long-ago major church schism about a single Greek letter in an obscure word or wars about land the size of a farm. I always want to ask about any conflict: Is the issue presented the real issue at hand? Is a battle about Halloween really a battle about Halloween? Could be. On the other hand, not likely.

My second reservation touches the heart of whole language, at least the way I understand it, and it is a major reason for my admiration for whole language. I am a Christian, and I take the Bible seriously, too. Like the boy's parents who disapproved of celebrating Halloween, I have loved the Scriptures all my life, not only as a splendid literary text but also as my trustworthy, infallible book of faith. By infallible I mean that it has never failed me.

But unlike some of these Christian opponents, I have also come to be convinced that whole language, under whatever name, is a jim-dandy approach to schooling, with many elements in substantial harmony with what I read the Bible to say about how I ought to love my learning neighbor as myself. I should think that at least some whole language teachers are driven by very similar biblical imperatives, often in an unarticulated way. Indeed, I know this to be the case, and I would hope that some of these leaders read this book.

Unless I have misunderstood all these years, I am under the impression that for whole language teachers there are neither winners nor losers, only a wide diversity of people all to be taken seriously as meaning makers—and Jesus taught me that before whole language teachers did. Gone are the days, at least largely, when teachers thought: If only they knew more English, had enough sleep the night before, were white and middle-class, had a good breakfast, did not watch as much TV or watched more uplifting programs instead, had chosen a more stable family, did not have one or more parents in jail or on drugs, had books at home, had been read to from birth, knew about paper and pencil, were not Down's syndrome, in a wheelchair, hearing-impaired, seeing-impaired, religion-impaired, traditions-impaired. . . . If only, if only, if only . . . then we could. . . .

Gone are the days when all I ever heard in staff rooms at recess was "those damned kids," by which was meant those who did not pliably walk the middle road of curricular compliance. Whole language has wrought miracles in changed staff room stories, retold ever more frequently at conferences and more and more in professional journals and books:

- "Listen to what Sally read; you wouldn't have believed it!"
- "You wouldn't think that Jevon had it in him, but he wrote . . . "
- "When my class finished, the parents stood and cheered."

These stories are more than evidence of better teaching. They are evidence of increased acceptance. These are works of faith, a belief not necessarily that all children are *equally* gifted in all areas, but that all are gifted in some way. That faith demands works, for without works faith is dead, as James writes in the Bible. Whole language is busy working out that faith. My own career in publishing has been my works of faith, imperfect, indeed in need of redemption, but meant to follow the example of how Jesus met people, all people.

Christians often disagree, and in public, and not all Christian educators and parents see it my way. At first I looked for opportunities to attend public meetings to challenge the views of those people and substitute my own views—much "better" views, of course. Fortunately, I never had much opportunity to substitute my carefully reasoned exegesis of basic biblical concepts, little opportunity to pull learned rank, so to speak. In many ways I am now glad that I did not land in combat zones. Over the last few years some searing disputes within the bosom of my own denomination and congregation have made me realize how futile an exegetical duel is in settling honest differences between people who see aspects of the world very differently.

The glasses of my Christian faith and other admirable humanist traditions have us see classrooms in very much the same way. The morning bell rings for school to begin, and you put yourself at the door for the morning greeting. What do you see? A block of 70s, a smaller block of 60s and another of 80s, a few 90s (bless their eager hearts), and a few below 50s (what am I going to do with them today?).

Or do you see this? Different sizes, shades, first languages, backgrounds, genders, demonstrated competencies, interests, gifts, temperaments, sureties, eagernesses . . . but learners all, and we are going to have a full learning day today. Even those who really do not want to be here for reasons we do not control are going to have a happy learning day.

The latter view is what whole language teachers see and what I see. Each day a new beginning and filled with promises. When we get knocked down, we help each other get up again. Each person a voice. Each voice a gift. Each gift a celebration.

But here is my point with all of this. When I hear some whole language teachers talk, and especially when I read the report of the Dr. Jan Jones CED workshop (Jones 1990), I do not hear and see quite the same attitude toward adults. I see and hear talk of winning and losing, mostly "they" are not to win and "we" are not to lose. I ask: Why one attitude toward children and another toward adults? As we bend to accommodate children, why can't we bend to accommodate parents? Why panic suddenly? Why tactics of dismissal? It does not seem to me to be "in keeping with the situation," as that marvelous line from *A Christmas Carol* has it.

An Old Problem

The central problem that we are addressing is not new. Our colleague James Moffett, for so long a trendsetter for so many of us, has documented his own long-standing pain about it in his book *Storm in the Mountains: A Case Study of Censorship, Conflict, and Consciousness* (1988). More than twenty years ago he intended his *Interactions* literature-based reading program (Houghton Mifflin) to be liberating and spiritual, a way of empowering teachers and students then hopelessly stuck in the nonlanguage of basals and workbooks. But he was met with fervent opposition, especially from born-again Christians in the mountains of West Virginia, a region, incidentally, which he knows well because of family connections. In fact, he loved those people in those days, and he seems to love them still. But they rejected him and in the end hated him.

So when I read Moffett's book or hear teachers' stories about what happened in school X and community Y or read about what has appeared in the *Congressional Record* and has been embedded in legislation, I bleed for teachers on the firing line. But I also bleed for those who do these things with at least a modicum of honest conviction. In fact, I wonder what has driven them to do what they do. I cannot accept that it is some sort of personal evil that affects "their side" but not "our side." Jesus tells me never to look past the beam in my own eye for the splinter in someone else's.

I need to interject something here so as not to have you get angry at me for the wrong reason. Under the right conditions, with battle lines clear and unequivocal, I can see myself joining your campaigns, lending whatever verbal abilities and powers of analysis I might have. In this chapter I simply ask: When? And when not?

Even when it is time to do battle, I cannot be happy simply to outmaneuvre those persecutors, either on local levels or in the wider arena of state/provincial and national politics. Some of our colleagues have become very clever at sketching out battle plans on local and broader levels, various mixtures of wile and of carrot and stick. But there is something crucial missing from that list of strategies. I do not encounter respect for our opponents as persons. I do not hear their voice honored, only their politics attacked. I thought that whole language people value voice, public voice, and that we do not ask first of all whether any voice is convenient, melodious, or harmonious. Voice, first of all, is legitimate. Christian is voice. Moffett's West Virginia mountain shouts were voice.

I am not talking about differences of opinion that can be resolved fairly readily, with people of moderation and an ability to see the other side, about children's books that raise touchy issues, or about parents who need to experience that what you give their children is what they really want for them. Nor am I talking about concerns for spelling, phonics, and grammar that can be translated into genuine issues of literacy, given time and a judicious cup of coffee.

I am talking about conflicts that feature two different languages, although both may be called English. "They" say that "you" are bad. As Moffett describes in his book (1988), his opponents believed that (authentic) children's books could make offspring critical of parents' values, rebellious even, could weaken the country, could prepare the children for the "Reds" and all other global varmint. They advocated a return to "American" and "Judeo-Christian" values. They demanded that schools keep on delivering the traditional civic faith, which their community saw as a strong reflection of their biblical faith, as it had always done for them and for their parents, too.

Those kinds of clashes are not about the competence of teachers, the appropriateness of curriculum, or the primacy of certain school subjects and the best way to teach them. They are, in my view, not even about censorship. These are harsh clashes about fundamental differences of what the "good life" is about. They are, I believe, about *fundamental clashes between forms of community still remnant in our cul-ture and the prevailing ideology of liberalism,* between communal rights and individual rights. Right now in our culture, individual rights are winning on broad fronts, and that is what makes communities so agitated.

Community is not even hinted at in the paragraph that I quoted about Halloween. There the conflict is simple: between that boy (with a bow to the parents) and the teacher, and the deciding factor is individual rights, the teacher's individual rights. But I put it to you that the real conflict is between the *community* to which those parents and boy belong and the individual teacher. Moreover, the conflict is between the Christian community to which those parents belong and the doctrine of individual rights. Two faiths at war—that is what the battle is, in my view. Those parents' enemy is liberalism.

Paul Marshall, a professor of political science at the Institute for Christian Studies in Toronto, recently stated:

> I believe that liberalism is the most potent force in the destruc-tion of Canada. In the pure form of such a society each person is taught that . . . all differences between people (sex, race, re-ligion) are irrelevant and therefore must be ignored in social life. . . . This type of society has many things to commend it. . . . But it is not a society which will retain communities or tradi-tions. (1991, 10–11)

"This type of society has many things to commend it. . . . " Anyone even vaguely familiar with the last thirty years of politics and legisla-tion in both Canada and the United States knows that laws and judicial cases involving individual rights have beneficially addressed issues of oppression: racial, gender, class, and other types. The job remains unfinished, but progress is clear.

"But it is not a society which will retain communities or tradi-tions." Or preserve the country that we know as Canada. Canada faces a short-term and crucial dilemma. One of its large provinces, Quebec, a community of North American French thought, language, and his-tory, is being threatened by the push of liberalist ideology in the form of a Charter of Rights which it so far has refused to accept for itself. The Charter of Rights enshrined in the Canadian Constitution says that all those who live within Canadian borders shall be individually equal before the law.

But Quebec says: We are French. French is language, and there-fore traditions, culture, and *community.* Communally we are different from you Anglos, and we want our definition of ourselves protected in law, or we will go it alone. You decide. We must be able to do communal things our own way, and we must be able to resist forces that undermine our identity, or we will disappear in the end. Do not ask us to privatize and individualize our real identity—that is the way of our cultural death.

The Charter of Rights is a typical liberalist document, for at its heart is the concept that a nation is made up of individuals whose relationships to the state must be scrupulously identical, certainly in theory. There can be no communities whose essence demands a unique place under the law. It cannot protect communities, except by allowing for anomalies that violate its own spirit and are therefore sure to be short-term.

For instance, our aboriginal people have certain unique hunting and fishing rights that are not available to other Canadians. That rankles the liberalist, Charter of Rights folks, and regular attempts are made to eradicate those rights. These days conservationist arguments are often invoked, but specific cases have always reflected current popular fancies. The drama of the Canadian case is obvious, that of most other cases is not. The last half-century has seen a gradual erosion of genuine community all over the Western world, as the spirit of liberalism has invaded our individual souls. For anyone interested in seeing the details of those claims fleshed out, I recommend a best-selling book written by a group of writers: *Habits of the Heart: Individualism and Commitment in American Life* (Bellah et al. 1985).

What is community? Whole language teachers often use the word to describe what we wish to develop in our classrooms. No problem here, as long as we understand the limits of the word in the way we use it: a group of children (plus one adult teacher) who work well together for about nine months and get to like and teach each other. My colleague Linda Cameron uses the term *collaborative coalition* instead, an apt phrase that captures the limits of time and commitment. She sees it as a group of people being collaborative around a common purpose, without anyone surrendering vital personal commitments.

Whole language teachers and learners might also use *community* to embrace our educator friends, those who share our beliefs about learning and teaching and who feel the need to huddle in the midst of other educators who may not even like us, let alone understand what we are trying to do.

But the authors of *Habits of the Heart* are more circumspect about their use of the term *community*, as I would want to be. When I think of community, I think about Dutch-Canadian Orthodox Calvinists. In Chatham, Ontario, where I live, my church is largely made up of post–World War II Dutch immigrants, and many have parents, siblings, and now children and grandchildren who attend the same type of church, sometimes the same congregation. Moreover, their English continues to show traces of the Dutch spoken by the original immigrants, including their regional dialects. They meet at Christian school and church meetings, both big elements in their communal identity. They shop at the thriving Dutch delicatessen for their cheese, cold cuts, and candies. The talk at birthday and other parties is incomprehensible to members of other communities, not because it is Dutch (it seldom is), but because the issues, shadings, jokes, and topics pertain to this particular community. That would include talk about issues of church and faith, and references to certain favorite parts of the Bible.

Above all, the members of this community recognize each other as having a shared history and a common descent from people who spoke their language. I used to write a monthly column in a weekly journal read by a lot of them, and I sometimes wrote stories about our lives before we came to Chatham, and after we came, and people in church would let me know that they knew what I meant. A lot of those stories would not mean anything to readers of this chapter.

In short, this group of Dutch people is typical of what *Habits of the Heart* calls community:

> Examples of . . . genuine communities are not hard to find. . . .
> They are ethnic and racial communities, each with its own story
> and its own heroes and heroines. They are religious communi-
> ties that recall and reenact their stories in the weekly and annual
> cycles of their ritual year, remembering the scriptural stories
> that tell them who they are and the saints and martyrs who
> define their identity. (Bellah et al. 1985, 155)

Of course, communities seen this way are mixed blessings. I will mention the fact that the members of my community do not read much or write at all. Actually, they exhibit little intellectual curiosity, resist changes in their church and family lives, and tend to judge harshly those members who rattle and roll the gates that keep members in and outsiders out. They spend enormous amounts of money on church and church-related "causes" but are, as a whole, a bit blind and deaf to the turmoil of the world, thinking that if people all over the world simply decided to live the way they themselves do, hunger, poverty, and misery would somehow disappear. The average family with children will spend $6,000–$10,000 a year to send each one to the local Christian school, which receives no government funding of any kind, yet those schools resist the very curricular and pedagogical renewal that their rhetoric would lead one to expect. They are little more than mediocre middle-class schools in whose parent newsletters the words *skills* and *discipline* had better appear regularly or the supporting community gets suspicious.

It is hard for a person like myself to belong. When I go to church, I leave a lot of myself at the door, for that part of me would carry an aura of the infidel to them. But belong I must, for it is community, and without it I feel lonely and naked in a world of lonely and naked people. I observe myself lapsing into Dutch, sometimes at the parties, or in the Chatham post office when I meet my builder friend Ray, my electrician friend Albert, or my insurance friend Jake. My now-retired steel fabricating plant manager friend Tom and I keep swapping stories about what it was like to be a boy during World War II—we both were. Albert, Tom, Ray, and Jake do not want liturgical renewal in the church, for they lead busy lives and want church to be a comfort zone. Those lovely people drive me up the wall sometimes. I hear them judge the world, and what they judge does not exist, or does not have the evil that they presume it to have. "Read," I silently scream at them. "You're ignorant, and ignorance is dangerous and un-Christian."

But they are community. For decades I fought to change them in places all over Canada—and they won, mostly. This community continues to teach its children and grandchildren legitimate limits and productive ways of living decent lives, even though I might find those lives a bit narrow and even blind in spots. Community provides borders and answers questions, a great gift to bewildered people living in a bewildering world. Indeed, some descendants break out of all of it. Some of those manage to keep their life whole. A lot of them do not.

My wife and I break out for some areas of our lives. While communities are a blessing, they are a mixed blessing. I cannot trust all of my life to community. For instance, my work has had to break itself free from their Christian school model. In education I have had to go it alone, and within the community I have had to pay a price for that choice.

Separation from a community is also discussed in *Habits of the Heart:*

> we live in a society that encourages us to cut free from the past, to define our own selves, to choose the groups with which we wish to identify. No tradition and no community . . . is above

> criticism. . . . So we live somewhere between the empty and the
> constituted self. (Bellah et al. 1985, 157)

Most North Americans no longer choose any community, but rely only
on individual choices for all aspects of their lives. Yet we cannot live
alone, and so the book also describes how we compensate.

While the liberalist language of growing up points to freeing
oneself from restraints such as family, work, and church, many people
act as if those prime communities are still important to them. Not long
ago I saw a television program on the Amish, on which was interviewed a former member, now a psychiatrist in Chicago. In my judgment the man had a hard time not crying, clearly about the losses in
his own life caused by his departure from the community.

Ironically, people who have bought into this individualist ideology with heart and soul tend to end up spending a lot of time and
money in various types of counseling. Community provides various
forms of intimacy. While ideologically individualists leave no room for
communal intimacy, their souls crave it, so they search for a suitable
confessional shingle and purchase human community in its professional form—every week one hour of intimacy for, say, $65. The expe-
rienced counselor authors of *Habits of the Heart* describe this
widespread phenomena in vivid detail.

I also sense that for a substantial number of whole language
teachers, this movement itself is a compensating attempt to gain intimacy, and whole language conferences have become a regular teacher-
community fix.

Our culture still retains many remnants of community. People
still gather around shared memories. Others compensate for a loss of
community in various ways. But the individual-rights ideology is
winning. Civil rights, but for individuals only. Allow no exceptions.
Believe what you will, but believe it in private.

So who are they, those frustrated, angry, sometimes lashing and
slashing Christians? They are believers in the Bible as a unique book.
Among themselves they will differ about what that means, but even
the milder and more ambivalent and dynamic Christian Bible readers
meet a point at which they decide that this book is fundamentally
different from all others.

They also see their communal life as a reflection of what they
hear the Bible tell them about marriage, family, government, school,
work, justice, sin, faith, grace, heaven. They tend to relativize life on
earth, which for them is mostly a vale of tears, a passing dispensation.
They hear the Bible describe them as pilgrims and as colonizers, and

the idea of moving on is clear in both images. They relativize human ideas and solutions to problems. They do not believe that earthly brokenness is fixable, ultimately, in human terms. With various degrees of eagerness, they await a new earth and a new heaven. If some renewal comes even on earth, it is the work of faith and the Holy Spirit, who may use human beings, even nonbelievers, but God is in control and wills it.

All this runs fundamentally counter to liberalist ideas, which are focused on this earth, with human beings the measure of all things and possessing the ultimate power to fix. The notion of universal schooling is essentially a liberalist idea, a belief that it is education and good ideas through which human society will be renewed, as John Dewey said in his preface to *Democracy in Education* (reprint, 1954).

Liberalism is winning. More and more these Christians sense that public life is demanding that they give up (or privatize, which for them is the same thing) citizenship in the Kingdom of God. They see public life coming at them as a fundamental attack on all the values that their community has held for generations.

The whole business gets even more complex for those segments of evangelical Christendom that have seen America as the embodiment of what God intended nations to be. American patriotism is probably the most spiritual patriotism in the world, which causes it to have an intensity and fervor which is a puzzle to many others, certainly to Europeans and even to Canadians. I cannot imagine an educational writer in any other Western country saying what James Moffett observed in his book or being taken seriously by readers when he wrote: "the United States has come closer to a Spiritual realization of government than any other country on earth" (1988, 104).

Now, I have met many Americans whose searing criticism of their own country demonstrates that they do not buy into that. On the other hand, I have watched, especially on TV, the massive patriotic outpourings of just such religious fervor. On the first Sunday of the Gulf War, when both President Bush and Secretary of State Cheney were televised going into church, they conveyed to viewers their belief that God is on the American side as always. As I watched them enter church, neither George nor Dick looked like a humble petitioner about to submit his actions and thoughts to a higher power. They looked like successful committee chairmen about to report to the chairman of the board about a mission that could not fail.

I am not saying that other Western leaders have not done the same thing in the past, but I am saying that I am unaware of any other such sustained notion of divinity of nationhood. The French statesman Alexis de Tocqueville wrote about it in his book *Democracy in America* (1830 [1954]), and while he admired it, he also warned against its potential excesses.

I have not yet said that the spirituality that Moffett discusses is necessarily Christian or linked to any organized religion at all. Moffett also wrote, "The great majority of the founding fathers were freemasons and Rosicrucians as well as Christians" (1988, 147).

There is a side to American Protestantism, especially within its fundamentalist, born-again wing, which comes close to identifying American patriotism with Christian faith. In the trappings of a human culture it spots the divine to the extent that aspects of national identity are thought to have been placed this side of the Atlantic as an example for all nations, and by God himself. The Stars and Stripes becomes another version of the cross. American individual freedom equals freedom in Christ. Every war is a Christian crusade. Such sentiments were expressed in an article written by an American for a Canadian audience in a then-Canadian magazine:

> God founded the great nation of America using Calvinists, not Jews or Roman Catholics. . . . Whatever is good in America, politically, economically, and socially is rooted in the faith and life of our earliest forefathers who gave birth to this nation in its incipient stages. (*The Christian School Herald* 1960, 3)

I know full well that such sentiments are not universally shared by all denominations, but this identification is widespread enough for me to regularly catch its presence, especially during the recent Gulf War.

Now my own prior knowledge, confirmed by *Habits of the Heart*, would question whether the U.S. founding fathers were Christians, but that is not the point here. These examples are important for signaling that the link between Christian faith and American nationhood is a strong one at least among some segments of the American people. And I believe that this link is a key to understanding how those opposed to whole language may become so strong in their actions and reactions.

For against the background of that link, schools, especially public schools, become the transmitters of American values, which are seen as biblical values. Schools are seen as, and in the past widely advocated being, the instrument of the state for the promotion of American national spirituality. In his book Moffett seems to be saying to his enemies: "I know what you want. It's the same as I want, and I want what our trusted forefathers, founding fathers, wanted: America the good, the true, and the beautiful. I'm giving it to you in my school program. Why can't you see that?" And the pages of his book bleed with the hurt of rejection. But those West Virginia born-again Christian mountain folk could not see that, and neither can many of their Christian peers today, urban or rural. For what is the perception of what is happening in America?

1. The body politic is sick, with politicians on the take and the country falling apart while the rich get richer and the poor get poorer.

2. Canada is not the only country in a desperate search for its own identity—MacNeil-Lehrer television interviews regularly point to the problem of a lack of national vision.

3. Church attendance is decreasing rapidly.

4. Business is playing too many dirty games with consumers, the environment, workers, governments. (Need I mention savings and loans?)

5. Academia is proclaiming one truth one week, and another truth the next, using statistics that we do not understand anyway.

6. The media are full of reports about how families have betrayed their members, through physical and psychological battering (including incest), breakup, alienation, and absence of intimacy.

7. Roughly 50 percent of North American marriages end in divorce.

8. George Bush proclaimed "a new world order" for international politics, a proclamation met with howls of derisive laughter around the globe.

9. The police are corrupt or powerless.

So when we meet the very hostile and the very docile in the parents of our students, we are probably meeting uncontrollable bewilderment about most of life. What has remained of personal safety, economic security, family loyalty, communal experience, personal wholeness, personal and institutional ethical standards, religious doctrines, truth in advertising, reliable goods, useful taxes, a country deserving patriotism, and a school that delivers the goods?

Schools have never been about skills and contents, but about the meaning of life and the future of the human race. Immigrants came to our shores and relied upon the schools to make their children into Americans and Canadians—which in practice seemed to mean some higher human race, some more virtuous, stronger, purer type of human being. The evidence is thick in the documents of the early days of public schools, as school promoters fought to establish their "holy institutions."

But schools no longer have a clear message, one contained in textbooks used by all, in lists of skills worked through by everyone, in one language. More and more schools, especially whole language schools, hang out the message that somehow the past has been wrong and the future is no longer guaranteed. I am not saying that whole language teachers personally hang out that message. But when they are seen as wanting to change the skills-based, textbook-dependent, and, to all intents and purposes, proven and tested curriculum that reigned when America was great and its institutions stable, then they are seen as "the enemy." Some of those parents see the trinity of church, country, and school being broken for their children. They see schools proclaiming the need for students to be independent thinkers, but they fear that what that means in practice is adults who no longer love God, country, and the primacy of the American people. The link between these three is broken by too many too different books and by children writing on topics of their choice.

What does it all mean? I have not tried to argue that the Christians whom I have described are right in all or even most of their views. Indeed, I have a profound skepticism about most of it, believing that we live in a post-Christian age and that the whole notion of Western Civilization being a Christian civilization is highly debatable anyway, at any time in history.

But the question of right and wrong is a liberalist, rationalist, technological, and scientific question, and not a community one. Liberalist ideology compels all views to be judged, and to be discarded if found wanting, or pushed back into the recesses of what people may think privately, deep inside themselves.

I would suggest that community views are not necessarily a teacher's to judge. I would invite teachers to learn to feel the community pain instead, as they always try to feel the pain of their students and colleagues. Can teachers respect those folks for their loyalty to their community, their history, and their Bible? Or must they push on without compromise, convinced that salvation comes mainly from their collection of children's books and teaching strategies? In that case they should not be surprised when they meet the kind of opposition that they do. There may not be a solution in specific circumstances. There may be times when you as teachers need to oppose and organize for opposition. I cannot tell you when. There are uncouth demagogues in the world who will use any community for their personal gain—the church is full of Jimmy Bakkers and Jimmy Swaggarts, and always has been, like the monk Tetzel who opposed Luther in the 1520s.

I am not arguing that we should not resist injustice and tyranny, and I would be happy to join Carole Edelsky's hotline if it made any sense for me to do that from Chatham, Ontario, Canada. I am only hoping that we will not get ourselves into a "them against us" stance all the time and perhaps sacrifice the children whom we profess to love by our insistence on both our rights and our superior insights, leaving the little ones bewildered between us and their parents.

The report to which I referred (Jones 1990) only sees opponents operating as a well-organized and well-financed bunch, with complex tactics. But can I convince teachers to see at least some of the opposition as a community under assault and in pain? Would teachers respect that? Would they make room for it? Would they restrain their own private wishes in the face of it? Would teachers trust somehow that even though they are able to quickly spot a community's liabilities, they know that it has substantial assets, assets that they could never share and that they might not even see?

I am asking for teachers to be *tolerating*. I choose that word over *tolerance* or *toleration* because I want a word that indicates a constant, lived experience of respect for others that is expressed in a deliberate and compassionate manner, living alongside things one dislikes, forever if need be.

Living like that is virtuous living, and close to impossible perhaps. Liberalist gospel also preaches the virtue of tolerance, but I am afraid that I see liberals pervert the potential depth of tolerance most often. Often liberals mean *indifference,* meaning *believe* what you want, I don't care. Or, believe what you want, but keep it to yourself. Sometimes liberals mean *tyranny*—believe what you want, but *do* what I believe. In Ontario that form of liberalism means that even though you may not believe the doctrines preached in the public school in your neighborhood, you must send your child there, or pay a crippling financial penalty. Or they *relativize* all views, including their own—you believe what you want, and I will believe what I want, and it is neither here nor there what anyone believes. Relativizing all things, yours and theirs, cannot be part of tolerating either.

I believe that the best of whole language points to *tolerating*: not only letting things be when you dislike them, but honoring and, if necessary, defending their existence, and that includes communities whose ideals you cannot share—sometimes at great cost or inconvenience to yourself.

Lillian Hentel points to "the emotional power of the group" as reason for the reluctance of some whole language teachers to enter a fray. I suggest that what she calls "emotional power" may well be the existence of genuine community, a shared history that commands loyalty over and above, and sometimes in the face of, new currents that keep coming. And those currents may be coming from you.

Not long ago I read a book called *Amish Literacy* (Fishman 1988), which is a perfect model of what I mean, for the author respected the community literacy already available and consciously refrained from trying to change it.

Do whole language teachers have to win? Do they have to fight back on all the issues that other people choose? Or could they sometimes, or often, go their way more placidly, living their own truth without having to force it on others, even if it is true, or seems true, that others force their own truths on these teachers and that they are not able to completely act out their own belief system every day?

I will make this prediction. As whole language grows in size and insight, more and more teachers will go the route that Nancie Atwell and Lucy Calkins have gone and will establish their own schools. They will come to realize that they do not have the right to push their beliefs and ideas onto others. They will fashion or find a community for which a school will be the representation, where parents send their children not because it is in the neighborhood but because the parents know what it is like and approve of it.

I believe that public schools, under even more assault for individual rights, will be weakened into institutions where nothing meaningful can be said anymore, for there will always be somebody to object to what someone else says or does, from the right or the left. Maybe the whole notion of public schools is an anomaly whose weaknesses are becoming apparent as more and more teachers enter them with definite, described, and passionately held belief systems that will clash with other equally passionately held belief systems about children, language, learning, and teaching.

Whole language teachers will be caught in the middle. They invite individual voice in their classrooms, but they must often deal with collective voice, with representative voice from outside the classroom. That is the real world in which we live.

Can whole language teachers under assault survive? Not easily, perhaps, but possibly. I hope so.

References

Bellah, R. N., R. Madsen, W. M. Sullivan, A. Swidler, and S. M. Tipton. 1985 [1986]. *Habits of the heart: Individualism and commitment in American life.* Berkeley: University of California Press. Reprint, New York: Harper and Row.

The Christian School Herald, July–August 1960.

de Tocqueville, A. 1830 [1954]. *Democracy in America.* 2 vols. Reprint, New York: Random House.

Dewey, J. Reprint, 1954. *Democracy in education: An introduction to the philosophy of education.* New York: Macmillan.

Fishman, A. 1988. *Amish literacy: What and how it means.* Portsmouth, N.H.: Heinemann.

Hentel, L. 1991. Commentary on the Dr. Jan Jones CED workshop of April 12, 1991. *Centerspace: The newsletter and bulletin for members of the Center for Establishing Dialogue in Teaching and Learning* 6 (May–June): 8–10.

Huizinga, J. 1924 [1969]. *The waning of the Middle Ages : Study of the forms of life, thought and art in France and the Netherlands in the 14th and 15th centuries.* London: Edwin Arnold. Reprint, New York: St. Martin's Press.

Jones, J. L. 1990. *What's left after the right? A resource manual for educators.* Self-published (written for the Washington Education Association and available from Janet L. Jones, 10871 S.E. Stevens Way, Portland, OR 97266).

MacCallum, E. 1991. Following the twisted trail of a book: Unfairly maligned. *Toronto Globe and Mail*, July 13.

Marshall, P. 1991. Search for Canada's soul a fool's quest. *Calvinist Contact*, June 28, 10–11.

Moffett, J. 1988. *Storm in the mountains: A case study of censorship, conflict, and consciousness.* Carbondale and Edwardsville: Southern Illinois University Press.

II Responsibility

In the introduction, we defined responsibility as the choice that professionals make to gain an understanding of the state of the field and to relate those understandings to their own practice. In this section David Doake pays heed to this concept of responsibility by exposing myths and espousing the realities of whole language theory and practice—necessary information for both detractors and proponents of whole language. Kathy Short illustrates how this responsibility is shouldered as she lets us see what personal change looks like as teachers encounter new theories, develop new beliefs, and connect them to practice. Ethel Buchanan, Constance Weaver, and David and Yvonne Freeman offer chapters that push forward the edge of what is known and what "can be" in education. Buchanan discusses how information on language use can impact something so traditional in education as spelling instruction. Weaver provides us with a new perspective on Attention Deficit Hyperactivity Disorders: a transactional view with theoretical and practical considerations. And the Freemans discuss how whole language theory impacts practice, especially when the focus is on bilingual students.

7 The Myths and Realities of Whole Language: An Educational Movement at Risk

David B. Doake
Acadia University, Wolfville, Nova Scotia

In an article in *Language Arts,* Maxine Greene (1988), in her usual insightful way, refers to the great value of sharing our own stories with the stories of others. When we do that on a universal basis, she claims, we may begin to be able "to share each other's dreams and develop a sense of communal responsibility for the world of tomorrow."

The phrase *communal responsibility* keeps ringing in my ears as I look around the world in which I live. What I see all too often is a world where competition reigns supreme, where a dog-eat-dog philosophy seems pervasively present, and where everything is based on a "here and now" view of life rather than looking to the effects on the future of what we are doing now. In her article, Greene refers to a prophetic observation made by the Nobel laureate Elie Wiesel at a gathering of his peers in Paris in January 1988, probably in reference to the ever-present possibility of a nuclear war (and still applicable today): "It is a question of saving humanity—or at least our humanity. We are all on a train that is running toward a precipice. We cannot change trains, so we have to slow it down." Greene comments: "For Wiesel, human beings define themselves not only by a 'thirst for truth' but by a sense of *responsibility*. If we can exert any control at all, he asked, how can we make sure that we will steer events 'towards the sun and not toward the abyss'"? (Greene 1988, 474–75).

When we examine the disastrous after-effects of Chernobyl and ponder the fact that there are fifteen nuclear power stations of similar design in the former Soviet Union, the train is still running. When we consider the prospects of the predicted alarming consequences of the "greenhouse effect" on the lives of the future inhabitants of this planet and the fact that countries such as the United States, Canada, and

Saudi Arabia refused, at an international conference in Geneva in 1990, to agree to *any* limits being placed on the emissions of gases that contribute to the loss of the ozone layer, another "All clear and full steam ahead" signal has been given to the train drivers. When we examine the results of a study conducted in Los Angeles on the lungs of a hundred children who lost their lives suddenly, and find that the lungs of 80 percent of these children had quite serious lesions and damage and that the lungs of 27 percent showed very serious damage, our train continues to belch out tons of lethal sulphurous gases with impunity. When we look carefully at the oceans of our world and think about the Exxon *Valdez* and similar disasters, about the millions of tons of waste being dumped in them every year, about the blatant destruction of all forms of marine life through overfishing and overhunting, our train does not stop at the ocean shore. Finally, when we link our thoughts about the burgeoning world population growth, about poverty, about the voracious swallowing up of valuable farmland by our ever-expanding cities and roads, about the widespread desertification of other lands, about the indiscriminate destruction of the rain forests, and about the constant presence of devastating famine in various parts of the world, our train appears to be bent on self-destruction. We seem to be gathering speed in our headlong rush toward Wiesel's abyss!

The oral tradition is no longer sufficient for us to "share our stories" as Maxine Greene would have us do. Even if we stand on street corners, shout our concerns, and offer creative solutions to the problems, only those in hearing distance have the opportunity for listening. We may even have the chance to have our voices heard at international assemblies, but unless what we say is written down, it will simply fade from memory with surprising speed. If our sense of communal responsibility is to transcend local, national, and, most importantly, international boundaries, and if we are going to share our concerns and work together on their possible solutions, we need a literate world in order for this to happen. More than ever before, we need active, vigorous, and fully informed literate communities, which choose their leaders on the basis of their demonstrated ability to turn our train away from the abyss, rather than continuing to select those who seem intent on helping the train gather momentum on its old tracks. The corporate magnates, their dependent political puppets, and their vacuous military generals would no longer be able to keep all the signals at "Go" should our votes be cast for a different set of criteria. A public that was genuinely literate could make certain that these forces would not be permitted to continue on their self-centered way but would insist on them being used for the common good. Scurrilous negative political advertisements would be ridiculed or ignored. The voting public would demand written evidence from those who chose to offer themselves for public office of their suitability to deal with the problems of the present and, more importantly, those of the future.

But we do not have a highly literate public. In fact, despite our universal system of education, we have a public that is mostly functionally illiterate or marginally literate (they can read and write with varying degrees of expertise, but only rarely do). Our school systems are not producing genuinely literate people who use reading and writing for all the necessary and desirable purposes of life. The causes for this do not all lie within the way that reading and writing have been (and are being) taught. The nonliterate environments of many homes must bear some of the blame. But no matter how inadequate children's home experiences have been with reading and writing in particular, the school has the ultimate responsibility to produce literate citizens. It has not been doing this, and the major reason lies in ways in which these language arts have been and are being taught. The philosophy of whole language has the power to turn that situation around, but it needs teachers who are thoroughly familiar with its principles and practices. A surface-level understanding will lead to surface-level implementation. The main purpose of this chapter is the identification and clarification of these dangers to an educational movement that could considerably reduce many of the limitations present in the system, not only in the area of language arts but right across the curriculum.

The Value of Being Literate

I am not one of those like Frank Smith (1989) or David Olson (n.d.) who seem to be taking the stance these days that being fully and functionally literate does not help our chances to make it in this world. Some of us may at times overstate the case for the values that accrue from being actively literate. We all know of cases where some people have never "made it" although they are well-read and write well. We can also quote cases of those who are not literate or actively literate, but who have been successful. One retired president of the United States provides us with a good example here. As long as you can read the script presented to you in a convincing way, that is sometimes enough. It is perhaps interesting to note that many of those who have made it in the political arena do not begin to write about their views and experiences until after they have left office, and only rarely does anyone get elected on the basis of what they have written. Mikhail Gorbachev may be an exception here, but then his "election" was one in name only.

I hold the view that in societies where being literate does play an important part in the growth and development of that society, those who cannot read and write effectively are almost always disempowered by their illiteracy. It is no accident, in my view, that countries that have high rates of literacy often seem to be very stable, caring societies. Look at Norway, Sweden, Finland, Denmark, and New Zealand, for example. There is no real poverty in those countries. The less advantaged people are usually found to be reasonably well-housed and well-fed. These countries have systems of universal free medical care, they have sufficient retirement pensions for all their citizens regardless of their economic status, and they have a system of universal free education *from the preschool age group right through to the university.* They also have relatively low crime rates.

Compare this with what is happening in the United States, which ranks about forty-ninth in the world in the literacy levels of its peoples. It has something like 60 million functional illiterates. There are some 35 million people living in the U.S. with no medical care. There are millions of people who are living in abject poverty, millions who are homeless, millions who cannot afford to send their children on to college because of the high cost of tuition. According to Peter MacLaren in his book *Life in Schools* (1989), 50–80 percent of all inner-city students drop out of high school. The Chicanos and the Puerto Ricans describe it perhaps more appropriately as being "pushed out." The consequences of schooling in the United States, according to MacLaren, are increasingly dependent on the social class of the child. "It remains the case that one in every seven Americans and more than one in every five children under the age of six live in poverty." Drugs and crime go hand-in-hand with poverty. Great wealth being flaunted in the presence of this chronic destitution provides the catalyst for these outcomes of hopelessness. The gap in real income between the lower 20 percent of the American families and the top 5 percent has nearly doubled in the past thirty years.

It is claimed in the United States that "anyone can reach the top." All that is needed is the desire, the energy, and hard work. But how much does it cost these days to become, for example, a senator? a congressperson? the president? I remain unconvinced by the argument that anyone in this country can make it to the top politically no matter how humble his or her beginnings. Sure you can make it to the top, but often as mouthpieces for the financial barons and the special-interest groups that have paid the bill to put you there!

There are countries, of course, that do have high rates of literacy but a pretty poor track record in caring for the less fortunate people who are controlled by their governments. Countries like South Africa and Israel, for example, have not demonstrated much humaneness over the years with regard to those disempowered peoples who live in those countries, and yet they have very high rates of literacy in their white or Jewish, "racially pure" populations. It is interesting to note that the press and the writers who support the disempowered peoples in those countries have been the target of censorship, and in many cases a total restriction has been placed on publishing. Often the writers have been imprisoned without trial, executed by "accidental" means, silenced forever. The written word does possess a power of its own, and this is quickly recognized by those who wish to maintain absolute power over a people.

Literacy *does* have a highly significant role to play in assisting in the healthy growth and development of a society. It provides its citizens with the opportunity to further educate themselves and thus to play a significant role in the building of that society. It provides them with a way of speaking out—of having their voices heard. Witness how the Canadian government eliminated the financial aid for higher education of its native peoples. Why? Could it be that the educated natives in that country are becoming too vocal by writing about their fight for justice?

Literacy also has a most important role to play in the survival of this planet. It is not who wins the armament race that is important. *It is who wins the education race.* It is only through having an informed and actively literate public that this world is going to be guided along the paths of survival and not, as Wiesel indicates, toward the abyss. A sense of "communal responsibility" on a universal basis cannot develop in a world where illiteracy is the millstone of over 900 million people. That population is growing even larger every year.

Some Obstacles to Change

Misinterpretation and Misrepresentation

I came to Canada from New Zealand in 1975. In 1977 I obtained a position in the School of Education at Acadia University in Wolfville, Nova Scotia. Along with people like Judith Newman, who was teaching at Dalhousie University, I tried to bring about substantial changes in the way in which parents and teachers go about the process of helping the children in their care learn to read and write. From the beginning, I have been aware that the kinds of things I and others have been saying, writing about, and often demonstrating have not always been interpreted in the way in which we wanted them to be. Not only has what I have been trying to communicate been misinterpreted, but it has often been distorted and sometimes even misrepresented. Some of these misrepresentations are now being used by those who mistakenly see the philosophy and practice of whole language as a dire threat to the well-being of education in Canada.

We now have a group of parents in the Shelburne area of Nova Scotia who have called themselves Parents Against Whole Language or PAWL. Their spokesperson totally misrepresents what whole language is all about. The sad thing about these people is that they refuse to visit the school which has become the focus of their attention. They have also refused to listen to anyone who is prepared to explain some of the reasons why the Education Department of Nova Scotia has officially recognized the philosophy and practice of whole language being used in its schools. They not only want whole language out of their school, but out of all schools in Nova Scotia! And their campaign is based on a few myths that have grown from a smattering of misinformation.

There are many generalized myths which already surround whole language. These are present in the minds of the general public, in the minds of the parents of children attending school, and in the minds of many teachers and administrators. These myths continue to fuel the fire of opposition to the growth of this highly significant educational movement. Already whole language is being blamed for a whole range of educational "problems." Grammar and spelling are two areas of the curriculum which receive a great deal of attention. Reading "skills," particularly in the form of phonics, also become a bone of contention.

Whole language has already become the whipping boy for those who want education to adhere to the old ways. These old ways are represented by a curriculum that is presented in a *step-by-step manner* and by classrooms where the students are supposed to learn *when, what,* and *how* they are told to learn; where teachers constantly *control* the so-called educative process; where *grades, competition, and the threat of failure* are constantly present and are used as weapons of control by teachers; where *passivity* reigns supreme; and where the *transmission-of-knowledge* model consistently dominates.

The sad thing about these proponents of traditional schooling is that they claim it has been successful in teaching almost everyone to read, write (and spell), and compute. "Look at us!" they state. "It worked for us!" And yet when asked, for example, how many of them *like* to write and whether they see themselves as competent writers, about 90–95 percent state quite emphatically that they "hate" writing and feel that they are "poor" writers. Many of them indicate that they have always "had trouble" with mathematics and spelling, and a surprisingly large number admit to reading books only rarely. But the "old ways are the best ways" motto prevails and closes the minds of many of these educational experts.

The Effects of "One-Shot" Inservice Presentations

Part of the reason for the development of the myths, misunderstandings, and misinterpretations that surround whole language may rest in the familiar "one-shot" nature of the inservice presentations that teachers frequently attend. There has often been little or no follow-up to what has been recommended. The experts come and speak. Teachers listen, seemingly attentively. Then they go back to their classrooms and continue to do what they have been doing for years, partly because of the one-shot nature of the presentation and partly for other reasons which I will elaborate shortly.

Further, the teachers' administrators rarely attend the presentations and so are not able to become part of the process of suggested change. In fact, they often deliberately stay away so that they will not have to even consider making any changes in the way in which their teachers teach.

Teachers and Their Self-Directed Learning

Teachers generally do not have easy access to textbooks or even educational papers. Sometimes their own experiences in learning to read and write have not made them into active readers and writers who constantly seek new knowledge through books and journals. Not enough teachers have read, for example, authors like Don Holdaway, Frank Smith, Jerry Harste, Ken and Yetta Goodman, Garth Boomer, Marie Clay, Margaret Meek, Donald Graves, Lucy Calkins, and Nancie Atwell.

In Canada, despite the fact that teachers are among the best paid teachers in the world (with an average salary at around Cdn$43,000), few teachers take out subscriptions for educational journals. The excellent National Council of Teachers of English journal *Language Arts* or journals of the Canadian Council of Teachers of English are seldom found in schools. Their own very good reading journal, *Reflections of Literacy,* is barely surviving with just a few hundred subscribers—very few of them elementary or secondary teachers. About all that many teachers seem prepared to read is the occasional newsletter which arrives at their schools, usually free of charge.

But one of the most powerful aspects of the change that many teachers are making in moving to a whole language perspective is that they are forming themselves into small teacher-support groups. Not only are these teachers *reading* in the wide range of professional litera-ture that is now available, but they are sharing their information with other teachers. Most importantly, many teachers are *beginning to write* about their experiences as whole language teachers. Not surprisingly, the greatest changes have occurred in those school districts where there has been a band of enthusiastic, informed, and energetic resource people who have continued to work diligently at helping their teach-ers change the way that they teach.

When the Change Is of a Major Dimension

The myths that have appeared in the form of an opposition to the whole language movement have also developed for another reason. Part of the problem is that the principles and practices of whole lan-guage are so very different from so many teachers' principles and practices. Although they may not have known it, their beliefs and assumptions about how children learn have been greatly influenced by Skinnerian-type behaviorists with their rat- and pigeon-condition-ing philosophies. The beliefs and assumptions which are the founda-tion of whole language are almost diametrically opposed to those that are espoused by the behaviorists.

For example, the knowledge that we now have about how children learn in general, and how they learn to read and write in particular, is very different from that held by many teachers who have followed, perhaps unwittingly, the Skinnerian line of thinking. Nowhere is this difference more evident than in the area of literacy learning.

Reading and Writing "Readiness"

When I have said at an inservice meeting that *there is no such thing as a period of reading readiness or writing readiness,* I have been looked at very suspiciously. When I state that children begin to learn to read as soon as they hear their first nursery rhymes or are read their first stories or are surrounded by written language in their first trips to the supermarket, I am looked at as if I come from outer space.

1. No reading readiness!
2. No teaching (and therefore learning) the letter names and letter sounds before children learn to read?
3. No learning of auditory discrimination skills?
4. No learning of visual discrimination skills?
5. No workbook exercises?

What am I supposed to do with these children every day? they ask. How can my students begin to learn to read before they have learned all these basic skills? You must be joking! I can't take you seriously!

1. No writing readiness!
2. No learning how to print the letters very carefully before they begin to learn to write?
3. No learning to spell words before they are asked to write using words?
4. No correcting their spelling mistakes?
5. No weekly spelling lists to learn and be tested on?
6. No formal grammar or punctuation lessons?

You must be out of your mind!

Despite the fact that I have made liberal use of audiotapes and videotapes and examples demonstrating children's natural growth as readers and as writers, the response has usually been: "Ah! But those children were all very intelligent and came from 'good' homes!" I counter with the information that Don Holdaway's work (1979) was carried out in inner-city schools with children who came from lower socioeconomic homes. I then describe my literacy recovery work done in 1983–84 with eleven- and twelve-year-old students who were abject failures in the school system (see Doake, in press). They all became readers and writers and no longer looked on themselves as failures. An aura of disbelief pervades the room, and I sense that there are some teachers who think that the results of this work have somehow been manipulated to show that the ideas work. Even when I outline the nine empirical studies conducted in six different countries reviewed by Warwick Elley (1991), the results of which demonstrated quite clearly that meaning-based, holistic approaches to second-language learning were superior to those of the skills-based model in every experiment, some still remain unconvinced. Indoctrination over many years is hard to counter.

Basal Programs

Again, when I have indicated that basal readers and their accompanying workbooks really have no place in our classrooms, I have often sensed a feeling of derision, disbelief, and sometimes anger run through my audience. When I recommend that our students be given freedom of choice in what they read, that classroom libraries should hold at least 500 to 1000 books, that all students need to be read to extensively and regularly from a wide body of high-quality literature, and that during the first few years in school, at least, the bedtime story has to be replicated through the use of enlarged print in our classrooms, disbelief reaches a peak.

1. No basal readers?
2. No formal teaching of that all-important hierarchy of skills for which the basal stories have been composed?
3. No workbook exercises that reinforce the learning of these skills?
4. No reading groups?
5. No grade retention for those who cannot pass their levels and/or standardized reading tests?

You don't know what you are talking about! It's time to go home!

But perhaps the most important part of the problem has been that teachers basically *do not want to change* what they have been doing over a period of years. The programs that they have been using have been designed by experts. The failure that some of their students have experienced, they believe, must have been the fault of the students since they as teachers did everything the manuals told them to do. In truth, those students who succeed frequently do so despite what is done to them in the name of instruction. The literacy-oriented nature of their home environments were quite possibly the main reason for their success—not the stultifying basal programs they had to endure.

Psychological Barriers to Change

There is another, perhaps more fundamental, reason why teachers find it difficult to move from using a curriculum that has been presented to them. It is closely related to the processes involved in bringing about change in any aspect of society, whether that change be inside or outside the education system. It is deep-seated. It is a similar kind of problem that Gorbachev met in the Soviet Union with his *Perestroika*. He found that the citizens of his country seemed incapable of accepting the changes that he wanted to implement. Many seemed incapable of making decisions, of taking more control of their lives, of taking more responsibility for the direction of their future and that of their country.

Gorbachev realized that the years of being told how to think and what to do, of having no freedom to choose or to make decisions about the task of improving their own living standards, had taken its toll. The power within his people to take up the challenge offered in a more free and open society had atrophied. His people were no longer capable of directing their own lives or even wanting to do so. Only through a new generation of citizens who have grown up in a freer and more open society might the goal of Gorbachev be realized.

How does this relate to Canada and the United States? Our teachers have come up through a school system that has tended to tell them what to learn, when to learn, how to learn, and even how much to learn. The reasons for students to learn have also been spelled out. They are learning to pass the tests, to qualify for grades, to earn university scholarships, to get a well-paying job. From the time students have entered school, their teachers, through the issuing of grades and through the provision of a highly competitive system based on a variety of methods of extrinsic motivation, have controlled them.

When I enter a lecture room with a new group of students, they sit and wait to be told when to start learning, even though they probably already have the course textbooks and know a fair amount about language arts through their own experiences. When I inform them that I will not be setting the topics on which they will be writing, they get upset. They become even more disturbed when I refuse to spell out how their papers are to be written or how long the papers should be. The next question they always ask is how much the paper is worth. I then describe how they will be expected to evaluate the effectiveness of their own learning and how they will be negotiating their own grade at the completion of the course, based on a set of criteria which we will work out together. Their discomfort reaches near panic levels. At the end of the course, however, they are almost always deeply appreciative of finally being given control over their own learning and the opportunity to develop an understanding of what it means to be an independent learner—and these students are studying for their second university degree!

We should not be surprised, then, when we find that our teachers often do not want to make changes in the way in which they teach. They do not want to take control of composing their own curriculum.

They do not want to move to a more open and flexible approach to teaching where they constantly have to take risks and try things out, to experiment, and even to make some mistakes. They do not want to relinquish to their students a lot of control over their own learning. They do not want each day to be different from the next. They do not want evaluation to be based on their own intimate knowledge of the curriculum and their understanding of where each student is with regard to his or her learning. They want standardized tests to do that for them—something standardized tests can never do effectively. The process of engaging in change, especially when it requires a major alteration of a system of beliefs and assumptions which have developed over many years, is difficult and demanding. We have to provide the opportunity for that change to come from within rather than trying to impose it from without.

Administrators and the Change Process

Sometimes educational administrators do not want teachers to be given power over the process of composing the curriculum. Many administrators do not want teachers to become fully professional, selecting the literature to use in their own classrooms for a range of purposes. These administrators do not want teachers to be responsible for the ongoing evaluation of the learning that is going on in their own classrooms. Why not? Basically because many administrators *do not trust their teachers* and do not think that the teachers have the ability to compose their own curriculum. These administrators think that chaos would reign supreme if this were to happen. They think that the systematic assembly-line approach to learning presently provided by our schools would break down and that, as a result, our students would emerge from the system "uneducated."

Fortunately, many administrators are now beginning to study how children learn, rather than focusing their attention on how to administer their schools. A school is often only as good as its principal, and we need more and more principals who are prepared to find out what is now known about human learning and the conditions that facilitate it most effectively. As a result, their teachers are gaining confidence, taking more risks in their own classroom practices, and bringing about productive changes in the way in which they teach.

Parents and the Change Process

Those teachers who are engaged in the process of making substantial changes in the way in which they teach—particularly the language arts—should realize that they may have a large proportion of parents who do not want any changes to be made in the way in which their children are taught. Parents, like those mentioned earlier in Shelburne, Nova Scotia, are generally suspicious of change in education. James Moffett pointed this out in the following way:

> . . . most parents still want schools to reinforce home training by inculcating their values, heritage and modes of behavior. (By the way, inculcate derives from the Latin verb meaning "to grind in with the heel.") Most parents want their children to stay the way they made them. . . .
>
> Parents who fear losing their children—and the majority do in some way—want the content of reading and writing to be controlled or made indifferent. Teach my children to read, but I don't want them to read this or this or this. Teach my children to write, but they don't need to delve into that or that or that. Just teach them to read and write so that they can get good jobs. Such an attitude, steering ambivalently between the necessity of literacy and the threat it poses, ultimately delivers to schools the message that they should teach youngsters to read just well enough to follow orders and to write well enough to take dictation. (1985, 52–53)

There are a lot of forces "out there" which are working against whole language permeating the education system in a productive manner. The myths that are being generated about it (sometimes quite deliberately by its opponents) are constantly working against the reality of whole language. Teachers, administrators, and teacher educators who have become convinced that the widespread acceptance of the philosophy and practice of whole language is desperately needed in a school system that seems to have lost its way in a maze of mandated curricula, a plethora of prepackaged programs, and the disguised monster of accountability, face an enormously difficult task in defusing opposition based mostly on misunderstanding. The place to start may be with a description of how "whole language" schools are different from the "traditional" ones that most people attended.

A Comparison between Whole Language and Traditional Environments

The changes that have to occur in moving from a traditional and formal mode of teaching to an approach that is based on the principles and practices of whole language are substantial. The main differences between the two approaches are summarized in Table 7.1. The characteristics of whole language classrooms need considerable elaboration

Table 7.1. Comparison of Whole Language and Traditional Classrooms

Whole Language	Traditional
1. *Genuine literacy-oriented classrooms*: books of all kinds, magazines, and newspapers; students' writing is honored and used; message boards; writing corner; reading corner.	1. *Pseudo-literacy-oriented classrooms*: sets of basal readers, workbooks, spelling lists, writing copybooks; textbooks (math, social studies, science); writing "notes" forbidden.
2. *Collaborative learning*: students share desks and share learning; freedom to talk and discuss; group study predominates.	2. *Isolated learning*: there are rows of desks; sharing is "cheating"; talking is forbidden unless teacher permits it; individual study predominates.
3. *Noncompetitive environment*: emphasis is placed on learning for learning's sake; no ability grouping or "tracking"; assignments are not given a grade or mark; no comparisons are made among students; an aura of trust pervades the classroom.	3. *Competitive environment*: emphasis is placed on learning to satisfy teacher's requirements; ability grouping and "tracking"; most assignments are given a grade or mark; marks and grades are made public; students are not trusted to learn, so an atmosphere of mistrust is generated.
4. *Teacher learns with the students*: a "reconstruction of knowledge" model of learning operates; questions come from students and teacher; there is no "one right answer."	4. *The teacher teaches*: "transmission of knowledge" model of learning operates; teacher controls questioning; few student questions except for procedural ones; the "tyranny of the right answer" is constantly present.
5. *Children read, write, and talk because they want to*: self-directed, self-regulated, and divergent learning is emphasized; motivation to learn is intrinsically based; control of learning is shared.	5. *Children read, write, and talk when the teacher says to*: teacher-directed, teacher-dependent, and convergent learning emphasized; motivation to learn is extrinsically based; control of learning remains with the teacher.
6. *Curriculum integrated as much as possible*: study of themes predominates; topics are relevant, and selection is "negotiated"; there are large chunks of time for study.	6. *Curriculum is fractionated* (Don Graves's "Cha-cha-cha" curriculum): timetable is divided into subjects; there are short periods of time for study; topics are selected by distant "authority."
7. *Meaningful, holistic, and purposeful learning is the focus*: relevancy, function, interest, and the needs and abilities of the students play a	7. *Abstract, skills-oriented, and meaningless learning the focus*: the curriculum is predetermined and prepackaged and may not match

Continued

Table 7.1. *Continued*

Whole Language	Traditional
major role in the nature of the curriculum; demonstration plays a key role in helping students learn, and teachers show their students that they love to read and write.	the needs and abilities of the students; learning is represented as "hard work," and teachers rarely show that they are readers and writers.
8. *Risk taking predominates*: experimentation and approximation are encouraged; feelings of confidence and competence grow; environment is essentially noncorrective; learning is pleasurable; students are actively engaged in the process of learning and develop independence; use of the imagination is emphasized.	8. *Little or no risk taking*: "get it right the first time" atmosphere; feelings of anxiety and insecurity grow; corrective atmosphere prevails; learning is seen as "hard work"; students tend to be passive, dependent learners; children's imaginations start to atrophy.
9. *Teacher composes own curriculum in association with students*: the negotiated curriculum operates within required guidelines where necessary.	9. *Teacher is dependent on a presented and predetermined curriculum*: students play no part in its composition.
10. *Evaluation is ongoing, informal, and process-oriented*: teachers possess intimate knowledge of each student's progress and potential; self-evaluation is the aim.	10. *Evaluation is periodic, formal, and product-oriented*: teachers possess knowledge of test scores; assessments are based on comparisons made with norms for each test used; self-evaluation is not considered.
11. *Teacher shares learning with other teachers*: meets regularly with other teachers; discusses results of reading, personal writing, and own teaching; adds constantly to professional library and subscribes to relevant journals; never satisfied with state of own teaching effectiveness; teaches reflectively.	11. *Teacher tends to work in isolation*: meets other teachers at required staff meetings and socially; rarely reads professional literature; does not write or discuss own teaching; possesses a limited personal library and does not subscribe to educational journals; is generally satisfied with own teaching effectiveness; teaches with little reflection.
12. *Parents and teacher collaborate meaningfully to help students learn*: parents understand and accept teacher's philosophy and practice; parents welcome changes being made and are informed about them; parents help in the classroom whenever possible.	12. *Parents and teacher rarely collaborate, follow "the teacher knows best" principle*: parents believe that their children should be taught in the way in which they were taught; parents suspicious of any change; parents will help in the school but not directly in the classroom.

and justification. Space does not permit that here, but I have done this in my forthcoming book, *Changing the Assumptions for Literacy Learning: A Revolution in Progress* (Doake, in press).

Bringing about Change in How Teachers Teach

So there is a lot to learn. Some teachers cope with the process quite easily since they have always wanted to make the changes. Others have to learn how to teach all over again. How well the legitimate practices of the new philosophy are implemented is dependent on a whole range of variables:

1. the commitment of the teachers
2. the extent of the teachers' understanding of the theoretical basis of the philosophy
3. the regularity with which teachers meet to share in their learning with others who are engaged in the same process of change
4. the ability of teachers to learn from what they are seeing happening with their students (the "teacher as researcher" model)
5. the degree of support and understanding that teachers receive from the administrators and parents

Becoming a whole language teacher will generally require learning of the transformational, ongoing kind that comes from within the learner as a result of experiences both direct and vicarious. It is obvious that change of this kind cannot and will not take place as a result of a few inservice sessions and demonstrations coupled with the use of some published whole language material. Hall and Loucks point out that the "implementation of innovations such as curriculum products and processes is not a bipolar use/nonuse phenomenon" (1977, 265). As a result of their research, they conclude that there are different "levels" of use of any innovation. They identify and operationally define eight levels: nonuse, orientation, preparation, mechanical use, routine, refinement, integration, and renewal (266–67). It is clear that research of the kind that Hall and Loucks have conducted is urgently required with whole language in order to determine whether this innovative philosophy of education is actually in use in the classrooms where teachers claim that it is and, if so, how it is being used.

In order to move to teaching based on holistic principles and practices, teachers have to be given the opportunity to study in some depth the theory and its implementation. They need the chance to discuss in detail the beliefs about learning and teaching on which it is based; they need to observe, to create and try out various teaching strategies, and to learn how to evaluate the effectiveness of these strategies through careful observation of the outcomes with their students. They cannot do all this alone. They need a mentor (or mentors) to guide them in their study. They need a support group of whole language teachers who are in various stages of developing whole language classrooms and who meet to talk, share, and learn on a regular basis. They need a principal and a curriculum consultant who will provide them with encouragement, guidance, and *time* in order to create a genuine, learner-centered classroom. Finally, they have to realize that what they are learning will never end—they will go on developing as whole language teachers for as long as they stay in the education system. Whole language teachers will never become bored with what they are doing because they never stop learning—they might get tired, but never bored! They continue to examine their assumptions and go on learning from their observations of and interactions with their students, their associates, and "the literature." Because almost every instructional decision is made with a different set of variables operating, the process never ends.

The most serious forces at work in undermining whole language are too often found in some of the practices that are occurring in classrooms where the teachers claim to be whole language teachers. *Of all the threats to the whole language movement, I see this as the most dangerous.* Why? For a very simple reason. When teachers claim to be whole language teachers but do not utilize the principles and practices of whole language in a legitimate manner, then their students will not learn in the way in which they are capable of learning—and whole language will reap the blame.

Like all movements in education, whole language is beginning to suffer from those who, for various reasons, do not grow and develop into genuine whole language teachers and—even more disastrously— from teacher educators who have adopted the philosophy in a superficial manner. I know one teacher who proudly stated to her student teacher: "I do just enough whole language to keep them [her administrators] off my back!" Whole language has become "the thing to do" in certain regions in Canada and is rapidly taking on the same mantle in the United States. The superficial adoption of the philosophy is its Achilles heel. It will not be long before whole language is blamed for everything that is wrong with our education system. Because one of its prime aims is to produce a highly literate and independently thinking public who will insist on being part of the process of governing their country, the conservative forces who wish to maintain and extend their power will use the myths which already surround whole language to consign it to the educational wasteland where other similar, potentially productive movements lie decaying.

What are some of these major myths that have infiltrated the principles and practices of whole language, and what are their realities? The following is a description of a few of what I see to be the major myths and realities at present. Additional ones will undoubtedly surface as the philosophy attracts more and more adherents and, probably, more and more opponents. They put the movement at risk, and unless their influence is reduced considerably, it is quite possible that whole language will be labeled as another educational fad which has no place in a "real" system of education.

The Myths and the Realities of Whole Language

Myth No. 1

Learning "naturally" has been interpreted literally to mean that the teacher does not need to teach.

The idea that children should be trusted as learners, that they should remain in control of their own learning, and that they will then learn "naturally" has been interpreted by many teachers and critics as a do-nothing approach to teaching. In the language arts, for example, teaching reading is seen as a process of reading regularly to the children and of providing them with access to interesting books. Teachers do not need to help children learn phonics, do not need to enhance children's comprehension skills, and do not need to assist them in learning how to gather information from expository texts. It will all happen quite "naturally." In writing, children will learn how to spell, to use grammar and punctuation correctly, and to write legibly through a process of osmosis as long as the teacher encourages them to write and occasionally responds meaningfully to what they have written. That whole language teachers do not teach spelling, grammar, and handwriting has become a very pervasive myth in the minds of many teachers, educational administrators, and parents.

The Reality

Whole language teachers do teach their students about written language, but they always do so within contexts that are meaningful and relevant and at times when they know their students will need and want to learn in order to communicate more effectively through written language.

While children who come to school after five or six years of growing up in a literacy-rich home may learn to read with very little direct help from their teachers, immersive procedures, in themselves, will not be enough for those children who arrive at school having never had a story read to them or who have had only limited experience of this kind. These children will have to have their interest in books and reading nurtured carefully and in quite specific ways. They will have to be helped to learn that the print on the page is permanent, that it is composed within certain directionality constraints, that it carries the message, and that words and letters are not the same. Their attention will be drawn to the differences and similarities in the ways in which words are put together. Graphophonemic cues will be used but not in isolation from meaning and language cues. Traditional workbooks and worksheets containing repetitive exercises will not be used, but teachers will take every opportunity to extend their students' knowledge about written language, especially when using enlarged print formats and through the students' writing. As they develop as independent readers, the opportunity is taken through individual conferences, small-group discussions, and whole class "mini-lessons" to enhance their abilities to comprehend at increasingly higher levels and to learn the skills involved in gathering information from content material. Optimum-time teaching becomes the quality that whole language teachers bring to their task most skillfully.

Spelling, grammar, punctuation, and handwriting are not left to chance either. In genuine whole language classrooms, students know that at least some of what they write is going to be read by others. Pieces that they select will be "published" in some form and will be shared. And just as we make sure that what we write for the public domain is both accurate at the surface level of written language and as clear as possible at the meaning and legibility levels, so do students in whole language classrooms begin to feel compelled to edit their work so that they meet these important criteria. They are assisted in developing an editorial conscience through regular conferences with their teacher and with their peers, where their attention will be drawn, in noncorrective ways, to any features of their writing which may be unconventional. But the emphasis will always be on their maintaining control over what they have written, and the strategies used to help them write in an increasingly conventional manner will be heavily weighted on the side of demonstration and on using what the student already knows, rather than on the side of correction. The aim will be to have students "read like a writer" so that they learn to read what they have written as if they were a member of their potential audience.

Whole language teachers do teach—actively, sensitively, and at opportune times. As Newman and Church point out, such teachers are always "on the alert for opportunities to present learners with challenges that gently push them beyond their current strategies and understandings (1990, 22). They are forever ready for the "teachable moment," and because they are so knowledgeable about their students' individual progress through careful and continuous observation, they usually know just when and how to intervene in order to help students grow still further. They are forever seeking new ways to teach more effectively and are meticulous in using cues provided by the students. The teachers and their students are integral parts of a creative learning environment.

Myth No. 2

All we really need to do with Big Books and other forms of enlarged print is to read them to the children a few times.

In 1978, I brought the first set of Big Books into Canada to be used by a teacher in New Minas Elementary School. Ashton Scholastic in New Zealand donated a set of their *Read It Again* series to be "tried out" in a grade-one classroom. The idea of using enlarged print formats with young children was not new. What was new was that the language of these materials was authentic, rich, and usually rhythmical. Teachers and publishers soon caught on to the idea, and now we have a plethora of Big Books and other enlarged print materials flooding our classrooms. But all too often they are being misused—especially with regard to their original purpose.

Sometimes Big Books are being used simply to entertain the children; they are read once or twice and then consigned to the bookshelf. They are not used to draw the children back to the story again and again, and all too frequently, the children do not go to a listening post to read along with an audiotape recording of the story as they look at smaller editions of the Big Book. Some teachers mistakenly try to make the children memorize the story, insisting on an accurate surface-level rendition of it. Most importantly, teachers are failing to use these materials for instructional purposes.

Once the children become familiar with the language of the book and can reproduce it with some degree of fluency, these teachers are not drawing their students' attention to the surface features of the print. They are not using the children's knowledge of the words of the story to go from the sounds to a visual representation of them and so begin to generate phonic knowledge. Similarities and differences in words, awareness of punctuation, recognition of interesting ways of expressing meaning through the use of various figures of speech, building word families, and so on are not seen as legitimate and important ways to make use of enlarged print.

The myth that Big Books and other forms of enlarged print should not be used for instructional purposes is widespread, and because of this, teachers are losing a valuable means of developing the rate at which their students will be able to become independent readers.

The Reality

Big Books were developed so that the bedtime-story situation could be replicated in the classroom. The first reading has got to be so enjoyable that the children will want the book to be read again and again. This rereading enables them *to gain control of the language and meaning* of the story. They are then able to reconstruct it for themselves using whatever language they have available. Approximation and experimentation are the key principles, coupled with self-directed and self-monitored learning. In the initial stages, the children may not have even developed the understanding that the print on the pages carries the story, but as this understanding grows through a variety of experiences with written language in functional ways, increased attention can then be given to teaching children about this form of their language.

Once the children are hooked on the book and are beginning to get control over its language, then teachers start drawing their attention to the print—to the *form of the language* (similarities, differences, patterns and families, suffixes and prefixes and their effect on meaning). Teachers also start looking at special linguistic features (alliteration, metaphor, simile, onomatopoeia). There is a great deal of teaching that can be done about written language through the use of Big Books.

Good examples of what can and should be done with Big Books and other enlarged print are contained in the teachers' guides for the original set of *Read It Again* Big Book series (Holdaway and Handy 1975). In his *Foundations of Literacy*, Holdaway (1979) also describes in some detail what they did with enlarged print as they experimented with the concept in schools in Auckland, New Zealand. The range of strategies that they used are clearly explained, and the responses of the children are provided.

Big Books and other forms of exciting and interesting enlarged print (e.g., poems, songs, chants, limericks) not only present teachers with a superb means of developing children's love of books and reading, but they also provide teachers with many opportunities for "the teachable moment" and contextually based learning.

Myth No. 3

Becoming a whole language teacher is not a particularly difficult task and can be achieved by attending a few workshops, visiting a whole language classroom in operation, and using a sourcebook of whole language activities.

If teachers see whole language as simply a matter of sharing the reading of some interesting Big Books, having the students write on self-selected topics every day, and keeping them busy for much of the time completing some carefully prepared activities obtained from some sourcebook, then the task of becoming a "whole language" teacher will not be a very difficult one. In a disturbing article in *The Whole Language,* Karen Dalrymple (1990), whose work has taken her into many classrooms in a variety of areas, wonders "if teachers, administrators, and publishers are using the term *whole language* without a full understanding of the philosophy." Some of the activities which she has seen used in the name of whole language teaching are as follows:

1. 379 Thermofax masters and 30 reams of ditto paper used by one "whole language" teacher in six months of school

2. Assigned worksheets sent home in thick packets, showing no indication of teacher response, comments, or communication

3. Silent "whole language" classrooms

4. "String-along" activities that carry on for weeks in a primary classroom

5. Publishers who use the term *whole language* for isolated skill work or teacher-directed activities that ignore the intelligence of children

"I shudder," Dalrymple comments, and then goes on to describe some conversations of "whole language" teachers who were discussing their students: "They're quiet, but they are not one bit creative"; "I wish the kids were a bit more enthused about learning" (this from a teacher using a group behavior-management plan for primary students); and

"This group just doesn't know how to listen so I quit reading aloud to them." Dalrymple voices her concern about the name of whole language and concludes that she is "just as concerned about young children's spirits and their attitudes toward learning as I was before the term *whole language* appeared in the literature" (1990, 426).

The Reality

Becoming a whole language teacher is a lifelong process—it starts with a comprehensive understanding of the system of beliefs about learning and teaching which contribute to the development of the philosophy and its implications for classroom practice.

As with any learning, the ease and speed of learning to become whole language teachers will be governed to a large extent by teachers' prior knowledge. If they start out learning about whole language from a system of beliefs about teaching and learning that is already grounded in a commitment to child-centered, experience-based education, then becoming genuine whole language teachers should not be overly difficult. If, on the other hand, teachers are coming from a commitment to teaching based on behavioristic principles, then the task will be much more demanding since the changes needed in their belief systems and teaching practices will be quite extensive.

Learning to be whole language teachers has to come from within. Gordon Wells's (1986) "reconstruction of knowledge" must be the process through which teachers learn. They have to learn through their own thinking, understanding, and commitment, and they should be aware that the inflexibility and occasional intolerance exhibited by dedicated and "enlightened" whole language teachers can in fact be counterproductive.

Teachers have to start composing their own activities and creating their own curriculum. There is nothing wrong with teachers going to published collections of whole language activities and sourcebooks of various kinds, but they have to start modifying, amending, and creating their own curriculum based on their understanding of the principles on which whole language is based. Ideally, teachers should form their own groups of Teachers Applying Whole Language (TAWL) and should critically examine any new activity book that comes on the market. In these groups, vigorous discussions, careful evaluations, and constant sharing of discoveries should take place. The principle to follow with regard to whole language activity books is to use them but not become dependent on them.

So becoming whole language teachers is not an easy task—but it is an exciting and uplifting one. Most importantly, it is a task that places great demands on the creative and imaginative abilities of teachers. Composing one's own curriculum is not as difficult as it sounds when teachers learn to take the lead from their students and to make productive use of students' inborn abilities and desires to take control of their own learning. The sense of learning together which pervades these kinds of classrooms brings a feeling of *communality* so necessary in our divided and divisive world.

Myth No. 4

"Learning problems" will disappear in whole language classrooms.

Whole language is being seen by some teachers as a magic wand. As long as teachers continue to wave this wand, all of their students will become successful independent learners. These teachers tend to avoid direct intervention with certain students because of a belief that this may not be appropriate in a whole language setting. They sometimes believe that if they simply give sufficient time to those experiencing some difficulty with their learning, everything will come right in the end.

The Reality

For some students, immersing them in a rich and stimulating learning environment and involving them in a range of meaningful experiences may not be enough. Although we will not depart from the basic principles of whole language, our teaching for some of our students must be more direct, must be aimed at developing specific understandings, and at times must be more intense. We will have to take quite specific steps to begin to identify at-risk children on entry to school and to provide these children with much more focused teaching for at least part of the day. Some children will require many hours of individual attention, something they may not have had during their preschool years. Making up for five or six years of limited and sometimes negative learning experiences will take a great deal of time and an enormous amount of energy and patience on the part of the teacher.

Myth No. 5

Whole language is fine for students of high ability, but children with special needs require a much more "structured" approach to learning.

Some teachers provide their high-ability students with plenty of opportunities to self-direct, self-select, and self-monitor their own learning but feel that they have to maintain control over the learning of their less able students. This usually means that what is to be learned is broken down into smaller, manageable units in a belief that this will make learning easier. Fewer errors will then be made, and less "unlearning" and relearning will have to be done. Resource or "remedial" teachers rarely see whole language principles and practices as being applicable to their work with children who experience difficulty in learning in school. They seem to assume that these students are incapable of taking control of their own learning and that the students will not know what they have to try to learn next.

The Reality

Whole language is just as important for the less able children as it is for the more able. The more control we try to exert over children's learning, the less control they are going to be able to develop for themselves. The same principles of learning have to apply no matter what the ability level of the learner is. The more we take what is to be learned and break it down into meaningless bits and pieces, the harder we make that learning since meaning and self-direction are at the heart of the process. The more we deny learners the opportunity to take risks in their learning, to experiment and approximate during the process, and to learn from their mistakes, the more cautious and dependent they will become.

Special-needs children do not need more structure and more control. They need more equality experiences and captivating demonstrations of what is to be learned. They need more freedom to explore and try things out for themselves, with the guiding and supportive hand of the teacher available when required. They need more time, more trust placed in them as learners, and more chances to prove to themselves that they can learn, just like everyone else—thereby avoiding denigrating labels which brand them as somehow being different. Whole language environments are probably even more important for children who have difficulty learning in school than for those who learn easily since the more able students will continue to direct much of their own learning no matter what is done to them in the name of instruction.

Myth No. 6

Whole language is suitable for only the early grades and is not relevant to the upper elementary school, the high school, or the university.

The developmental learning principles on which whole language is based certainly were used first in kindergarten and in the other early grades. Since "real" learning starts in the later grades of the elementary school and grows in importance further up the system, it cannot be left in the hands of the learner; instead it has to be controlled by the teacher. Students cannot really be trusted to select, regulate, direct, and monitor what they learn. The transmission-of-knowledge model has to prevail since what is to be learned has to be clearly defined and presented, with products of this learning measured subsequently.

The Reality

If the principles and practices of whole language are not applicable to education in general, it does not deserve to be recognized as a legitimate educational movement. Of course it applies to all levels of learning. We learn best when what we are learning makes sense to us and is relevant to our lives; when we are able to exercise at least some control over what is to be learned; and when we are actively involved in the process. Our learning becomes most effective when we are able to self-monitor and self-correct as we proceed. As learners, we have to be continuously responsible for our own learning and be free to self-direct, self-select, and self-regulate as we engage in the process. These kinds of principles are important at all levels of learning. Since they function naturally, effectively, and universally outside the classroom, it is reasonable to suggest that they should also be present in all our elementary and high school classrooms as well as in our tertiary education institutions.

If teachers at the junior and senior high school levels would shift from their transmission-of-knowledge view of teaching to a reconstructionist one in which students are left in control of their own learning, the present unacceptably high dropout rate from secondary schools would almost certainly be reduced quite dramatically. Perhaps even more significantly, the principles and practices of whole language are beginning to be found in some courses at our universities. Until the greater majority of the professors responsible for presenting teacher-education programs begin to demonstrate the effectiveness of the philosophy through their own practices, many beginning teachers will continue to teach as they were taught, and the widespread change needed in classrooms above the early grades will not become a reality.

Myth No. 7

Whole language applies only to the language arts and not to other areas of the curriculum.

The label given to this philosophy is misleading. It is not unusual to find teachers teaching holistically during the language arts period on their timetable and moving directly to the transmission-of-knowledge model when they teach mathematics and science, for example. Even when they use a theme-based approach, most of what the children do originates from the teacher's careful planning. The children are simply manipulated into doing what has been organized for them. In Canada, we already have some school boards mandating what themes will be studied in certain grades and how many should be studied in a year.

The Reality

The Suzuki method has shown, with incredible clarity, the tremendous advantage to be derived from having children (and very young children at that) learn to play the violin holistically. In physical education, learning to play games such as basketball is best started with the children experiencing the enjoyment of playing the game before any specific attempt is made to have them learn particular skills. We learn to drive a car through some loving and trusting soul who takes us out on the highway and lets us drive—very inexpertly at first. Human beings learn best when they engage in the whole process before they start concentrating their attention on learning the parts.

Mathematics is probably one of the worst taught subjects in the curriculum. The traditional step-by-step method of having students complete computations and problems of various kinds, following exactly the model presented by the teacher, continues to produce dependent learners who are lost in a mathematical maze when left to their own devices to solve a new problem that may not quite fit the procedures taught. And yet, mathematics lends itself to holistically based learning through providing children, for example, with the opportunity to explore mathematical relationships with all kinds of concrete materials, by having them develop their logical powers through working out the solutions to puzzles and games, and by using their knowledge in relevant and useful ways.

In their use of themes, teachers should be using the ideas of Kieran Egan (1986), who suggests that the story form provides the opportunity for students to use their imaginations to resolve the "conflict" situation established when beginning to study a topic. For example, if the students were starting a study of "the community," after an initial brainstorming to find the reasons why we tend to live in communities, the binary opposites of survival and destruction could be used as the conflict to be resolved. Not only do students seek to discover the benefits of living together, but they also examine the destructive aspects of living in towns and cities (such as the eating up of valuable farmland for buildings, pollution, crime, the loss of a sense of small community). The final task is for students to use their creative powers to solve this conflict situation so that their world will be a better place in which to live. The use of thematic studies in this manner no longer consists of gathering information and/or simply completing the process according to the teacher's plan.

For too long now the curriculum planners have worked at dividing learning into a number of self-contained segments with little effort being made to help students understand the importance of the relationships among the various "disciplines." Whole language, with its heavy emphasis on integrated collaborative learning and on the interrelated and interdependent nature of life on this planet, is providing an opportunity to slow down and eventually reverse this divisiveness—before it is too late.

Myth No. 8

The publishing industry is to be trusted—what they produce in the name of whole language materials will be useful.

We now have basal series being published that are labeled not as basal series but as "literature anthologies beautifully suited to whole language classrooms." Some even have accompanying workbooks of "whole language activities." We now have "complete whole language programs" with Big Books, accompanying fictional readers, poetry readers, content readers, and recommended themes to study. Some of these published materials are being mandated for use by school boards. Whole language is rapidly becoming equated with an activity-based curriculum, with the teachers' task being to come up with interesting and exciting activities for the children to complete every day. They rush to presentations at conferences which indicate that "a variety of whole language activities will be described."

The Reality

You cannot have a "whole language" basal program. Whole language teachers have to maintain control over their own curriculum. They have to learn to be selective from the plethora of materials that are flooding the market in the name of whole language. They have to maintain their independence, their spontaneity, and their creativity. Their students' interests and needs dictate the direction for at least some of their curriculum.

The activities used have to grow out of what is being studied or done in the classroom. A Big Book might be spontaneously turned into a play to be acted out or a song to be sung. A story that has been read might lead to writing other stories like it. A social studies topic might lead to a trip to the museum, which may then lead to other field trips or visits of various people to the classroom. The range of activities to be used will come from the creative powers of the teacher and the children, and although many of the activities will be planned quite meticulously, others will emanate instinctively from the children's imaginations. No set of readers and their accompanying "activity guides" produced by some distant "expert" can ever hope to consistently provide for needs of children or teachers at the time that they are needed.

Myth No. 9

Evaluation is not important in whole language classrooms.

Because whole language teachers spurn the use of standardized tests and de-emphasize any form of product-oriented measurement, it is thought that they are not concerned with assessing the progress that their students are making. If possible, whole language teachers will reject the use of grades, but if grades have to be used, these teachers will emphasize that students self-evaluate their own learning. This causes additional conclusions pointing to a certain "sloppiness" in their approach to evaluation.

The Reality

Whole language teachers are much more interested in the processes that their students are learning to use rather than in the products of learning. One of teachers' prime goals is the development of students' ability to evaluate the effectiveness of their own learning as objectively as possible.

Central to any whole language classroom is what Yetta Goodman has called "kidwatching" (1985). Through careful and regular observation and interaction with their students, teachers learn a great deal about what and how students are learning. They also become very aware of why students may not be making the kind of progress that they perhaps should be making. Such teachers do not see the scores obtained on a standardized test as being a valid, reliable, or useful indication of what any student is learning.

As a result of their "kidwatching" activities, teachers continue to grow in their understanding of how learning takes place and what they can do to assist it. They become very aware of teaching strategies that work for some students but not for others, and they also learn which strategies are not productive and therefore need to be discarded or modified. Because these teachers develop an extensive repertoire of information based on the work of their students, they are able to communicate clearly to parents the kind of progress that their sons or daughters are making. They are also able to support their observations with practical, understandable, and relevant examples of each student's work.

Unless students learn to self-evaluate effectively, the education system has not served them in the way in which it should have. As individuals, we have to learn to assess not only how well we are doing in our learning but also where we could be going wrong. The only way that this can happen is by engaging in the process on a regular basis. Whole language teachers spend a great deal of their time engaged in individual conferences with their students in which the teachers help the students examine carefully what they have produced and share with students what they have discovered about the students' learning in noncorrective ways. The emphasis is on assisting the students to find out how they are learning, where and why they might be going wrong, and how they might improve what they are doing. The overall aim is to establish a range of criteria through which students can continue to learn to self-evaluate the effectiveness of their own learning.

Whole language teachers are constantly evaluating the progress of their students and are doing so in profoundly sensible and productive ways.

Conclusion

Whole language, if implemented true to the assumptions about learning on which it is based, will change the course of education in Canada and the United States. It is not just another method of teaching reading and writing—it is a philosophy of teaching that should pervade everything we do in our schools as teachers, students, and parents. It has unlimited potential if it is given the opportunity to grow from a base of well-informed teachers and parents. *It is at risk when half-truths form its foundations.*

The change is already gaining a strong foothold through the energy and application of a relatively small group of teachers. Its power to develop students as enthusiastic, capable, and independent learners is most easily found in numerous primary grades. It is beginning to penetrate the upper grades in elementary schools, too often, however, in inappropriate forms. It has yet to make any significant inroads into the most traditional and conservative areas of our education system: high schools, colleges, and universities.

The transmission-of-knowledge model of learning continues to reign supreme in those institutions for one easily identifiable reason: the teachers, instructors, and professors do not know any other way to teach and are not really interested in even considering that there might be a more effective way to fulfill their educative function. Until that change comes about, these institutions will continue to produce too many graduates who could be described as "educated cripples" since they seldom continue to pursue learning for learning's sake in their future lives. They will read only when they have to. They will write even more rarely, and those who cannot write will have others write for them. Their voices will never be raised in protest. Their thoughts of how we should change our way of life will remain undeveloped.

But when students who have come through their elementary classrooms being taught by genuine whole language teachers reach the upper levels, pressure will be put on the education system to change. The students themselves and their parents may well provide that pressure. It is to be hoped that Krishnamurty's cry will become their cry:

> . . . implicit in right education is the cultivation of freedom and intelligence, which is not possible if there is any form of compulsion with its fears . . . it is only when we begin to understand the deep significance of human life that there can be true education, but to understand, the mind must intelligently free itself from the desire for reward which breeds fear and conformity. (1981)

We will not commence to steer ourselves toward the sun and away from the abyss until we have a society that persistently demands that its leaders change their ways, until those who are voted into public office are there because they have demonstrated their concern about the evils which beset this world and a commitment to eradicate these evils, until the value system that gives direction for that change is based on a sense of *communal responsibility on a worldwide basis*. The military commanders, with their constant drive for more power, will not contribute to that change. Indeed, they will pervert it with the misleading cry for a mythical "security" and "strength through power." The business leaders of this world, with their addictive profit-making policies and vast political influence, will certainly not contribute to that change. The search for more gullible markets and cheaper labor forces in the Third World will continue. The efforts of business leaders to consumerize the minds of the public will continue unabated.

It will be only through a system of education that aims to cultivate "freedom and intelligence," in the real meaning of these words, that we will at least begin to slow down our rush toward destruction and maybe start to reverse our direction. The philosophy and practice for that education system are already available. Its raw materials are in our schools at the moment. All we need is for teachers from the kindergarten to the university to realize that it is what they do in their classrooms that will make the difference. All we need is for them to take up the challenge to bring about major changes in the way in which they teach. All of us have the responsibility to see that this happens.

References

Dalrymple, K. 1990. In the name of whole language. In *The whole language evaluation book,* ed. K. S. Goodman, Y. M. Goodman, and W. J. Hood. Portsmouth, N.H.: Heinemann.

Doake, D. B. In press. *Changing the assumptions for literacy learning: A revolution in progress.* Portsmouth, N.H.: Heinemann.

Egan, K. 1986. *Teaching as story telling: An alternative approach to teaching and curriculum in the elementary school.* London, Ontario: The Althouse Press.

Elley, W. B. 1991. Acquiring literacy in a second language: The effect of book-based programs. *Language Learning* 41 (3): 375–411.

Goodman, Y. 1985. Kidwatching: Observing children in the classroom. In *Observing the language learner,* ed. A. Jagger and M. Burke-Smith. Newark, Del.: International Reading Association.

Greene, M. 1988. Research currents: What are the language arts for? *Language Arts* 65 (5): 474–80.

Hall, G. E., and S. F. Loucks. 1977. A developmental model for determining whether the treatment is actually implemented. *Educational Research Journal* 14 (3): 263–76.

Holdaway, D. 1979. *The foundations of literacy.* Sydney, New South Wales, Australia: Ashton Scholastic.

Holdaway, D., and L. Handy. 1975. *Read it again: Teacher's manual.* Auckland, New Zealand: Ashton Scholastic.

Krishnamurty, J. 1981. *Education and the significance of life.* New York: Harper and Row.

MacLaren, P. M. 1989. *Life in schools.* Toronto: Irwin.

Moffett, J. 1985. Hidden impediments to improving English teaching. *Phi Delta Kappan* 67 (1): 50–56.

Newman, J. M., and S. M. Church. 1990. Myths of whole language. *The Reading Teacher* 44 (1): 20–26.

Olson, D. R. N.d. Mythologizing literacy. Unpublished manuscript, Ontario Institute for Studies in Education, University of Toronto.

Smith, F. 1989. Overselling literacy. *Phi Delta Kappan* 70 (5): 353–59.

Wells, G. 1986. *The meaning makers: Children learning language and using language to learn.* Portsmouth, N.H.: Heinemann.

8 Moving toward a Literature-Based Curriculum: Problems and Possibilities

Kathy G. Short
University of Arizona

The recent increase in the publication of children's books and professional books and workshops on the use of literature provides evidence that children's literature is playing an increasingly important role in classroom life. As educators attend conferences and workshops and hear about literature-based programs and strategies, they often get excited about new possibilities and, for the moment, ignore the problems. When they return to the classroom, however, they can find themselves overwhelmed by the problems of trying something new or taking a different perspective on what they are already doing. They lose sight of the new possibilities for learning and focus on the problems instead.

As educators bring literature into the classroom and into children's lives in more powerful ways, they must deal with new issues as well as new potentials for learning. I believe that many of these problems and possibilities arise, not so much from how we view literature or how well we implement a particular idea, but from broader questions about curriculum and the roles of teachers and students in the classroom. To be literary in a classroom, we need more than books or kits. Being literary is not just what we do but the perspectives we have toward what we are doing—ways of looking at literature and how literature can be read and used, ways of viewing children as readers, and ways of looking at the classroom community, curriculum, and learning.

The possibilities and problems that I discuss in this chapter grow out of many different conversations and experiences with other educators. My area of teaching and research is children's literature, and so I have spent a great deal of time thinking, talking, and working with different groups of teachers. One group includes teachers who have taken a series of university courses on children's literature. Over the past four years, we have had many conversations about the issues and potentials that they face in their teaching situations. For the past three years, I have also been part of two school-based study groups, and much of what I share here comes from that experience. Tucson Unified School District moved from a traditional basal approach to a literature anthology and sets of literature books several years ago. Teachers were offered a one-day workshop to make this transition, hardly sufficient considering the range of their experiences with literature—from teachers who already had strong programs built around literature to teachers who occasionally read aloud to their students. As an alternative to traditional inservice programs, the district agreed to explore study groups as a way to support teachers. Ten to fifteen teachers from each of two elementary schools, Warren and Maldonado, meet every other week after school to talk and think together about the issues that concern them as teachers. At the end of each study group session, the group decides what their focus will be for the next meeting. I have also spent time working with these teachers in their classrooms. Each summer, a group of teacher researchers meets to analyze the study group experience and the issues being discussed within these two groups (Short et al. 1992).

Based on these conversations and experiences, I want to raise a number of issues about the problems and possibilities as educators move to more fully integrating literature into classroom life. All of these issues involve examining the move toward a literature-based curriculum within a broader curricular and theoretical framework. The first issues are related to the role that literature plays within the curriculum, and the other issues involve examining our questions about how to use literature in the classroom from both practical and theoretical perspectives.

The Role of Literature in the Curriculum

Literature has often been viewed as a better way to teach reading. This view of the role of literature, however, limits its potentials within the curriculum. There are at least four major roles that literature can play within the curriculum: literature as a way to learn language, literature as a way to learn other content, literature as a way of knowing about the world, and literature as a way of knowing about social, political, and cultural issues. Within each of these roles, children can be involved in both extensive and intensive experiences with literature. By exploring a broader range of roles and experiences with literature, new potentials for learning and connection are made available.

Literature as a Way to Learn Language

Many elementary teachers see literature as a way to learn language: to learn how to read and write. For them, literature has replaced the basal as a way to teach reading. Literature discussions and experiences such as shared reading and guided reading with Big Books and predictable books often focus on the reading strategies that students are using and how these strategies relate to different kinds of literature. Literature is integrated into writing workshops to help students explore different writing styles and writing strategies, such as getting an idea, starting a story, using dialogue, and revising for an audience.

When students in Leslie Kahn's sixth-grade classroom wrote only "shopping mall" and "gang" stories, she involved them in literature circles with poetry and author studies which focused on authors of informational books. By exploring authors such as David Macaulay, Aliki, and Mitsumasa Anno, students were exposed to a variety of formats and styles of writing that they could use during writing workshops for their own pieces. Roxanne Lung and Clay Connor were concerned about whether their students were developing useful reading strategies for informational books, so as students read historical information books and biographies, the two teachers often pulled the class together for short discussions about their students' strategies for reading these books. The class examined both the genre of informational books in terms of the organization and structures of these books and their own strategies as readers.

Literature as a Way to Learn Other Content

Some teachers see literature as a way to learn other content and thus organize literature experiences around themes and topics that are part of current studies in science, social studies, and mathematics. Their discussions about literature often focus on what is being learned through literature and how that compares to their learning from other sources.

Junardi Armstrong and I used read-aloud and literature group experiences as part of her second graders' exploration of ecosystems and the desert. The students met in small groups to read from text sets, a set of related books such as fiction, nonfiction, and poetry on rain forests. The different texts in these sets brought in a variety of perspectives and types of stories and information related to each group's topic and supported students in exploring a range of aesthetic and efferent stances (Short and Armstrong 1993). Sandy Kaser involved her fifth graders in an exploration of family histories using a wide range of literature experiences as well as interviews with family and community members. Students combined novels, picture books, and stories from their own childhood and that of their parents and grandparents to explore issues of family, culture, and world conflict.

Literature as a Way of Knowing about the World

Some teachers also realize that literature is itself a content area, a way of knowing about the world that differs from other ways of knowing, like science or history. Ralph Peterson, Mary Ann Eeds, and Karen Smith have been instrumental in raising our awareness of this perspective. They argue that we have been so busy *using* literature for other purposes that we have lost sight of literature having value in and of itself (Peterson and Eeds 1990; Smith 1990). Louise Rosenblatt (1978) has helped us see that through literature readers are able to experience life in a different way and to live inside the story world in ways that transform them. In terms of the classroom, this perspective justifies pure enjoyment of literature—just to read and enjoy a book without having to respond to it through discussion or writing or relate it to a curricular study. The stories may be shared during read-aloud or independent reading experiences or discussed in literature circles. Literature discussions from this perspective focus on giving readers the chance to share their "lived through" experiences and to discuss the literary devices and personal connections used by authors and readers to create those experiences.

Often literature experiences which highlight this perspective occur in literature circles where a small group of students reads and discusses a shared piece of literature. Because the story is shared, the students can focus on their different interpretations and responses to the story and can look in depth at literary elements such as characters and themes. In a literature circle on Jean Craighead George's *Julie of the Wolves* (Harper and Row, 1972), sixth graders in Kaylene Yoder's classroom explored themes related to survival, death, communication, and culture as well as talking about information on Alaska, wolves, and Inuit cultures. They also debated their differing responses to and interpretations of the ending (Kauffman and Yoder 1990). Pamella Sherman engaged her first graders in literature circles on Tomie de Paola as an author and illustrator. The children's discussions included personal connections to their own lives as well as comparisons across the different themes, topics, and characters of de Paola's stories and an in-depth analysis of his illustration style and how that communicated meaning to them.

Literature as a Way of Knowing about Social, Political, and Cultural Issues

Teachers are also currently exploring how literature is a way of knowing about social, political, and cultural issues. While this focus is similar to literature as a way to learn other content, it specifically grows out of personal social, political, and cultural experiences. Critical theorists point out the necessity of consciously examining how our thinking is influenced by the community and world in which we live and the need to examine social issues such as homelessness, prejudice, cultural diversity, and living at peace with others. The intent is both to understand in different ways the problems in the world around us and to examine our histories in order to find our own voices. Society is dominated by particular voices and points of view that deny anyone else a voice. Literature is one way to begin to reflectively and critically consider other ways of thinking about the world and to look at our own histories in light of global complexities.

Some of the students in Caryl Crowell's third-grade bilingual classroom were concerned about the Gulf War, so she put together a text set of picture books on war. Students read and discussed the books, most of which dealt with the Holocaust. Through their discussions they were able to make many connections to the Gulf War and to look more critically at what was occurring (Crowell 1993). As Kathleen Crawford's fourth-grade students discussed Mildred Taylor's *Roll of Thunder, Hear My Cry* (Dial Press, 1976) in a literature circle, they focused on the prejudice experienced by the characters in the book. They also began to explore how they still face prejudice in their school and community and how they are often silenced in the same ways as the Logan family.

Highlighting a Perspective

Obviously these four perspectives are not mutually exclusive, and more than one is present during any experience in a classroom. But one of these perspectives is usually highlighted at any one time, and the perspective being highlighted changes the kinds of experiences planned for the classroom and the understandings of the readers involved in that experience. My concern is that often one of these roles is highlighted to the exclusion of the others, and thus the perspectives offered by a range of roles are not available to children. Too often in education we divide ourselves into different camps or corners, arguing the validity of a particular perspective. Some educators see literature only as a way to teach reading and therefore limit the possibilities for connections across the curriculum and within children's own lives. Instead of arguing which perspective is most important, educators need to consider the need for all four perspectives and how each role changes the experiences and the potentials for conversations and thinking in a classroom. The decision of which role is highlighted at any one time should be related to the goals of the curriculum and the strengths and needs of the particular learners.

The Role of Extensive and Intensive Literature Experiences

Within each of these roles, students need to have both extensive and intensive experiences with literature (Peterson and Eeds 1990). When I first began exploring literature, my goal was for kids to learn to love reading. I focused on reading aloud, having sustained reading times where children read books of their own choice, and engaging in fun projects with literature. Many of the teachers in the study group joined the group because they wanted to "motivate" their students and create more interest in reading for pleasure and for students' own purposes. These extensive experiences allow children to enjoy books and to become proficient readers. However, I had another goal as a teacher: for students to become critical readers and thinkers. I knew they could read widely and enjoy reading but still not think critically about their reading. I wanted them to think deeply about what they were reading and to connect what they read with their lives as well as to use reading to gain new perspectives on themselves and the world.

I began to explore literature circles with teachers in a number of classrooms. In these literature circles, small groups of students read and discussed shared books or text sets. Instead of answering questions, they talked about their responses to what they read as they explored and revised with others their "rough draft" understandings about literature. The dialogues were exciting, and students responded critically to literature. Their discussions made it obvious to us that we did not need programs or kits to develop critical thinking. These intensive literature experiences dominated the classroom, and we soon realized that students were not having a chance just to sit back and enjoy what they read without having to talk about it to someone else. As we thought about our lives as adult readers, we realized that only a small portion of what we read is discussed intensively with others. So we went back to our classrooms and looked for a better balance of intensive and extensive experiences.

In examining this issue of balance, we realized that primary teachers tended to exclude intensive experiences, assuming that young children needed predictable books and shared reading experiences. Children constantly revisited books, but for the purpose of developing fluency and reading strategies, not intensively considering meaning. We realized that they needed to see reading as a critical thinking process from the beginning, and we explored reading quality picture books aloud to children so they could discuss the books in small groups or with the class. The predictable books that they were able to read independently rarely supported an intensive consideration of meaning and life issues. In contrast, students in the intermediate grades often engaged primarily in intensive experiences and rarely had time to simply enjoy a good book and develop fluency and flexibility as readers.

All of us as educators have a tendency to find something that works or is exciting and to focus on it to the exclusion of everything else. Both extensive and intensive reading play essential roles in children's development as fluent and thoughtful readers who use reading as a way to live and change their lives. Through these experiences, the possibilities are increased that students will become literate lifelong learners who both enjoy and think critically about their reading.

Connections across Theory and Practice

When we first began the study group, we did not have a specific focus beyond exploring issues related to literature and curriculum. Most of us assumed that we would discuss practical issues related to implementing literature groups in the classroom. By the second meeting of the study group, however, we were discussing a wide range of issues and concerns, and visitors to our group would probably not have identified our focus as literature.

One of the tasks of the research group was to list the particular issues, questions, and topics that came up in discussions during the study group sessions and visits to classrooms. We quickly realized that those questions and topics covered a tremendous range. There were many questions about literature discussion groups, such as how to organize and set them up, what kinds of materials to use in the groups, how to support discussions and talk about literature, what to do with the rest of the class while kids were in literature groups, and how to handle presentations or projects. We talked about issues such as whether it was appropriate for students to reread books, whether to attend to reading levels and difficulty, and use of the literature anthology. We talked about writing and issues such as conferencing, revising, editing, social talk, offering invitations, noise level, and spelling. We talked about the reading process and teaching about language. We talked about ways to organize the classroom and looked at different ways to schedule the day. We talked about integrating the curriculum, making connections across the day, and involving students in their own research. We talked about district mandates, particularly in relation to evaluation. We talked about communication with parents. We also talked about collaborative curriculum, and how teachers and students together can negotiate the curriculum as well as establish structures that support students in pursuing their own learning. We talked about ourselves as learners reflecting on our own thinking and the difficulty of changing beliefs and practices. We talked about whole language and whether it was a way of thinking, a set of methods, or a fad. We spent a lot of time on evaluation, exploring field notes as a way to capture some of what was happening in the classroom. We also discussed portfolios as an alternative to report cards and standardized tests in reporting to the district and parents.

These topics ranged from very practical concerns with materials, student behavior, and instructional strategies to theoretical questions and reflections. As I read this list over and over, I became convinced that we often look at our questions from too narrow a perspective and that when we explore only the surface-level question, the same question keeps emerging, just in different forms.

One question that came up frequently in the study group and the courses I teach is, "How do you get the kids talking in literature groups?" Teachers are concerned about how to move students beyond retelling the story, engaging in social talk, and staring at each other, to in-depth, critical dialogue about a work of literature. They are also concerned about how to redefine their role in the group from directing the discussion by asking questions, to facilitating discussion among group members.

Within the study group, we addressed this question by examining practical strategies and concerns. We talked about the need for social talk in any group as a way to establish contact and feel at ease.

The study group always started with fifteen to twenty minutes of social talk and informal sharing before we could move into our focus for that session. We talked about our need to share and "muck around" before focusing our discussion on a particular issue, and we realized that children had the same need. The "mucking-around" time encourages children to share their aesthetic responses and allows a wider range of connections to be shared. While the ideas that they share are often tentative and half-formed, these ideas are an essential part of the process and help students find something worth discussing in greater depth.

We also discussed particular strategies that took the focus off the teacher as the director of discussions, such as having students share their initial responses to or feelings about a book and then brainstorming a web or list of possible topics that could be discussed in more depth. Because students used this web to decide at the end of each day what they would discuss at their next literature circle, they felt the responsibility to be prepared for that discussion. In addition, we discussed having students write responses or draw sketches of what the story meant to them and bring those to the group as a way to start discussion.

The question about how to get students talking in literature circles, however, kept coming up again and again, both in the group and in classes at the university. I began to ask, "Why? What's so hard about dialogue? What are some of the issues behind that question? What other questions or issues are embedded within this one question?"

Changing Our Beliefs and Theories

As I talked about these questions with teachers, we realized that one issue was the theories of the individuals involved in the groups. Both students and teachers bring to the group particular views about learning that can make discussion groups difficult. Because of their past experiences, most students expect to be told what to learn and think and to be asked questions to which there is only one correct response. Learning has been an isolated individual task for them. Even when they are in groups, they may work with other students but rarely think with others. For literature circles to be successful, students must change their beliefs about learning and see learning as an active, reflective, and social process.

Some students have been in classrooms where they were encouraged to be active learners but were never asked to reflect on and talk about their learning and thinking. They have had many extensive experiences with literature through reading aloud, independent reading, and shared reading, but they have not intensively explored their understandings of what they read. Initially they find literature circles difficult because they need time to learn how to put their thoughts into language to share and explore with others.

For many teachers, literature circles involve changes in their beliefs about reading and learning. They have to move away from viewing learning as an individual cognitive process which is directly taught. If we believe that learning is active, then all learners must have a voice in determining the direction of the curriculum and of their own learning. This perspective means a major change in the social relationships within the classroom and the school and signals a move toward a collaborative view of curriculum. Curriculum is negotiated within the classroom, not determined outside the classroom.

Traditionally, curriculum is created outside the classroom and imposed on teachers who in turn impose it on students. Most of us experienced school as a top-down hierarchial model of passing down information, skills, and pieces of knowledge. Textbook companies are currently developing literature-based programs that are based on this model with questions and workbook exercises (now called journals) for students to answer on pieces of literature. This movement is frightening because previously the "good" books were left alone, and the basal stories were ruined through workbooks and questioning. Now we have the potential of ruining good pieces of literature.

Because students' voices were not heard in this model, the focus in education has shifted to students and listening to their voices so that their experiences, needs, and interests are brought into the classroom. This focus on students has led many people to a liberal model of curriculum where the teacher stands back and lets the curriculum unfold by following student interests. The curriculum is seen as child-centered and as emphasizing trusting in the learner. What we found was that this focus on students led teachers to ask the painful questions: "Then what's my role as a teacher? Why am I here?" Teachers found themselves "letting go" to the point where their voices were no longer heard in the classroom. They were afraid to make suggestions, plan whole-group experiences, ask questions, or teach directed lessons for fear of "taking over" student learning. They wanted to live actively as learners in their classrooms with their students, but they felt that there was no room for their thinking, connections, and creativity. As we talked together in the study group, we realized that we had just created another hierarchy, one with students at the top. What we needed to do was to move beyond hierarchy to collaborative relationships.

A collaborative curriculum allows everyone to have a voice in constructing the curriculum. As teachers, we bring to the classroom our understandings based on experiences, district expectations, and outside experts, but we do not impose them on students. Students bring their understandings and interests, and together we negotiate and create curriculum. Teachers do carry the major responsibility for establishing a learning environment that is conducive to the growth of the specific students in that classroom. But students are also involved through choices which allow them to be active in their own learning processes and through reflection on their learning and the classroom learning environment, as shown in Figure 8.1. Darcy, a third grader in Gloria Kauffman's classroom, reflected on the influence of a collaborative environment on her learning:

> Last year, we did workbooks. I didn't like it because I didn't have to think. This year we create our own workbooks through webbing, charting, and lit logs. I feel more comfy without workbooks. I am thinking more.
>
> This year we are all teachers and learners, meaning that the teacher gives us ideas and we give the teacher ideas.
>
> Last year we were assigned seats but this year, we sit at tables and are not assigned seats. We are responsible for getting our work done so we are careful to sit somewhere where we can work.
>
> We don't have levels of reading. We are all valued equally. And our thinking is valued.

A collaborative curriculum is not teacher-centered or student-centered, it is *learning*-centered. This curriculum is much harder to deal with as teachers because our roles are no longer clear-cut. As we negotiate the curriculum with our students, we constantly shift the roles that we are taking, depending on their expertise, needs, and interests.

For us, the question of "How do I get kids talking in literature groups?" was based on exploring collaborative curriculum. Behind that question are other questions that involve redefining our roles as teachers, such as: "How do I facilitate, support, and sometimes direct student learning? How can I facilitate without silencing student voices? How do I listen to and involve students more powerfully in making decisions about their own learning and the curriculum?"

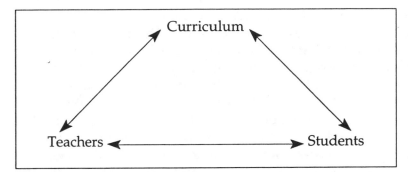

Figure 8.1. Model of collaborative curriculum showing the interaction between curriculum, teachers, and students in a whole language classroom.

Establishing Structures and Functions for Learning

As we explored these questions, we realized that we needed to establish structures that support students in their learning but that do not restrict their voices or take away their choices. We also found that we needed to be careful that the structures we established to support student learning did not become a set of procedures or a list of rules to follow. When students did not understand the reasoning behind those structures, they became inflexible rules. For some students, the writing workshop is a set of procedures rather than a support for their own writing processes: they do two sloppy copies because that is what they are supposed to do, not because their story needs revision to make it more powerful.

Story grammars have been popular as a way to facilitate dialogue about literature. Students do need an understanding of how stories are structured, but these exercises are usually "fill in the blanks" with little meaning to students. The same is true of the question-filled "journals" that accompany commercial literature anthologies. Students are asked to answer page after page of open-ended questions. Instead of one right answer, there are now two or three right answers—hardly a significant change.

Whether students view a list of suggestions as procedures rather than a demonstration of possibilities seems to depend on whether they participate in creating that list. The first time that Becky Williams began literature circles with her first graders, she wrote a list of suggestions on the board for what they might discuss, such as share your favorite part or discuss the ending of the story. Students, however, used these ideas as a checklist, going around the circle and having each person answer each item. When Becky realized what was happening, she quickly erased the list from the board. The next day she had students brainstorm what *they* thought they might talk about. She also had students come together after their literature circles for a class discussion so they could hear what other groups were discussing and brainstorm solutions for any problems in the groups. By making these small changes and having students generate the list of suggestions, she found that they used the lists as a place to get ideas for discussion *if* they needed them. In Sandy Kaser's classroom, fifth graders created a list of what they talk about with their friends after going to a movie. As they moved into their first literature discussions, I noticed that a number of students were using the list on the board to guide their discussions when they needed support.

The issue of function is an important distinction in whether the structures established to support learning become procedures. As teachers, we need to ask ourselves, "What purpose does this activity or role serve for students? Do they see that purpose as valuable in their own learning?" Without an understanding of purpose, the activity is something that students do for the teacher, instead of part of how they think. Many of the activities and experiences included in classrooms serve the function of control, rather than inquiry and learning. Both the traditional and liberal models of curriculum emphasize control and ask the question "Who is in control?" In a collaborative model, however, the focus is not on control but on inquiry, on learning.

Literature logs are often used to make sure students are not fooling around or to have something for evaluation. Both of these purposes have a control function. Because the logs are primarily being used to control student behavior, they often become the focus of contention and frustration for both students and teachers. For some students, these logs are a punishment for having read a book, and they put little time or thought into writing entries because they are only "for the teacher." Logs should support students in thinking and reflecting on their responses to literature and in preserving those responses to share with others. The logs help students prepare for literature circles and so can take different forms, such as stick-on notes, sketches, webs, or charts rather than only written responses. When logs are viewed from this perspective, they become functional for students as well as teachers. Both students and teachers might also use them to evaluate the students' growth in response, but they have a learning function that makes that response worth evaluating.

The same issue of control versus inquiry is involved in some teachers' use of activities and centers to keep students busy while they are not in literature circles. These activities often fulfill a control function rather than pushing students' understandings and learning. Some of the projects that students complete as part of literature circles are "cutesy"—fun for students to do rather than allowing them to continue thinking about their responses to a book through other communication systems. When everyone is asked to make a diorama or do a puppet show rather than developing their own responses, students tend to see the activity as teacher-directed rather than meaning-directed. In essence, these centers and activities can become just as meaningless as the stacks of worksheets that formerly were used to keep students occupied. Making a diorama can be powerful or meaningless, based on the purpose for that activity and whether it allows students to continue thinking through their understandings of a particular book, or whether it simply fills time.

In the study group, we spent several months talking about field notes in the literature circles: what they were, how to take them, how to focus the notes, what to do with them once you had them, and how to use them to develop your own categories and checklists. I was surprised by how long the group focused on this topic. I was ready to move on, but the teachers in the group obviously wanted to continue discussing field notes and trying to take notes in their classrooms. Finally, someone in the group asked, "Why are we discussing this? Why would you even take field notes?" So we spent some time talking about why to take field notes and suddenly realized that what was driving the group was their focus on how to build a collaborative curriculum with their students. They needed other ways of knowing their students. If teachers are not just instituting a set of procedures or basing the curriculum on test scores and district directives, then they need other ways of knowing about what is happening in the classroom. They could not build a collaborative curriculum without new ways of "seeing" their students. Field notes provided the teachers with a chance to systematically look at what was happening in the classroom and gain many insights into their students. Because field notes took on a real function for both teachers and students, they began to be integrated into daily classroom life. Through field notes, some teachers were able to find more powerful ways to bring theory and practice together in their teaching.

As long as the structures and functions of activities continue to focus on control, then changes in classrooms will be minimal. When the central focus is placed on inquiry and involving learners in mean-ingful learning experiences based on their needs and interests, then the potential exists for changing the basic structures and learning environ-ments of schools. When learners are engaged in learning that they find meaningful and in which they have a voice, many of the control issues which now dominate schools will be reduced. While it would be idealistic to argue that control issues disappear, at least they would no longer be the basis for every decision made in schools. Children do not come to school to be controlled, but to learn.

Examining Our Learning as Adults

Through our discussions in the study groups, we also came to realize that what we believe about learning for children is also true about our learning as adults. If we believe that learning is both active and reflec-tive, then we have to bring theory and practice together in our own learning. Despite all the rhetoric, theory and practice continue to be separated in education. University educators are seen as the source of theory, and classroom teachers as the source of practice. While I am a university educator concerned with theory and research, I am also a teacher. I constantly struggle with how to create powerful learning environments in my university classrooms. Classroom educators are not only teachers, but theoreticians who reflect on their teaching and beliefs about learning, reading, and children.

As educators, we found that we were constantly trying to be both active and reflective learners—to bring together our beliefs and our practices. We realized that those of us who were strong in practice but did not reflect on our beliefs and theories had no way to create our own curriculum because we were dependent on others for new ideas. Others of us who had strong theoretical understandings and were not putting those theories into practice were constantly frustrated because of the violation of our theories and the uncertainty about how to change our practice. We also saw that the process of connecting theory and practice was especially difficult for those who were changing both beliefs and practices at the same time. Often these teachers felt that they were not standing on solid ground of any kind or even that they had no sense of what questions to ask.

Teacher Sandy Kaser reflected on the difficulty of changing both beliefs and practices at the same time:

> It's enormous when you're changing your philosophy and your
> practices every day. You're just thinking through all this and

working with kids and helping them and you're not sure where it's going to end up. I'm not even sure what's happened this quarter. It's scary and exhausting. I can have a really good day but I have a headache because I have to think so hard all the time.

The belief that all learners need to be both active and reflective led us to question hierarchial structures and to look for more collaborative ways to create curriculum with children. If we believe that the classroom should be based on collaborative relationships and not hierarchies, then the same should be true about our relationships with other educators outside the classroom. There are so many hierarchies in education that even if we begin to explore how to collaborate with students, other hierarchies continue to affect our teaching. These hierarchies include the next grade's teachers, the principal and other school administrators, and district and state curriculum and testing mandates.

In dealing with these hierarchies, we must get beyond a "them versus us" perspective and must act with, rather than react to, administrators. In the study group we discussed the issue of teachers being asked by the school district to use evaluation measures that came from a different theoretical perspective than the curriculum mandates. As teachers, we have the tendency to react by complaining loudly, by doing the minimal to get the district off our backs, or by giving in to the mandate. Through our discussions, we realized that just as each of us has conflicting beliefs and practices, so does a district. Teachers need to work with district administrators to deal with those conflicts. Because we knew that the district wanted to develop the use of portfolios, the group began to brainstorm ideas for portfolios that would have a strong student self-evaluation component as well as communicating to other teachers and parents and meeting district needs for reporting. Teachers did not look at portfolios in defiance of the district but in recognition of the need for alternatives within the district, of being able to say, "This is what we are thinking through and why," in the hope that the district might recognize their efforts.

As educators, we need to deal with the issue of how we develop mutual respect for each other rather than resorting to power plays within hierarchial relationships. While we may not develop collaborative relationships, at least we can develop relationships based on respect for each other's roles and responsibilities. Collaboration involves both parties being willing to collaborate and requires much time spent thinking and talking together. Neither of these requirements are always possible within schools.

We need to realize, however, that administrators cannot just leave teachers alone to do whatever they want, no more than we would leave our students alone to do what they want. Administrators have certain responsibilities that require a need for particular kinds of structures and information. As educators, we need to consider how we can build those structures together and find ways to provide the needed information. In turn, administrators need to develop ways of really hearing teachers and students and should not focus on just their own needs.

If we believe that the structures and activities that we introduce into the classroom must have a function, then the same holds true for administrators. The problem with many evaluation measures used by districts is that they have no function in the classroom. We need to develop measures that have a function for both administrators and teachers. Administrators often ask teachers to turn in weekly lesson plans. Frequently the function of submitting the lessons is to control teachers, rather than to encourage them to reflect on their teaching and to provide a place for keeping track of their plans and thinking. In many ways, this issue is similar to those raised for literature logs. If teachers and principals can work together at lesson plans and the purposes for those plans, they can find ways of creating plans that have a function for both teaching and administration.

Within the study group, we found that the more we were able to "live the process" and experience a more collaborative learning community among ourselves, the more we wanted to establish that same kind of community with our students. The integration of theory and practice took on new meaning because we had a different sense of the potentials within a collaborative learning environment.

Teaching and Learning as Processes of Inquiry

Above all, what has become most important to me as an educator and learner is the realization that learning is a process of inquiry—of searching out the questions that matter in my life and the lives of my students. I value literature in the classroom because it brings life into the classroom. Literature invites students to take different perspectives on their own lives and helps them discover and explore questions about their lives and about the world around them.

As teachers, we are also inquirers, trying to find and answer our own questions. The process of inquiry will bring us some answers, but it will also bring us new questions—the sign of a positive learning experience, not that something is wrong with us. Field notes, tapes, transcriptions, and the search for categories have been seen as standard practices used by university researchers to gather and analyze data. Because teaching is an inquiry process, teachers need those same kinds of tools, not just to report to others, but for their own learning.

Until we view teaching and learning as processes of research and inquiry, the changes being made in schools will be short-lived. The movement toward more use of literature and literature circles, writing workshops and writing notebooks, and broad curricular themes and concepts will be just a focus on activities and procedures to be implemented. We will remain at the mercy of the next "fad" just as much as our students are at the mercy of the next teacher, when they have not taken control of their learning. It is only when we see ourselves as inquirers—learners who are able to systematically go about finding and posing our own questions and exploring possible answers to those questions as well as finding new questions—that we will really be able to move and change our classrooms.

Once learners experience inquiry and develop their own purposes for learning, they find ways to keep that learning going. Steven, a first grader, had discovered the power of writing in his own life and was determined to continue writing. As we discussed the role of writing when he grew up, he told me, "Even if I'm a truck driver, I'll come home at night and write because writing is so important to me." He was determined to keep learning through writing, and I knew that even if no other teacher facilitated his writing, Steven would continue writing.

Margaret Valfre, a teacher in several university classes, told me:

> This is the first time it ever occurred to me that I had a right to my own agenda for teaching and learning. I never even considered it. I always accepted everyone else's agenda—my administrators' or my professors'. Now that I've experienced what it is like to follow my own agenda, I'm not willing to settle for anything less—not in my personal life or professional. I know that I will have to take other courses to finish my degree where I won't be able to set my own agenda, and I'm not sure what I'm going to do about those courses. I do know that now that I've experienced it for myself, I can't ever go back and just accept what others tell me to think.

Valfre still has many conflicts in her beliefs and practices that she wants to work through, but she will find her way because she is an inquirer. She has a need to learn and understand and to ask her own questions, which will allow her to slowly create a powerful learning environment in her classroom.

When we see ourselves as inquirers, we take a different perspective on the problems that we as teachers encounter. Roxanne Lung, one of the study group members, commented that the group had allowed her to understand that "if you believe in something, you keep on going even if it doesn't work out right away." Previously she had abandoned ideas that did not immediately work in her classroom.

The classrooms of the teachers in the study group have not become sudden showcases or exemplars for literature-based teaching and collaborative curriculum. We probably could have made dramatic changes in the schools. I could have put together and had teachers implement a set of procedures, a formula for literature circles, and a schedule. But the changes would have been surface level and dependent on me. Now it is too late. The educators in these schools have taken charge of their learning and would strongly resist "experts" bringing in prescriptive programs.

If we are going to continue learning as teachers, then we need the same kind of learning environment that our students need: a place where we can be inquirers. Our schools need to become places that facilitate the inquiry and dialogue among all learners—teachers, students, and administrators.

I want to go back to the title of this chapter, "Moving toward a Literature-Based Curriculum: Problems and Possibilities," and redefine *problems* and *possibilities*. If we take the perspective of being an inquirer, then *problems* are not something "bad" or "wrong." They are the questions and issues that we seek out as learners. They are what we want to understand and explore. *Possibilities* are the options, the wide range of answers and new questions that we develop through inquiry. We will never find the perfect way to teach. Instead, inquiry provides us with an open and exciting process of continuing to grow as learners and teachers.

References

Crowell, C. 1993. Living through war vicariously with literature. In *Teachers are researchers: Reflection and action*, ed. L. Patterson, C. Santa, K. Short, and K. Smith. Newark, Del.: International Reading Association.

Kauffman, G., and K. Yoder. 1990. Celebrating authorship: A process of collaborating and creating meaning. In *Talking about books: Creating literate communities*, ed. K. Short and K. M. Pierce. Portsmouth, N.H.: Heinemann.

Peterson, R., and M. Eeds. 1990. *Grand conversations*. New York: Scholastic.

Rosenblatt, L. 1978. *The reader, the text, the poem: The transactional theory of the literary work*. Carbondale: Southern Illinois University Press.

Short, K., and J. Armstrong. 1993. Moving toward inquiry: Integrating literature into the science curriculum. *The New Advocate* 6 (3): 183–99.

Short, K., K. Crawford, L. Kahn, S. Kaser, C. Klassen, and P. Sherman. 1992. Teacher study groups: Exploring literacy issues through collaborative dialogue. In *Forty-first yearbook of the National Reading Conference*, ed. D. Leu and C. Kinzer. Chicago: National Reading Conference.

Smith, K. 1990. Entertaining a text: A reciprocal process. In *Talking about books: Creating literate communities*, ed. K. Short and K. M. Pierce. Portsmouth, N.H.: Heinemann.

9 Spelling for the Whole Language Classroom

Ethel Buchanan
Language Arts Consultant, Winnipeg, Manitoba

My teaching career went through two stages: the cocoon stage and the butterfly stage. In the cocoon stage I taught so well that, for the first time, my class beat the neighboring school in a phonics test. Mind you, my students did not read much; sometimes they did not have a chance to do any real reading at all. They were so busy on the prereading and post-reading activities that they had little time to read anything apart from the two pages that they had to read with me. The children who needed to read the most had the smallest amount of time left for reading. As a result of the phonics test, the children felt good because they had done so well, and I got the reputation of being a good teacher for doing things that had little, if anything, to do with real teaching.

After a number of years of this cocoon-like existence, I did smarten up a bit, or at least I had a principal who made me smarten up. One day in the staff room I was moaning and groaning about how sick I was of the basal program that I was using. One class had to be twenty pages behind another class, and class three, the sparrows or whatever they happened to be called, had to be twenty pages behind the middle group. This was the routine that we were expected to follow. The children in the third group were expected to get excited over a story that every child in the whole room already knew by then; and so did I, believe me. When I had finished complaining on this particular day, the principal said, "Well, Ethel, why don't you do something about it?"

Although I had been apprehensive about working with this principal, being with her and accepting her challenge was certainly one of the best things that ever happened to me. She not only challenged me to come up with a plan; she also offered support and encouragement every step of the way. She allowed me to get rid of the basal readers and workbooks, to use trade books that the children selected, and to have the children work on group and individual projects of their choice. This was a form of individualization similar to our present-day version of whole language teaching. There must have been critics of what was going on because all this happened almost twenty-five years ago, and such actions were almost unheard of in our division at the time, except perhaps in small, select, special classes of "gifted" children. I am very grateful that in later years I had a chance to thank Miss Jefferies for giving my pupils and myself a chance to move beyond a cocoon stage into a more joyous, alive, and self-fulfilling butterfly stage.

It was during this time that the children in my grade-two class taught me a lot about sharing and the value of sharing. Every day at a quarter to four, in a flash, our room was tidy, our desks were cleared, and the children who had something to share were ready at the front of the room, sitting on little chairs that I had been able to scrounge from the kindergarten room. We all looked forward to this part of the day and the magic of sharing. The things that the children shared were varied; sometimes they shared a marvelous word that they had found—one they could use in a sentence, spell, and write on the board. They knew how to use the word in a context; they had discovered it and made it their own.

Another thing that I learned at this time was the value of individual conferencing, of setting aside a special time when a child knows that he or she will have your undivided attention. I had thirty students and was able to conference with each one approximately every six days. The thing about conferencing is that you cannot accomplish it in five or ten minutes unless you are prepared for the conference. In my case, it meant taking the student's work folder home the night before his or her conference and examining it. In preparing for a spelling conference, you look to see what is happening with the student's spelling, searching out patterns of misspellings, finding out what words the child uses frequently but is unable to spell, and observing those words that the child can spell in standard form. The words in this latter group may provide the key to helping the student spell other words that he or she wants to spell. At this time you also pick up information about students who have similar needs and plan a group mini-lesson for these students. Both the most successful student and the student having the most difficulty deserve the teacher's undivided attention for a planned period of time. Finding time for conferencing is not difficult in a classroom where children are accustomed to working independently, whether they are reading, writing, or working on projects.

What I want to share here is based on my own experience. It is also based on what I have learned from a good many people, including James Beers, Sandra Wilde, Frank Smith, Ken and Yetta Goodman, Orin and Donna Cochrane, and other wonderful teachers. It is also based on the best teacher-educators of all, the children themselves. Ken Goodman often comments on how much he has learned from children, and other teachers would no doubt concur.

The Learning Process and Learning How to Spell

When we speak about learning how to spell and spelling instruction, it is very important that we do so in the context of the child's life and environment. We know that a child learns best when certain conditions exist: when the learner has his or her physical needs met; is nurtured, loved, and capable of giving love; is respected by others; feels good about himself or herself; understands the nature of what he or she is trying to do; and has adequate prior knowledge.

Usually, learning begins with a demonstration by a significant other. The child sees someone for whom he or she cares doing something, and the child decides that he or she would like to be able to do that task or activity. It certainly is not always that simple; sometimes it takes much more. James Britton says that one of the most important jobs for a teacher is "to light the fires of a child's intent." A teacher's own interest and curiosity about words can often light the fires of a child's intent to learn to spell.

Intention to do something has to be tied to the belief that one is capable of doing that thing and is willing to risk doing it. In order for children to be willing to risk doing something, they must understand that it is all right to make mistakes, that making mistakes is a natural part of learning. Our students will believe this if we look at their mistakes qualitatively, praising them for the part of a misspelled word they have spelled correctly and providing them with minimal cues to spell the rest of the word. We do this in the context of the child's own meaningful writing, but we never interrupt the writing process to do so, unless the child asks. We encourage the correction of spelling at the editing stage of writing, not during the initial writing period during which nothing should interrupt the formulation and recording of ideas.

Demonstration, intent, and the belief that one is capable of doing something are all part of motivation to learn. Now we come to the learning process itself: doing something, or testing one's hypothesis about how to do something, receiving feedback, and integrating what has been learned into what one already knows. Frank Smith has frequently said that we have learned nothing unless we can relate it to something else that we know. A child needs to attempt to spell a word (that is, to test his or her hypothesis about how to spell the word), to receive feedback, and then to relate what he or she has learned about the spelling of a particular word to what he or she knows about the spelling of other words. Learning to spell, like learning anything else, involves thinking. It is not merely a matter of memorizing lists of words.

When teachers regard spelling as a thinking process based on prior knowledge, they realize that many of the words that young children write will inevitably be misspelled. They also recognize that using functional or inventive spellings gives children the power to get their ideas down and to learn about the writing process; in fact, they become writers. At the same time, the teacher models standard spelling while being careful not to be concerned about spelling during the writing of a rough draft, or during the revision of ideas and how they are expressed and organized.

I do believe that standard spelling is important. I believe that if anything is going to defeat the whole language movement, it will be the way we handle spelling. I have just come from working in a school and have heard the remarks of some parents. Even though this is a school in which every teacher, supported by the principal, is emphasizing spelling within the context of students' meaningful writing and reading, a few of the parents still believe that spelling is not being taught unless it is a subject isolated from other aspects of language learning.

Criticism is coming not just from parents of school children, but also from the business community and other educators. Whole language teachers must satisfy their critics, or their critics will take charge of programs. When critics say that whole language teachers do not care about how kids spell, we must convince them that we do care, that we understand how the ability to spell develops, and that we are providing appropriate feedback. We must be able to present evidence of our students' growing ability in learning to spell. We must help parents and the general public to understand the roles of both standard spelling and functional or inventive spelling; help them to see that we allow our students to use approximations of spelling as they learn to spell, in the same way that they, as parents, allowed their children to use approximations of oral language while learning to speak.

We must help parents to realize that misspellings are not random, but are based on the knowledge that the child has. Janet Potter, a grade-one teacher, told me how one of her students had spelled the word *went* as "YT." What the student was doing made sense to Potter as she compared the movements of the mouth, tongue, and jaw when she said "went" and when she said "Y-T." The student was making connections between what she knew about producing a word and producing certain letters of the alphabet.

How one predicts the spelling of a word depends on the prior knowledge that one is able to bring to the process. This could include the use of knowledge about sound production ("Y-T" for *went*), rules governing sound-symbol relationships (putting a silent *e* in *ride*), how meaning affects the spelling of a word (*explain*, therefore *explanation*), and about words that follow the same spelling convention (such as doubling the final consonant before adding a suffix).

It takes years of experience to build the kind of knowledge (most of it implicitly built from many experiences in writing and reading) that enables a person to spell, with a high degree of success, many words that he or she has never spelled before. During this time, one's beliefs about what is involved in spelling undergo some major changes. Learning to spell is therefore a developmental process. As teachers, we need to understand this and to have some knowledge of the developmental stages through which our students pass so that we are able to provide the kind of feedback that will help them operate more effectively at their particular stage of development and move beyond that stage to a more advanced one.

How Literate Adults Use the Spelling Process

We predict the spelling of a word using graphophonic cues (sound-symbol relationships). We know, because of our experiences, that these cues are not always reliable. We have heard about research in which computers, which were programmed with many rules about sound-symbol relationships, still misspelled many more words than students who knew few of these rules in an explicit way. We have read in Frank Smith's (1978) study that a total of over two hundred spelling-sound correspondences were identified in just 6,092 one- and two-syllable words used by nine-year-old children; that 166 rules and 45 exceptions to the rules governing vowels and consonants and another 69 rules for grapheme units could be identified using this small sample of simple words. In other words, the connection between sound and symbol is a complex one. We know that such things as dialect, meanings, and spelling conventions interfere with the use of graphophonic cues. The comedian Gallagher once had a routine in which the word *tomb* was pronounced to rhyme with *bomb*. This mispronunciation corrected, the word *comb* was then pronounced to rhyme with the now-correct *tomb*. The progression continued with other mispronunciations or misspellings, such as *fomb* for *foam* since it is pronounced to rhyme with *comb*.

We predict the spelling of a word using semantic (meaning) and syntactic (grammar) cues, and we know from experience that these cues often override phonic cues. We use word meanings to help us spell homophones such as *there, they're,* and *their.* We use meaning units within words (*telephone, telegraph*) to help us with difficult unstressed vowels. We are familiar with inflections that show plurality, possession, comparison, and change in subject, tense, or time. We look at the words within compound words, and we recognize blends, such as *smog* from *smoke* and *fog.* We are able to go back to the meaning of contractions to help us place the apostrophe correctly. We use meaning to help us spell the suffixes in words such as *hostess* and *stewardess.* We have learned spelling conventions such as function words having two letters, but not other words (*in, inn; by, buy*). We have learned some of the conventions about when to double consonants when adding a suffix, but this is still one of the most prevalent spelling problems for even advanced spellers.

We confirm or disconfirm our attempts at spelling. Some combinations of letters rarely or never occur, and when we try to write them, it feels unnatural and awkward. Here the muscular sequence encourages us to check out the spelling. In other cases, our store of knowledge about how the spelling system works helps us to confirm or disconfirm a particular spelling. This is probably one of the side products of reading, although very rapid readers may not acquire as much power from this confirming technique as those who read less rapidly. Auditory memory is another confirming technique. Some people have a keen auditory memory for the rhythm of the oral spelling of a word. Mnemonic devices are another technique. An example of a mnemonic device in spelling is the deliberate mispronunciation of a word in such a way that it provides a cue to the spelling of the word. Such references as dictionaries and computers offer further assistance. I use a spelling-check program on my word processor, but it lets me down by being unable to suggest the correct spelling of some words which may have only one letter out of place and by accepting any spelling that is the correct spelling of a word although it may not be a word that is acceptable in the context of the writing. I can check out an almost endless number of alternatives in my dictionary, while my word processor stores only a few. In any case, the more I know about the spelling of words, the more effectively I am able to use either the spelling checker or the dictionary.

We relate or integrate what we have discovered about the spelling of a word with what we know about the spelling of other words. We form a network of associations among words which assists our memory and sets out pathways to aid recall when memory fails.

How Our Students Use the Spelling Process

Our young students have neither our knowledge nor our understandings about how the spelling system works. They can use only what they know about the spelling of words and their own beliefs about how to spell. By identifying patterns of misspellings, and also by noting students' successes in predicting standard spelling, researchers have discovered stages of development through which children progress as they journey toward the final stage of learning to spell.

Perhaps it is necessary at this time to explain that the word *stage* is being used here to indicate that there are periods during which students use only one specific technique to spell all the words that they are using. Many things are happening, but it becomes clear from an analytical examination of numerous misspellings that threads or patterns of misspellings emerge; that these patterns follow a sequence; and that as children develop as spellers, the predominant pattern of their misspellings changes, and the power to remember and to predict standard spellings grows.

I read *Developmental and Cognitive Aspects of Learning to Spell* (Henderson and Beers 1980) when it was first published, and was somewhat skeptical of the idea of developmental stages in learning to spell. Since that time, I have analyzed hundreds of misspellings made by elementary students. It has become very clear to me that these students were not simply trying to remember how a word was spelled, but that they were creating their own systems about how to spell words, based on their own discoveries and what they believed to be true about how to spell. It also became obvious that the same patterns of misspellings occurred even though the children making them had different teachers using different approaches to teaching reading, writing, and spelling.

I became overwhelmed with a sense of the power that very young children have within themselves to express their ideas in writing using a method of spelling that no one had taught them but that grew out of the things they had discovered for themselves. Young children are able to use their own cues about how to spell and are able to write messages that we can actually read. They demonstrate, in an awe-inspiring way, that they are thinkers.

The great bonus that comes out of understanding something about the developmental aspects of learning to spell is the connection that we now can make between spelling instruction and the real world of what children know and are practicing in their attempts to spell.

Many of us have benefited from learning about miscue analysis from the work of Ken and Yetta Goodman, Dorothy Watson, Carolyn Burke, and others. Miscue analysis is a form of analyzing how students are using the reading process. Teaching strategies to help students use the process more effectively are always a part of reading instruction for those who use miscue analysis. We look at misspelling analysis in the same way. Once we understand how a student is using the spelling process of predicting, confirming, and integrating spelling, we can use this information to help the student become a better speller. We can provide the kind of feedback that the student requires. All language learning requires feedback, but it is most important in learning to spell because writers are presented with a blank piece of paper, and how they represent their ideas graphically must come from within themselves or from some source beyond the pencil and paper. Print provides feedback to the reader; but it is absent for the writer, at least until he or she has attempted to write a word.

The Pre-phonetic Stage

At one time, many of us did not regard young children's early drawings and scribbles as having anything to do with learning to spell. We now understand their significance due to the research and writing of people like Ferreiro and Teberosky (1982) and Temple, Nathan, and Burris (1982). Children at the pre-phonetic stage represent objects and ideas symbolically through their drawings and scribbles. Even though they are trying to represent objects and ideas and not the words that stand for them, these children have taken the first major step in learning to spell.

Instructional Strategies for Pre-phonetic Spellers

Teaching strategies for pre-phonetic spellers have the following two goals.

To encourage writing. Make sure that a variety of writing materials is available to children, and respond to their efforts. Do not interfere, but observe any changes in the groupings of their scribbles, in the ordering of any symbols that they use, or in their use of letters when these occur. Model writing.

To make connections. Help young children make connections between the words used for objects and ideas and how these words are represented in writing. Label things. Use name labels for lockers and possessions. Put children's names on their writing papers, write the names of the people about whom the children talk, play games with name cards. Respond to the request "How do you write ———?" Take dictation from the children about their drawings, and write their ideas on experience charts. Have the children memorize poems and nursery rhymes, and then present the poems and rhymes in print on chart paper. Read to the children every day, and encourage parents to read to their children and to model personal reading and writing activities.

The Early Phonetic Stage

Because of their own experiences with print, and from watching others read and write, children begin to realize that words themselves, not objects or ideas, hold the key to spelling. The amazing thing is that they do not use the sound of the word, but how they produce the word. They make a connection between what happens with the mouth, tongue, and jaw when they say the names of the letters of the alphabet, and what happens with the mouth, tongue, and jaw when they say a particular word. It is unlikely that they are aware that this is what they are doing. At this time, children might write the letter *f* for *off*, *prk* for *park*, *brdr* for *brother*, *jp* for *jump*. Their writing may look something like that in Figure 9.1: "I want some candy." Gradually vowels will appear, and more letters will be used to represent a word as children begin to move into the advanced phonetic stage.

The Advanced Phonetic Stage

Advanced phonetic spellers begin to try to reflect every change that occurs in the production of words, and they begin to use quite a few vowels when they write. As there are no names of the letters of the alphabet that are the same as the short vowel sounds in words such as *bet, up, sat,* and *hit*, children are likely to write these words as in Table 9.1. (Although some letters are not produced in exactly the same way

Figure 9.1. Writing sample of a young child at the early phonetic stage.

as the names of the letters of the alphabet, there are strong similarities.) A pattern of advanced phonetic spelling can be seen in the following writing sample:

> Abta Wan I Go To my frAS Home
> I SAD TO my MOM KAN I SLep OVr
> My [mom] SAD OK BAt Be Good
> I DADE
> We SLep tpGATr JASt me AND my frAD
> WAN We WoK up I SAE a BrD LAINg eggs
> The Egg was green
> WAN I Et BArst my FAD PK 1 Egg
> I SAD Pt It BK
> WAN HeS PAT It BAK the Brd Bet Hhr fAGr
> I WAt HOMe

Instructional Strategies for Phonetic Spellers

Teaching strategies for both early phonetic and advanced phonetic spellers have the following two goals.

To help children use phonetics more effectively. Throughout our lives, how sounds are produced is a part of spelling words, but these cues are of limited value and often lead to the kinds of misspellings seen in the above examples. In the early stages of spelling, sound production cues are the main cues available to children. Therefore, make sure that

Table 9.1. Common Phonetic Spellings of the Short-Vowel Sounds

Word	Phonetic Spelling	Explanation
bet	bat	*e* is pronounced like the name of the letter *a*
up	ip	*u* is pronounced like the name of the letter *i*
sat	sit	*a* is pronounced like the name of the letter *i*
him	hem	*i* is pronounced like the name of the letter *e*

they know the names of the letters of the alphabet. Encourage young students at this stage of their development to play with alphabet cards, magnetic letters, and alphabet blocks. Have them produce alphabet scrapbooks and sing alphabet songs. Label things and notice the letters at the beginning and end of some words when doing experience charts. Play "I Spy," and use students' name cards in many ways, perhaps categorizing them by initial or final letters. Do not ignore the fact that students must know something about the alphabet in order to attempt to spell anything, but avoid using the above activities in a way that is reminiscent of traditional drill methods.

To help children move beyond the phonetic stages to using actual sounds to help them spell. Take dictation from the children for experience charts and captions for the children's own drawings. Read simple Big Books over and over again with the children. Have them memorize nursery rhymes, poems, and songs, and when they know the words well, present the print on a chart. Read and talk about environmental print seen on walks outside, throughout the school, and within the classroom. Print simple morning messages, and talk, write, and read about the weather or the day's timetable. Above all, at this and every stage that follows, read to the children every day, and provide time for all children to read and write, even beginners. Provide experiences which will enrich their lives, develop concepts, and extend their vocabularies. Talk to parents about what you are doing, and why you are doing it.

The Phonics Stage

Phonics has to do with generalizations or rules about sound-symbol relationships. As children move into the phonics stage, the major pattern of their misspellings changes from misspellings caused from using phonetics (sound production cues) to misspellings from using phonics. When students begin to use phonics, they try to reflect every subtlety of pronunciation, and write such things as *riade* for *ride* and *wene* for *when*. They spell words in the way in which they hear the words pronounced and thus write *budder* for *butter* and *hafta* for *have to*. They have seen a combination of vowels used to represent certain sounds but do not know which combination of vowels to use, and so they may write *nies* for *nice*, or *tode* for *toad*. They will double consonants where a single consonant is needed, and use a single consonant where a double consonant is required, as in *latter* for *later*, or *pas* for *pass.* They overgeneralize, writing *whent* for *went* because they have just learned to spell *when.*

Although they know one vowel will not do in certain kinds of words, they are confused about the placement of vowels and may write *tierd* for *tired, daer* for *dear, freind* for *friend.* They have trouble with unstressed vowels and may write *compny* for *company* or *reluctent* for *reluctant.* (This is a problem that haunts many older writers who have not moved to the next stage, where meaning becomes an important cue in the spelling of words.)

Instructional Strategies for Phonic Spellers

Teaching strategies for phonic spellers have the following two goals.

To help children use phonics more effectively. Use poetry in which the rhyming words end in different strings of letters to help students develop the understanding that the same sound may be represented in different ways. Use selected poems to show that many words that rhyme end in the same string of letters. When helping a student with the spelling of a word, suggest another word that has the same spelling pattern and encourage the student to add other words that fall into the same orthographic pattern. When a student asks how to spell a word like *though,* provide the cue needed, likely the *-ough* ending. Also suggest another word that has this orthographic pattern but is pronounced differently, such as *rough.* These *-ough* words can cease to be a problem when students keep a record of the words as they are encountered and consider the words as having the same spelling pattern. Encourage students to play with words in the way H. R. Wittram (1966) does with *A maker of boxes,* which becomes *a baker of moxes, bong loxes, bare squoxes,* and so on. This is a fun way to draw attention to how words are constructed. List in a special place a few words that cause problems for a number of students in the class and make the students responsible for the correct spelling of these words whenever they edit their writing. Recategorize brainstormed words according to spelling patterns. Always, no matter at what stage of development a student may be, insist that he or she attempt the spelling of the word before you give any assistance.

To help phonic spellers change. We want phonic spellers to begin to use syntax and meaning when spelling words. The natural way to get into this is through the spelling of homophones (*pear, pare, pair*), contractions (*can't, don't*), and word derivations (*please,* therefore *pleasant*). Deal with these when they occur in the child's own writing.

The Syntactic-Semantic Stage

At this stage, the student has come to the realization that meaning and grammar provide important cues which, in many cases, take precedence over sound cues. Because the focus in this chapter is on primary students, who are just beginning to move into this stage, I discuss it very briefly. The focus of instruction is on word meanings, meaning units within words, and meaning units shared between words. Particular attention needs to be paid by teachers to the spelling of *too*, *there*, and *their*, because these three words are the most misspelled words throughout the elementary grades. Some strategies which will help the students use meaning in the spelling of words follow.

Draw attention to root words: for example, when students spell *interesting* as *intrasting*, have them think of the root word *interest*. If they spell *usually* as *usaly*, help them go back to the root *usual*. If they spell *minerals* as *minnerals*, and *mining* as *minning*, have them think of the root word *mine*. When they omit the apostrophe in contractions, have them write the contraction in its full form and then place the apostrophe where they think a letter is missing. For example, if they write *dont*, have them write *do not* in full; then have them write the shortened form, putting in an apostrophe where a letter has been dropped.

By this stage, students will spell many words in standard form. When they do misspell words, these are often words that contain more than two syllables. If this is the case, have students clap out the syllables or say the word, breaking it into syllables. For example, if they spell *presentation* as *presentaion*, have them say *pre-sen-ta-tion* to help them spell the word. We noticed that one grade-five student spelled correctly almost all the words that she used in a long story about a new teacher in the school, but when she tried to spell *secretary*, she wrote *starity*, and when she tried to spell *principal*, she wrote *presple*. Her other spellings indicated that she probably had enough knowledge to spell these words correctly with little help, but she was confused because she had not broken the words down into manageable parts.

Syntactic-semantic spellers use more suffixes when they write, and so they need to formulate rules for themselves about spelling conventions, such as doubling a final consonant when adding a suffix. One student wrote *shopping* at first in her story and then later wrote *shoping*. She was ready for some guidance in formulating a workable rule, which could be done by the teacher telling her that the correct spelling is *shopping*, asking her to write *shopping* in her spelling notebook, suggesting another word that was similar, such as *dropping*, and encouraging the student to add other words that she encountered in which the final consonant was doubled when a suffix was added. Then the student could formulate and test her own hypothesis about when consonants should be doubled. The same type of procedure could be used for words such as *preferred* and *preference,* where accent governs the doubling of the consonant *r.*

Spelling Evaluation

So far in this chapter I have discussed the following:

1. A philosophy of learning in which learners are regarded as thinkers bringing what they know to the process

2. A theory of learning to spell which is consistent with the learning process

3. The major patterns of students' misspellings that change as students acquire new information and insights about spelling

4. Strategies to help students become more proficient in what they are trying to do, and strategies to help students develop new understandings about how to spell

Evaluation will identify a student's level of spelling development and will reveal growth in spelling ability. Misspelling analysis is a form of spelling evaluation which will do both. It can be done informally on an ongoing basis, but there are advantages to doing a formal misspelling analysis. Data are recorded in an organized form and can be used to show parents how we evaluate a student's progress and how we use information from the evaluation to provide the kind of instruction most appropriate for the student.

There is space to give only a very brief introduction to misspelling analysis here. Those who wish to explore it further can find an explanation, examples, and forms for recording, assessing, evaluating, and reporting spelling in *Spelling for Whole Language Classrooms* (Buchanan 1989). In order to find out how students are using the spelling process, we code each aspect of a misspelling using one or more of the following categories:

1. The misspelling is *phonetic* (*kam* for *came, wat* for *went*).

2. The misspelling is related to using *phonic cues* (*whent* for *went*).

3. The misspelling is the wrong form of a homophone (*pear* for *pair*).

4. A suffix is misspelled (*laught* for *laughed*).

5. The misspelling has to do with the root within a word (*expli-nation* from ignoring the root *explain*).

6. The misspelling has to do with punctuation (*dont* for *don't*). Note that miscues coded 3, 4, 5, and 6 all indicate the student is not using *meaning cues.*

7. Standard spellings. Here we record most of the correct spellings of beginning writers, or significant standard spellings of more advanced spellers. (We would record, for instance, the correct spelling of the words *furnish* and *furnished* if the student had misspelled *furnishing* as *furnashing.*)

8. We note apparent misspellings which are due to faulty penmanship, such as the connections in cursive writing between *b, w, v,* and *o* with other letters, and problems with cursive writing of *m* and *n.*

In misspelling analysis, we code about forty misspellings and record correct spellings taken from unedited pieces of the student's writing. When we do this, we clearly see the major pattern of the student's misspellings, and we have the data for working out percentages of errors caused from a student's use of phonetic and phonic cues and from not using meaning cues. Our evaluation is complete once we have: (1) recorded our evaluation from the analysis; (2) compared this evaluation with earlier evaluations; (3) noted our observations about the student's feelings about spelling, willingness to take a risk, interest in spelling, use of resources, willingness to do quick spelling checks and to edit, and ability to identify possible misspellings; (4) noted plans for instruction based on the evaluation; and (5) written a brief overall evaluation in which we noted the following:

1. *The student's progress*—the purpose of this is to draw attention to the student's accomplishments over a period of time.

2. *The student's progress in terms of the teacher's expectations of students in that grade*—the purpose of doing this is to make sure that parents understand what is happening. We must be honest with parents, but we also must help them respect, support, and encourage learners who are doing their best. Making mistakes rarely means that students are not trying. Both teachers and parents must realize that making mistakes is a natural part of learning. When we are critical of students for making mistakes, we discourage them and make them unwilling to risk, and we thus inhibit the learning process. We must take mistakes as our cues for the type of instruction the student needs (Buchanan 1989, 89).

Strategies to Use with Elementary Children at Every Stage of Spelling Development

Recently I had a satisfying and enriching experience with the staff of Chapman Elementary School in Winnipeg, Manitoba. Together we planned and held an evening with parents on the teaching of spelling. The staff had already had a series of meetings with parents to explain other aspects of their curricula. Spelling was chosen as the subject for this meeting because some parents had expressed their concern that spelling was not being taught. They believed this to be the case because the formal spelling period had been dropped, and they thought the teacher "did not care how the kids spelled."

At the meeting, I briefly introduced my philosophy of learning and talked about the spelling process and learning to spell. The teachers then talked about strategies that they were using to help their students develop as spellers. Most of the strategies listed below were used throughout their school, and the examples given are all from their students.

Always remember that all children are different. This is not, of course, a specific strategy, but it is the key to all teaching. Some of the differences are obvious, but even children who appear to be at the same "level" have different strengths and needs. Pat Kozak, the grade-one teacher, did what many grade-one teachers do on the first day of the term. She asked her children to draw. Figure 9.2 demonstrates the range of artistic development for children in the same class.

Model standard spelling. Be careful to spell, in standard form, words on charts, brainstormed words, and other examples of your writing around the room. Encourage the children to draw your attention to any misspellings that you may happen to make. When you display students' work that has not been edited for spelling, label it in some way, such as "Our Rough Drafts." Respond to children's writing, modeling the correct spelling of some words that they have misspelled. Joanne Jaeger's response to the writing of one of her grade-two students is shown in Figure 9.3.

Write good-morning messages. Write messages on the chalkboard, leaving blanks for some of the words. You might provide an occasional letter at the beginning of a missing word or supply an interior letter. Good-morning messages may be very simple, perhaps a greeting and some comment about the weather, or a message about something that is going to happen on a particular day. The message

Figure 9.2. Drawings made by four grade-one students on the first day of school.

could be a review, with key words omitted, of a social studies or science unit that has just been completed. Shawna Bradley, the grade-five/six teacher, wrote the dialogue shown in Figure 9.4, omitting the words *going, come, coming, hope, getting, hoping, thinking, skip, skipping,* and *go* to see if her students could spell these words correctly and if they could then formulate an hypothesis about adding *-ing* to different one-syllable words.

Enjoy a poem of the week. Poetry, rhymes, and chants are fun. Everyone has a favorite poem. Find a poem you love, and chances are good that your students will enjoy it, too. Read it to them. Reread it

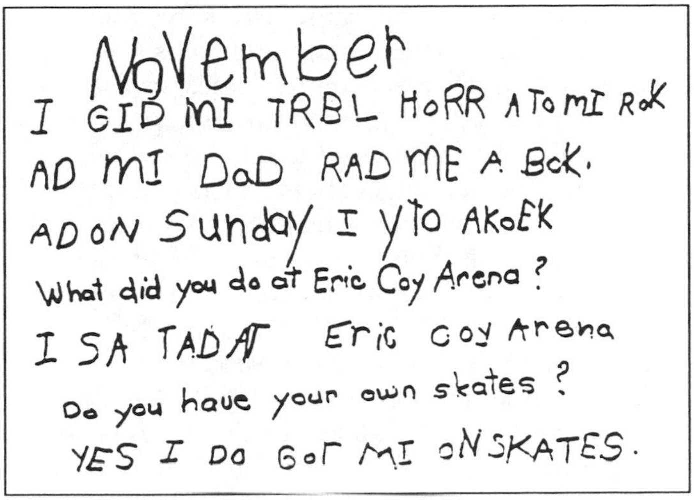

NoVember
I GID MI TRBL HoRR ATo MI RoK
AD MI DoD RAD ME A BoK.
AD oN Sunday I yTo AKoEK
What did you do at Eric Coy Arena ?
I SA TADAT Eric coy Arena
Do you have your own skates ?
YES I DO Gor MI oNSKATES.

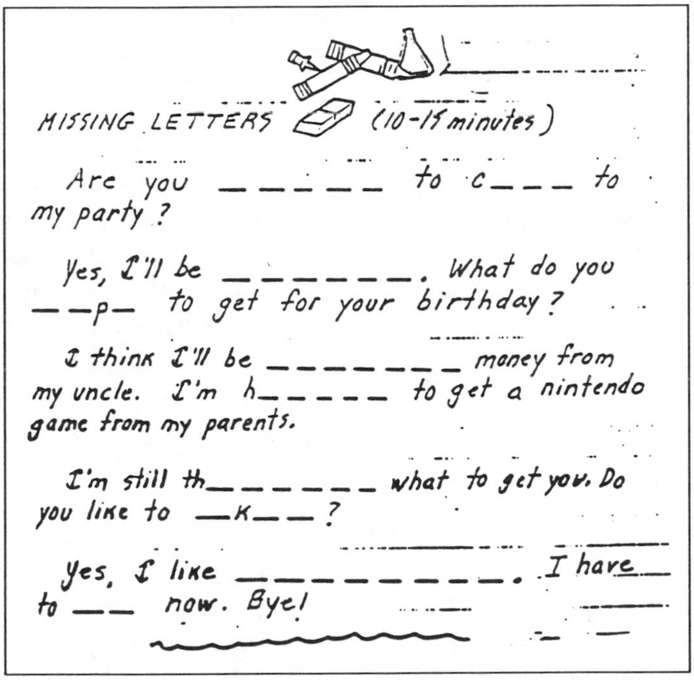

MISSING LETTERS (10-15 minutes)

Are you _ _ _ _ _ to c_ _ _ to
my party ?

Yes, I'll be _ _ _ _ _ _ _ _. What do you
_ _p_ to get for your birthday ?

I think I'll be _ _ _ _ _ _ _ _ money from
my uncle. I'm h_ _ _ _ _ _ to get a nintendo
game from my parents.

I'm still th_ _ _ _ _ _ what to get you. Do
you like to _ K_ _ ?

Yes, I like _ _ _ _ _ _ _ _ _ _. I have
to _ _ _ now. Bye!

Figure 9.3. Written dialogue between a grade-two student and a teacher.

Figure 9.4. Incomplete dialogue for grade-five/six students to fill in.

and let them fill in the words when you pause. Print the poem on a chart and read it with the children every day, perhaps as a response poem, having groups or individuals read different lines; or use it as a choral reading, or as a chant if suitable. Sometimes, when you know your students have internalized a poem, ask them to write their comments about the poem and the spelling patterns of rhyming words they have observed. Figure 9.5 shows the comments that one of Karen Kroft's grade-three students wrote about the poem of the week.

Some poetry books or works in verse that you might enjoy using in your classroom are *The Lady with the Alligator Purse* by Nadine Bernard Westcott (Little, Brown, 1988), *Oodles of Noodles* by Margaret Roc and Allan Stomann (Hodder and Stoughton, 1987), *Blue Frog and Other Poems* by Orin Cochrane (Whole Language Consultants, 1982), *Under the Sunday Tree* by Eloise Greenfield (Harper and Row, 1988), *The Day the Goose Got Loose* by Reeve Lindbergh (Dial Books for Young Readers, 1990), *Annabel Lee* by Edgar Allan Poe (Tundra Books, 1987), *The Cremation of Sam McGee* by Robert Service (Kids Can Press, 1987, and in numerous poetry collections), and *Sitting on the Farm* by Rob King and Bill Slavin (Kids Can Press, 1991).

Do daily edits. Do not overdo these or make the task long and boring. On the chalkboard, write a few sentences containing the kind of errors on which you would like to have the students focus because of the misspellings that you are finding in their writing. As the students arrive in the room, have them try to locate all misspellings and suggest correct spellings. Some examples of possible errors are listed below:

Hellow

smil

did anyone brig there hamburger mone or book order?

it is fryday i hop u hav a good week end

Have students identify likely misspellings. When students have finished a rough draft, ask them to look it over and circle words that they believe are misspelled. One teacher encourages students to try out a few different possible spellings and to identify the one most likely to be correct. Sometimes a partner helps with this. It is revealing how successful students are at identifying their own misspellings. This activity provides good material for an individual spelling conference. A draft written by one of Joanne Jaeger's grade-two students appears in Figure 9.6, with misspellings circled by the student.

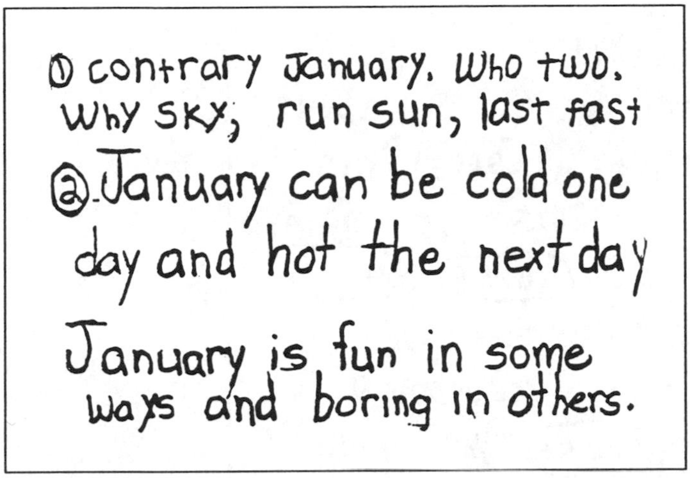

① contrary January. Who two.
Why sky; run sun, last fast
②.January can be cold one
day and hot the next day

January is fun in some
ways and boring in others.

Figure 9.5. Written comments of a grade-three student about the poem of the week.

Have students think about spelling. Pat Kozak asked her grade-one students to indicate what they did to help them spell words. Some of their responses are given below:

> I sound the words and letters.
>
> I copy them from the good-morning letter.
>
> I see them in different places: good-morning letter, poems, books.
>
> Practice writing my words in my weekend news. By rhyming words. My first was cat. I learned rat and bat. I look for words in newsletters.
>
> I get words everywhere: chalkboard, poems, and walls.

These students knew and used the available references. Karen Kroft asked her grade-three students to write what they thought she expected of them in regard to spelling. The following response provides important information about one child's own spelling development and attitude toward spelling:

> Mrs. kroft expects me to take my time when i'm spelling and not to rush. Also to do the best i can. I am doing really well spelling. Now i only have a coplc of words in my journail.

Initiate a discussion about spelling with those students who you think are ready for it. You could prepare a variation of Carolyn Burke's reading inventory and ask for students' responses to questions such as the following:

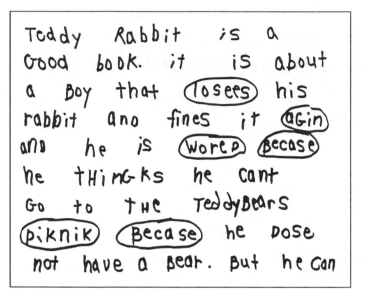

Figure 9.6. Likely misspellings in rough draft identified and circled by its grade-two author.

- When you are writing a rough draft and don't know how to spell a word, what do you do?
- What is standard spelling? Is it important? Why, or why not?
- When should you edit for spelling?
- What are some tricks you use to help you spell difficult words?

Hold individual spelling conferences. Many brief spelling conferences occur spontaneously as students seek a teacher's help while self-editing (and sometimes during the writing of a rough draft, although it is not a good idea to encourage this). A possible scenario for a spontaneous spelling conference appears below:

1. The student asks the teacher how to spell a word. The teacher asks the pupil to attempt to spell the word.

2. If the student misspells the word, the teacher supplies minimal cues to help the student write the word in standard spelling.

3. The student records the word and a related word (which may be suggested by the teacher) in a spelling notebook or on a chart. The words may be entered in a category such as a subject area, a theme, a spelling pattern, a word root, homophones, or a spelling convention, such as dropping *e* before adding *-ing.*

Teachers with whom I have discussed the idea believe there is value in scheduled spelling conferences as well as spontaneous ones. They identified the following benefits: empathy grows between teacher and student; the teacher can pay attention to the specific needs of the student; and the conference has a focus, is dynamic, and demonstrates to the student that standard spelling is important.

Adhering to the following description will help ensure successful spelling conferences:

1. The teacher understands the spelling process and how the ability to spell develops.

2. A schedule for spelling conferences has been drawn up in advance.

3. Before the conference, the teacher has examined a variety of writings done by the particular student and has a clear picture of the patterns of the student's misspellings and an idea of the extent of the student's repertoire of standard spellings.

4. The teacher has prepared a brief mini-lesson based on his or her observations. The purpose of the lesson is not to tell the student how to spell particular words, but to help the student develop insights as to how the spelling system works, using the student's own spellings as a starting point.

5. The student has assumed the responsibility of submitting to the teacher prior to the conference his or her spelling notebook and a portfolio of his or her own writing. Included in the portfolio should be a rough draft that the student has written, one in which the student has tried to identify his or her misspellings and has offered what he or she thinks are possible correct spellings. Both a student's first attempt at spelling and subsequent attempts at correcting misspellings supply information to the teacher.

6. The student leaves the conference believing that he or she does know something about how to spell and that he or she has learned something new.

7. A record of the conference is kept, preferably using the student's spelling notebook. When a conference is planned, a lot can happen in just five minutes. Instead of having a twenty-minute spelling period each day, try having four five-minute spell-

Figure 9.7. Pages from the spelling notebook of a grade-one student.

ing conferences while other students in the room are reading, writing, or working on projects. The accumulative benefits will surprise you.

Have students keep spelling notebooks. The spelling notebook might be used for categories of words from the child's writing, as is demonstrated by the pages from a notebook of one of Pat Kozak's grade-one students shown in Figure 9.7. The spelling notebook also might be used for recording spelling problems. Students from Karen Kroft's grade-three class and Shawna Bradley's grade-five/six class recorded

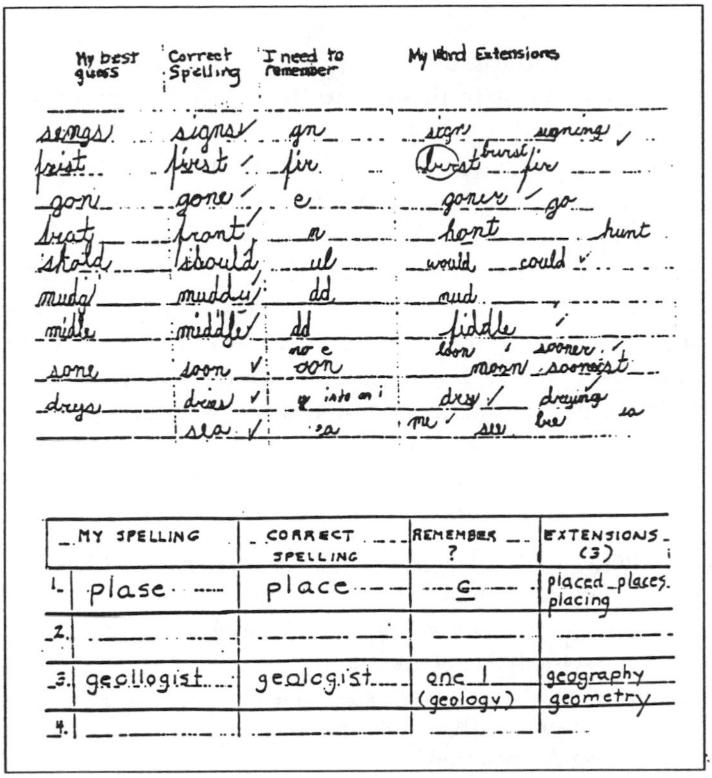

Figure 9.8. Pages from spelling dictionaries of a grade-three student (top) and a grade-five/six student (bottom).

spelling difficulties in the notebooks shown in Figure 9.8. Other entrees could be problem words listed for editing purposes, words that the students have categorized in preparation for writing, words with which students have received help, other words following the same orthographic patterns or observing the same convention, and words that are derivations of words that students have already learned.

What goes into the spelling notebook differs for each individual student and is dependent on the students' needs and the patterns of their misspellings. The notebook can be used as a record of one spelling conference and to open the next conference. Above all, items put in the notebook are to be referred to again. I like the idea of children occasionally sharing with partners what they have put in their notebooks and what they have learned as a result.

Conclusion

These general strategies are adaptable to any grade level and can focus on any aspect of spelling that is indicated by the students' own writing.

Having contact with teachers and hearing about what they are doing in their classrooms is always an inspiration to me. I was particularly excited about what was happening in Chapman School because all the teachers were working to improve spelling standards in their school and were doing this in the context of real reading and writing activities. They were adapting strategies to suit the children in their various classrooms. They were sharing their experiences with each other and with the parents of the children whom they taught.

References

Buchanan, E. 1989. *Spelling for whole language classrooms.* Winnipeg, Manitoba: Whole Language Consultants.

Ferreiro, E., and A. Teberosky. 1982. *Literacy before schooling.* Trans. Karen Goodman Castro. Exeter, N.H.: Heinemann.

Henderson, E. H., and J. W. Beers, eds. 1980. *Developmental and cognitive aspects of learning to spell: A reflection of word knowledge.* Newark, Del.: International Reading Association.

Smith, F. 1978. *Understanding reading: A psycholinguistic analysis of reading and learning to read.* 2d ed. New York: Holt, Rinehart and Winston.

Temple, C. A., R. G. Nathan, and N. A. Burris. 1982. *The beginnings of writing.* Boston: Allyn and Bacon.

Thomas, V. 1974. *Teaching spelling.* Agincourt, Ontario: Gage Educational Publishing.

Wilde, S. 1989. Looking at inventive spelling: A kidwatcher's guide to spelling, part 1. In *The whole language evaluation book,* ed. K. S. Goodman, Y. M. Goodman, and W. Hood, 213–26. Portsmouth, N.H.: Heinemann.

Wittram, H. R. 1966. A maker of boxes. In *Sounds of laughter* by B. Martin, 70–91. New York: Holt, Rinehart and Winston.

10 Understanding and Educating Attention-Deficit Students: A Systems-Theory, Whole Language Perspective

Constance Weaver
Western Michigan University

I begin this chapter by describing the hyperactivity of six-year-old Donald, who was brought to an Attention Deficit Hyperactivity Disorders clinic because all the teachers and school staff who had contact with him described him as being in constant motion; his classroom teacher, "though loving and patient, was exasperated by his intensity and drive." Donald's parents did not experience similar problems with him at home, but they brought him to the clinic because Donald's private school informed them that he would not be allowed to return to the school unless his hyperactivity was brought under control (Gordon 1991, 8–9). Experts at the clinic discovered, however, that Donald was bored at school. As psychologist Michael Gordon summarizes:

> It turns out that his favorite academic pursuit was teaching himself Chinese characters in the hope that one day he might travel to the Orient with his father (who was a college professor of languages). Donald was not about to attend to math problems he was able to manage in preschool when the lure of more stimulating material was at hand. When the teacher forbade his "doodling," he could not tolerate the daily tedium and decided to keep himself busy in more provocative and disruptive ways. (14)

This chapter was first published in 1991 in the Concept Paper Series of the National Council of Teachers of English.

Balanced against this story of overly hasty diagnosis of an attention-deficit disorder is the story of a child whose disorder remained
undiagnosed until high school. After a major suicide attempt, sixteen-
year-old John was hospitalized for depression. As his mother later told
the psychiatrist, yes, one of John's teachers had indicated that he had
a short attention span. But when John's second-grade teacher said that
he seemed to have a short attention span since he did not finish his
work, his mother pointed out that he found the work boring and that
he was quite capable of sustaining attention to something that interested him: in fact, he had recently spent three hours intently looking
for snails in the stream in Milham Park.

John's school years had passed fairly uneventfully until sixth
grade, when his teacher suggested private tutoring because this obviously bright child was receiving a D on a research project that he had
not completed. At the teacher's suggestion, her mother, a retired
teacher and experienced tutor, was hired. What ensued were expen-
sive hours spent jumping on the trampoline, practicing handwriting,
and trying to learn to organize his work. Somehow John finished
middle school on the honor roll. In high school, however, his work
quickly began to deteriorate. His ninth-grade algebra teacher commented that he was one of those people who might come up with a
new mathematical theorem but never get around to publishing it. The
next math teacher simply failed him in algebra time and again. John
demonstrated that he was quite capable of doing A+ work on creative
projects, while failing tests on detailed, factual material—even within
the same class. After two years of worsening depression, John attempted to commit suicide after admitting to his mother that when she
went to parent-teacher conferences that evening, she would find that
he had slipped from A to C work and worse in second-year French,
which he was taking for the second time. While hospitalized, John was
diagnosed as having an attention-deficit disorder.

The story of the initially misdiagnosed case of hyperactivity is
from Michael Gordon's *ADHD/Hyperactivity: A Consumer's Guide*
(1991). The story of the undiagnosed attention-deficit child is from my
personal experience. The John in this case is my son.

This personal experience has led to my professional interest in
what is at present officially known as Attention Deficit Hyperactivity
Disorder or ADHD (American Psychiatric Association 1987). My first
reaction to the psychiatrist's suggestion that John might have an attention-deficit disorder was disbelief. John clearly was not very hyperactive, and he repeatedly received A's and A+'s on major projects when

I helped him think through what needed to be done, guided him in developing a series of deadlines, and then supervised his completion of the work. Furthermore, I had read articles in the mid-1970s suggesting that there *was* no such disorder as "hyperactivity." This was a myth devised by parents and especially teachers who just could not, or would not, cope with the individual needs of the rambunctious and bored child. There was even a book called *The Myth of the Hyperactive Child: And Other Means of Child Control* (Schrag and Divoky 1975) that I vaguely recalled hearing about. Furthermore, as a whole language educator, I had become convinced that labeling children as disabled usually does more harm than good (e.g., D. Taylor 1990; Heshusius 1989; Poplin 1988a; and Coles 1987). Of course I was not about to accept the psychiatrist's tentative diagnosis.

But being a scholar as well as the parent of a child who was clearly in trouble, I began to read: a book on depression, articles and pamphlets on Attention Deficit Disorder (as it was then called), and even a book or two intended for pediatricians rather than the general public. What I found led me to reconsider not only the diagnosis of my son, but my previous knee-jerk tendency to consider all labeling of children as necessarily more harmful than beneficial. In a similar vein, I invite skeptics to willingly suspend disbelief long enough to consider the possibility that a simplistic rejection of labels might be an inadequate and unhelpful response to the cluster of behaviors sometimes labeled as Attention Deficit Hyperactivity Disorder.

In the following pages I first discuss social criticisms of the origin and consequences of the concept of ADHD and then suggest why a systems-theory reconceptualization of ADHD might be more practical as well as more satisfying theoretically. After discussing the concept, diagnosis, and "treatment" of ADHD in more detail, I concentrate upon effective strategies for educating students with an alleged Attention Deficit Hyperactivity Disorder.

Social Perspectives on ADHD

Clearly, the prevailing concept of ADHD is a medical one: those exhibiting significant problems in maintaining attention and restraining impulses are said to have a *disorder*, which implies some sort of malfunction within the individual. Until recently, however, the evidence for a biological basis to such behaviors was sketchy, and even now it is not conclusive. No wonder, then, that social critics have seized upon ADHD as one symptom of cultural values that they find reprehensible.

Schachar (1986) points out, for example, that the concept of "hyperkinesis"—which is the historical antecedent of today's ADHD—developed shortly after the turn of the century, when Darwin's concept of "survival of the fittest" was frequently invoked to explain and justify socioeconomic inequities that must surely, so the argument ran, develop from constitutional weaknesses in the poor. More generally, physiological differences were sought as explanation and justification for class differences. Thus physical evidence of brain damage leading to hyperactive behavior in a *few* individuals led to subsequent hypotheses of minimal brain damage or minimal brain dysfunction as the cause of hyperkinetic and related behaviors, even when no corroborating evidence was available.

Given the inconclusiveness of the evidence for a physical basis to a hyperkinetic syndrome, Schrag and Divoky raise different social criticisms in *The Myth of the Hyperactive Child* (1975). They are understandably concerned with a society and educational system that have so narrowed the definition of "acceptable" behavior and of "learning" that increasing numbers of children cannot succeed except by being labeled "deviant," with lowered expectations as to what constitutes learning and success. To the degree that parents try to fit their children into such an educational system and society, they are reinforcing that system and set of values, according to Schrag and Divoky.

Schachar points out, too, that positing a hyperkinetic syndrome in the absence of conclusive physiological evidence amounts to salving our individual and collective consciences. The concept of the hyperkinetic syndrome "has provided educators, politicians and parents with an explanation of failure of their children that imputes no failure or stigma to the school, parents, child or society" (Schachar 1986, 36). In short, the concept of ADHD assuages our guilt by absolving us of responsibility.

Selectively citing certain research studies, Coles derides the notion of a neurological factor in ADHD as a prelude to arguing that learning disabilities—both alleged and actual—are caused by environmental factors. He argues persuasively that if "the structural forces and relationships in the interactivity that produces educational failure are not addressed, challenged, and changed, the educational 'poor' will be with us forever" (1987, 213). (For other valid criticisms, see the well-researched 1989 article by Kohn).

The problem is that however well justified, these criticisms of the concept of ADHD offer no *immediate* hope or help to the children whose difficulties with attention, impulsivity, and hyperactivity are forever getting them into difficulties: at home, at school, on the playground, and in a myriad of social settings. In fact, Schrag and Divoky strongly imply that it is better to let our children fail than to help them succeed within such a flawed social and educational system. Few parents or teachers would willingly accept that alternative.

I suggest that what is needed is a *both/and* perspective: a perspective that simultaneously acknowledges the validity of the social criticisms and works toward changing society, but at the same time acknowledges and attempts to alleviate the very real difficulties of the children in our homes and schools right now—and the difficulties of those who live, work, and play with them. Each approach supports the other; they are two sides of a coin. It is only natural that some of us will be drawn more to the former task, and some to the latter.

Both/And Thinking: The Implications of a Transactional Paradigm

In my writings, I have often contrasted a mechanistic, "transmission" paradigm of education with the "transactional" paradigm that underlies whole language (Weaver 1985, 1988, 1990); others have used different terms for essentially the same paradigms (e.g., Heshusius 1989; Poplin 1988a, 1988b). According to the transactional, "relational" paradigm (Weaver 1991), learning is not simply transmitted from teacher to student, nor—at the opposite extreme—does it simply occur autogenously, out of the individual himself or herself. Learning requires transactions with an external environment: hence the emphasis on collaborative learning among whole language educators.

Historically, one of the "recent" antecedents for this way of thinking comes from quantum physicists, who study the behavior of particles smaller than the atom. Shortly after the turn of the century, they discovered that light is either a particle or a wave, depending upon how its characteristics are measured—or how the scientist "transacts" with the external environment. Or to put it differently, light is *both* a particle *and* a wave, depending upon how we view it (Zukav 1979).

I suggest that this *both/and* way of thinking is part of the intellectual heritage of a transactional paradigm, and part of the philosophical underpinnings of whole language—a philosophy of education that is further clarified by example in the discussion of how ADHD students can be educated more effectively.

A Systems View of ADHD

What does it mean to take a *both/and* view of ADHD? I think it means at least four things:

1. While trying to change the educational and social system to be more accepting of individual differences, we need to recognize that this will by no means solve all the problems caused by ADHD behaviors. Railing against the system is not enough: we also need to help the individual child and those who surround him or her.

2. It means recognizing that while ADHD may be characterized as difficulty in responding to certain kinds of expectations and demands, it may nevertheless have origins in the individual's neurological functioning—in biology and physiology.

3. It means recognizing that even the biological and physiological aspects of ADHD may stem from environmental rather than genetic causes, though heredity does often seem to be a factor.

4. It means not just "treating" or attempting to change the behavior of the individual, but changing our expectations and demands and our ways of interacting with the child, adolescent, or adult who exhibits ADHD behaviors.

This is in effect a general systems view (von Bertalanffy, as discussed in Davidson 1983), a view that rejects simplistic cause-effect reasoning and linear explanations, a view that sees causes as multidimensional and multidirectional: in short, a view compatible with and contributing to a whole language philosophy of education. See Figure 10.1 for a visual representation of this system's view of ADHD and the complex interrelationships that give rise to and alleviate ADHD behaviors.

Toward an Understanding of ADHD

Before continuing, it is important to note that children may have an attention-deficit disorder without impulsivity and hyperactivity. Girls, especially, seem more prone to this kind of attention difficulty (e.g., Lahey and Carlson 1991; Epstein et al. 1991).

Attention Deficit Hyperactivity Disorder, however, is characterized by problems in restraining impulses as well as in focusing and maintaining attention. Conservatively, it is estimated that 3–5 percent of the school-age population (probably from 1.4 to 2.2 million students) have such an attention deficit (Barkley 1990, 61). The hyperac-

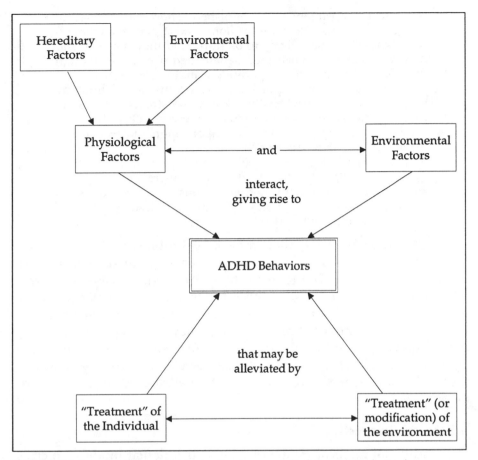

Figure 10.1. A *both/and* systems-theory model of the genesis and alleviation of ADHD behaviors.

tivity associated with ADHD is related to, and may very well stem from, the difficulty in restraining impulses. Barkley, a psychologist who is an expert on ADHD, calls this difficulty "behavioral disinhibition" (41–43).

In general, ADHD individuals appear virtually unable to resist acting upon impulses, including impulses to do something (anything!) other than boring schoolwork. These individuals—children, adolescents, and even adults—seem unable to use what they know about the social inappropriateness or probable consequences of their actions to control their behavior. As Barkley comments:

> Children may engage in disruptive, aggressive, or destructive behavior in the classroom—even though they know they're

likely to be reprimanded or punished. They may engage in dangerous actions or activities at home and at play, even though they "know" they are likely to be hurt. And they may say and do things that antagonize and alienate their peers, even though they "know better" and desperately want to be accepted.

Adolescents may impulsively exceed the speed limit by huge margins, even when they know the streets are heavily patrolled, when they've previously received tickets for such excesses, and when they "know" that one more violation could result in losing their driver's license.

Adults may engage in impulsive buying, even though they "know" their family cannot afford their extravagances, their spouse will be distraught by their actions, and one more such incident could be the last straw leading to a divorce they emphatically don't want. (41–43)

Of course, each situation reflects a complexity of factors, and people who do not have ADHD will also engage in such seemingly self-defeating actions. But to reiterate, ADHD individuals seem virtually *unable* to regulate their behavior by its likely consequences. They frequently seem unable to *choose* how they will act, based on what they know about how other people will react. They seem to be at the mercy of their emotions and impulses, which in turn are often reactions to the environment. Clearly the cause of ADHD behaviors cannot be attributed solely to the individual, but must be attributed to the environment as well.

A Medical Perspective

The traditional medical model of ADHD is a deficit model, which is why whole language educators and others have tended to reject the notion that there is such a thing as ADHD. Nevertheless, there is growing evidence that intractable impulsivity, hyperactivity, and inattentiveness may result from neurological structure and/or functioning. However, we might more appropriately think of *differences* in functioning, rather than deficits—and of quantitative rather than qualitative differences (Shelton and Barkley 1990, 214). These quantitative differences give rise to behaviors along a continuum, from what is socially desirable and functional for the individual to what is socially intolerable and self-defeating. Viewed this way, a medical perspective makes a valuable contribution to a broader systems view of ADHD.

Some recent studies suggest differences in size or functioning of different aspects of the central nervous system (Hynd et al. 1991; Klorman 1991). Blood flow studies and recent studies using high-tech procedures like Brain Electronic Activity Mapping (BEAM), Magnetic Resonance Imaging (MRI), and Positron Emission Tomography (PET) increasingly link ADHD to underfunctioning of certain neural pathways within the central nervous system (Barkley 1990, 29; Shelton and Barkley 1990, 211). Other lines of research suggest that what causes this "underfunctioning" may be an insufficiency of certain brain chemicals, most notably certain neurotransmitters like dopamine and norepinephrine (Zametkin and Rapoport 1987). A recent and widely publicized study by Zametkin and his colleagues at the National Institute of Mental Health used PET scans to confirm earlier findings of reduced glucose metabolism in the brains of ADHD adults, compared with others—particularly in the premotor cortex and the superior prefrontal cortex (Zametkin et al., 1990).

While there is no clear-cut evidence as to exactly what aspects of brain structure or functioning seem to be implicated in ADHD, researchers seem to be converging on evidence that ADHD behaviors derive from a biological/physiological condition, with heredity often a factor in a child's development of ADHD. I base this conclusion on a wider range of studies than those discussed in Coles (1987), including several studies that are more recent. Other causes may include brain damage, pregnancy factors (e.g., maternal consumption of alcohol) and birth complications, toxins (especially lead), infections, and diet. Sensational claims have been made about food additives or sugar causing hyperactive behavior (e.g., Feingold 1975), but a sizable body of research has failed to confirm these as common causes of ADHD (see discussions in Barkley 1990, 95–100; Gordon 1991, 69–72). Clearly, though, environment as well as heredity may contribute to the particular neurological functioning that seems to be a major component of ADHD.

This, then, is a succinct description of the medical contribution that I think must necessarily constitute part of a systems theory of Attention Deficit Hyperactivity Disorder—with a focus on *differences*, however, rather than deficits. And yes, I do think ADHD exists, with a neurological factor contributing to this social phenomenon: even though it is constantly being defined and redefined by the experts, even though researchers do not completely understand its causes or the mechanisms by which it operates, and even though there are significant disagreements as well as a significant degree of consensus within the field (Shaywitz and Shaywitz 1991). After all, there seems to be no more uncertainty or controversy about ADHD and what to do about it than there is about reading and how—or whether—to teach it.

A Sociological Perspective

As previous examples indicate, environmental factors may play a role in the genesis of ADHD, as well as in its definition and diagnosis. In addition, social and situational factors play a role in the maintenance and treatment of ADHD. For the moment, I focus on the maintenance of ADHD behaviors. People and situations can make it *harder* for ADHD individuals to restrain impulsive and hyperactive behavior and to pay attention, or they can make it *easier* to exercise self-control and maintain attention. The following excerpt from a session with a therapist provides an all-too-typical example of how a parent can exacerbate a teenager's ADHD behavior. The therapist's comments begin to clarify how, in systems theory, ADHD is viewed as an inter-action between the characteristics of the individual, on the one hand, and the demands, expectations, initiations, and responses from the external environment, on the other hand. In this case, we see how the mother exacerbates the teenager's predisposition:

> *Therapist:* So what are the major problems at home?
>
> *Mrs. Cohen:* Matthew's bad temper. He gets really angry for no good reason. Then he curses, yells, and is totally out of control.
>
> *Matthew:* You're full of it, Mom! I don't do that! You're just a nag!
>
> *Therapist:* Wait a minute, Matt. I know you feel strongly about this, but I have to check out something with your mother first. Give me a play-by-play description of a recent temper outburst.
>
> *Mrs. Cohen:* I said, "Don't you have homework?" He said, "No," and I said, "Come on, your teacher says she always gives homework. Tell us the truth." And . . .
>
> *Matthew:* See, there she goes bugging me and thinking I'm always lying.
>
> *Therapist:* Matthew, I know you feel strongly. And I can see how when your mom puts you on the spot about homework, you come out slugging.
>
> *Mrs. Cohen:* Doc, you got it. He actually ended up pushing and hitting me last night.
>
> *Therapist:* So, when you say that Matt loses his temper easily, you are talking about something between you and Matt, not just Matt. You ask nicely first. He doesn't answer. So you turn the screws a bit and press him, suggesting he is lying or holding back on you. He clobbers you back. We

> are looking at a sequence of communication between the two of you, not just one person losing his temper, right?
>
> *Mrs. Cohen:* I guess so, but it's his ADHD that makes him do it, not my question.
>
> *Matthew:* There she goes again, with that ADHD shit! Next she's going to tell you about Ritalin, "the miracle drug."
>
> *Therapist:* Matt, sounds like you get pretty mad and sarcastic when your mom blames your ADHD for everything. Mrs. Cohen, a person with ADHD is like a tightly stretched guitar string. The string can break if you pluck it too hard, but it must be plucked to break. Matt may be more likely to explode because of his biology, but it still takes your statement to set him off. And with the guitar, if you pluck the string just right, you can make beautiful music. You and Matt have the potential to get along with more harmony, even if his ADHD makes him like the tight string. This is a two-person problem. We need to change how you two communicate, not just Matt and not just Mom. (Robin 1990, 471–72)

Here we see the therapist reframing the problem: ADHD does not merely reside within the individual. Rather, it arises as the individual transacts with the external environment. In this sense, ADHD is something like Louise Rosenblatt's metaphorical concept of the "Poem," the meaningful rendering of a text (1978). A text has the *potential* to mean, yet meaning does not reside within the text: it arises as a reader transacts with the text and is influenced by various kinds of context. It is similar with ADHD: an individual has the *potential* for certain behaviors that characterize ADHD, but the extent to which and the ways in which these are manifested depend somewhat, and sometimes a lot, upon the external environment.

Situational demands can have a profound effect upon ADHD behaviors. For example, research clearly demonstrates that ADHD children have great difficulty attending to tasks that they find boring, such as completing dittos and worksheets. They find it much easier to attend to tasks that they find stimulating and meaningful. While some critics and even clinicians have assumed that such situational variation might automatically rule out a diagnosis of ADHD, other researchers have suggested that variation across situations might even be considered a defining characteristic of ADHD (Barkley 1990, 49). In other words, it may be primarily ADHD individuals who find it virtually impossible to complete boring tasks, yet somehow (or sometimes) they find it possible to complete what genuinely interests them.

At any rate, what emerges is a picture of ADHD as a "system" involving both individual characteristics and environmental influences. Within the life of an individual who is biologically/physiologically predisposed to certain kinds of behaviors, various forces intersect and interact: parents, teachers, and peers, for example; or home, school, neighborhood, and community. These participate in creating what is *perceived* as ADHD. It is a *both/and* phenomenon: both biological/physiological and sociological, involving the individual in transactions with society. Though I came to this systems conceptualization of ADHD independently, I have been pleased to discover that this is an emerging perspective among some psychologists who are experts on ADHD (Anastopoulos, DuPaul, and Barkley 1991; Barkley 1990; Robin 1990; Robin and Foster 1989; E. Taylor 1986; implicit also in Gordon 1991). See, in particular, Russell Barkley's *Attention Deficit Hyperactivity Disorder: A Handbook for Diagnosis and Treatment* (1990), a compendium and analysis of extant research that served as a major resource for this chapter.

Characterizing ADHD

The American Psychiatric Association is in the process of revising the "official" criteria for diagnosing ADHD. It seems likely that the forthcoming fourth edition of its *Diagnostic and Statistical Manual* will list the defining characteristics under two relatively separate behavioral dimensions, Inattention-disorganization, and Impulsivity-hyperactivity (e.g., Lahey and Carlson 1991).

Drawing upon and extrapolating from various sources in the professional literature, including the third edition and the third edition, revised, of the *Diagnostic and Statistical Manual,* I have developed my own partially idiosyncratic list of behaviors characteristic of ADHD. The *impulsivity* that now seems to be the major characteristic of ADHD can manifest itself in various ways, such as the following:

1. Difficulty in obeying rules—which may lead to difficulty in obeying the law

2. Interrupting people, calling out in class, talking incessantly in movies and while watching TV

3. Speaking irritably and angrily to people, with little or no provocation

4. Hitting others, or in some other way acting out negative emotions toward them

5. Responding impatiently or angrily when needs and wants are not immediately met, and when expectations or routines are changed; low tolerance for frustration

6. Tendency to do whatever catches interest and attention at the moment, regardless of consequences

7. Difficulty modifying behavior in the here-and-now to achieve desirable goals, particularly long-range goals

8. Tendency to be quarrelsome, argumentative; overly sensitive to teasing or criticism

Some of these characteristics are more typical of those defining an "Oppositional Defiant Disorder" than of those *officially* characterizing ADHD itself, but they occur in about 40–60 percent of ADHD individuals, particularly boys (Fletcher, Morris, and Francis 1991; Barkley 1990, 433; Szatmari, Boyle, and Offord 1989). To me, at least, these characteristics seem related to difficulty in refraining from acting upon impulses, particularly impulses triggered by emotion.[1] By the time the fourth or fifth edition of the *Diagnostic and Statistical Manual* is published, subtypes of ADHD will probably be specified—including, I expect, a subtype with oppositional and/or conduct disorder (Cantwell and Baker 1991; Dykman and Ackerman 1991). Meanwhile, Table 10.1 presents the current *Diagnostic and Statistical Manual* characterizations of ADHD, Oppositional Defiant Disorder, and Conduct Disorder, all of which co-occur with some frequency, but are not the same.

To be considered as having ADHD, children must exhibit not only impulsive and hyperactive behavior but difficulties in *focusing and maintaining attention.* The attention-related problems may also manifest themselves in a variety of related ways, such as the following:

1. Difficulty in attending to what someone is saying; easily distracted

2. Difficulty in listening to instructions; particular difficulty in grasping instructions consisting of several steps

3. Difficulty in settling down to work on a task

4. Difficulty in organizing work

5. Difficulty in attending to a task without being distracted or without getting restless or fidgety

6. Tendency to shuttle from one activity to another instead of focusing on one activity and completing it

7. Difficulty in following through on work until it is completed, particularly when the task involves several steps or requires sustained attention over a period of time

8. Tendency to regard lots of things as "boring," apparently because they require such an effort of concentration

Of course, each individual is unique in his or her particular constellation of characteristics.

It is important to realize that for those with ADHD, their various problems with impulsivity and attention may be severe and pervasive enough to cause difficulties in doing schoolwork, to create problems with parents and siblings at home, to create barriers to making friends and being accepted socially, to create problems on the job later on, and sometimes to get them in trouble with the law. Thus ADHD is a handicapping condition in general, not a learning disability or even a learning "difference." Furthermore, it is now recognized that at least

Table 10.1. Diagnostic Criteria for ADHD, Oppositional Defiant Disorder, and Conduct Disorder

Attention Deficit Hyperactivity Disorder	
1. Fidgets	9. Difficulty playing quietly
2. Difficulty remaining seated	10. Talks excessively
3. Easily distracted	11. Interrupts others
4. Difficulty waiting turn	12. Does not seem to listen
5. Blurts out answers	13. Loses things needed for tasks
6. Difficulty following instructions	14. Engages in physically dangerous
7. Difficulty sustaining attention	activities
8. Shifts from one uncompleted task to another	
Oppositional Defiant Disorder	
1. Argues with adults	5. Acts touchy or easily annoyed by
2. Defies adult requests	others
3. Deliberately annoys others	6. Angry or resentful
4. Blames others for own mistakes	7. Spiteful or vindictive
	8. Swears
Conduct Disorder	
1. Has stolen without confrontation	7. Has deliberately destroyed others'
2. Has run away from home overnight at least twice	property
	8. Physically cruel to animals
3. Lies	9. Has forced someone into sexual
4. Has deliberately engaged in fire setting	activity
	10. Has used a weapon in a fight
5. Truant	11. Initiates physical fights
6. Has broken into home, building, or car	12. Has stolen with confrontation
	13. Physically cruel to people

Source: American Psychiatric Association, *Diagnostic and Statistical Manual of Mental Disorders,* 3d ed., rev. (Washington, D.C.: American Psychiatric Association, 1987).

70–80 percent of the children diagnosed as ADHD are likely to exhibit many of these characteristics in adolescence, to a degree inappropriate for their age group, and an estimated 50–80 percent are likely to exhibit problems with impulsivity and inattention in adulthood as well (Barkley 1990, 114 and xi, respectively; see also Kane et al. 1990).

In sum, a definition and characterization of ADHD rests significantly upon what is functional for the individual within society. In effect, ADHD is a disorder defined by the expectations of society—an *interpretation* of behaviors that may have a biological/physiological basis, but that are certainly exacerbated by some kinds of environmental conditions and alleviated by others.

Assessing ADHD

As the opening anecdote illustrates, hyperactive behavior is not necessarily indicative of ADHD, nor is all failure to maintain attention or to inhibit impulses. Even for the trained clinician, it is not always easy to distinguish ADHD from other kinds of disorders, disabilities, or physical or emotional problems. Therefore, any attempt to diagnose ADHD, or to rule it out, should include at least the following: (1) extensive interviews with parents, the child, and, ideally, the teacher(s); (2) behavior-rating scales completed by parents and teacher(s); and (3) a medical examination. Where feasible, these can be supplemented by observations in natural settings and/or by laboratory tests of attention. But high-technology procedures like PET scans are not reliable enough for diagnosis, however appealing they might be (Shelton and Barkley 1990; Barkley 1990).

By themselves, neither the subjective behavioral rating scales nor the "objective" laboratory tests of attention are completely reliable as diagnostic tools (e.g., Barkley 1990, 328–34). To a significant degree, ADHD remains within the eye of the beholder, and different beholders see different things. Nevertheless, a clinician experienced with ADHD can usually make a fairly reliable diagnosis by considering various sources of information in concert with one another. Clearly, diagnosis is an art rather than a science—but then, so is our profession, teaching.

As an aid to diagnosis, there are quite a few behavioral checklists that can be used by parents, teachers, or both, keeping in mind that symptoms should be present to a degree inappropriate for the child's age and sex (Barkley 1990, 61–62). In his research compendium titled *Attention Deficit Hyperactivity Disorder,* designed as a practical guide for clinical practice, Russell Barkley (1990) describes and critiques a number of these checklists. One, for example, is based directly upon the current *Diagnostic and Statistical Manual*'s fourteen criteria for diagnosing ADHD. Parents and teachers are asked to rate the child with respect to each of these behaviors. Does the child exhibit the behavior not at all? Just a little? Pretty much? Very much? This is one of the rating scales that has been shown to discriminate ADHD children from learning-disabled and normal children, as well as to differentiate ADHD children from those who have problems with attention but not with impulsivity or hyperactivity (DuPaul 1990). This checklist and a number of others are included in a collection of procedures and forms for the clinician (Barkley 1991). Also valuable is the Copeland Symptom Checklist for Attention Deficit Disorders (Copeland and Love 1990), though it must be used with caution because some of the behaviors are symptomatic of often-related problems rather than of attention deficits per se.

Note that there is a crucial difference between the way learning disabilities are generally diagnosed and the way ADHD is diagnosed. Learning disabilities are attributed to children mainly as a result of their scores on decontextualized tests of isolated skills. In contrast, ADHD is diagnosed primarily when there is a mismatch between the expectations and demands of *everyday life* and what the child seems capable of doing. A diagnosis of ADHD may be typically less "objective," yet considerably more *real*.

Treatment of ADHD: A Systems-Theory Model

Consistent with the *both/and* systems-theory model developed here, "treatment" of ADHD will be considered under two separate headings, one dealing with the individual and the other dealing with the environmental aspects of the "system."

Treatment of the Individual

Unfortunately, the most certain statement that can be made about treatment of ADHD is that there is *no* treatment that consistently or typically produces long-term effects. This is consistent with the hypothesis that the disorder has a neurological basis or, more specifically, a biochemical basis. To date, even the chemical treatments for ADHD, such as Ritalin, work only for a few hours at a time, and unevenly at that. And both behavioral and cognitive approaches also seem to have limited effects, seldom generalizing or transferring to times or situations other than when the training programs are in effect (Pfiffner and

Barkley 1990, 538–39). Indeed, recent research suggests that most ADHD children are likely to demonstrate a significant degree of impulsivity and inattentiveness into and probably throughout adulthood, despite treatment during childhood and possibly adolescence. Again, these observations are consistent with the hypothesis of a neurological factor.

Research indicates that medication complemented by cognitive or behavioral therapy is more effective than any of the three common treatments alone. Next I briefly discuss each of these three approaches and then turn to a systems concept of ameliorating the behavioral omissions and commissions associated with ADHD.

Medication. Despite the controversy over Ritalin initiated by the Church of Scientology in the late 1980s (Baren 1989; Barkley [1990] references many of the original sources in his discussion, 34–36), its effectiveness and reasonable safety have been demonstrated in hundreds of research studies (but see Anastopoulos, DuPaul, and Barkley 1991; Whalen and Henker 1991). And though parents and teachers may rightly be concerned about "drugging" children to improve their behavior, using chemicals to stimulate brain functioning is perhaps no more reprehensible than using chemicals to stimulate, simulate, or improve any other aspect of bodily functioning.

Clearly there have been abuses in overprescribing Ritalin for children who do not genuinely have ADHD, and in not adequately determining the appropriate dosage or monitoring the drug's use. And clearly there is the possibility of negative side effects, most notably the possibility of initiating or exacerbating nervous tics (Tourette's syndrome), though this serious problem is relatively rare. On the other hand, 70–80 percent of children with ADHD do appear to exhibit a positive response to central nervous stimulants (Ritalin, Cylert, or less often Dexadrine), an improvement significantly greater than that perceived with placebos (DuPaul and Barkley 1990; Gordon 1991), and greater than the effects of most other treatments alone. That is, these medications typically reduce impulsive and hyperactive behavior and increase attentive behavior during the few hours for which each dose is effective.

Other medications, notably Impramine (a tricyclic antidepressant), have been used successfully with some children, especially those for whom the stimulants are ineffective or inappropriate. However, the effects of tricyclics on ADHD and the possible side effects are not nearly as well researched as those of the stimulants (see, for example, Gordon 1991).

Because of their efficacy and the relative ease and cost of medication therapy, stimulants are increasingly seen as the treatment of choice by many professionals and parents. However, it must be reiterated that the effects are only temporary, that no medication (to date) cures ADHD, and that, ideally, medications should not be the only therapy.

Cognitive Techniques for Self-Control. The logic behind cognitive behavior therapy is to help children develop self-control of their behavior, instead of relying on external controls: to get them to "stop, look, listen, and think" before acting. Based on the work of the Russian neuropsychologist Luria (1966) as well as others, these approaches emphasize the need for helping impulsive children develop self-directed speech to guide their responses to immediate problem situations (Barkley 1990, 31–32). These and a variety of other cognitive techniques are described and discussed in Pfiffner and Barkley (1990). Unfortunately, the effective cognitive strategies and behaviors that children have been able to exercise under laboratory conditions have generally not transferred to home or school situations. In short, cognitive training has not been successful in helping children develop an inner locus of control (Abikoff 1991; Pfiffner and Barkley 1990, 538–39). This again is consistent with the hypothesis that the root cause is neurological, a result of brain chemistry and functioning.

Barkley suggests that these self-control techniques are most useful when taught to parents and teachers, who can remind children to rehearse the procedures when situations requiring impulse control seem about to arise. He also suggests that these methods be combined with reinforcements for the children's self-controlled behavior.

Behavioral Modification Techniques. Neither cognitive nor behavioral modification techniques have proved as effective alone as stimulant medications, though either or both are valuable adjuncts to medication and may be the treatment of choice for some children—or by some parents. Behavioral management seems more effective than attempting to teach cognitive control, again consistent with the hypothesis of an underlying neurological factor. That is, the hypothesis of an underlying physiological cause would also explain why children are typically more able to respond appropriately to *external* controls via behavioral modification than to develop *internal* controls.

And yet, external control via behavioral modification also proves extremely difficult. Frustrated parents and teachers have been known to observe that their ADHD children seem to respond to neither reward nor punishment (e.g., Wender 1987). In fact, a lack of conventional response to reward and punishment seems to be a defining characteristic of ADHD (Barkley 1990, 67–73). To be successful with ADHD children, rewards and punishments (such as "response cost"—the withdrawal of a reward) have to be unusually—one might say incredibly—consistent, immediate, frequent, highly motivating, and modified often in order to maintain motivation (Pfiffner and Barkley 1990, 503–5). In short, successful behavioral modification of ADHD children proves extremely difficult.

Given that a whole language philosophy of learning draws upon cognitive psychology and embraces a cognitive perspective on learning, this difficulty with behavioral modification might be what whole language educators would expect—or even hope—to find. However, attempts to develop and maintain ADHD children's self-control seem even less successful, at least with time-limited, laboratory-type training situations.

Treatment of the Environment

Each of the preceding "treatments" for ADHD has dealt with changing the individual considered to have Attention Deficit Hyperactivity Disorder. A systems approach also involves altering the demands, expectations, and interactional patterns with the environment. One example is the way that the therapist was beginning to work with Matt's mother in the previous excerpt from a therapy session. He was helping her understand how her behavior elicited characteristic ADHD responses from Matt.

A systems-theory model of ADHD emphasizes the fact that the individual is not solely responsible for ADHD behaviors. Rather, they arise from the interaction—or transaction—between certain characteristics of the individual and the external environment, including people, places, situations, and events. Thus, ADHD behaviors can be alleviated by changing the external environment as well as by changing or treating the individual.

Educating ADHD Students

From a *both/and* systems point of view, teachers and schools as well as parents must change how they interact with ADHD students and what they expect and demand of them. The traditional classroom requires of the ADHD student everything that he or she is not good at: sitting still and not talking, concentrating on dittos and other skills work that the student finds boring, and not acting or speaking impulsively. Because the demands of the traditional classroom are so difficult for ADHD students to meet, perhaps it is not surprising that most of the professional literature on the schooling of ADHD students focuses almost exclusively on managing their behavior. This is unfortunate, leading many teachers to conclude that ADHD students can (at best) be only managed, not educated.

Whole Language: A Systems Perspective and Approach

Whole language classrooms, by contrast, reflect a *systems* philosophy of education, adjusting the curriculum to meet the needs and interests of students more than pressuring the students to fit into a predetermined curriculum. There are several specific ways that whole language teachers are likely to make both learning and living easier for ADHD students in their classrooms.

1. Whole language teachers are particularly sensitive to the interests, abilities, and needs of their students, both collectively and individually. They shape the curriculum with and in response to the students, instead of expecting the students to cope with a prepackaged curriculum. And they attempt to meet the needs of individual students. This is particularly important for ADHD students.

2. Whole language teachers emphasize all students' *strengths.* They find ways of using students' strengths to alleviate, compensate for, or avoid accentuating their weaknesses. Emphasizing strengths is especially important for ADHD students, since they are so often criticized for their shortcomings. This aspect of whole language teaching is particularly important for boosting self-esteem and self-confidence.

3. Whole language teachers are alert for ways in which they can alleviate students' difficulties and work around their weaknesses. Recognizing that ADHD students typically find it difficult to complete written work, even that which is highly interesting to them, whole language teachers may try to provide ADHD students with computers and word-processing programs. A computer helps these students complete their work before attention fades, and it avoids the problem of poor handwriting that typically plagues ADHD students. Whole language teachers may also encourage the use of a spelling checker for final drafts, knowing that many ADHD students have particular difficulty with spelling.

4. Whole language teachers avoid worksheets, workbooks, and isolated skills work—a particular blessing for ADHD students, who find it extraordinarily difficult to concentrate on such work.

5. Whole language teachers provide many opportunities for students to choose learning experiences that are meaningful to them: to choose what books to read, to decide what to research and investigate, to determine what to write and how to write it, for example. It is significantly easier for ADHD students to concentrate on tasks that they find interesting and meaningful.

6. Whole language teachers encourage students to think not only critically but creatively, and to engage in learning experiences that foster such independence of thought and expression. This is especially important for many ADHD students, who are often among the most creative and divergent thinkers in the class.

7. Whole language teachers allow and even encourage a significant degree of mobility in the classroom, as students locate resources, confer with peers, move from one learning center or area to another. They also tend to be tolerant of individual students' needs to fiddle with something, move their feet, or sit or lie in unconventional positions as they work. Recognizing that ADHD students may have strong needs to engage in activities that involve the hands or body, whole language teachers may be especially likely to provide for these needs through various curricular activities: hands-on math and science, creative drama, even music and dance, along with art.

8. Whole language teachers organize for collaborative learning: students working together on projects, sharing what they are reading and writing, helping each other solve problems, and so forth. Discussion and conversation are valued aspects of a whole language classroom, another blessing for ADHD students. As students work collaboratively, whole language teachers can help ADHD students develop self-control and social skills, while helping other students come to understand and accept the problems of ADHD students and begin to respond to them more positively.

9. Whole language teachers minimize the use of formal tests, but when such tests must be administered, they attempt to adjust to the needs of ADHD students as well as others. Some ADHD students may work impulsively; they need help in slowing down, thinking about, and checking their answers. Other ADHD students need extra time (even on standardized, timed tests), because their difficulty in

concentrating slows them down. Whole language teachers typically minimize the use of test scores in evaluating students, which is particularly important for ADHD students because they are rarely able to demonstrate their strengths on formal tests—standardized or otherwise.

10. Whole language teachers tend to communicate frequently with parents, encouraging them to share their understanding of their child, to work together for the child's success, and even to participate actively in facilitating classroom learning experiences. Such close collaboration with parents can have particular benefits for the ADHD student.

Clearly, whole language learning and teaching reflect a *both/and* transactional concept of learning: a systems-theory approach.

Other Teacher and Classroom Modifications

Most of the aforementioned tactics and techniques are more common in whole language classrooms than in traditional classrooms. However, there are several ways that all teachers knowledgeable about ADHD may help their students who have difficulty with impulsivity, hyperactivity, and attention. Again, such adjustments to the needs of the student reflect a systems concept of education. However, it should be noted that several of the following adjustments would help *many* students, not just those with Attention Deficit Hyperactivity Disorder.

1. Teachers may help ADHD students (and others) develop strategies for minimizing the effects of emotion-controlled, impulsive behavior. When a student is inclined to keep arguing with the teacher or with a peer, for example, the teacher can indicate that *both* parties need to take "time out" to regain self-control. This defuses the situation, but it does not lay blame exclusively on the ADHD student. The same approach can be taken when the student has impulsively engaged in other disruptive or aggressive behavior that will later need to be discussed and dealt with.

2. Knowledgeable and sensitive teachers avoid shaming or laying a guilt trip upon ADHD students when they have behaved inappropriately. Knowing that self-control is difficult and often impossible for these students, the teachers remain sympathetic to the students while rejecting the behavior. For the same reason, they ignore or avoid making an issue of minor disruptions.

3. To help students grasp instructions, teachers may adopt such strategies as the following: (a) obtaining eye contact with an ADHD student before giving instructions, or before repeating instructions for the benefit of that student; (b) writing instructions on the chalkboard and making sure that the ADHD student has copied them correctly; (c) writing down instructions for the ADHD student; (d) checking to be sure that the ADHD student understands instructions before beginning a task; and (e) issuing a complex set of instructions one step at a time.

4. Recognizing the difficulties that ADHD students have in settling down to work and sustaining their attention to a task, sensitive teachers will keep ADHD students' homework to a minimum: by providing for work to be completed during class, for example, and even by assigning them less homework than other students. Having worked extensively with schools to help ADHD students, psychologist Michael Gordon suggests no more than 30–45 minutes of homework for ADHD children in the elementary grades, and no more than an hour or so for older children (Gordon 1991, 132).

5. To make sure ADHD students are organized to do whatever homework *is* required, teachers may need to make sure that such students have homework assignments written down, that they understand these assignments, and that they leave school with the materials needed to do their work. Teachers may see that such students have an assignment notebook, check the students' progress daily, and work with parents to see that work is accomplished. ADHD students often need such support even when the "homework" involves something in which the student is highly interested.

6. Recognizing that ADHD students may not be able to take as much responsibility for their own work as many other students, teachers may collaborate with their students to develop an organizational plan for completing major projects and then to develop a series of intermediate "due dates" and an assignment calendar. Subsequently, teachers may supervise and monitor the students' completion of each step of the work.

7. Teachers and parents may establish a "note-home" program, according to which the teachers report on certain agreed-upon concerns: typically on work completed or not completed and turned in. Even high school ADHD students may need this kind of monitoring system daily. To make it work, parents may have to establish a reward and response-cost program, with response cost (withdrawal of a re-

ward) occurring if the note or form from the teacher is not brought home completed. For suggestions on how to set up such a program, see Pfiffner and Barkley's chapter in Barkley (1990); Copeland and Love (1990) include some sample forms.

8. Teachers may provide a quiet space with few distractions for ADHD students to complete written work that is to be done independently. This includes tests.

9. Recognizing that ADHD students are especially frustrated by departures from the expected, knowledgeable teachers provide a classroom environment and routine with predictable structure and clear and consistent expectations. This provides security for *all* students: a safe environment in which to take the risks necessary for learning.

10. In general, knowledgeable and sensitive teachers will find ways of enabling the ADHD student to succeed in school, regardless of problems with impulsivity, hyperactivity, and inattention. This may require soliciting additional help for the student, even occasionally to the point of removing the child from the regular classroom. (More on this below.)

These strategies reflect a systems perspective by adjusting the environment and environmental demands to meet the needs, capabilities, and limitations of the student, instead of just applying the Procrustean-bed technique to the individual who does not fit. This approach to the education of ADHD students is implicit in Michael Gordon's *ADHD/Hyperactivity: A Consumer's Guide for Parents and Teachers* (1991), previously mentioned as an excellent resource for both parents and teachers. (Other valuable resources are listed in the Further Readings section at the end of this chapter).

In responding to teachers' concerns that making special adjustments for ADHD students would not be fair to the other students, Gordon argues that "fairness isn't when everyone gets the same, but when everyone gets what he needs" (Gordon 1991, 125). It is a persuasive argument. Even whole language teachers may need to adjust their expectations in order to minimize or work around the limitations of the ADHD student and to provide the support needed for success.

A Whole Language Approach to Behavior Problems

In a somewhat different vein, the story of how a sixth-grade teacher named Steve dealt with a problem situation illustrates how teachers can lead ADHD children and other students with behavior problems toward taking increasing responsibility for their actions. The anecdote is from Mark Collis and Joan Dalton's *Becoming Responsible Learners* (1991), an excellent resource.

In this situation, Tanya and Troy, both known for temper outbursts, were each struggling to gain possession of the video's remote control. Steve told them to put the control down, and Troy did let go, but Tanya then lifted it above her head and hurled it against the wall, yelling defiantly. I focus just on how Steve dealt with the problem of the broken video control: "I'm too angry to talk now," says Steve, "sit here until we all calm down enough to talk sensibly about this." Five minutes later he returns to Tanya, reminding her that he will be contacting her parents about the incident because one of their class rules is that parents will be called when equipment is broken. Soon after initiating this discussion, Steve encourages Tanya to admit that she broke the remote control.

> "What can we do about the remote control?" Steve asks.
> "I could fix it," Tanya offers.
> "That's one idea, can you think of another?" prompts Steve.
> "I could pay for a new one, or take it home for Mum or Dad to fix," the ideas come more quickly.
> "Have you any more ideas, Tanya?" Steve adds after a little pause.
> "No," replies Tanya.
> "So we have three ideas. You could fix it yourself. You could pay for a new one or you could ask your parents to help you fix or replace it," Steve summarizes. "Which of those ideas do you think you'll be able to do?"
> "Well, I don't think I could fix it myself, " Tanya says looking at the pieces scattered across the floor. "And I haven't got enough money to buy another one."
> Tanya pauses and looks down at her toes avoiding any eye contact with Steve.
> "So which idea will work for you," prompts Steve.
> "I could ask Mum and Dad to help me fix it or get another one I suppose," she answers reluctantly.
> "So asking Mum and Dad to help you fix it or replace it will best solve our problem of the broken remote?" Steve queries.
> "Yeah," Tanya replies a little more confidently.
> "Well, you talk to your Mum and Dad tonight and we'll get together tomorrow and see how you went. Remember I'll be talking to them this afternoon so they'll be expecting you to talk about what happened today pretty soon after you get home, right?" Steve adds smiling.
> Tanya looks up and smiles faintly, "Right" she affirms. (Collis and Dalton 1991, 31–33)

In this incident, Steve demonstrates "shared ownership" and responsibility, encouraging Tanya herself to consider ways of making amends for the damage that she has done. This is but one example from *Becoming Responsible Learners* of how teachers can help students take more responsibility for their learning *and* their behavior.

Collis and Dalton present at the outset what they consider to be three major classroom leadership styles: teacher ownership and control, shared ownership and control, and child ownership and control. They recommend and demonstrate shared responsibility, with gradual release of responsibility to the children, yet continued flexibility in responding to changing situations. See Table 10.2 for the application of this model to the control of behavior. Though such an approach will not necessarily be more effective than psychologists' cognitive behavior training in producing long-lasting effects, it has the decided advantage of being of longer duration (the entire school year) and of occurring in a naturalistic setting. Furthermore, the teacher can always retreat to a greater degree of shared control for a time, later relinquish some control again, and repeat this pattern as necessary.

Some ADHD students may never be able to entirely avoid incidents in which strong emotion leads them to be impulsively hurtful or

Table 10.2. Classroom Leadership: Behavior

Teacher Ownership	Shared Ownership	Child Ownership
1. Strong teacher control	1. Shared control	1. Strong child control
2. "I decide what you will do"	2. "Let's decide together"	2. "You decide what you will do"
3. External control based on authority	3. The teacher invites: negotiation/input, responsibility, and cooperation	3. Internal control based on self-direction/discipline
4. Teacher is responsible for behavior	4. Children are learning both independence and interdependence in order to behave appropriately	4. "I'm responsible for how I behave"
5. Children are dependent on the teacher	5. "I am responsible for my behavior and I care about the behaviors of others"	5. Children are independent of teacher

Source: M. Collis and J. Dalton, *Becoming Responsible Learners: Strategies for Positive Classroom Management* (Portsmouth, N.H.: Heinemann, 1991), p. 33.

destructive, but they *can* learn more effective ways of dealing with the problems that their actions cause.

Additional Educational Services for the ADHD Student

In order for both ADHD students and their classroom teachers to survive, they may need some additional help from the school. In particular, the classroom teacher may need help assisting students with time-consuming organizational tasks (e.g., Pfiffner and Barkley 1990, 521–23, 531–34; Gordon 1991, 111).

Public Law 94-142 guaranteeing special-education services does not specifically mention Attention Deficit Disorder *alone* as a condition qualifying children for those services. However, the Office of Civil Rights within the federal Department of Education has ruled that AD(H)D students are guaranteed special educational services by Section 504 of the Rehabilitation Act of 1973, if their condition substantially limits their ability to learn or to benefit from the regular educational program (Gordon 1991, 117; Copeland and Love 1990, 12). During 1991, additional guidelines were being developed by the Department of Education to guarantee students the right to special educational services solely on the basis of Attention Deficit Disorder (with or without hyperactivity). Federal legislation is being drafted to support that guarantee.

Here are some ways the school might provide support to such students and their teachers:

1. Provide an appropriate chunk of time at the end of the school day for the student to meet one-on-one with the resource room teacher, or someone else appropriate, in order to go over the tasks and assignments on which the student had difficulty focusing during class and to make sure that the student is all set to do assigned homework. This academic support person could also help the student plan for completing larger projects and monitor the student's progress, relieving the classroom teacher from this sort of task.

2. Provide at the end of the school day someone to make sure that the student has his or her "note home" form appropriately completed and signed by the teacher.

3. Provide an after-school supervised study hall for ADHD students and others needing such structure to complete their homework before leaving the school grounds.

4. Provide a classroom aide whenever there are three or more ADHD students in a class, with the aide's first priority being to work with these children.

5. Provide other pull-out or pull-in programs, as needed.

Many of these services could be performed by an aide rather than a fully credentialed teacher. Indeed, significant help might even be provided by administrative staff, a guidance counselor, a parent volunteer, an older student, or even a peer "buddy." Cost would be minimal, perhaps even nil, but such additional help might make the difference between school failure and school success for many ADHD students. The importance of this kind of assistance can scarcely be emphasized enough.

Placement in a special-education class is likely to be needed for only a few ADHD children who are *severely* disruptive or aggressive, or who have other special needs that cannot be met by regular classroom instruction supplemented with additional assistance. The chance of school success for the majority of ADHD children can be greatly enhanced by a systems approach, with the student supported by the classroom teacher and both student and teacher supported by the school as a whole.

A Systems Perspective and Whole Language

It is undeniably true that many of our nation's children have been overdiagnosed, overlabeled, and consequently underappreciated and undereducated. Denny Taylor's *Learning Denied* (1990) offers a prime example of that, documenting a school's absolute refusal to see a child's learning strengths and growth, while dwelling upon his alleged disabilities. Given stories like this—and many of us could share our own—it is no wonder that many educators are suspicious of labels like ADHD. Furthermore, recognition of ADHD as entitling a student to special educational services can, unfortunately, serve to provide for such students the same skills-oriented education that has often characterized special-education pull-out programs. Special services do not *guarantee* that the ADHD student will receive appropriate understanding or educational support.

What holds significantly more promise, however, is a systems approach, both to defining ADHD and to dealing with it. A systems perspective encourages us to view ADHD as a socially dysfunctional cluster of behaviors that may be caused by the environment interacting with an individual who may have certain biological predispositions toward these behaviors. ADHD represents a set of less-than-optimal *relationships* between the individual and the environment. We can improve these relationships, then, not only by changing the individual but by changing the environment: by modifying how we interact with the person as well as what we expect or demand of him or her. That is, we can take the *both/and* stance and approach that logically follows from systems theory.

Because whole language theory reflects a *both/and* stance toward responsibility for learning and a conviction that teachers need to work *with* children to help them control their behavior appropriately, whole language teachers may be particularly effective with ADHD students. They will be all the more effective, I think, if they consider that ADHD may involve a neurological factor—that is, if they at least entertain the possibility that their ADHD students may have biologically based difficulties and limitations that make it important for teachers to offer appropriate understanding and some of the aforementioned kinds of support for learning.

ADHD and Learning Disabilities: A Systems Theory and Transactional Paradigm

For the theoretically minded, I want to add some comments on ADHD and learning disabilities, discussing both in the context of theories and paradigms.

As noted previously, ADHD differs significantly from learning disabilities in being diagnosed primarily on the basis of difficulty in meeting the demands and expectations of daily life, rather than on the basis of standardized tests. Additionally, ADHD behaviors often manifest themselves across a spectrum of social situations, not just in settings where students are expected to manage or master certain kinds of skills tasks. Furthermore, there is more evidence—at least indirect—for the operation of a neurological factor in ADHD: unlike learning-disability behaviors alone, ADHD behaviors are alleviated by medications, for the majority of individuals. Because of such differences, I would argue for considering ADHD as a condition—or rather, a set of interrelationships—that *affects* education, rather than as a learning disability.

On the other hand, a systems perspective or theory of learning disabilities is at least as appropriate as a systems theory of ADHD. It may be even more appropriate to consider learning disabilities within the context of environmental influences, if indeed there is less evidence for a neurological factor in so-called learning disabilities.

In his critical examination of learning disabilities, Gerald Coles objects—rightly, I think—to what he calls a "reductionist and determinist neurological thesis" accounting for learning disabilities (1987, 134). But he seems to embrace an equally reductionist interactivity theory, according to which all learning differences are environmentally caused—even those involving neurological factors. Perhaps, but I think the causes may sometimes be more complex than that (as does Heshusius 1989). Or in other words, I resist this opposite kind of reductionism.

If I am more convinced than Coles of the existence of a neurological factor at least in ADHD (having considered a wider range of evidence than what he cites), I am nevertheless equally convinced of the need for reconceptualizing learning failure in terms that place primary responsibility on the schools and a society that tacitly expects and accepts a significant degree of educational failure. As Heshusius (1989) indicates, this concept of disabilities as a social construct is gaining increased attention within the field of special education (e.g., Carrier 1983; Sleeter 1986; see also Wixon and Lipson 1986, Goodman 1982, and other articles within that same journal issue; see also the May 1991 issue of *Topics in Language Disorders*). And with this understanding comes increasing recognition that we need to examine how the environment contributes to the genesis, diagnosis, maintenance, and treatment of alleged learning disabilities and conditions like ADHD.

In short, I join theorists like Poplin and Heshusius in rejecting a mechanistic paradigm of education and the models that reflect it: the medical model, the psychological process model, the behaviorist model, and the cognitive/learning strategies model (Poplin 1988a). And I likewise join them in espousing the *transactional paradigm that underlies whole language instruction* (Poplin's "holistic/constructivist" paradigm, 1988b; Heshusius 1989). Whole language rejects the "blame the victim" stance typically associated with the admission of a neurological factor in learning differences (e.g., Stires 1991; Dudley-Marling 1990; Rhodes and Dudley-Marling 1988). Whole language educators decry such failure-oriented assumptions and practices of our schools and attempt to foster the success of all students, viewing them as capable and developing rather than incapable and deficient (Weaver 1990). Thus, in educating ADHD students and all other students, whole language reflects a systems theory of education within a trans-actional paradigm.

Postscript

I do not know the fate of Donald, the six-year-old who preferred teaching himself Chinese characters to doing the boring schoolwork assigned by his teacher. But I can give you an update on my son John.

In July of the summer in which he was hospitalized and diagnosed as having an attention-deficit disorder, I broached with his psychiatrist the subject of John's returning to school in the fall. "Why, Connie," the psychiatrist said, "there isn't any place for him in our schools." No place for my son? I was shocked. "He obviously can't succeed in regular classes," the psychiatrist continued, "and he doesn't really belong in a special-education class." To make a long story shorter, I discovered that our city had recently developed an alternative high school for students who had dropped out for a semester or more. There was less pressure, classes were smaller, and, most crucially, John had time in most of his classes to complete his homework. He graduated with mostly A's during his last year and honors certificates in both algebra and English (creative writing). After a brief fling with a nearby junior college—where, predictably, he could not sustain his organizational skills and attention to homework well enough to succeed—he has recently graduated with high honors from a two-year electronics engineering program at a technical school. As of this writing, John is at the top of his class in a third-year program that will culminate in a Bachelor's of Applied Science. He has found a professional area of interest and an educational program with characteristics that meet some of his most crucial needs. Perhaps most critical is the fact that he previously had homework in only one subject a night.

John's recent educational success offers testimony to the effectiveness of a systems concept of ADHD and a systems approach to meeting the educational needs of ADHD students.

Note

1. Currently, the "official" criteria for diagnosing ADHD are those listed in the revised third edition of the American Psychiatric Association's *Diagnostic and Statistical Manual* (1987). My list of behaviors associated with impulsivity might result in characterizing some children as ADHD who more clearly reflect characteristics of an "Oppositional Defiant Disorder," with only a few ADHD tendencies. Since oppositional, defiant behavior is more com-

mon among lower socioeconomic, nonmainstream children (Barkley 1990), the most inappropriate effect of using my list diagnostically might be to overdiagnose ADHD among children of lower socioeconomic status.

References

Abikoff, H. 1991. Cognitive training in ADHD children: Less to it than meets the eye. *Journal of Learning Disabilities* 24:205–9.

American Psychiatric Association. 1980. *Diagnostic and statistical manual of mental disorders*, 3d ed. Washington, D.C.: American Psychiatric Association.

———. 1987. *Diagnostic and statistical manual of mental disorders*, 3d ed., rev. Washington, D.C.: American Psychiatric Association.

Anastopoulos, A. D., G. J. DuPaul, and R. A. Barkley. 1991. Stimulant medication and parent training therapies for Attention Deficit–Hyperactivity Disorder. *Journal of Learning Disabilities* 24:210–18.

Baren, M. 1989. The case for Ritalin: A fresh look at the controversy. *Contemporary Pediatrics* 6 (January): 16–28.

Barkley, R. A. 1990. *Attention Deficit Hyperactivity Disorder: A handbook for diagnosis and treatment.* New York: Guilford Press.

———. 1991. *Attention Deficit Hyperactivity Disorder: A clinical workbook.* New York: Guilford Press.

Cantwell, D. P., and L. Baker. 1991. Association between Attention Deficit–Hyperactivity Disorder and Learning Disorders. *Journal of Learning Disabilities* 24:88–95.

Carrier, J. G. 1983. Explaining educability: An investigation of political support for the Children with Learning Disabilities Act of 1969. *British Journal of Sociology of Education* 4 (2): 125–40.

Coles, G. 1987. *The learning mystique: A critical look at "learning disabilities."* New York: Fawcett.

Collis, M., and J. Dalton. 1991. *Becoming responsible learners: Strategies for positive classroom management.* Portsmouth, N.H.: Heinemann.

Copeland, E. D., and V. L. Love. 1990. *Attention without tension: A teacher's handbook on attention deficit disorders (ADHD and ADD).* Atlanta: 3 C's of Childhood.

Davidson, M. 1983. *Uncommon sense: The life and thought of Ludwig von Bertalanffy, father of general systems theory.* Los Angeles: J. P. Tarcher.

Dudley-Marling, C. 1990. *When school is a struggle.* Richmond Hill, Ontario: Scholastic.

DuPaul, G. J. 1990. The ADHD Rating Scale: Normative data, reliability, and validity. Unpublished manuscript, University of Massachusetts Medical Center, Worcester.

DuPaul, G. J., and R. A. Barkley. 1990. Medication therapy. In *Attention Deficit Hyperactivity Disorder: A handbook for diagnosis and treatment*, ed. R. A. Barkley, 573–612. New York: Guilford Press.

Dykman, R. A., and P. T. Ackerman. 1991. Attention Deficit Disorder and Specific Reading Disability: Separate but often overlapping disorders. *Journal of Learning Disabilities* 24:96–103.

Epstein, M. A., S. E. Shaywitz, B. A. Shaywitz, and J. L. Woolston. 1991. The boundaries of Attention Deficit Disorder. *Journal of Learning Disabilities* 24:78–86.

Feingold, B. 1975. *Why your child is hyperactive.* New York: Random House.

Fletcher, J. M., R. D. Morris, and D. J. Francis. 1991. Methodological issues in the classification of attention-related disorders. *Journal of Learning Disabilities* 24:72–77.

Goodman, K. 1982. Revaluing readers and reading. *Topics in Learning and Learning Disabilities* 1:87–93.

Gordon, M. 1991. *ADHD/Hyperactivity: A consumer's guide for parents and teachers.* De Witt, N.Y.: GSI Publications.

Heshusius, L. 1989. The Newtonian mechanistic paradigm, special education, and contours of alternatives: An overview. *Journal of Learning Disabilities* 22:403–15.

Hynd, G. W., M. Semrud-Clikeman, A. R. Lorys, E. S. Novey, D. Eliopulos, and H. Lyytinen. 1991. Corpus callosum morphology in Attention Deficit-Hyperactivity Disorder: Morphometric analysis of MRI. *Journal of Learning Disabilities* 24:141–46.

Kane, R., C. Mikalac, S. Benjamin, and R. Barkley. 1990. Assessment and treatment of adults with ADHD. In *Attention Deficit Hyperactivity Disorder: A handbook for diagnosis and treatment*, ed. R. A. Barkley, 613–54. New York: Guilford Press.

Klorman, R. 1991. Cognitive event-related potentials in Attention Deficit Disorder. *Journal of Learning Disabilities* 24:130–40.

Kohn, A. 1989. Suffer the restless children. *Atlantic Monthly*, November, 90–100.

Lahey, B. B., and C. L. Carlson. 1991. Validity of the diagnostic category of Attention Deficit Disorder Without Hyperactivity: A review of the literature. *Journal of Learning Disabilities* 24:110–20.

Luria, A. R. 1966. *Higher cortical functions in man.* New York: Basic Books.

Pfiffner, L. J., and R. A. Barkley. 1990. Educational placement and classroom management. In *Attention Deficit Hyperactivity Disorder: A handbook for diagnosis and treatment*, ed. R. A. Barkley, 498–539. New York: Guilford Press.

Poplin, M. S. 1988a. The reductionistic fallacy in learning disabilities: Replicating the past by reducing the present. *Journal of Learning Disabilities* 21:389–400.

——. 1988b. Holistic/constructivist principles of the teaching/learning process: Implications for the field of learning disabilities. *Journal of Learning Disabilities* 21:401–16.

Rhodes, L. K., and C. Dudley-Marling. 1988. *Readers and writers with a difference: A holistic approach to teaching learning disabled and remedial students.* Portsmouth, N.H.: Heinemann.

Robin, A. L. 1990. Training families with ADHD adolescents. In *Attention Deficit Hyperactivity Disorder: A handbook for diagnosis and treatment,* ed. R. A. Barkley, 462–97. New York: Guilford Press.

Robin, A. L., and S. L. Foster. 1989. *Negotiating parent-adolescent conflict: A behavioral family systems approach.* New York: Guilford Press.

Rosenblatt, L. M. 1978. *The reader, the text, the poem: The transactional theory of the literary work.* Carbondale: Southern Illinois University Press.

Schachar, R. J. 1986. Hyperkinetic syndrome: Historical development of the concept. In *The overactive child,* ed. E. Taylor, 19–40. Philadelphia: J. B. Lippincott.

Schrag, P., and B. Divoky. 1975. *The myth of the hyperactive child: And other means of child control.* New York: Pantheon.

Shaywitz, S. E., and B. A. Shaywitz. 1991. Introduction to the special series on Attention Deficit Disorder. *Journal of Learning Disabilities* 24:68–71.

Shelton, T., and R. A. Barkley. 1990. Clinical, developmental, and biopsychosocial considerations. In *Attention Deficit Hyperactivity Disorder: A handbook for diagnosis and treatment,* ed. R. A. Barkley, 209–31. New York: Guilford Press.

Sleeter, C. E. 1986. Learning disabilities: The social construction of a special education category. *Exceptional Children* 53:46–54.

Stires, S., ed. 1991. *With promise: Redefining reading and writing needs for special students.* Portsmouth, N.H.: Heinemann.

Szatmari, P., D. R. Offord, and M. H. Boyle. 1989. Correlates, associated impairments and patterns of service utilization of children with Attention Deficit Disorder: Findings from the Ontario Child Health Study. *Journal of Child Psychology and Psychiatry* 30:205–17.

Taylor, D. 1990. *Learning denied.* Portsmouth, N.H.: Heinemann.

Taylor, E. A., ed. 1986. *The overactive child.* Philadelphia: J. B. Lippincott.

Weaver, C. 1985. Parallels between new paradigms in science and in reading and literary theories: An essay review. *Research in the Teaching of English* 19:298–316.

——. 1988. *Reading process and practice: From socio-psycholinguistics to whole language.* Portsmouth, N.H.: Heinemann.

——. 1990. *Understanding whole language: From principles to practice.* Portsmouth, N.H.: Heinemann.

——. 1991. Whole language and its potential for developing readers. *Topics in Language Disorders* 1 (3): 28–44.

Wender, P. H. 1987. *The hyperactive child, adolescent, and adult.* New York: Oxford University Press.

Whalen, C. K., and B. Henker. 1991. Social impact of stimulant treatment for hyperactive children. *Journal of Learning Disabilities* 24:231–41.

Wixson, K. K., and M. Y. Lipson. 1986. Reading dis(ability): An interactionist perspective. In *The Contexts of School-Based Literacy*, ed. T. E. Raphael, 131–48. New York: Random House.

Zametkin, A. J., T. E. Nordahl, M. Gross, A. C. King, W. E. Semple, J. Rumsey, S. Hamburger, and R. M. Cohen. 1990. Cerebral glucose metabolism in adults with hyperactivity of childhood onset. *The New England Journal of Medicine* 323:1361–66.

Zametkin, A. J., and J. L. Rapoport. 1987. Neuro-biology of Attention Deficit Disorder with Hyperactivity: Where have we come in 50 years? *Journal of the American Academy of Child and Adolescent Psychiatry* 26:676–86.

Zukav, G. 1979. *The dancing wu li masters: An overview of the new physics.* New York: Bantam.

Further Readings

References for Understanding Principles of Whole Language

Edelsky, C., B. Altwerger, and M. Flores. 1990. *Whole language: What's the difference?* Portsmouth, N.H.: Heinemann.

The Elementary School Journal, November, 1989 (special issue on whole language).

Goodman, K. 1986. *What's whole in whole language?* Richmond Hill, Ontario: Scholastic; Portsmouth, N.H.: Heinemann.

Gursky, D. 1991. After the reign of Dick and Jane. *Teacher Magazine* 2 (9): 22–29.

Newman, J., and S. M. Church. 1990. Myths of whole language. *The Reading Teacher* 44 (September): 20–26.

Pace, G. 1991. When teachers use literature for literacy instruction: Ways that constrain, ways that free. *Language Arts* 68 (January): 12–25.

Stephens, D. 1991a. *Research on whole language: Support for a new curriculum.* Katonah, N.Y.: Richard C. Owen. (Describes in detail much of the research giving rise to and supporting whole language.)

———. 1991b. *Toward an understanding of whole language.* Technical Report no. 524. Champaign, Ill.: Center for the Study of Reading, University of Illinois.

Weaver, C. 1990. *Understanding whole language: From principles to practice.* Portsmouth, N.H.: Heinemann.

Readings and Resources on Attention-Deficit Disorders

Publications

Barkley, R. A. 1990. *Attention Deficit Hyperactivity Disorder: A handbook for diagnosis and treatment.* New York: Guilford Press. (This 747-page book offers a thorough, research-based discussion of ADHD, its assessment, and treatment.)

Children with Attention Deficit Disorders (CHADD) Education Committee. N.d. Attention Deficit Disorders: A guide for teachers. (Available from CHADD; see address below.)

Copeland, E. D., and V. L. Love. 1990. *Attention without tension: A teacher's handbook on Attention Deficit Disorders (ADHA and ADD).* Atlanta: 3 C's of Childhood. (Includes several potentially useful lists and forms.)

Gordon, M. 1991. *ADHD/Hyperactivity: A consumer's guide for parents and teachers.* De Witt, N.Y.: GSI Publications. (Humorous, yet professional; this is "must" reading.)

Wender, P. 1987. *The hyperactive child, adolescent, and adult.* New York: Oxford University Press. (Readable and insightful.)

All of the books above, and many other books and tapes, are available from the ADD Warehouse, 300 Northwest 70th Ave., Suite 102, Plantation, FL 33317. Call 1-800-233-9273 to order or to obtain a catalogue.

Parent Support Groups

CHADD National Headquarters
499 Northwest 70th Ave.
Suite 308
Plantation, FL 33317
1-305-587-3700

>   CHADD (Children with Attention Deficit Disorders) is the largest national parent support group and has many local groups; it publishes a monthly newsletter and a biannual journal.

ADDA
4300 West Park Blvd.
Plano, TX 75093

>   ADDA (Attention Deficit Disorders Association) is another national group, again with local support groups.

Legal Right to Education

For current information on the legal rights of AD(H)D students to receive special educational services, contact your regional office of the U.S. Department of Education, Office for Civil Rights. Addresses and phone numbers are provided in Copeland and Love, *Attention without Tension* (above).

In most, if not all, states, there are groups similar to Citizens Alliance to Uphold Special Education (C.A.U.S.E.) in Michigan. This is a powerful advocacy group that can help parents obtain the special services to which their children are entitled. For information on C.A.U.S.E. or on advocacy groups in other states, write 313 South Washington Square, Suite 040, Lansing, MI 48933, or call 1-800-221-9105.

11 Whole Language Principles for Bilingual Learners

David Freeman and Yvonne Freeman
Fresno Pacific College

Whole language. It's everywhere. Professional journals are filled with ads for whole language materials and articles about whole language. Experts offer whole language seminars. School districts are making the transition to whole language, and inservices for school staffs feature experts on whole language.

With all this publicity, it is hard *not* to have heard something about whole language. But different people in different places have heard very different things. Is whole language Big Books? process writing? thematic teaching? a revolt against basal readers and phonics? just good teaching? the latest fad? In addition to the question "What is whole language?" has come a second question, "Who is whole language for?" Again, the answers seem to differ. In some schools, whole language is only for the top students. In others, whole language is reserved for students who have not been successful in traditional programs, including students identified as limited English proficient. We believe that whole language is good for all students but especially important for those students whose first language is not English.

Some writers refer to students who speak English as a second language by the official label, LEP (limited English proficient); however, we regard that label, like many other labels, as negative. Ken Goodman (1986) has referred to such students as "severely labelled," and we agree. We use the term *bilingual* in referring to second-language learners because we are talking about students who come to school speaking a language other than English. These students, in whole language classrooms, are encouraged to maintain their first language as they develop proficiency in English. The goal for whole language teachers of second-language speakers is for their students to become fully bilingual and biliterate.

Whole language teachers need to be knowledgeable about working with bilingual students because the number of bilingual students has increased dramatically over the last few years. Demographic projections suggest that the number of bilingual students in the United States and Canada will continue to increase. In the United States, for example, between the 1985–86 school year and the 1989–90 school year, the second-language population increased from 1.5 million to 2.1 million. Figures in the state of California help us project a continued increase in the number of second-language students in the rest of the United States. In the 1989–90 school year, 862,000 California students were identified as limited English proficient. In fact, while the second-language school population of the U.S. was 1.5 million in 1985, it is predicted that California alone will have 1.4 million second-language learners by 1995 (R. Olsen 1989).

Whole language is an approach to teaching, learning, and curriculum that is especially effective in classrooms that have students with diverse linguistic backgrounds. It is based on theory and supported by research. For our own understanding, we have defined this approach in terms of seven principles that we try to follow (Y. Freeman and D. Freeman, 1992). While we believe that teachers who follow these principles provide teaching that is good for all students, we are particularly interested in how the principles apply to bilingual students, so we will draw our examples from that population.

1. *Lessons should proceed from whole to part.* Students need the big picture first. They develop concepts by beginning with general ideas and then filling in the specific details.

2. *Lessons should be learner-centered because learning is the active construction of knowledge by students.* Whole language focuses on the whole student. Lessons begin with what the student knows, and activities build on student interests.

3. *Lessons should have meaning and purpose for the students now.* Students learn things that they see as meeting a present need. They should reflect upon what they are learning and be able to apply what they learn to their life outside, as well as inside, of school.

4. *Lessons should engage groups of students in social interaction.* When students share their ideas in social settings, individual concepts are developed. Working in groups, students also learn the important life skill of collaboration.

5. *Lessons should develop both oral and written language.* Especially for students learning English as a second language, the traditional view has been that the development of oral language must precede the development of literacy. However, involvement in reading and writing from the start is essential for developing academic competence and actually facilitates listening and speaking as well.

6. *Learning should take place in the first language to build concepts and facilitate the acquisition of English.* Use of the first language is the best way to make the input comprehensible. What students learn in their first language is then also available to them in English because they understand the concept and only need the English to express the concept.

7. *Lessons that show faith in the learner expand students' potential.* Teachers who believe in their students, including their bilingual students, plan activities that show their faith in the learner. All students can learn if they are engaged in meaningful activities that move from whole to part, build on students' interests and backgrounds, serve their needs, provide opportunities for social interaction, and develop their skills in both oral and written language.

In the following sections, we discuss each of these principles separately, using examples of how the principles look in action in classrooms with bilingual students. We should add that many of these classrooms are not official bilingual classrooms. Not all of the students in these classrooms are bilingual. In many cases, the teacher has students from a mixture of language backgrounds, including students whose first language is English. Because these teachers are "kidwatchers" (Y. Goodman 1985), however, they involve *all* their students, including their bilingual students, in meaningful learning as they follow whole language principles.

Principle 1

Learning goes from whole to part. The process of acquiring a first or second language involves moving from whole to part even though it sometimes does not look that way on the surface. In oral language, for example, young children or second-language learners often use one-word sentences. These single words give the impression of part-to-whole learning, but, in fact, they express whole ideas. For instance, a young child saying "Milk" could be trying to express one of several different thoughts: "I want some milk," "I spilled my milk," or even, "The milk is over there." Language learners always begin with a whole idea, and as language develops, they fill in the parts by adding more words to their sentences.

Written language also develops from whole to part. Beginning writers often represent a whole word with a single letter. As students continue to write, they add more letters and move toward conventional spelling. Manuel, a fifth grader who recently arrived from Mexico, took an English spelling test in which he wrote correctly the first and last sound of every word. Thus, he wrote, "bs" for *birds* and "sf" for *save* and "ls" for *laws*. Unfortunately, his teacher did not see what Manuel was doing and counted every word on his fifteen-word list as wrong, rather than recognizing that his writing was developing naturally from whole to part.

Students in whole language classrooms read and write whole texts because their teachers know that complete stories are easier to read than short, adapted pieces, and whole stories are easier to write than simple sentences or paragraphs. Linda, a high school Spanish teacher with many years of experience teaching ESL, is convinced that her students can read and write whole stories in Spanish early in their first semester. She begins by telling the story of her own family, using pictures and realia. She writes in Spanish about her family on the overhead projector. She includes lots of vocabulary as she tells the story. Then students bring in pictures of their families, write about them, and share their stories with one another. Linda's lessons move from whole to part. She starts with the general concept of family and then helps students develop the specific vocabulary and structures needed to describe their families.

Instead of having students learn language and content from part to whole, teachers like Linda organize their curriculum around theme cycles (Edelsky, Altwerger, and Flores 1991). These theme cycles can be based on concepts called for by state or district guidelines. One bilingual first-grade teacher, for example, spent much of the year developing the concept of "community" by having his bilingual students, who had experienced both city and country living, compare and contrast the country and the city (Y. Freeman and Nofziger 1991). A fourth-grade teacher with a classroom of Southeast Asian and Hispanic students developed the important theme of "prejudice" with her immigrant students following suggestions from the state *History—Social Science Framework* for grade four, "California: A Changing State."

Thematic cycles help bilingual students because when they know the overall theme, they come to recognize related vocabulary and can predict content much more easily than when topics change frequently.

Using the students' first language is another way that whole language teachers can support content learning and start with the whole. In classes with many second-language students, the teacher, a bilingual paraprofessional, or a peer supplies the whole in the students' first language by giving an overview of what they will be studying in their second language. Without this overview, second-language learners are often lost and miss opportunities to learn both content and language. Picture, for example, a kindergarten class with several Spanish-speaking children in the first weeks of school. The monolingual English-speaking teacher suggests that the class go on a tour of the school, interview the principal, secretaries, the librarian, custodial staff, and cafeteria personnel. The children will take pictures of the people to whom they talk and the places that they visit around the school and then will make a class book. The teacher brainstorms questions with the children for the interviews. The Spanish speakers are lost through all the planning and are confused as the class gathers for their tour. At each stop the teacher tries to get those children to listen, but they are distracted and do not pay attention. In fact, it is not until after the pictures are developed and the class begins to make their school book that the non-English-speaking children realize what the purpose of the whole trip was.

The entire scenario can be easily changed. If a Spanish-speaking aide, parent, cross-age tutor, or even classmate explains in Spanish what is about to happen, the children will understand the purpose of the tour. They will probably pick up key vocabulary as the teacher introduces important school figures. The children now have an opportunity to predict not only what is happening but also the meaning of the English-language words that they are hearing. They can also respond to the activity by producing their own class book in Spanish.

An overview in the first language is helpful in the lower elementary grades, but it is even more valuable and critical in content-area classes. Second-language learners in the upper grades often must be able to understand content without many extralinguistic cues such as visuals and hands-on activities. A biology teacher, for example, could have someone explain in the student's first language that the class will be studying the functions of the heart and its various parts. Then, as the discussion with charts and models proceeds, those students understand the general topic and pick up both content concepts and the related English vocabulary. In social studies, bilingual students studying the westward movement can better understand the content and purpose for a simulation activity in which they take on the personalities of different pioneer families if they first are given an overview in their first language.

Whole language teachers, whether working with one or more than one language, try to be sure that second-language learners are provided with lots of contextual support as they learn. Teachers have students read and write complete stories and reports as they explore topics organized around a central theme. Whenever possible, students are given an overview in their first language of what is about to be studied. In this way, these teachers follow the first principle of whole language: their lessons go from whole to part.

Principle 2

Lessons should be learner-centered because learning is the active construction of knowledge by students. A second important principle of whole language for bilingual students is that learning should be student-centered rather than teacher-centered. This principle is summarized in one of Bil Keane's "Family Circus" cartoons. When Billy and his younger sister, Dolly, return home after school, Billy explains to their mother that school would be better without "that lady up front talkin' all the time."

The idea of the teacher as the source of all knowledge standing up front and directing instruction is the traditional image. However, whole language teachers follow John Dewey's advice that "The child is the starting point, the center, and the end" of all curriculum decisions (1929). While the curriculum in all classrooms should start with the learner, it is especially important for teachers with bilingual students to make their classes learner-centered. Unfortunately, with second-language learners, there is sometimes the temptation to have a teacher-centered classroom because the teacher has the English proficiency that the students need. It is important to remember that second-language learners are not deficient simply because they do not speak English. They bring a rich and varied background of experiences and talent to the classroom.

When teachers build on the strengths of second-language learners, all students benefit. Recently, a teacher education candidate at our college was observing a learner-centered classroom when a new student arrived. Steve wrote about his observation experience:

The teacher had a new student who came from Ethiopia and spoke no English. She could not speak Amharic . . . but rather than allowing him to languish, she chose to allow him to teach the class enough Amharic so that they could all communicate a little bit. The children got excited about discovering a new language. This led to the teacher doing a unit on Africa complete with a wall-size relief mural of the entire continent. The end result was that the Ethiopian student was treated as a valued part of the class. He was able to contribute the richness of his culture while learning about his new home.

Teachers such as this one have many ways of making their classrooms less teacher-centered and more learner-centered. We would like to suggest two ideas: questioning strategies and student publishing. Clark has pointed out that curriculum should involve students "in some of the significant issues in life"; he therefore encourages teachers to design their curriculum around "questions worth arguing about" (1988, 29). He suggests questions for different age groups including several that would be especially relevant for immigrant students: "How am I a member of many families?" (K–1); "What are the patterns that make communities work?" (2–3); "How do humans and culture evolve and change?" (4–5); "How does one live responsibly as a member of the global village?" (6–8).

Sizer draws on the same idea by suggesting that organizing around "Essential Questions" leads to "engaging and effective curricula." In social studies, teachers responsible for teaching U.S. history might begin with broad questions, such as, "Who is American?" "Who should stay?" "Who should stay out?" "Whose country is it anyway?" (1990, 49). Sizer suggests larger questions for long-term planning and smaller, engaging questions to fit within the broader ones. For example, an essential question in botany might be, "What is life, growth, 'natural' development and what factors most influence healthy development?" A small engaging question might be, "Do stems of germinating seedlings always grow upwards and the roots downwards?" (50).

Of course, in a whole language classroom, it is important not only that the questions are relevant to the students but also that they come from the students. One teacher, Kelly, and her students, many of whom come from Hispanic backgrounds, had been working on the theme of drugs. Their broad question was, "How do drugs affect my life?" As they explored this topic, Kelly and her students looked at the surgeon general's warning against smoking and the effects of tobacco on health. The question of why people would still buy and smoke cigarettes despite the medical evidence arose naturally from the students during discussion. The students asked, "How does the media (in English and Spanish) use propaganda to encourage smoking?" They brainstormed what ads they had seen, cut out ads from English and Spanish language magazines and newspapers, interviewed people, and then wrote their own ads against smoking.

When teachers help students raise questions, they often find that the students know a great deal and that many of the students' questions are the ones that the teachers were hoping to raise anyway. However, by involving the students as Kelly did, teachers help them take ownership of their learning. As a result, students contribute much more than they would if the teacher made all the curriculum decisions.

A second idea for making learning student-centered that is especially appropriate for second-language learners is through the publishing of the students' own stories. Many teachers with immigrant students have discovered that students need to tell about their experiences, and that they can do this through writing. We have seen newsletters, individual books published for the classroom library, whole class books, books for school distribution, books published with hardback covers, and even professionally published books. All of these help bilingual learners share their experiences with others. For example, a student named José wrote the following paragraph about his first day at an American school:

> My first day of school, I was very embarrassed in my class. Another problem, I don't even know any words in English. When the teacher talk to me, I don't understand. But I have luck, because in the class was a person who speak Spanish, and he translate me. I was embarrassed, because they change me to another class. But this never happen again, because I learn a little bit English. (Jackson 1990)

When bilingual students are involved in a learner-centered curriculum, teachers focus on what their students can do rather than what they cannot do. This process builds student self-esteem and also raises teachers' expectations. In a learner-centered classroom, the potential of bilingual learners is expanded.

Principle 3

Lessons should have meaning and purpose for the students now. Research has shown that children learn their first language because it serves a purpose for them (Halliday 1984; Smith 1983). Babies' first words are ones that identify primary caregivers—"mama," "dada," "bapa"—or immediate needs that they have—"agua," "wawa." These needs are similar in different cultures. For Hmong children, for example, common early words are "mov" (food/rice) and "mis" (milk). As children grow older, they continue to learn the language that is necessary for them to get what they need.

In the same way, second-language students learn the language that they need in order to function in different social settings, including school. Katie's pre-first-grade class planned and took a trip to the pizza parlor. Later, Khmer-speaking Mak contributed to brainstorming for the class newsletter with his first spoken word in English: "pizza." Another teacher, Joan, reported on one of her first graders who spoke no English: "Roberta wasn't too interested in reading from the books we had, but being the people person she was, she soon learned to read the names of all the kids on our sign-in sheet!" Teachers and researchers (Cummins 1981) have found that second-language students learn the English expressions used in playground games or other social situations before developing more formal classroom English. It is not surprising that social language develops first; it serves students' immediate needs.

As educators, we realize that it is important for all students to develop academic language as well as social language. Unfortunately, in many classrooms academic language develops slowly because the curriculum is future-oriented. Students are told to study because "some day you are going to need to know what is being taught today." Kindergarten gets children "ready" for first grade, first grade prepares children for second, and this future orientation continues through high school or even college. The problem with this future orientation is that human beings learn things when they see a need for them. We can relate this principle to our own lives: it was not until we bought our own computer and had a problem using it that we were willing to sit and study the manual.

In whole language classrooms, teachers create situations where academic language serves all students' immediate needs. For example, when students misbehave, Jane Jones, the language arts mentor teacher for Parlier Unified School District, asks them to write to convince her that they should be excused from punishment. Miguel's piece shows how persuasively this second-language student can write in English when the writing serves an immediate purpose for him:

> Mrs. Jones I am sorry that I misbehaved in detention I want to play flag football very much. My team is counting on me to play They need me because they want to win the game I am their

only punter. I won't behave that way next time. I am really sorry
I really, really want to play. Pretty please If I would have know
that it meant not play football, I would have tried hard to
behave my self I know now. I am very sorry I will try to be good
so I wont be in detention I know that you are a nice lady I am
counting on you to let me play.

For teacher-assigned writings prepared in class, Miguel never writes
more than two or three controlled sentences. Though the piece above
shows he has not yet mastered all the conventions of writing in English, Miguel does know how to present an effective argument. This
assignment led to authentic writing (Edelsky 1989). When students are
given authentic assignments, they are more willing to take the risks
involved in using a second language.

Another authentic assignment that many bilingual students find
personally meaningful is pen pal letters. Teachers have found that
students of all ages who are reluctant to read or write regular classroom assignments will enthusiastically read pen pal letters and spend
long hours working on written responses. The following letter, written
in Spanish by a first grader to her older pen pal, not only shows an
authentic social purpose for writing, but also demonstrates the use of
the complex conditional verb form *gustaría* (would like). This young
girl uses the form naturally when writing for a real purpose.

Caro eres buena me gustaría cono ser te me gustarí leerte un
cuento bai

[Caro, you are (a) good (person). I would like to meet you. I
would like to read you a story. Bye.]

Immediate meaning and purpose are important for all students,
but especially for students who speak English as a second language.
Whole language teachers know that these students will develop English in the functional context of meaningful use. Teachers cannot put
academic content on hold until students master English. Instead, these
students need to be engaged in activities through which they can
develop concepts in their first language and learn both English and
academic content. When bilingual students are given authentic activities that build on their personal experiences and interests, they become
successful in school.

Principle 4

Lessons should engage groups of students in social interaction. Whole language teachers organize for interaction. They know that language

plays a key role in the learning process, and they create situations in which students use language for a variety of purposes and with a variety of people. In these classrooms, students frequently engage in social interaction rather than working individually. Ken Goodman explains why this is so important: "Language becomes the social medium for the sharing of thoughts; it creates a social mind from individual minds and thus greatly magnifies the learning ability of any one person" (Goodman et al. 1987, 33).

Both the physical setup of the classroom and the kinds of activities that are planned can facilitate or inhibit social interaction. When desks are pulled together or tables are available, students can work in small groups. When the room is set up in straight rows facing the teacher, social interaction is inhibited. In some classes, students move from one part of the room to another and work with different classmates; in other classes, students remain in one location and are asked not to talk with their neighbors. If students collaborate to explore questions and solve problems together in math, social studies, and science, they interact socially. On the other hand, if students are asked to complete worksheets or read chapters and answer questions individually, there is little opportunity for interaction.

In classes where students do shared readings or read with a peer or cross-age tutor and then discuss their books during literature studies, they experience interaction. In classes where there are three reading groups and where two groups do individual seat work while students in the third group read one by one for the teacher, there is little interaction. In whole language classes, students regularly interact not only with their teacher and classmates but also with other people, including administrators, parent volunteers, guest speakers, pen pals, and cross-age tutors. This social interaction is particularly important for students who are developing English proficiency (Enright and McCloskey 1985).

One especially effective way of promoting social interaction is through cross-age tutoring. Although there are different kinds of tutoring programs, all these programs create situations in which students can develop language and concepts as they interact with one another.

Kay, a bilingual resource teacher in a rural farming community, has promoted an exciting cross-age tutoring program model that has been extremely successful. At her middle school Kay has offered an elective course the last period of the day entitled "Teachers of Tomorrow." At the beginning of the year she recruits students at the orientation assembly, explaining that she needs students who speak another language so that they can be teachers to the younger students. This year Kay recruited twenty seventh- and eighth-grade students, several of whom had recently arrived from Mexico and others who speak Punjabi. These students read, write, and talk with forty-three first-, second-, and third-grade Chapter 1 students twice a week. The Teachers of Tomorrow read Spanish and English literature, discuss books, and write in interactive journals with their students. The tutors are encouraged to use their native languages, so the sounds of English, Spanish, and Punjabi are heard throughout the sessions. In addition, in order to evaluate their own teaching, the middle school students also keep journals in which they reflect on the younger students' progress. Both the older and younger children benefit. The older students feel good about their leadership roles and also see a need for both English and their native languages in the future. Several are now planning to become bilingual teachers. The younger children are supported in their first language and also see the older students as positive role models.

Another example of the value of social interaction comes from Charlene's fourth-grade classroom. Her students, many of whom were immigrants from Mexico and Southeast Asia, prepared a unit on oceanography to present to other classes in the school. Groups of children became experts on different sea animals of their choice. They read about the animals, visited an ocean aquarium, wrote about their sea animals for a class book, made models of the animals to scale, decorated their classroom like an ocean, and then presented their knowledge to other classes and to parents who came to visit the student-created ocean aquarium on display.

When students share their ideas and their knowledge in social settings, individual concepts are developed within a social context. Personal inventions are shaped by social conventions (K. Goodman 1986). Whole language classrooms buzz with a kind of controlled noise. Students, both those who speak English as a first language and those learning English as another language, are constantly talking with their classmates and their teachers, using the language or languages that they possess. They are learning as they engage in authentic social interaction.

Principle 5

Lessons should develop both oral and written language. While most mainstream whole language teachers recognize the importance of helping students develop both oracy and literacy from the start, this principle runs counter to traditional ESL methods in which oral language is established before written language. Many materials for teaching ESL provide separate lessons or even separate books for listening, speaking, reading, and writing. Often, for older students, there are even separate classes for each of the four areas.

Whole language teachers understand that it is unnatural to teach the four modes separately. When students are involved in meaningful, authentic activities, they naturally have many opportunities to speak, listen, read, and write. Pam teaches fourth grade in a farming community where the school population is about 85 percent Hispanic. Her description of a class project provides an excellent example of a teacher encouraging students to use all four modes:

> I remember one time this year, I heard a group of students complaining that the cafeteria only offered chocolate milk once a month. I told them instead of complaining about the matter they should try to do something about it. So a group of about seven students got together and brainstormed how they could change the matter. They investigated the cost of both regular and chocolate milk and found the cost difference to be very small. They then surveyed other students to see if they agreed that chocolate milk should be served more often. They then presented their information to the head of the cafeteria who, by the way, found it very delightful that the students would do so much work to change the serving of milk. She agreed to serve it more often. (She did not realize that the students even wanted chocolate milk!)

The students in Pam's classroom solved a real problem in their lives at school. In the process of investigating milk prices, surveying other fourth-grade classes as well as the fifth-grade classes, and organizing their argument to present to the head of the cafeteria, they talked and listened to one another, read information about milk, made lists, and wrote survey forms. If the second-language learners in Pam's class had been limited to oral English, they would not have been able to participate fully in this learning experience.

The idea that oral language should precede the development of literacy for bilingual students comes from the observation that children acquiring their first language speak before they read and write. While it is true that young children develop oral language first, what they are really doing is developing the kind of language that most immediately meets their needs. Written language allows people to communicate across time and space, but a two year old communicates about the here and now, so reading and writing do not serve a meaningful function. On the other hand, bilingual students need to use written language in school in order to succeed academically. If these students have to wait until their oral production of English is flawless before developing literacy, they fall behind their native English-speaking classmates in academic content areas.

Katie is a teacher who recognizes the importance of getting all her students, including her second-language students, to read and write as early as possible. She was teaching a pre-first-grade class in a large inner-city school in Fresno, California. Her second-language learners came from Mexico, Vietnam, Laos, Cambodia, and India. She had several Hmong students, so when the school district announced that a Hmong storyteller was available who could tell "The Three Billy Goats Gruff" in Hmong, Katie jumped at the opportunity to invite him to her classroom.

Before the storyteller arrived, Katie read her entire class several versions of "The Three Billy Goats Gruff" in English, and the students discussed the story enthusiastically and acted out parts. When the Hmong storyteller arrived, he was surprised that Katie wanted the entire class to hear the story told in Hmong. The children listened attentively and followed along, delighted when they recognized the sounds of the goats crossing the bridge with the "trip-trap, trip-trap" sound effects in Hmong.

After hearing the story, Mo, one of Katie's Hmong students, began to write and read in both English and Hmong. The next day he drew in his journal a picture of a goat on a bridge and labeled it in English, "3BLE GOT GRF" (Three Billy Goats Gruff). Mo realized that he could communicate in both oral and written language. In his next daily journal entry, he became a "teacher" of Hmong to Katie. He drew pictures of a book and different articles of clothing and labeled the drawings in his invented spelling of his own Hmong language. Below the pictures and Hmong words, he wrote in English "theys are mog log wich theys are the thine to me" (These are Hmong language. These are the things to me.) Katie responded by telling him how much she liked reading and learning Hmong. Mo demonstrated not only a pride in his first language and culture but also an enthusiasm for school and learning his second language. Through reading, listening, speaking, and writing, Mo showed that he was becoming an empowered biliterate.

Principle 6

Learning should take place in the first language to build concepts and facilitate the acquisition of English. Katie recognized the importance of building on her students' first language and culture. Even though she was not able to speak the primary languages of her students, she found ways to support all of her students.

All teachers recognize the importance of helping their students develop competence in English. It seems logical that the best way to develop English is to immerse students in an environment where they hear, speak, read, and write English each day. The idea that "more English leads to more English" is logical, but it is not psychological. Whole language teachers with bilingual students are familiar with the research that shows that the fastest way for students to develop both academic concepts and English is through their first language (Collier 1989). In fact, use of students' primary language helps develop English more rapidly than exclusive use of English.

We acquire language when we receive comprehensible input, messages that we understand (Krashen 1987). If students enter our schools speaking languages other than English, and if English is the language of instruction, then the students may simply not understand enough English to acquire English. In order to learn a second language, we need to have an understanding of what is being said or read. For example, it is nearly impossible to learn Portuguese simply by listening to the Portuguese radio station when the listener does not understand anything that is being said!

Use of the first language, then, can help make all instruction, including the instruction in English, more comprehensible. In the discussion of the first principle, we discussed how bilingual students who are given a preview of the lesson in their first language have a better chance of understanding the lesson in English and also learning English. If they also have a review of the lesson in their first language, they can clarify concepts and attempt to make more sense out of the English instruction. In addition, when they are also given opportunities to discuss what is going on with their classmates in their first language during the lesson, they can resolve questions and better follow the English instruction. Each of these ways of using students' first languages helps them understand content and acquire English.

Cummins (1981) has explained that if we believe that more English leads to more English, we must believe that each language is stored separately in the brain, that we have a separate underlying proficiency for each language. Those who think that we have a separate underlying proficiency must believe that something learned in one language cannot be transferred to a second language. Cummins argues that we have instead a common underlying proficiency and that concepts learned in one language transfer to the second language. We do not have to learn a concept like addition all over again in English after we have learned it in Spanish. What we need is a way to express our understanding in the new language. The more fully our first language is developed, in both oral and written form, the easier it is for us to develop a second language.

Even when schools offer instruction in students' primary languages, they often rush students into English too soon. Research has shown that while students develop the ability to converse in English in about two years, it takes much longer, from seven to ten years, for students to develop academic competence in English, even when they have continued first-language support (Collier 1989). Yet, most bilingual programs transition students into English after two years. A review of successful bilingual programs revealed that students showed success in content areas and in English because they received long-term support in their first language (Krashen and Biber 1988).

Bilingual students who receive instruction in their own first language from qualified bilingual teachers are most likely to succeed. However, only a small percent of bilingual students are in classrooms with bilingual teachers. Whole language teachers who are not bilingual can still support their students' first languages. Vince, a monolingual English-speaking teacher, teaches in Fresno, California. He recalls his experience with a Lao student:

> Chai came into my fourth-grade classroom directly from the camps in Southeast Asia. She was the first second-language student I was to come in contact with who felt good enough about her native language writing skills to employ them in class. . . . When she was finished writing a piece, she would read it to other Lao speaking students in my class who would give suggestions on the content and share their ideas with her in Lao.

Vince encouraged Chai to continue writing in her first language. During that first year in the United States, Chai never did speak or write in English. The following year some of Chai's friends told Vince that "she's speaking English so much and she writes it, too." As Vince admitted, "My first reaction was not one of achievement, it was rather a question of what the fifth-grade teacher had done that I hadn't done to get Chai to come this far along." As Vince studied the research in second-language acquisition, he began to understand better why his initial decision to allow Chai to write in Lao had been a good one. As Vince put it, "Only later did it dawn on me that those early opportunities that empowered Chai were a big part of why she was comfortable speaking and writing English so soon after her arrival." Vince gave Chai the time that she needed to develop her first language as she acquired English.

Not all teachers can provide students with instruction in their own primary language, but all teachers can find ways to support that first language. Below we list ten tips that we have found helpful for monolingual teachers who work with bilingual students (Y. Freeman and D. Freeman 1991a).

> 1. Arrange for bilingual aides or parent volunteers to read aloud literature written in the primary languages of the students and then to discuss what they have read.

> 2. Plan for older students who speak the first languages of the children to come to the class regularly to read to or, with the younger students, to act as peer tutors. For example, sixth-grade students might come to a first-grade class two or three mornings a week to share reading. This often proves beneficial to the older students as well as the younger students. Younger students can choose books to read to older students on certain days.

> 3. Set up a system of pen pal letters written in the students' primary languages between students from different classes or different schools.

> 4. Have students who are bilingual pair up with classmates who share the same primary language but who are less proficient in English. This buddy system is particularly helpful for introducing new students to class routines.

> 5. Invite bilingual storytellers to come to the class and tell stories that would be familiar to all the students. Using context clues, these storytellers can convey familiar stories in languages other than English. Well-known stories such as "Cinderella" have counterparts (and often origins) in non-English languages.

> 6. Build a classroom library of books in languages other than English. This is essential for primary-language literacy development. At times, teachers within a school may want to pool these resources.

7. Encourage journal writing in the first language. A bilingual aide or parent volunteer can read and respond to journal entries. Give students a choice of language in which to read and write.

8. To increase the primary-language resources in classrooms, publish books in languages other than English. Allow bilingual students to share their stories with classmates.

9. Look around the room at the environmental print. Include signs in bilingual students' first languages as well as articles and stories in English about the countries from which the students come. One teacher made bookmarks which were laminated and left in a basket for visitors. On one side was a proverb in English, and on the other side was the equivalent proverb written in a language other than English.

10. Have students engage in oral activities such as show and tell using their own first language as they explain objects or events from their homelands.

Principle 7

Lessons that show faith in the learner expand students' potential. When bilingual students enter schools where English is the language of instruction, they are tested for English proficiency. Many of them are labeled LEP (limited English proficient) or NEP (non-English proficient). Once students are labeled, teachers may respond more to the label than to the student. Labels like LEP suggest that the student is limited in some way, and instruction may be planned with that limitation in mind. If the students also begin to see themselves as somehow limited, they may develop low expectations for themselves, and those low expectations may confirm some teachers' beliefs that the students are deficient. In this way a cycle of failure can be set up.

On the other hand, when teachers look at bilingual students as a source of enrichment for their classrooms and treat them as an asset rather than a liability, the students often develop positive feelings about themselves and set high goals for themselves. Many teachers who see their bilingual students as an asset refer to them as PEP (potentially English proficient) rather than LEP as a first step toward viewing them positively and overcoming damaging labels (Hamayan 1989).

One of the problems with focusing on students' lack of English is that teachers may delay involving the students with meaningful content until the students develop English proficiency. ESL classes may focus on learning language for its own sake rather than using language to accomplish meaningful purposes. In *Crossing the Schoolhouse Border,* Olsen (1988) reports on interviews with a number of students who did not find ESL classes meaningful:

> Here ESL is a bad word to be called. At first I liked ESL because the other kids and the teacher were nice to me not knowing English. But I want to get out now. (9th grade Vietnamese girl)

> I was two years in ESL and I didn't like it. My English level was not that low, but they treat you like your level is so low and you are stupid. (12th grade Salvadoran girl)

Students such as these want to be engaged in meaningful content-area learning with others their age. They do not want to be labeled and treated differently.

Nevertheless, if students are struggling with English, they will not succeed in a mainstream class unless the teacher makes a special effort to make the content comprehensible to them. One way for teachers to make sure that all their students understand the concepts being explored in the classroom is by sheltering instruction (Y. Freeman and D. Freeman 1991b). Below we list several sheltering techniques that teachers have used to make content comprehensible for all their students, including their bilingual students:

1. Use visuals and realia.
2. Move from the concrete to the abstract.
3. Use gestures and body language.
4. Speak clearly and pause often.
5. Say the same thing in different ways.
6. Make frequent comprehension checks.
7. Have students explain main concepts to one another as they work in pairs or small groups. They could do this in their own first language. Then have students report back to the class.
8. Have students read and write about things that are relevant and important to them and their own lives.
9. Keep oral presentations or reading assignments short.
10. Use cooperative activities (Kagan 1986) more often than lectures or assigned readings.

If possible, preview the content in the student's first language, perhaps with the assistance of a bilingual aide or another student. Then, if possible, review the completed lesson in the student's first language.

Perhaps more important than these sheltering techniques to make the content comprehensible is the attitude that teachers have toward their students' culture and language. Whole language teachers see the diversity in their classrooms as an opportunity to expand on their personal experiences with both language and culture. Instead of subscribing to the melting-pot image, these teachers see their students as part of a great patchwork quilt. The diverse languages and cultures that bilingual students bring to the classroom can provide additional beauty in classes where teachers celebrate diversity. In *Embracing Diversity*, a book about thirty-six teachers successfully "embracing the diversity" of California classrooms, Moyra Contreras describes her approach to bilingual students: "My role is to respect the kids as they come into the classroom as opposed to trying to change them into something they are not" (L. Olsen and Muller 1990, 28). When educators have this alternative view, bilingual students are seen as valuable, important, contributing members of every classroom community.

Unfortunately, many types of assessment used with bilingual learners cover rather than uncover their strengths. It is extremely difficult for schools to change their view of bilingual learners and for bilingual learners to value themselves when they are labeled by inappropriate evaluation instruments. Standardized tests of all kinds tell educators what students cannot do but give little information about what they can do. Many whole language teachers who have faith in their students' abilities have developed alternative methods of evaluation that are more consistent with their views of teaching and learning.

Portfolio assessment is one tool for evaluation that is good for all students but especially for bilingual students (Y. Freeman and D. Freeman 1991a). Below we provide information about portfolios for second-language learners that might be helpful to teachers considering portfolio assessment.

What is a portfolio? A portfolio is a box or a folder which contains various kinds of information that has been gathered over time about one student.

What goes into students' portfolios? Portfolios are most commonly considered a collection of students' formal and informal writing. However, portfolios might also contain audiotaped and videotaped recordings of students' science, math, or art projects; programs from music and drama events; social studies reports; teacher/parent observation notes; lists of books read with dates and notes; and lists of activities in which the students are involved outside of the classroom. For second-language students, samples are collected in both the students' first and second languages.

Who are portfolios for? Portfolios are for teachers, all support personnel that work with the students, the students themselves, parents, and administrators.

Why is portfolio assessment important for second-language students? Research shows that it takes five to seven years for second-language learners to achieve on a par with native speakers of English when growth is measured by norm-referenced standardized tests (Cummins 1989). However, bilingual students learn much more than what standardized tests show. Portfolios provide examples of students' abilities and growth over time in their first as well as second languages.

Who decides what goes into portfolios? Students and all teachers working with the students make choices.

How often do things get put into portfolios? This varies, but at least once a month. Some teachers and students put things into their portfolios weekly and then at the end of each month choose which things are to be left in.

What do portfolios show teachers and administrators? Portfolios show student growth over time, student interests, student strengths in their first as well as second languages, and the effectiveness of the present curriculum for each student.

What do portfolios tell students? Portfolios show students what they have learned, what they spend time and energy on, and what they need to work on more.

What do portfolios show parents? Portfolios show parents what their children are learning, what they are doing in school, what kinds of activities are valued in school, and what kinds of activities the parents can do at home to support learning.

What are the advantages of portfolios over other types of evaluation? Portfolios involve students and allow them both to show and to see their progress over time. Instead of highlighting what students cannot do, portfolios allow students to show what they can do without time restraints.

Portfolio assessment has benefits for everyone. Teachers can see their bilingual students' strengths and growth. By looking at the work that students keep in their portfolios, teachers can see which activities are most effective with their second-language learners. Portfolio assessment offers the kind of evaluation which can "form, inform and reform curricula and programs rather than fragment learning into isolated elements" (Barrs 1990).

Conclusion

Of all the principles for whole language teachers of bilingual students, we believe that faith in the learner is the most important. Supporting students' primary languages, providing comprehensible content for these students, and finding ways such as portfolios to assess student progress are all ways to put faith into action. When whole language teachers have faith in the learner, they follow the other principles that we have discussed: they teach from whole to part; they begin with the students and build on students' strengths; they involve students in meaningful content; they help students become bilingual and biliterate as students develop both oral and written language; they encourage learning in each student's first language; and they encourage students to engage in purposeful social interaction. Teachers who have faith in the learner help bilingual students reach their potential as learners.

References

Barrs, M. 1990. The Primary Language Record: Reflection of issues in evaluation. *Language Arts* 67 (3): 244–53.

Clark, E. 1988. The search for a new educational paradigm: Implications of new assumptions about thinking and learning. *Holistic Education Review* 1 (1): 18–30.

Collier, V. 1989. How long? A synthesis of research on academic achievement in a second language. *TESOL Quarterly* 23 (3): 509–32.

Cummins, J. 1981. The role of primary language development in promoting educational success for language minority students. In *Schooling and language minority students: A theoretical framework*, 3–49. Los Angeles: Evaluation, Dissemination and Assessment Center, California State University, Los Angeles.

——. 1989. *Empowering minority students.* Sacramento: California Association of Bilingual Education.

Dewey, J. 1929. *My pedagogic creed.* Washington, D.C.: The Progressive Education Association.

Edelsky, C. 1989. Bilingual children's writing: Fact and fiction. In *Richness in writing: Empowering ESL students*, ed. D. Johnson and D. Roen, 165–76. New York: Longman.

Edelsky, C., B. Altwerger, and B. Flores. 1991. *Whole language: What's the difference?* Portsmouth, N.H.: Heinemann.

Enright, D. S., and M. L. McCloskey. 1985. Yes, talking! Organizing the classroom to promote second language acquisition. *TESOL Quarterly* 19 (3): 431–53.

Freeman, Y. S., and D. E. Freeman. 1991a. Portfolio assessment: An exciting view of what bilingual children can do. *BEOutreach* 2 (1): 6–7.

——. 1991b. Ten tips for monolingual teachers of bilingual students. In *The whole language catalog*, ed. K. Goodman, L. Bird, and Y. Goodman, 90. Santa Rosa, Calif.: American School Publishers.

——. 1992. *Whole language for second language learners.* Portsmouth, N.H.: Heinemann.

Freeman, Y. S., and S. Nofziger. 1991. WalkuM to RnM 33: Vien Vinidos al cualTo 33. In *Organizing for whole language*, ed. K. Goodman, Y. Goodman, and W. Hood, 65–83. Portsmouth, N.H.: Heinemann.

Goodman, K. 1986. *What's whole in whole language?* Portsmouth, N.H.: Heinemann.

Goodman, K., E. Brooks Smith, R. Meredith, and Y. Goodman. 1987. *Language and thinking in school: A whole language curriculum*, 3d ed. Katonah, N.Y.: Richard C. Owen.

Goodman, Y. 1985. Kidwatching: Observing children in the classroom. In *Observing the Language Learner*, ed. A. Jaggar and M. T. Smith-Burke, 9–18. Newark, Del., and Urbana, Ill.: International Reading Association and National Council of Teachers of English.

Halliday, M. A. K. 1984. Three aspects of children's language development: Learning language, learning through language, and learning about language. In *Oral and written language development research: Impact on the schools*, ed. Y. Goodman, M. Haussler, and D. Strickland. Urbana, Ill.: National Council of Teachers of English.

Hamayan, E. 1989. *Teach your children well.* Oak Brook, Ill.

Jackson, W., ed. 1990. *New Americans.* Fresno, Calif.: Yosemite Middle School.

Kagan, S. 1986. Cooperative learning and sociocultural factors in schooling. In *Beyond language: Social and cultural factors in schooling language minority students*, 231–98. Los Angeles: Evaluation, Dissemination and Assessment Center, California State University, Los Angeles.

Krashen, S. 1987. *Principles and practice in second language acquisition.* Englewood Cliffs, N.J.: Prentice Hall.

Krashen, S., and D. Biber. 1988. *On course: Bilingual education's success in California.* Sacramento: California Association of Bilingual Education.

Olsen, L. 1988. *Crossing the schoolhouse border: Immigrant students and the California public schools.* San Francisco: California Tomorrow.

Olsen, L., and N. Mullen. 1990. *Embracing diversity: Teachers' voices from California classrooms.* San Francisco: California Tomorrow.

Olsen, R. 1989. A survey of limited English proficient enrollments and identification procedures. *TESOL Quarterly* 23 (3): 469–88.

Rigg, P., and V. Allen. 1989. Introduction. In *When they don't all speak English,* ed. P. Rigg and V. Allen, vii–xx. Urbana, Ill.: National Council of Teachers of English.

Sizer, T. 1990. *Student as worker, teacher as coach.* New York: Simon and Schuster.

Smith, F. 1983. *Essays into literacy.* Portsmouth, N.H.: Heinemann.

III Practice

In light of what we know about education, what action do we take? That is the question posed by the concept of practice, and each author in this section suggests a different answer. The point of this section is not to suggest "how to do it," but rather to sample what others have done. Yetta Goodman begins the section by exploring what it means to embrace a multicultural perspective: how this perspective plays out in the classroom and what it means when one "takes seriously the language and culture of the learner." She not only provides a historical context for how multicultural issues have been dealt with, but she invites us to examine our own beliefs. Wendy Hood and Nigel Hall both recount the impact that whole language theory has on their practices—Hood as a kindergarten teacher moving to a new assignment in second grade, replete with challenges and solutions, and Hall as a researcher discovering the ability that very young children have to engage in written dialogue. Mary Kenner Glover discusses the role that caring plays in her whole language school. Sarah Hudelson and Irene Serna provide an engaging description of how young Spanish speakers take their first steps as writers in Spanish and English and relate how the school setting supports these writers' efforts. Carolyn Ewoldt reports on her observations of deaf and hearing-impaired students and teachers. Her focus is on how meaning is negotiated and disrupted during a specific language event—that of shared reading. We close with Rudy Engbrecht's narrative chronicling the difficulties that were encountered and the rewards that were reaped along the route that one teacher traveled as he abandoned one educational orientation in favor of another. It is a piece of writing that mirrors the change that many of us have undergone as a result of having old beliefs challenged, abandoned, and supplanted with those more elegant, liberating, and practical.

12 One among Many: A Multicultural, Multilingual Perspective

Yetta M. Goodman
University of Arizona

Multicultural education is as important for teachers and other adults in our society as it is for the students in our classrooms. In fact, I want to argue that unless teachers are actively involved in continuously learning about multiculturalism, their students' knowledge and experiences will be seriously limited.

Thoughtfully organized whole language curriculum is immersed within a multicultural perspective because it takes seriously the language and culture of the learner. Both whole language and multicultural education call for a view of students as capable learners. Concern for multicultural education provides opportunities and experiences to view with understanding the various perspectives and beliefs expressed by our students, their parents, and their communities and helps teachers begin to appreciate that within every community there is a culture that can inform the student and the school (Moll et al. 1990). Within a multicultural framework, we respect each other, recognize our similarities, debate our multiple perspectives, accept and celebrate our differences, and are constantly involved in exploring the strengths and influences that all the members of our world community contribute to our own growth and well-being.

Multicultural education is equally important for all groups of students and their teachers, whether they are part of the dominant cultural group or members of various parallel cultural groups within the society. I borrow the term *parallel culture groups* from my colleague Rudine Sims Bishop to avoid the misnomer of the term *minority*. Each cultural group, regardless of its position in society, has a tendency to be ethnocentric in its orientation. As we find ways to understand each other, every group benefits. Author Ralph Ellison has made this point in a most eloquent way:

If you can show me how I can cling to that which is real to me,
while teaching me a way into a larger society, then I will drop
my defense and my hostility, but I will sing your praises and I
will help you make the desert bear fruit. (Quoted in Riessman
1967, 47)

In the past year, I have had a number of experiences that have
heightened for me the importance of and need for multicultural education for all of us—adults and children. There have been repeated
editorials in daily newspapers raising specters of disaster for American schools because there are school districts, universities, and colleges that are finding ways to provide a broader base and deeper
understanding of history and culture than the one which has been
typically available to students, especially through standardized textbooks. These editorials seem to deny multiple perspectives concerned
with ways of knowing, believing, and valuing.

George Will was one such journalist who sounded an alarm,
speaking against "compensatory history that preaches the virtues of
the oppressed by exaggerating their achievements." In an editorial
appearing in the *Arizona Star* in 1991, entitled "Multicultural History
Becomes a Political Tool," Will indicated that such a view suggests that
"There's always an Irishman at the bottom of it doing the real work."
He means that in such presentations of history, ethnic groups exagger-
ate their achievements in the grand scheme of things. He suggests that
this kind of teaching is politically motivated without acknowledging
that teaching from only a European/Western tradition is equally politically motivated.

Another experience occurred at a whole language conference
that I attended in Massachusetts. Of the over two hundred people
there, two participants complained that there was "too much multicultural content" at the conference; "too much about the Holocaust and
various minority groups"; and "not enough content for middle class
white kids."

A continuous experience that I have related to the look of surprise that I get from people when I mention how much I loved living
in Detroit. I spent my years in Detroit learning from friends and colleagues from different racial and ethnic groups. Those fourteen years
have had a lasting influence on my professional life as well as my
personal life.

Through these experiences and other similar experiences, it is
obvious that we have a long way to go and much work to do to free
ourselves from biases and prejudices. Myths about others are often

established by the educational system, even in professional literature and in the classrooms of universities and colleges. Because of the need for all of us to understand the nature of prejudice, which I believe stands in the way of strong multicultural education, I want to discuss multicultural education not only from the point of view of what it means for curriculum in the classroom but what it means for each and every one of us concerned with whole language.

Multiculturalism: A Curriculum for Problem Solving and Democracy

James A. Banks of the University of Washington in Seattle has written widely on multicultural education (Banks 1988; Banks and Banks 1989) and is thoughtfully critical of what he calls the contributions and ethnic-additive approaches to multicultural curriculum. These approaches add ethnic heroes, holidays, or customs to the ongoing curriculum by simply adding a book, a unit, or a course without examining how what is being studied impacts major issues and movements in society. Rather, Banks suggests that it is necessary to understand "the nature, development and complexity" of society by examining how different perspectives, frames of reference, and content from the various groups interrelate and impact the world as we know it. In addition, once we discover that there are problems occurring because of these complexities, then we need to become actively involved with our students in solving the problems as members of a democratic society. It is not enough just to *know*—we must act on that knowledge. That is the nature of a democracy. Our programs must move our students to action. I believe through meaningful activity or experiences more powerful and long-lasting learning occurs.

Using Literature for Extending Multicultural Experiences

I want to share some of the things I have read that have helped me consider different perspectives, frames of reference, and content. Reading about others and understanding their perspectives allows us to expand and enrich our world. My purpose is that these ideas may not only impact your ideas about multiculturalism but also may point to ways in which such expansions will impact the classroom. I am concerned that teachers who do not continuously add to their own knowledge about the worlds of others cannot develop a multicultural curriculum that will seriously affect the thinking and actions of their students. Without taking multicultural issues seriously, we may add nice units about others to the curriculum, but these will not provide the transformations necessary to recognize the complexities of our world and to explore the ways of participating in the problem solving necessary to make the significant changes that will impact all of our citizens.

It has been through these readings that I constantly keep myself sensitive to issues of people who have different views of the world than I do, who see the world in very different terms because they have less money than I do, who speak a different language than I do, or who come from a family that believes very differently than I do. It is too easy for humans to see the world from just their own point of view. The passage from Ralph Ellison quoted above suggests to me that if I as a teacher can constantly reconsider these issues of difference, then I can take what I believe and what I know and share them with my students. I will also be in a position to recognize the ways in which our lives are similar as well as different. If my students see that the way I act (not just what I say) reflects a multicultural view and my acceptance and respect for every one of my students regardless of age, race, creed, national origin, language, or gender, then they will be comfortable and able to reach out and understand my world, and the world of their students as well.

The more we read and the more we try to discover the backgrounds of the students whom we teach, the more opportunities we will have to dispel the myths that strongly influence the way in which we teach.

Looking Historically

By examining historical documents, it is possible to gain glimpses into the ways in which myths about various individuals and groups are developed and maintained. I have always been amused by an article written in 1905 about Jewish immigrant children. It is interesting to note the misconceptions and overgeneralizations that this middle-class, well-educated teacher had about the new Jewish arrivals in New York schools. There are teachers and other authors writing about the children of the poor today who lack the sensitivity and insight of the African American author Jessie Fortune. Although she writes eloquently about the plight of Jewish immigrant children, she perpetuates the myth about Jews and money:

> Unlike the best Hollander, the Jew does not seem to take naturally to cleansing or scrubbing; his sole aim seems to be earning

> money, and all household duties are subservient to this purpose, so that as often as not the dining room, parlor and sitting room serve as a tailor shop or work shop. . . . they are interesting children to know. Some of them are very beautiful, physically and temperamentally, and some are quite the reverse . . . one grows to have an interest in their development which one would never imagine feeling when one first views the swarms of them playing around the streets. (Fortune 1905, 6–7)

Another historical examination that can be enlightening for our own knowledge and for our students' relates to major anniversaries and celebrations. In 1992 we observed the 500-year anniversary of Columbus's trip to the Americas, which led to many accounts in the popular press that were useful in the classroom. Many groups legitimately raised questions about who really discovered America and when and about the nature of Columbus's contributions to the New World and the Old World. I do not want to deny Columbus his due, but a feature article in *U.S. News and World Report* entitled "America before Columbus" (1991) suggests an interesting way to explore the issue of the Americas and who lived here during which periods of time. It provides a broadened framework from which to explore the contributions of Columbus by presenting not just the impact of the Old World on the New but also the contributions made to the Old World from the New. A publication for children called *Rethinking Columbus* (1991) focuses on helping readers examine the sources of readily accepted beliefs about Columbus, many of which are critiqued from a variety of points of view. By using these resources, students and teachers broaden their views about the variety of concerns related to the development of the Americas.

In the past there have been fairly few children's picture books concerned with life in the Americas before Columbus, but the 500-year anniversary of Columbus's sailing has sparked the publication of numerous books documenting this period from a wide range of perspectives. Teachers and their students may write their own accounts as they research this period.

Biographical Accounts

Many of our students come to school with backgrounds that are very different from North American culture and language. Eva Hoffman's *Lost in Translation: A Life in a New Language* (1985) helped me understand the powerful transitions that such people are called on to make. Hoffman emigrated with her family to Vancouver, British Columbia, from Poland in 1959 and felt as if she had moved from paradise to exile as she exchanged cultures and languages. She recounts the intensity of her innermost emotional and intellectual responses to these major changes in her life. Hoffman relocated again to attend college in Houston, Texas, and then moved into the intellectual literary world of New York City, where she is now an editor for the *New York Times Book Review.* This is a poignant personal narrative for those concerned with discovering how anyone who crosses over from one culture to another and from one language to another feels emotionally and intellectually. It helps to sensitize us to our students and to their parents, whether they come from overseas to this part of the world, from a reservation to an urban metropolis, or from a big city to the mountains of Colorado. Those who identify with Eva Hoffman must take into account what would happen to any of us as we move from culture to culture, from language to language, from society to society. We take our old selves with us and must make peace between the two or more worlds that are coming together for us. Hoffman uses language in a most powerful and sensitive way to reveal to us the impact that the complexities of being bilingual has on understanding both our old and new worlds.

This is described poignantly as she recounts the response to her own and her sister's Polish names by the school teacher who

> has seen too many . . . come and go to get sentimental about a name. Mine—"Ewa"—is easy to change into its near equivalent in English, "Eva." My sister's name—"Alina"—poses more of a problem, but after a moment's thought . . . the teacher decides that Elaine is close enough. My sister and I hang our heads wordlessly under this careless baptism. (105)

Hoffman also helps to awaken her readers to what happens to any bilingual learners when they come to see the differences in their perceptions and conceptualizations in one language and the other:

> "River" in Polish was a vital sound, energized with the essence of riverhood, of my rivers, of my being immersed in rivers. "River" in English is cold—a word without an aura. It has no accumulated associations for me, and it does not give off the radiating haze of connotation. It does not evoke. (107)

Multiple Languages, Genres, and Forms

Perhaps one way to get us all to think simultaneously of the differences and the similarities of language and literacy in the world is to bring into our classrooms languages that we do not understand. We need to become exposed to the multilingual nature of the world as well as to multiculturalism.

Classrooms should include resources that appear in many different languages. Picture story books in such languages as Japanese, Spanish, Hebrew, French, and Vietnamese, among others, should line our bookshelves. With our students, we can explore the differences and similarities of the multiple types of written languages and illustrations that are published in the world. We can examine versions of the same books that appear in different languages and can compare them in a variety of ways. We can invite speakers of those languages to read aloud to our classes. Children can follow along if the books are familiar to them; if the children are not familiar with the material, translations of words or actions can be provided.

Examining Our Own Biases

I believe another multicultural concern that can be affected by literature is recalling and understanding the injustices inflicted on one group of people by another. What are the sociocultural and political conditions that allow one group of people to reduce others to nonentities? In my own Jewish tradition, we often recite on the Passover holiday, "remember that you were once slaves in Egypt and teach this diligently to your children," so that we can be vigilant about those who forget the lessons of various tyrannies committed over the years. The last ten years have seen a growing number of books written for children about the Holocaust caused by Hitler and the Nazis. *Rose Blanche* by Roberto Innocenti (Taborti and Chang, 1985) is a picture story book that captures this horrible time in a way that encourages even young children to talk about and wonder about what happened. But we also need to be concerned about the treatment in the United States of various parallel groups over the years. We can institute time for the discussion of current events in our classrooms and can use magazines and newspapers extensively as well as books to explore these controversies.

Melor Sturua, a political journalist for *Izvestia* for over forty years who is now working on his autobiography at the University of Minnesota, quotes Chekhov by saying that all his life "he squeezed the slave out of himself drop by drop" (1991). Sturua uses this metaphor to explain the influence of Stalin over the Soviets. I would like to use the metaphor to help us all to recognize the attitudes and values that we need to squeeze out of ourselves drop by drop in order to establish a classroom community in which multiculturalism will have a chance to flourish and have a real impact on the lives of our students.

In 1991 Ron Somers, a sportswriter for the *Arizona Star*, reviewed a new publication called *I Had a Hammer: The Hank Aaron Story* by Hank Aaron and Lonnie Wheeler (HarperCollins, 1991). Somers quotes Aaron, who began to receive the vilest hate mail when he was closing in on Babe Ruth's home-run record: "The Ruth chase should have been the greatest period of my life, and it was the worst. I couldn't believe there was so much hatred in people. It's something I'm still trying to get over, and maybe I never will. I know I'll never forget it, and the fact is, I don't want to." The review ends: "That's the compelling theme of the book. He [Hank Aaron] appears to transcend racism by becoming a sports hero. Yet he is forever haunted by the hatred he faced just because he had black skin and could hit a ball over a fence" (Somers 1991).

In addition to the issue of racism, the language used is another concern that I would explore with students. The reproduction of one of the hate letters in the newspaper article reads: "Hey nigger boy, We at the KKK Staten Island Division want you to know that no number of guards can keep you dirty (expletive) nigger (expletive) alive" (quoted in Somers 1991). What is interesting is that the expletives that are not printed are probably words that my students and I use without much thought, but the word *nigger* is one that I always hesitate saying, even in settings such as this one where it serves an important purpose. Yet in the newspaper, common swear words are omitted and a term of great derision is allowed to stand.

A biography called *Sorrow's Kitchen* that was written for adolescents by Mary E. Lyons has helped me gain access to a range of concerns about racism, feminism, and dialect variation. In this unusual and powerful biography, Lyons not only tells the history of a great writer and anthropologist, Zora Neale Hurston, but embeds the stories and folklore written by Hurston within the chronology of the biography.

This book enlightens the reader about African American writers during the 1920s. It explores why a woman who writes passionately about her southern roots, language, and experiences was rejected by other African American authors, mainly males. Hurston was part of the Harlem Renaissance in the 1920s, which Lyons describes: "Harlem became a cultural magnet that attracted unknown musicians and artists. . . . Here they were free to develop their artistry and become part of the 'golden legend' of Harlem" (Lyons 1990, 34). Harlem attracted poets and novelists who, in a ten-year period, wrote some of the most memorable literary works of this century.

Hurston, who went to Howard and Columbia Universities, had poor and rural southern roots. Even at Howard, a prestigious all–African American institution, she was different—a woman from the rural South, which allowed her to create "unforgettable folk characters and speech." However, many African American writers, such as W. E. B. Du Bois, Ralph Ellison, and Richard Wright, were unhappy when blacks were portrayed "as common folks working in bean fields" (97). To them, racial stereotype included folklore and writing in dialect. In 1973, author Alice Walker rediscovered Hurston as an important literary figure.

Hurston's books, some fictional with the flavor of folktales and others anthropological research accounts, provide a rich description of the culture, language, beliefs, and religious orientations of rural southern African Americans at the beginning of this century. Mary Lyons brings this significant figure to adolescents and their teachers.

Multicultural education should be the central theme in social studies and literacy education. It allows our studies of history, geography, political science, government, archeology, and anthropology, among others, to include wide ranges of perspectives. It suggests that in order for students to become active, democratic adult citizens, they must be able to understand and take part in the controversies that represent a diversity of perspectives.

Call to Action

One book that documents the notion that problem solving concerning multicultural issues includes action is a Venezuelan book titled *La Calle Es Libre* (The Streets Are Free) (Kurusa 1981). This book helps teachers and students realize that the solutions to many problems rest in the hands of each and every member of the society. It clearly explores the need that people have to act in concert with others in order to solve their own problems.

The children in this book live in a poverty area of a big city. They have no place to play in their community of crowded streets and houses. With the help of a librarian and an aggressive newspaper reporter, the children confront city officials and organize their parents. After going through a series of problematic events, they eventually are able to have their own *parque*. They invite all to their free park with a sign on the fence that reads:

El parque es libre
Pasen todos
Muy felices.

All students, including those from the middle class, need to explore what contributions come from the many and varied groups with whom they share this world. They need to experience what collaboration and interdependence can accomplish. As schools and teachers organize for a powerful multicultural curriculum involving various parallel cultural groups, it is necessary to explore the role of power, what happens to those who face a sense of powerlessness, and the ways in which power is shared in a democracy.

Literature is a place to start such understandings and a place to which the teacher and the students return time and time again for new insights and understandings. They can assume responsibility collaboratively to respond to issues which rise out of the literature. Students and teachers may find that they need to rewrite the text in new ways to more accurately reflect the realities of the present or to discover unusual new texts.

But we cannot build a strong multicultural curriculum until we are committed to understanding the many lessons available to us from the many groups that we face in our classrooms. We need to see each of our students as representatives of their own cultural lives. We need to be willing to rejoice in the cultures represented in our classrooms and to learn from them so that our students will in turn find reason to learn from us. It is really in the hands of each and every one of us to take responsibility to actively and democratically build a multicultural curriculum.

References

America before Columbus. 1991. *U.S. News and World Report,* July 8.

Banks, J. 1988. *Multiethnic education: Theory and practice,* 2d ed. Boston: Allyn and Bacon.

Banks, J., and C. Banks, eds. *Multicultural education: Issues and perspectives.* Boston: Allyn and Bacon.

Bigelow, B., B. Miner, and B. Peterson, eds. *Rethinking Columbus: Teaching about the 500th anniversary of Columbus's arrival in America.* 1991. Milwaukee: Rethinking Schools.

Fortune, J. 1905 [1975]. Among the children of the East Side Jews. Reprint, *Jewish Currents* 29 (2): 4–7.

Hoffman, E. 1985. *Lost in translation: A life in a new language.* New York: Penguin Books.

Kurusa. 1986. *La calle es libre.* Caracas, Venezuela: Ediciones Ekare Banco del Libro.

Lyons, M. 1990. *Sorrow's kitchen: The life and folklore of Zora Neale Hurston.* New York: Charles Scribner's Sons.

Moll, L., C. Velez-Ibanez, J. Greenberg, and K. Whitmore. 1990. *Community knowledge and classroom practice.* Final Report no. 300 87-0131. Tucson: University of Arizona, Office of Bilingual Education and Minority Language Affairs.

Riessman, F. 1967. *Blueprint for the disadvantaged.* New York: Anti-Defamation League.

Somers, R. 1991. Book review in *Arizona Star,* July 28.

Sturua, M. 1991. *Parade Magazine,* July 28.

Will, G. 1991. Multicultural history becomes a political tool. Syndicated column in *Arizona Star,* July 18.

13 Beginning Literacy in English in a Whole Language Bilingual Program

Sarah Hudelson and Irene Alicia Serna
Arizona State University

Many of us who work in bilingual education fight constantly for the acceptance, valuing, and use of languages other than English in the classroom. It seems that we are always arguing that learners will not be disadvantaged because they are learning in a language other than English, that becoming literate in a language other than English will assist with literacy in English, and that using one's native language does not make a person a threat to the American way of life. When focusing specifically on children in preschool and elementary school settings, many seem to make the assumption that if children do not speak English, somehow they are unable or not ready to learn. Also disturbing is the claim made frequently that if children learn in a language other than English, they will never become English users, that somehow they are doomed to a life of monolingualism. Such a result is certainly not the intent of bilingual programs; further, this has not been our experience as we have worked with children in bilingual education classes.

Our impression has always been that learners have gradually and naturally started to use English or added it on to their native languages. In fact, a greater problem has been that learners will begin to *refuse* to use their native languages and move exclusively into English, with a resulting loss of language resources that we so desperately need. Given our sense that adding on English has not been a problem for learners, we decided to examine some data from a whole language bilingual program in which we (along with Yvonne Montiel) have been involved for the last two years. While our major purpose has been to document the literacy development of Spanish-speaking children through a series of three-year case studies, we also have been collecting instances of English language use among our case study children. Our intention in this chapter is to share some of our findings.

We start by setting the context for the samples, by describing the site where we have been working. William T. Machan School is a public elementary school in Phoenix, Arizona. The neighborhood around Machan is becoming increasingly Hispanic as more families move north from Mexico, Guatemala, and Honduras, seeking economic opportunities and refuge from civil strife. Presently, about 65 percent of Machan's population is Hispanic, and Spanish is spoken in many homes. About 40 percent of the children are designated as Spanish dominant. The school population is quite transient. It is not unusual for 25–30 percent of the children in any room to enroll and withdraw from the school within the course of an academic year.

When Dr. Lynn Davey, the principal, arrived in 1986, the instruction at Machan was highly traditional and focused on the utilization of basal readers, sequentially based math texts, and content-area textbooks. Since her arrival, Davey has been working to recruit to the school teachers with a whole language philosophy and to help teachers implement a whole language philosophy in their classrooms. A grant from the Arizona State Department of Education that focused on increasing the achievement of "at risk" children at the K-3 level has assisted in this effort and has brought the services of Kelly Draper to Machan. Draper works with the primary teachers on a regular basis and has been most instrumental in helping to put into practice a whole language philosophy. Most of the teachers at Machan believe that learning occurs most effectively in settings where children are asking questions, solving problems, constructing meaning, and taking risks. Children are involved in meaningful content study where they utilize and interact with a variety of materials, texts, and audiences. Literature forms the basis for classroom reading, and writing for multiple purposes and audiences is at the core of what children do.

With regard to bilingualism and whole language, the school maintains a philosophy that children initially should become literate and learn school content in their particular native language or in the language in which they feel more confident (in this case, Spanish); then they should use the abilities developed in the native language to construct meaning in another language, English. Machan has a transitional bilingual program, the goal of which is that the children will be able to do their learning in English by the fourth grade. Since 1989, we have been spending quite a bit of time at Machan on a research project designed to provide documentation about how Spanish-speaking children, within the context of a whole language bilingual program, construct literacy in their native language. We began by working with selected children in both kindergarten and first grade at Machan, and we moved with those children into the first and second grades, and then into the second and third grades. (In spite of Machan's high transiency rate and the fact that the school boundaries changed midway through our study, seventeen of the twenty case study children remained at Machan.)

Although we have been attending to the Spanish-language literacy development of our case study children, we and the classroom teachers in whose rooms we have conducted our research have also been fascinated and charmed by the children's voluntary use of English. So, to borrow a phrase from Harste, Woodward, and Burke (1984), we would like to share with you some language stories which provide literacy lessons for all of us working in bilingual education. We have grouped the stories based on the generalizations that we think may be made from them.

The first story comes from kindergarten. Right before school ended, one of the bilingual kindergarten teachers asked the children in her class to write letters to next year's kindergartners to tell them what to expect in kindergarten. The children set to work. One of our case study children, Juan, a Spanish-dominant child who usually chose to sit with other children who were writing in Spanish, on this day sat with a small group of English speakers. When he finished his letter, he carried it to his teacher excitedly and announced that he had written his letter in English. The letter read like this: "bernr-bCDReBReREde." He then read to the teacher what he had written: "Dear kindergartner. She is a good teacher and pretty, too." Then he showed the teacher the bottom of the page and announced: "Mira, teacher, también escribí mi nombre en inglés." He had written his name in English by substituting a *y* for the *j*. In this particular bilingual kindergarten, the majority of the children were English speakers. Juan's teacher was a native English speaker, although she spoke Spanish fluently in the classroom. Most probably, Juan had concluded that there was a good chance that many of the incoming kindergarten children would be English speaking—so he wrote to them in English.

Another story pertaining to Juan had occurred a short time earlier. For weeks Juan had been working on a complex story, "Los Osos Malos." This was an adventure story about some evil bears who chased Juan, intending to eat him. When Juan captured one of the bears and took him home, it turned out that the bear was a boy in a costume. The final version of his story was shaped and typed by Irene, and Juan created illustrations to go along with it. When it was ready, Juan read it aloud to the class. After he had read it in Spanish, he went back through the story and translated it orally into English for the members of the group who did not know Spanish. Once again, he demonstrated that he realized that he needed to make his work understandable to an English-speaking audience.

When Juan moved into first grade, he had two teachers who worked as a team, one with whom he worked on Spanish language arts and mathematics in the mornings, and another with whom he worked on thematic units in science and social studies in the afternoons. Although both teachers were bilingual, the teacher he had in the morning came to be thought of as "la maestra de español" (the Spanish teacher), because she used Spanish exclusively in the mornings. Additionally, the afternoon thematic-unit work was designed to be time for English as a second language, where children, grouped heterogeneously in terms of language dominance, would work together studying content of interest to them and using English (at least part of the time) to investigate the content. Early in the year the children were studying sea animals. In his learning log one day, Juan wrote about an animal that he had been studying, "Eso asrk" and read aloud, "We saw a shark." Then he added orally in Spanish, "en una escoba pasando en frente de la luna" (on a broom passing in front of the moon). Because Juan associated English with his content work, he tried to write in English. But clearly his Spanish was much more developed than his English, as the additional description in his native language demonstrates. With the teacher's encouragement, he went back to writing his learning log entries in Spanish.

In another bilingual first grade, Alicia had decided to create a book, an expert project, all about Barbie dolls since she owned several of them. With Irene's help, she spent several weeks constructing the text for this book. It was full of facts about the different kinds of Barbie dolls that Alicia owned, how they were alike and different from each other. Irene worked with her on producing and revising the text, and Irene entered the text into the computer and printed it out. One day, Alicia shared the book with some of her classmates, both Spanish-dominant learners and English speakers. For the benefit of the English speakers, she summarized in English the information that she had written in Spanish. But one English-speaking child complained that she could not read this book since it was written in Spanish. What could be done about that? The solution: translate the book into English. But the task of translating a twenty-page book seemed a vaunt-ing one to this very capable first-grade child. So she proposed to Irene that she herself would translate the book orally into a tape recorder and that Irene would transcribe her words into written form using the computer. Irene complied, and thus a translation of the Barbie book became a reality.

To celebrate the publication of some of the first-grade authors' books, Alicia's teacher arranged an authors' tea, at which selected authors read their works to other children. Alicia was one of the authors honored at the tea. She read to small groups of both Spanish speakers and English speakers. When doing so, she knew without asking whether to read in Spanish or English, and she insisted on reading her entire book in one language or another.

Second-grader Arturo had been in the bilingual program since kindergarten. His first-grade experience had been with the teacher dubbed "la maestra de español," the designated Spanish language arts teacher. When he moved into second grade, the makeup of the class changed somewhat in that there were more English speakers in the room, and the English and Spanish speakers stayed together all day for instruction. This meant that there was more English used in the class. Additionally, Arturo's teacher was not a native Spanish speaker, although her Spanish was excellent. All of these factors may have influenced Arturo, early in the school year, to assume that he should interact with her in English whenever possible, or even, perhaps, that he should use only English for his schoolwork. This is one explanation for the fact that his first journal entries were in English though he was a child who was still more fluent in Spanish than he was in English. His first entry was the following:

> bearmsc—
> buyuLaek Fars or Sneiks
>
> [Dear Mrs C—
> Do you like frogs or snakes?]

As his teacher continued to work in Spanish, however, Arturo quickly switched back into Spanish for his journal writing. Later in the year Arturo once again demonstrated his sensitivity to the language of his interlocutor when he wrote a letter to a friend who had left Machan for another school. This child was an English speaker who did not speak Spanish. So Arturo had to write his letter in English, which he did. Using basically Spanish orthography, he composed a text which made clear how he felt about his friend.

> Dear jimmy, I mist jou sow moch ver du eu Lib uiarnt yu coming bac we d misiu Tichur dyt tu Hector Tu I lov iu jemmy sensirali
>
> [Dear Jimmy, I miss you so much. Where do you live? Why aren't you coming back? We all miss you. Teacher did too. Hector too. I love you, Jimmy. Sincerely]

Another example of sensitivity to audience occurred one day when Arturo's teacher was working with the children on how to write informational pieces, which she called reports, as a part of their thematic unit work. On a chart, the teacher had written out a sequence of steps in English and was sharing it with the children in English, when one of the Spanish speakers indicated that he did not understand. Immediately, Arturo and three other children began to translate her chart orally sentence by sentence for the child who did not understand the English. The translation was remarkably accurate.

For years linguists working in the area of bilingualism have demonstrated the sensitivity that bilinguals have with regard to the issue of language choice (Grosjean 1982), that is, if I am a bilingual, which language do I use? One of the factors that affects language choice is the language ability of the person with whom one is interacting. Bilinguals tend to be highly tuned in to the language abilities of their interlocutors, and they either choose the language of the interaction carefully before beginning or they switch into the language in which they think their interlocutors are most comfortable (Valdez-Fallis 1978). There is a lot of evidence that this happens with children as well as with adults (Genishi 1976; McClure 1977). While most of the work previously reported has been with regard to language choice and code switching in face-to-face conversation, the examples given here suggest that the sensitivity applies to the realm of written language as well. The children whose work is used here have demonstrated a sensitivity to the language abilities of others either specifically or generallly. They realize that they need to use one of their languages (Spanish) to communicate with some audiences and another of their languages (English) to communicate with other audiences. And they are willing to do this—even though English is their second language, even though they are more fluent in Spanish than in English, and even though they have not had formal literacy instruction in English. We also recognize that their eagerness to use English may also reflect their awareness that English is the language of status in school. English is the expected language for learning in school (Edelsky and Hudelson 1982).

Let's return to kindergarten to examine some language stories that illustrate another point. In one of the bilingual kindergarten classes, the teacher initiated home journals or diaries with some of her Spanish-speaking students. She gave the children blank journals, like the ones that they used in school, to take home, and she explained that the purpose of these journals was to give them an opportunity to keep a record of some of the things that happened to them at home. She also explained that some people keep journals or diaries as a way of reflecting on their lives. The activity was a voluntary one, and the children did not need to return the journals to school unless they wanted to do so. One of the kindergartners, Cecilia, really enjoyed this activity, and she brought in her home diary to share with the teacher. In one of the entries Cecilia described a trip to the store to purchase new shoes. From the illustration it became obvious that the shoes had been purchased at JC Penney's because she carefully printed "JC Penny's" at the top of her picture. She spelled the English name of the store with only the second *e* missing. She also used an English apostrophe accurately.

We noted a similar phenomenon with Arturo in the second grade. One day he wrote a fiction story in Spanish about a leopard who walked into a laundry looking for food and proceeded to wash himself in one of the washing machines. The illustration of the story again struck us, as we noticed that he had written the word *laundry* in English ("landri") rather than using the Spanish *lavanderia*, which appears in the body of his story. In the neighborhood around the school, there are signs in English for laundries—but no signs in Spanish.

In many of the stories and journal entries of children in both first and second grade, there were also references to computer games such as Nintendo (spelled "Nintendow" or "Nitendo") and Super Mario Brothers ("SuprMario Bradrs"), toys such as Barbie ("Barbi," "Barvi"), cartoon heroes such as Spiderman ("Spdrmn"), Superman ("Suprman"), Teenage Mutant Ninja Turtles, Bart Simpson, and the Barn Yard Commandos, and English-language movies that the children rented from video stores, such as *Bambi* and *The Wizard of Oz*. While sometimes the labels were rendered in invented spelling, most of the references were spelled with standard English or almost standard spelling.

For us, the significance of these English inclusions is that they make clear that these becoming-bilingual children live in a culture where English is all around them, particularly if one takes into account the popular culture of the mass media, including child consumerism.

Whether we approve or not, this is a reality for children. To use Judith Lindfors's (1987) terms, children use what is salient and interesting to them and make careful observations of the world around them. Carole Edelsky (1986) has noted that the bilingual writers she studied used data from past language experiences to make hypotheses about how to represent English as compared to Spanish texts. Yetta Goodman and her colleagues (Goodman and Altwerger 1981) have demonstrated that both native speakers of English and ESL learners develop an early awareness of print in the environment around them. The children with whom we are working corroborate these findings. Non-English-speaking children living in Phoenix (or in many other urban centers) are surrounded by English print; English is a reality in their lives. It is only natural that in their creative construction of oral and written language, they will attend to this language data, to this input, and will use it to meet some of their needs.

In addition to these items of child or consumer culture and environmental print that made their way into the children's writing at the lexical level, there were other occasions where the children used English-language terms within a Spanish text. For example, Lilia, a second grader, wrote frequently in her journal about playing "basque-boll" (basketball), utilizing Spanish orthography and spelling as she pronounced English. Arturo also used English words within his Spanish journal entries. In one example he wrote to ask his teacher what she had done during the recent spring break: "Ms C. que iso por Sprina vacasiones" (Ms. C, what did you do for spring vacation?). At another time he asked her to explain an English term she had used: "Ms. C me puede desir que es grandet por favor" (Ms. C, could you please tell me what is grounded?). He also used English for special effect when he appealed to her to help him look for a missing watch: "Ayúdame por favor plis. Si no me mama me mata." (Help me please, please. If not, my mother will kill me.) These examples suggest that some of our young writers were engaging in written code switching at the lexical level for particular purposes: because an item had a particular meaning or association in English (the terms *basketball* and *spring vacation* convey special meanings that Spanish translations would not); because the writer sought information about a particular English word; and because the addition of the English *please* to the Spanish *por favor* might carry with it more persuasive impact. Perhaps the children's tacit understandings about code switching in face-to-face conversation might carry over to some small extent into their written language use.

So far we have grouped our language stories under three basic categories or themes: children's sensitivity to audience and their use of English to meet this sociolinguistic reality; children's awareness of and interaction with English print in their daily living; and minimal utilization of lexical-level code switching (mentioned by Edelsky in her 1986 examination of bilingual children's writing development). A fourth group of stories we have clustered under the category of free experimentation with writing in English. By this we mean that some of the children we have been studying would, from time to time, produce a piece in English, without any special need or external pressure to do so, but, it seemed to us, basically because they felt like writing in English, because they had confidence that they could do it, and/or because they wanted to try out their English. Arturo was the second-grade learner who did this most frequently. You will remember him as the child who began his second-grade journal entries in September by writing in English because of his sensitivity to the fact that English was being used in his room with much greater frequency than it had been in previous years. Although he quickly switched into writing in his daily journal in Spanish, from time to time during the school year he moved into English for an entry or two and then back into Spanish. In January, for example, he explained to his teacher that he preferred drawing to writing:

> Ms —— I gradr drau I downt laic Too raet uel I du rait a letol David p es gouengtu let me gus a case Dd of Nintendow
>
> [Ms. ——, I'd rather draw. I don't like to write. Well, I do write a little. David P is going to let me use a cassette of Nintendo.]

Arturo and his teacher carried out a series of exchanges about who could beat the other at playing computer games such as Nintendo and Super Mario Brothers. His teacher had written him in Spanish that she was going to beat him because she had been over to her cousin's house to practice Super Mario Brothers. Arturo responded in English in some detail, claiming that there was a game at which he could beat her:

> Wi waso se about that Ms —— Teal jur casen tu bring His NintendoTuscul or cutt ju sab. The prinses ud Fair gur I cut
>
> [We will see about that Ms. ——. Tell your cousin to bring his Nintendo to school. Or could you save the Princess Wood Fairy? I could.]

His teacher responded in English, and then Arturo switched back to Spanish. Then again in March he addressed her in English, pondering the quantity of writing that he wanted to do in his journal and asking what the class would contribute to the monthly display of children's work in the school office:

> Ms —— I em sore vecas I vgin pag #1 but I em going too riet Fast soo I cot Beng paiaj #2
>
> [Ms. ——, I am very sorry because I begin page #1 but I am going to write fast so I could begin page #2.]
>
> Ms —— gooatar we gointupud in the o fes now I en in paig #2
>
> [Ms. ——, what are we going to put in the office? Now I am in page #2.]

Arturo also experimented with writing a story in English during the writer's workshop time. As Sarah sat with him one day in March, he told her that he was getting ready to write a story in English. Until this time all of his story writing had been in Spanish. When she expressed surprise, he informed her that sometimes he liked to write in English and sometimes in Spanish. When asked if he could also read in English, he indicated that he could. Arturo wrote down the title of his story and the first sentence: "Once upon a time der was a many fron japen." He used an appropriate story beginning in English, down to his use of English orthography. He then asked Victoria, the English-speaking girl sitting next to him, how to spell the word *he*. She told him, and he began the second sentence. When he proceeded to ask Sarah for spelling assistance, she asked him how he thought the words were spelled, and he was comfortable predicting both on the basis of Spanish orthography and on the basis of what he was figuring out about English spelling. He stopped writing after the second sentence, and Sarah asked him what his story was going to be about. He told her that it was going to be about this man fighting with someone. Victoria then suggested that he could continue by writing, "One day he was walking," and she showed him that he could use the word *once* to figure out how to spell the word *one*. He took her suggestion as far as "One day he," and then he went off on his own. Over the next several days he worked on his story, until he resolved the conflict of the man looking for his kidnapped wife. He then went back to writing in Spanish. His final story was the following:

> Once upon a Tlme der was a man Fron japen He Woos bere strong and brab One day he gada call From Hec Frand and He sed my wife has ben ced nap He sed do not move soo he ran to Hes Friend's House with Hes gun Heran to Hes car Wen He was at Hes Frands Haws Hes Frand sald Lowpan gads mi waif so He gaa mad and he sad get iun naif we are going to Lopans labr

tore camn gita geden The car man soode gwent to Lopans
labratore but wen de uer der The deding no were tu go. Peple
wr troeeing rocs at dem and the god mad the jump in from the
windo in said and they found Lopan but he got away and they
nevr Faund His waf. The End

[Once upon a time there was a man from Japan. He was very
strong and brave. One day he got a call from his friend and he
said my wife has been kidnapped. He said do not move. So he
ran to his friend's house with his gun. He ran to his car. When
he was at this friend's house his friend said Lowpan got my
wife. So he got mad and he said get one knife. We are going to
Lowpan's laboratory. Come on. Get in the car, man, so they
went to Lowpan's laboratory but when they were there they
didn't know where to go. People were throwing rocks at them.
And they got mad. They jumped in from the window inside and
they found Lowpan, but he got away and they never found his
wife. The end]

After her translation of the Barbie book, first-grader Alicia also
continued to experiment with English by translating some of her journal entries word for word from Spanish to English. Since her teacher
was bilingual and most of their journal correspondence over the year
had been in Spanish, there was no need in terms of audience for her to
do this. Our interpretation is that she enjoyed the challenge of translating and was having fun experimenting with writing in English.
One example of her translating ability is the following line by line
translation:

Yo quiero tomar awa Sra ——
I want a drink of water Mrs ——

Un diente se me esta moviendo proque se me ba caer
A tooth is crecet [crooked] because its going to fallen out

When the children first began to experiment with English writing, their orthography was influenced heavily by Spanish. In making
use of the linguistic resources available to them, a major resource was
what they already knew about how to create readable text in Spanish.
But as they read more in English and made inquiries of English speakers, their orthography began to reflect efforts to use English spelling
generalizations. Additionally, there was a Spanish-dominant child
who in kindergarten used English letter names to assist her in writing
Spanish. Lorena had been in a preschool program the year before she
entered Machan, and most of her instruction in that setting, including
work on the names of the letters of the alphabet, had been in English.
So when she began to use the alphabetic principle to write, she made

use of English letter names as well as Spanish graphophonic corre-spondences. For example, she spelled *castillo* one time as "aSkato," using the English letter *k*, since Spanish makes almost no use of that letter; she used the English letter *E* to spell the Spanish word *y*; and she spelled *castillo* another time as "ksteo," using the English letters *k* and *e*. Thus Lorena's experimentation with English involved the con-struction of Spanish text using both the Spanish and English alphabets.

The idea of experimentation is one that is central to the creative constructionist view of language and literacy development. The young writers with whom we have been working have demonstrated over and over again that they are actively involved in figuring out how the written system of Spanish works. As they develop confidence with that system and as they see themselves as writers, they begin to experi-ment with some English. What has struck us most about this is that the children do not see this as anything extraordinary. When asked who has taught them how to write (or, for that matter, how to read) in English, they shrug their shoulders and note that they have taught themselves. And indeed they have. They are the ones who are engaged in the work of becoming literate, regardless of the language.

To this point, almost all of the examples used have involved children's forays into writing in English. But in these bilingual class-rooms, the Spanish speakers also began to experiment with reading in English. The major context for the Spanish speakers to become inter-ested in reading English was that of the teachers reading to children. On a daily basis, teachers shared literature with children in both Span-ish and English, choosing books based on their literary merit, on their relationship to some content or theme that the children were learning about, and, in some cases, on their predictability. Initially, not all of the Spanish-speaking children wanted to hear stories read in English. Our classroom notes corroborate that several times Cecilia (the child who wrote "JC Penny's") protested vociferously when her teacher brought out a book to share in English: "en inglés, no maestra; en español" (in English, no teacher; in Spanish). She was not the only one to protest. However, as the year progressed, we noticed changes in the children's responses to English stories. Initially, to facilitate construction of mean-ing, the kindergarten teachers would summarize the story in Spanish, either before they read it in English or as they read it. Later, they no longer needed to translate, because the children could understand enough English to follow stories in English. The Spanish-speaking children, however, almost always responded to the stories in Spanish. With more exposure to English, the children became increasingly more comfortable responding to stories in English, although there were never sanctions against them responding in Spanish, and sometimes they responded in both languages.

In terms of the Spanish speakers actually reading English-language books, we documented in our notes that after an adult read the children a story and it became a part of the classroom library, the children were quite likely to pick it up and construct meaning from it. What was familiar would probably be read, read in the sense of constructing meaning using any or all of the language cuing systems, with more success than what was unfamiliar. Lorena frequently cornered Irene so that she could read to Irene an English-language animal alphabet book that her teacher had shared in class one day. This book became one of her favorites, and when she had time to browse among the books in the library corner, she often chose that book, particularly if she could read it to or with someone else.

In the second grade, the books that the children chose most frequently to experiment with during DEAR (Drop Everything and Read) time were those that the teacher had read and that were predictable in more than one way. Second-grader Juanita's list of books for DEAR time included the titles of such predictable books as *I Know an Old Lady Who Swallowed a Fly, The Three Little Pigs, Tikki Tikki Tembo, Caps for Sale, Noisy Nora,* and *Old MacDonald Had a Farm.* When the children read these books independently, they were doing so without a background of formal reading instruction in English. They were experimenting with English. As with their writing, the children were applying what they knew about reading from their experiences in reading Spanish. They certainly used the graphophonic cuing system of Spanish as a way of predicting what the English would sound like. In terms of pronunciation, the children's early English often sounded as though they were pronouncing nonsense. But in spite of this surface inaccuracy, for all of the readers there was some construction of meaning. Early on in their independent reading of books, the children were more comfortable talking in Spanish about what they had read. Later they became more able to retell the story in English.

Second-grader Juanita also taught us a lesson about not making assumptions about children's construction of meaning in a second language based upon a single book. Juanita had been reading regularly in English for several months and participating in literature study sessions in English as well as Spanish. One day, as part of our data collection, Sarah asked her to read an unfamiliar book. She agreed and read aloud William Steig's *Brave Irene* (Farrar, Straus and Giroux, 1986).

When she had finished, she did a satisfactory job of retelling the basic plot, but she omitted a lot of the details. Sarah decided to ask her what her favorite part of the story was. Juanita opened the book to the pages that illustrated the party that the duchess gave after Irene arrived with the beautiful dress made by her mother. As she examined the illustration she commented, "All the ladies look the same." She was right; they did all look alike. Sarah commented that perhaps that was the way William Steig drew his characters. Until then, Juanita had not realized that *Brave Irene* was written by William Steig. She told us that her class had been studying a lot of Steig's books. Her favorite was *Doctor DeSoto* (Farrar, Straus and Giroux, 1982), which she had read in a literature study with a group of children. Juanita proceeded to overwhelm me with details about that book and what she had liked about it. For whatever reasons, *Doctor DeSoto* was a much more memorable book to Juanita than *Brave Irene,* as demonstrated by this transcription of her retelling:

S: What's your favorite Steig book?

J: *Doctor DeSoto.*

S: What do you like about it?

J: The guy he put a sign up that he couldn't—he couldn't—attend—that he was a doctor of the teeth—and he put up a sign that no cats or dangerous animals. And the wolf he was down down down and he said that he really needed to see a dentist because he had a bad tooth. And the woman said let him come in. So the man make him come in. Then the wolf came in and Doctor DeSoto told him to take off his things and then he said he had a rotten tooth so the lady put him this medicine. She put it so it could not hurt when he took it out. And he went to sleep. When he was asleep the lady gave him the thing to take off the teeth. And so they put it over. It was a fishing pole. He pulled it out. The wolf said, "I'm bleeding." And so they put like rolls of cotton, something like that, right here in his mouth, so it will stop bleeding. And the man told him to come tomorrow to put another teeth in it. So the wolf came the other day. And it was a gold teeth. So eat him? Then he closed his mouth with Doctor DeSoto in it. Then he opened it: "Just kidding." Then Doctor DeSoto said, "We can't play jokes right now." Then he put the teeth in it, and the other girl she gave him glue and the man said, "It's a special potion for you so your teeth could—don't end quickly." The teeth that he just put in there. And he put it on him and it was glue. And he said, he goes, he was gonna say, "Thank you" but he couldn't because as

> Doctor DeSoto said it was gonna be sticky so he didn't say,
> "Thank you." He said "Tak yu."

In addition to stories, some of the children began to use English language expository—informational texts as resources for content learning. When Arturo's class studied China, the children brainstormed what they already knew about China and then listed some aspects of China that they wanted to learn about. Arturo had decided that he wanted to do some investigation of Kung Fu. He asked several questions: How do they fight Kung Fu? How do people train for Kung Fu? What are the signs of Kung Fu like? How do people learn Kung Fu? What are Kung Fu uniforms like? Then he found a book in English about Kung Fu and proceeded to read to answer his questions. His answers, written in Spanish, make it clear that he found some information, and that some information was not available. His written Spanish served as a demonstration of his understanding of the English book.

> Como pelean ConFoo ai muchos tipos de Cong Fu Ti He i Cong
> Fu Ti He tocas con quien estas peleando Cong Fu si pega salas
> personas y Wing Chun le pusieron ese nomvre porque asi se
> llama el omvre de el que inbento Cung Fu
>
> [How do they fight Kung Fu? There are a lot of types of Kung
> Fu, Tai-chi and Kung Fu. Tai-chi you touch the person you're
> fighting with. Kung Fu you hit the people. And Wing Chun got
> its name because that's the name of the man that invented Kung
> Fu.]

As with the writing samples, what we have just related in terms of reading English as a second language is not new. Ken and Yetta Goodman (1978) and Pat Rigg (1977, 1986) have revealed many of the same phenomena as they have worked in reading English as a second language with readers having a variety of native languages. These literacy stories confirm their findings about how children actively work to construct meaning from texts, about children's differential involvement with varied texts, and about how children reveal more of the meaning that they have constructed when they are able to use their native languages as well as English. Perhaps what is most significant is these children's interest in experimenting with English and their utilization of English, as well as Spanish, as a way to mediate their own learning.

And so our language stories are done. We now need to ask, so what? What significance do these stories have? What lessons do they offer us? We think that there are several lessons that they teach us about children who are becoming bilingual/biliterate:

1. Becoming-bilingual/biliterate children are sensitive to language, aware of what is happening around them linguistically, and tuned in to the realities of different languages.

2. Becoming-bilingual/biliterate children are interested in English; they see English as purposeful for them.

3. Becoming-bilingual/biliterate children whose native-language literacy development has been valued and supported, as has been the case in this whole language bilingual program, have confidence in themselves as readers and writers. As they begin to view themselves as readers and writers, they begin to experiment with their new language (in this case, English). Their experimentation involves using the resources of their native languages to figure out how to express themselves in their new language. The children who are the most fluent readers and writers in Spanish are the ones engaging in the most experimentation with English or adding on of English.

4. Becoming-bilingual/biliterate children are individuals with varying personalities, interests, needs, rates of language and literacy development, and responses to school. So not all children respond in the same way to invitations or opportunities to experiment with English. And not all children respond on the same timetable. Juanita chose to read a lot in English, but she did very little individual writing, at least in the context of school. Arturo enjoyed experimenting with writing in English, especially when it suited some particular purpose. Other children, at the end of first or second grade, were not yet as interested in using English on such a sustained basis. The children's teachers understood and accepted these individual differences.

5. Perhaps most importantly, the becoming-bilingual/biliterate children in these classrooms are in control of their learning, including their learning of English. By this we mean that their teachers were interested in their learning and using English but were not obsessed by it. They believed that the children had time for the task; so they allowed and encouraged and even celebrated children's experimentations, but they did not force them. The children chose to begin to use English; they were not told they had to. The teachers' primary goals were strong native-language literacy development and the learning of significant content. The teachers wanted the children to see themselves as active, inquiring learners and to use language for learning. To use one of Bonnie and David Freeman's (1989) whole language principles, the teachers had faith in the learners and in the fact that they would

learn both content and English. We would submit that these learners are doing just that.

References

Edelsky, C. 1986. *Writing in a bilingual program: Habia una vez.* Norwood, N.J.: Ablex.

Edelsky, C., and S. Hudelson. 1982. The acquisition (?) of Spanish as a second language. In *Bilingualism and language contact: Spanish English and Native American languages,* ed. F. Barkin, E. Brandt, and J. Ornstein Galicia. New York: Teachers College Press.

Freeman, V., and D. Freeman. 1989. Whole language approaches to writing with secondary students. In *Richness in writing: Empowering ESL students,* ed. D. Johnson and D. Roen. New York: Longman.

Genishi, C. 1976. Rules for code-switching in young Spanish-English speakers: An exploratory study of language socialization. Ph.D. diss., University of California, Berkeley.

Goodman, K., and Y. Goodman. 1978. *Reading of American children whose language is a stable rural dialect of English or a language other than English.* (NIE-C-00-3-0087). Washington, D.C.: U.S. Department of Health, Education, and Welfare.

Goodman, Y., and B. Altwerger. 1981. *A study of the development of literacy in preschool children.* Tucson: University of Arizona, Program in Language and Literacy.

Grosjean, F. 1982. *Life with two languages: An introduction to bilingualism.* Cambridge, Mass.: Harvard University Press.

Harste, J., C. Burke, and V. Woodward. 1984. *Language stories and literacy lessons.* Portsmouth, N.H.: Heinemann.

Lindfors, J. 1987. *Children's language and learning,* 2d ed. Englewood Cliffs, N.J.: Prentice Hall.

McClure, E. 1977. *Aspects of code-switching in the discourse of bilingual Mexican-American children.* Urbana, Ill.: University of Illinois at Urbana-Champaign, Center for the Study of Reading.

Rigg, P. 1977. The miscue-ESL project. In *Teaching and learning ESL: Trends in research and practice,* ed. H. D. Brown, C. Yorio, and R. Crymes, 106–18. Washington, D.C.: Teachers of English to Speakers of Other Languages.

———. 1986. Reading in ESL: Learning from kids. In *Children and ESL: Integrating perspectives,* ed. P. Rigg and D. S. Enright. Washington, D.C.: Teachers of English to Speakers of Other Languages.

Valdez-Fallis, G. 1978. *Code switching and the classroom teacher.* Arlington, Va.: Center for Applied Linguistics.

14 Providing Time for Flowers: A Curriculum Vision for the Twenty-first Century

Mary Kenner Glover
Awakening Seed School, Tempe, Arizona

ast spring, as I was struggling to find a focus for this chapter, I sat at my desk taking care of school responsibilities. I was typing our school newspaper. Amidst the work submitted for publication was the article and illustration by Jacob shown in Figure 14.1. I was immediately attracted to it, initially because of the delightful simplicity of the drawing, but then later for the writing as well. As I continued working on the newspaper, I could not get Jacob's piece out of my mind. I kept thinking that what he had written about was much more than just how to plant flowers. I began to see that his piece could be taken on a number of levels:

- It is a topic in which Jacob is interested (gardening), and he wants to share his knowledge.
- It is a reminder to slow down and take time to nurture things of beauty in our world, which we often view as unnecessary "extras."
- It can be taken as a metaphor for our work as teachers with children, caring for them and giving them what they need in order to grow.
- It is about caring for the natural wonders around us which are precious and vulnerable.

The idea of caring appeared to be a recurring theme in each layer of meaning in Jacob's article. I thought about its presence in schools and classrooms that are alive and its absence in those classrooms in which teachers and children are just going through the motions of teaching and learning. It seemed that an examination of caring and its influence on the climate of schools and classrooms would be a worthwhile process.

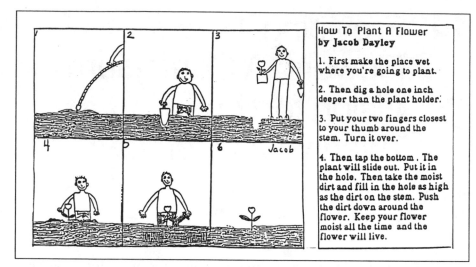

Figure 14.1. "How to Plant a Flower," from *The Seed News*, April 1991, Awakening Seed School, Tempe, Arizona.

Milton Mayeroff, in his book *On Caring* (1971), describes the major ingredients of caring. He writes that true caring involves:

Knowing: having a sense of others, knowing who they are and what their powers and needs are.

Alternating rhythms: having a sense of when to act or not to act, and learning from the past when each is appropriate.

Patience: enabling others to grow in their own time and way.

Honesty: seeing others as they are rather than how we want them to be, and knowing that how we act and feel must match how others really are.

Trust: having faith that others will grow in their own time and way, and trusting our own capacity to care.

Humility: having an attitude of knowing that there is always more to learn from others.

Hope: feeling that the present is alive with possibility and that some situations are worthy of commitment.

Courage: having the willingness to step beyond safety and security, having learned from the past and staying open to the present.

I began to think about the presence of caring in my own school, Awakening Seed School, and how these elements of caring operate. They seem to be present at several levels.

At the family and school level, there are parents who show that they care for their children by consciously choosing a setting where their children will thrive with teachers who know how to nurture them. Teachers nurture parents, too, as they offer assistance and guidance to parents in the complicated process of educating their children. In turn, parents support their children's teachers by driving on field trips, helping with fund-raising, assisting in the classroom, actively participating with at-home reading and assignments, and providing resources for studies.

At the staff level, administrators demonstrate care for teachers by talking jointly with parents when issues arise, by being advocates for teachers at board meetings, by taking care of management details so teachers can teach, and by arranging time off for personal and professional development. The perspective of teachers is respected and honored by the administration as teachers have the opportunity to offer input on policy issues and school operation procedures. Furthermore, two of the administrators in our school are also classroom teachers. Through firsthand experience they know and care about what happens each day in classrooms.

Caring is present among teachers as well. It is not uncommon to see two or three teachers gathered informally after school, asking advice from each other, exchanging ideas. Teachers plan multiple age-group events together, such as buddy reading or field trips. There is an attitude of sharing ideas rather than hoarding them, with teachers viewing each other as resources rather than as competition or a threat. Teachers draw on each other's strengths and share their passion for their work. They strive to make school an interesting place for children by furthering their own professional growth. Involvement in local teacher support groups such as the Center for Establishment of Dialogue in Teaching and Learning (CED) is another way that teachers at our school not only expand their knowledge base but also make that connection with other teachers outside of our immediate school community.

In addition to caring for each other, teachers, above all else, care for children. Each day the ideas and interests of children are honored by their teachers. Those ideas are incorporated as an integral part of the daily classroom life. When three and four year olds made a list of their favorite books, their second-grade buddies used the list as a guide for choosing books to read to them. When chicken pox broke out in the spring and became the topic of discussion in every class, it was decided that Inbal's piece on chicken pox should be the lead article in the school newspaper (see Figure 14.2). The passionate interest that many of the children have for sports was honored by featuring several of their articles in the newspaper as well, such as Darvá and Justin's piece titled "School Baseball":

> Baseball is on Wednesdays after school. Girls and boys go. You have to sign up before you join. You have to be good while walking. Don't bring a ball because you might lose it. Make sure you bring a mitt. Make sure you bring a bat. Don, Sandi, Steve, and Terry take care of you. Don't walk too fast when you are going to the park. You have to have another kid with you when you go to the park. The other kid has to be either younger than you or older than you. When you get to the park you can choose if you want to play T-ball or baseball. Don't break your bat. Never ever cheat. Slide to the base if you have to. You only run on your third hit. Hit the ball hard. Do not steal a base. Stay awake.

By focusing on children's strengths rather than their deficiencies, teachers show that they care. The work of Pat Carini, a renowned educator from Vermont, has certainly influenced the thinking of many local teachers in this way. When I struggled with a class that was quite active and restless, she helped me to see that their strength was in their ability to use their hands, to be actively curious. My respect for their rich sense of humor led me to choose books for reading aloud such as Beverly Cleary's *Ramona the Pest* (William Morrow, 1968), which allowed that sense of humor to go to work.

Teachers care for their students by serving as role models for learning how to care about others. When children see their teachers being respectful of other people and their ideas, they become that way themselves. David recognized this quality in Steve, a volunteer at our school, and honored him by writing the following paragraph:

> Steve does not just teach baseball. He teaches football, basketball, juggling and yoyoing. He volunteers. He does not get money for it. Steve used to be the P.E. teacher with Peter Ting. He is the start of love in our school.

Additional modeling is provided for children through content studies which focus on individuals who have dedicated their lives to caring for others. Individuals such as Martin Luther King Jr., Mahatma Gandhi, and Harriet Tubman are featured in yearly studies about human rights. Children learn that caring sometimes involves paying the high price of one's life in order to improve the quality of life for others. Children are given opportunities to express their under-

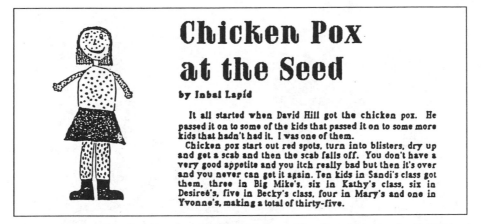

Figure 14.2. "Chicken Pox at the Seed," from *The Seed News*, April 1991, Awakening Seed School, Tempe, Arizona.

standing of this sacrifice through poetry, drawings, and conversations with one another.

Teachers also help children to care about learning by expecting good scholarship. They teach children to work hard and set their own high standards. Furthermore, teachers enable children to see that in putting forth their best efforts, they will not only enjoy the process of learning but will often end up with a high-quality product. The beautifully handcrafted books that children make and publish at our school are examples of this.

Caring finds its way into our school in other ways as well. Teachers enable children to see that in addition to caring about learning and what it takes to be a good citizen, they must begin the practice of caring within their immediate school world. This includes caring for their classmates, teachers, and other children in the school, people who come in contact with the school in various ways, and the school facility itself. One way in which students show that they care about each other is through notes they write to and on behalf of each other. When Jillian was student of the week, her classmates wrote short greetings to her on a poster. She took the time, on the poster itself, to respond to each of their comments (see Figure 14.3). On another occasion, when Inbal and Andrea noticed that their classmate Michael had been behaving in a way which concerned them, they wrote a note to his mother (see Figure 14.4). At the end of the school year, when it was time to say good-bye to their reading buddies, Andrea wrote the following thoughtful note to her four-year-old buddy, Mya: "I liket Haveing you

Figure 14.3. Poster honoring Jillian as student of the week.

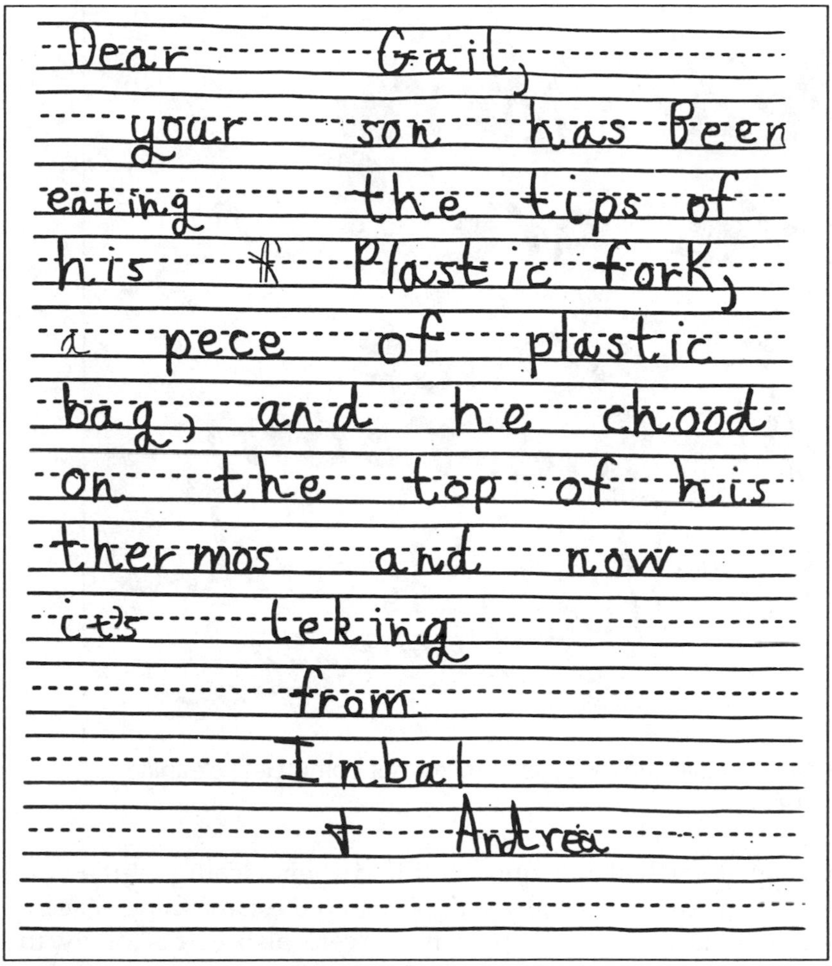

Dear   Gail,
     your   son   has been
eating   the   tips   of
his   *   Plastic   fork,
a   pece   of   plastic
bag, and   he   chood
on   the   top   of   his
thermos   and   now
it's   teking
from
Inbal
+   Andrea

Figure 14.4. Inbal and Andrea's letter to Michael's mother.

As a Buddy. How did you like me? Are you Comeing Hear next Year? I am. WHat DiD You Like Best About Buddy Reading?" In giant letters at the top of the page, Andrea wrote "Ceep ReadIng In the Sumer!" All of these notes demonstrated a level of caring felt between children within the classroom and in the school.

The note writing was not limited to other children. It extended to their teacher as well. The morning after my car window had been shattered by a flying rock from the playground, Izaak left three dimes on my desk and a note that read, "Here is 30¢ to go with your window." When Caitlin and her classmates fell short on their cleaning efforts while I was gone, she left a note to let me know that they cared,

Dear: Mary
We are sory
We DiDnot
git the room
Totlly Cleandup
Love Caitlin

Figure 14.5. Caitlin's letter of apology for not completely cleaning the classroom.

even though they had not quite fulfilled their cleanup duties (see Figure 14.5). In both cases, the notes expressed the same thing—caring.

Individuals outside of the school were also cared for by the children. David suggested that each child write a letter to his ailing grandmother who had just recently moved into a nursing home. The entire class eagerly responded, knowing from their weekly visits to a local nursing home what David's grandmother might be feeling. The weekly visits, as part of an intergenerational program called Community, helped the children develop a more loving, compassionate attitude toward the elderly. Caitlin's end-of-the-year poem bid good-bye to her nursing home friends (see Figure 14.6). Johnny's log entry about his visit with Venna demonstrates the level of caring that grew between friends young and old (see Figure 14.7):

Dear Mary

I went up to Venna. I said we are going to make a picture of Halloween today. She said, "What's Halloween?" I said, "Hal-

Good-bye, My Friend

Good-bye is the way
that the Englishmen say
Adios
says the Mexican
But there is only
one way
to say it
the friendly-like way
Good-bye, my friend
See you again some day

Figure 14.6. Caitlin's poem saying good-bye to her nursing home friends.

loween is when you dress up in a costume and try to scare people." And the next thing I knew . . . Venna was on top of my back!!! She scared me pretty good alright. And I got to push a resident back to their room. It was fun!!!

A natural outgrowth of caring for people in our immediate circle of friends associated with school has been a rapidly increasing awareness of world issues and the people affected by those issues. Environmental issues have always been a concern of students at our school. Some time ago, Sarah was studying about pollution and wrote to Senator Barry Goldwater to express her concern (see Figure 14.8). Last year, the three and four year olds were exploring ways to help the environment. They decided they could make signs to post around the school that would remind others not to waste water and paper towels. Duncan's sign helped us all remember that by saving water at school there would be more water in the future for him and for his family (see Figure 14.9). Along with environmental concerns, children had strong responses to the war in the Persian Gulf. Their sense of caring for what was happening in the world was expressed through their poetry (see Ryan's poem in Figure 14.10) and their letters to President Bush (see Jessica's letter in Figure 14.11). Knowing that their voices were respected by their teachers and peers, they felt they had a responsibility to express their opinions. Feeling empowered as citizens, they were learning that as individuals we can make a difference, even by responding in the smallest of ways.

When I returned my attention to Jacob's article for our school newspaper, his final statement stuck in my mind: "Keep your flower

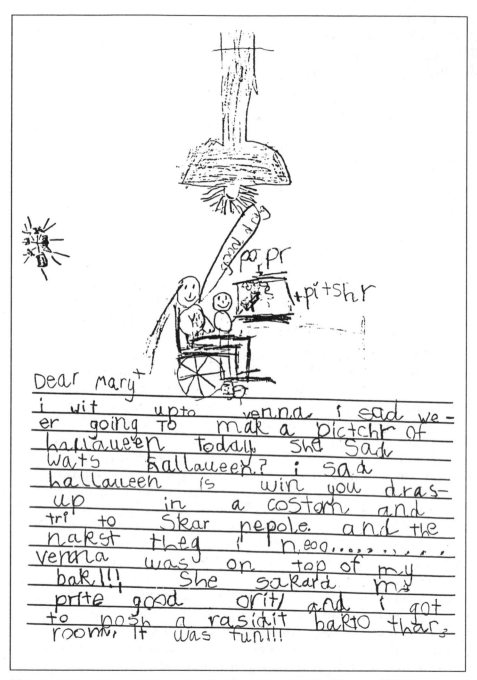

Figure 14.7. Johnny's log entry about visiting a friend in a nursing home.

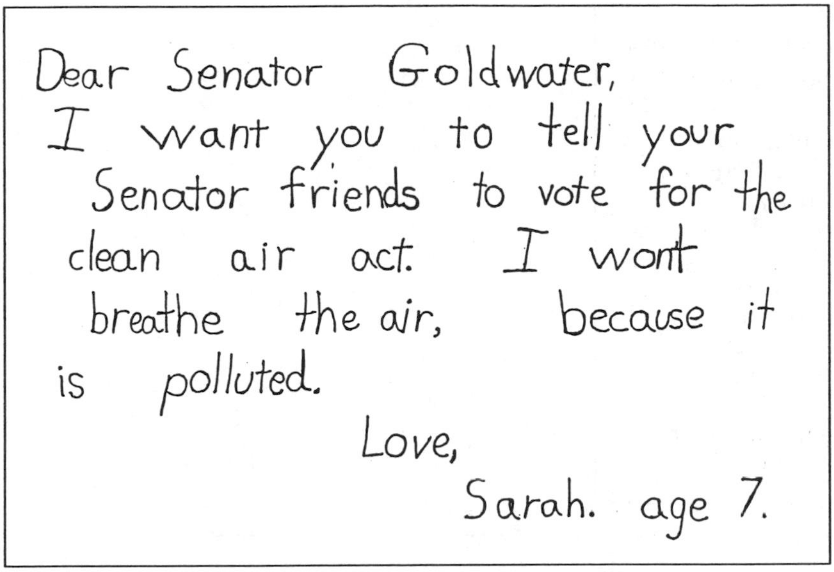

Dear Senator Goldwater,
I want you to tell your Senator friends to vote for the clean air act. I wont breathe the air, because it is polluted.
                              Love,
                                    Sarah. age 7.

Seed tip: By turning the water off while soaping up your hands and then turning it back on again just long enough to rinse, you will be doing your part to conserve water!

Me and my family swimming.
by: Duncan

Figure 14.8. Sarah's letter to Senator Barry Goldwater.

Figure 14.9. Duncan's sign advocating water conservation.

All the People Dying

the war seems
it
will go on on
and on
in my heart
all
dying dying
and
a golden heart
broken
with all
the
people dying in
my heart.

February 7, 1991

Dear Mr. Bush,

I am affected by the war. I'm sad, too. So are my classmates. I would like you to stop the war. My friends and I are not the only ones that are affected. Others are too, even adults. So please stop the war. It will really help. I never thought that I would see a war in my life. Why did you make the deadline Martin Luther King's birthday? Wasn't he a peacemaker?

Your friend,

Jessica Rodd

Figure 14.10. Ryan's poem about the Gulf War.

Figure 14.11. Jessica's letter to George Bush about the Gulf War.

moist all the time and the flower will live." I realized that the "moisture" he wrote about is, indeed, caring: It is that sense of caring we have for our students and for our work. It is our passion for learning and for helping others to learn. It is caring that fills up our classrooms. It is the books in our libraries, the displays on our walls, and everything we learn and talk about each day. It is what we as teachers care about and value and, in turn, what we teach our students to care about and value. It is our belief that what we do in our classrooms will make a difference in the world of tomorrow. It is our hope for the future and our courage to do what we know is right.

As I thought about Jacob's article, I also thought about *America 2000* (Alexander 1991), President Bush's educational plan for the twenty-first century. It includes six goals to be achieved by the year 2000:

1. All children in America will start school ready to learn.

2. The high school graduation rate will increase to at least 90 percent.

3. American students will leave grades four, eight, and twelve having demonstrated competency in challenging subject matter including English, mathematics, science, history, and geography; and every school in America will ensure that all students learn to use their minds well, so they may be prepared for responsible citizenship, further learning, and productive employment in our modern economy.

4. U.S. students will be first in the world in science and mathematics achievement.

5. Every adult American will be literate and will possess the knowledge and skills necessary to compete in a global economy and exercise the rights and responsibilities of citizenship.

6. Every school in America will be free of drugs and violence and will offer a disciplined environment conducive to learning.

While I think these goals are ambitious, I think we need to look beyond the surface to see why we have not achieved them before now and what is necessary to meet them in the future. I have a hunch that it has little to do with achievement and accountability and much more to do with plain old-fashioned caring. As we move into a new century in just a few years, I think we need to take a good hard look at where our priorities lie. I believe that less emphasis needs to be placed on being first or being the most competitive, and instead we need to place children and their genuine needs and interests at the heart of every decision we make. Until we can concentrate our focus on that which will enable children to lead happy and healthy lives, knowing that they are loved and cared for on all levels, it will be difficult to get them to do much of anything, much less eliminate drugs and violence. When children know that they can trust us to provide them with a world which is safe, then they will also be able to care about their environment and its people and to respond as productive citizens. When we make the passions and interests of children the central content of our curriculum rather than phonemes, digraphs, and standardized tests, then we will begin to see achievement. When children know that we are sincere in creating schools which have as their focus stimulating, thought-provoking learning rather than control and discipline, then *they* will lead the way and show us how the schools of tomorrow should be. They will be able to face the future with hope and courage, two of Mayeroff's major ingredients of caring (1971).

Another publication that comes to mind is a small book called *The Grandpa Tree* (Donahue and Strawn 1988). It was given to me by a friend who had recently moved to Colorado and who called it her first "Colorado book find." It is the story of a tree's life cycle, from the seedling stage to the time when the trunk falls to the earth to decompose and become rich soil for future trees. As the tree is about to crash to the ground, it speaks to the younger trees: "Now I am needed on the ground, to be a home for rabbits, and food for flowers. So, my children, remember the youth. As they need room to grow, leave them a world where their branches can spread as freely and greatly as yours do now."

In a simplistic way, this story expresses what I have been trying to say about caring. If we really care about our children and their future, we *will* leave them a world where their branches can spread freely and greatly.

References

Alexander, L. 1991. *America 2000: An educational strategy*. Washington, D.C.: U.S. Government Printing Office.

Donahue, M., and S. Strawn. 1988. *The Grandpa Tree*. Boulder, Col.: Roberts Rinehart.

Mayeroff, M. 1971. *On caring*. New York: Harper and Row.

15 The Triumphs and Tribulations of a Whole Language Teacher

Wendy Hood
Warren Elementary School, Tucson, Arizona

I taught kindergarten for seven years. A whole language kindergarten. The kind of place you would want your kid to attend. A child-centered classroom that promoted literacy learning, self-esteem, decision making, community building. The kind of class that they never pulled special kids out of because it was "kinesthetic, tactile, and multisensory" (whatever that means). I published articles about that classroom in *Learning* and *The Whole Language Evaluation Book.* Pat Rigg wrote about me as a special teacher in *The Whole Language Catalog.*

Now I am not saying all this to sing my own praises but rather to let you know that I was feeling pretty good about myself as a teacher—a whole language teacher. But after seven years, for a variety of reasons, I decided it was time to move on. Cautiously I submitted applications for openings at other schools within my own district. I only applied for positions at schools that I knew were supportive of whole language. This was not easy, as principals were posting job descriptions stating that applicants "must be able to implement whole language, literature-based instruction, manipulative math, cooperative learning, Essential Elements of Instruction, and Assertive Discipline." (All for one job!)

With a lot of luck and a little seniority, I found myself reassigned to second grade at Warren Elementary School, a school moving toward whole language under the direction of Dr. Myna Matlin as principal. I was thrilled. I knew that I would have the support that I wanted/needed/craved to create my second-grade Xanadu.

Grand Plan

I spent my summer thinking, pondering, planning, and jumping out of bed in the middle of the night to jot down new ideas. I spent my money every time that I saw something perfect for my new second grade.

All the theory that I knew about literacy and learning would be put into practice with my class of thirty-two seven- and eight-year-old students. I would use large blocks of time. There would be choice. The kids would be at the core of the program. I would be the facilitator of learning providing opportunities and resources matched perfectly to my students' evolving interests and needs.

I would do writing samples, anecdotal records, and running records from day one. We would do process writing; hands-on math; shared, guided, and independent reading; literature study; interactive dialogue journals; thematic units; hands-on science; integrated social studies; and choice, lots of choice.

"Second graders are so much bigger than kindergartners," I kept saying. "They can read. They can follow directions. They can unbuckle their own pants when they go to the bathroom!"

I went in early to set up the physical environment of the classroom, arranging it as in Figure 15.1. I was really pleased with the results. Myna had gotten me some extra bookshelves, and we had both agreed that tables would work better than desks. The focal point of the classroom was the library, which I positioned in the very center of the room. I believe that the placement of the teacher's desk communicates the teacher's role in a classroom. My desk was tucked away in the corner next to the bathroom.

I had no storage space at first for the kids' belongings, so I made what I called the "cubby wall"—a stack of cardboard boxes taped together. Most were old book-club boxes. I used a razor to cut openings on the sides and alternated them so the openings faced either direction to ease congestion. It was a rather ugly looking structure but quite functional, for a while. Myna said that she would try to get me some real cubbies.

Then the first day of school arrived along with thirty-two eager kids. My plan for the first day of school was to have the kids dive right into the routine that we were going to establish. In the center of each table were blank journals. The day would begin with journal writing as the kids self-selected their seats and settled in. Then we moved to group time on the rug. I introduced my favorite song, we chatted a bit, and we chose class chores. I read Mike Thaler's *The Teacher from the Black Lagoon* (Scholastic, 1989). My favorite part is when Derek whines, "We haven't had fractions yet." The teacher beckons him to her desk. "Derek stands by her desk. 'This is a whole boy,' she smirks. She takes a big bite. 'This is a half a boy. Now you've had fractions.' "

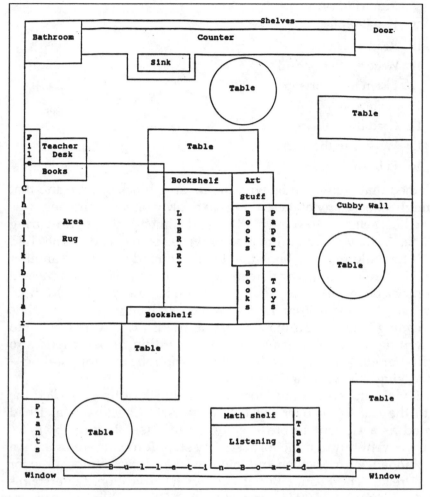

Figure 15.1. Classroom diagram for Wendy Hood's second-grade classroom.

After the story, I directed the kids' attention to Language Arts Choices, a list of the following activities:

1. Read a book
2. Write a story
3. Read poetry
4. Write poetry
5. Read with a friend
6. Illustrate a story
7. Revise a story

8. Read riddles
9. Write riddles
10. Read a magazine
11. Write a letter or card
12. Listen to a storytape
13. Write a song
14. Read the walls
15. Work with the teacher
16. Publish a book

I explained that we would be working in a big block of time and that they might choose any of these things to do. My only requirement was that the kids select both some reading and some writing to do during that time. As they moved off to read or write, as they chose, one child asked if he could read the book that I had just read aloud and another asked if I had more books by that author. When Joey, who had browsed the library a bit, returned to inquire, "Do you have any Robert Munsch books?" my heart was jumping for joy. I looked about the room. Kids were reading books alone, in pairs, and in triads. Kids were writing in their writing notebooks. Some were even writing cards or letters to their first-grade teachers. Inside my head the refrain kept running— "It's working! It's working!"

Toward the end of our language arts block of time, I called the kids to the rug to go over the Language Arts Checklist that I had designed as a student record-keeping system (see Figure 15.2). Together we went through the form step by step. It took more time than I had planned, far more time, but that was okay. It was almost time for lunch. I read "The Peanut Butter Sandwich" from Shel Silverstein's *Where the Sidewalk Ends* (Harper and Row, 1974), establishing our Poetry Break Before Lunch time.

After lunch, I read the first chapter from *The Twits* by Roald Dahl (Knopf, 1981). The kids began to think I was really weird. My plan was to use our after-lunch block of time as theme study time. I figured that it was a good idea to get the kids started by having them share about themselves. We began a week-long All about Me theme with the kids writing autobiographies, cutting out pictures of favorite things from magazines, drawing self-portraits, and so on. By the end of the week, we would cover our big bulletin board with these items under the caption "We are Room 3."

With our first day drawing to a close, I shared the letter I was sending home to their parents. As the kids filed out and one child

Language Arts Checklist					
Name _____ Date _____					
	Monday	Tuesday	Wednesday	Thursday	Friday
Read (what I read)					
Read to a friend (name)					
Read to an adult (name)					
Write in my journal					
Write (what I wrote)					
Writing conference					
Edit my writing					
Publish my writing					
Read to the class					
Listen to a tape					
Illustrate a story					

Figure 15.2. Language Arts Checklist form for student record keeping.

hugged me, I overheard another say to his buddy, "I guess we don't get P.E. in second grade." Oops! I knew I had forgotten something!

I sat down to reflect on that first day. Except for forgetting to take the kids outside all day, everything went well. In my dialogue journal with Myna I wrote, "It worked. It worked!" She responded with the query, "Had you expected that it wouldn't?" Maybe I had.

Things continued to go well that first week. I managed to do a running record on every kid and conference with them all on the drafts of their autobiographies, collect a freewriting sample, and learn everyone's name. Everything was not necessarily perfect, but I learned from that.

I learned that it takes seven year olds longer to write down what they did than it took to do it.

I learned that providing "Publish a book" as a choice before "Write a story" is completed invites kids to staple blank pages into a cover and *then* sit down and think of what to write.

I learned that it takes a long, long time to respond genuinely to thirty-two journals.

I learned that some second graders still have trouble with their buckles.

I learned that it takes more than a teacher's good intentions to create a community of learners.

I learned that by the second week of school, the honeymoon was over.

From Freedom to Chaos

I spent most of our journal-writing time that second Monday morning policing student behavior. While most of the kids were writing, one group was arranging and rearranging walls made from binders to keep others from peeking; one child stood sharpening a pencil down to a stub; another group was huddled over someone's new Ninja Turtle; and José had lost his journal and spent the whole time looking for it. It took ten minutes to get the kids to come to our group time, during which most of the kids seemed disinterested in the story.

Language Arts Choices time was even worse. I had done my running records, evaluating the kids' miscues and reading strategies, so I was ready to start pulling small groups together for guided reading strategy lessons. Once the kids appeared engaged in activities, I called together my first group. While we read *Fantail, Fantail* by Margaret Mahy (Ready-to-Read [Wellington, New Zealand], 1983), a patterned story about a bird that is offered a variety of foods and that refuses them all until a fly is served, one girl wrote a love letter to a boy; another boy wrote a hate letter to a different girl; one boy sketched Ninja Turtles while his buddy looked on; others built a fort of chairs and books; one child sat in a chair and did nothing; and José continued to look for his journal, recruiting an ever-growing crew of supporters to help him in his search. A few kids, very few kids, were actually reading or writing; a small group of girls were quietly singing "Down by the Bay" with some enlarged text cards; a couple of boys discovered a junior atlas and were pouring over it; Melba was engrossed in a novel. Then the noise level started to grow and grow and grow!

I invited my group to respond to *Fantail, Fantail* by making their own books—gluing food pictures onto paper plates and writing their own words. Several other kids wanted to join in that activity, but they had not read the story and declined an invitation to do so. That's when the whining started: "How come they get to do that but all I get to do is read?" Oh no!

The kids were driving me crazy. They drove me nuts for three days. It got worse and worse, louder and louder. Soon even Melba wasn't involved in reading or writing. I could not get through a group session without the noise levels going through the roof.

I gave up working with groups and spent my time policing behavior, saying things like, "If you kids make me act like a police officer, I can't be a teacher." In my dialogue journal with Myna, I wrote nothing. I was too exhausted by the end of each day. But if I had not been so tired, I would have written, "It's not working."

When I complained about things to my teacher husband, he suggested that I "show 'em what it can be like. Assign 'em seats, give 'em each a huge stack of worksheets, and make 'em sit and work silently all day. They'll come 'round." "I can't," I responded. "Everyone has to compromise their philosophy a little bit once in a while," he said. "No" I explained. It was not that I *would* not do that, but that I *could* not do so. I certainly did not own any worksheets, and there was not a workbook to be found in the whole school. I had already checked. I was stuck. Whole language or bust.

I spent that week blaming the kids. "Those kids won't clean up. They won't make choices. There are too many in there. If only I had fewer kids, it would work." As the week wore on and what should have been ten-minute cleanups turned into forty-five-minute madhouses, I felt like a dogsled driver trying to hold back a scatter harness hitched with eager canines. Whoa!

I became discontented not only with classroom behavior and activity, mine and the kids, but also with my own thinking. At first I was angry with myself, "If I'm such a good teacher, why won't the kids shut up?" Soon I was chastising myself, "Why do I allow this to happen and to continue to happen?" Fortunately that brought me around to exploring a new question, "What is it I am doing and have done that has promoted what is going on in my classroom?" The students had mistaken permission for freedom as a license for chaos.

Pulling in the Reins

First I explored what I had done wrong. I had provided too much choice too soon. I had established neither my expectations nor acceptable norms for those choices. I had not wanted to lecture kids on all the rules and procedures for everything, so I did not. But I also had not provided effective, appropriate alternatives, such as modeling or demonstration.

I had evaluated the kids' reading, writing, and other academic abilities, but I had not taken sufficient time to evaluate their decision-making strategies, group dynamics, or experience with self-direction and choice. I also realized that I was still thinking of the class as mine rather than ours.

I reevaluated my underlying beliefs about learning and literacy, and I reviewed developmentally appropriate practices for seven and eight year olds. I did not want to abandon choice, so I needed to think through issues relating to student empowerment and teacher control. And I could not go against my knowledge about how literacy is learned.

With all this in mind, I began to restructure the classroom.

Restructuring Freedom

I confess that there was one day where I required the kids to sit in one spot and sit quietly. But they did not do worksheets. They wrote in journals, read silently, wrote stories, and did math. Okay, maybe they did one or two math worksheets—but that was all. I also asked them to write what they knew about the earth. As Figure 15.3 demonstrates, Joey knew that "the Earth turns." Somehow in the previous days of chaos, we had managed to brainstorm what the children wanted to study during second grade. Amazingly, it all related to earth. More amazingly, I had previously selected earth as our overarching theme for the year. What a coincidence. We closed that day with a discussion about choice and responsibility in a democracy.

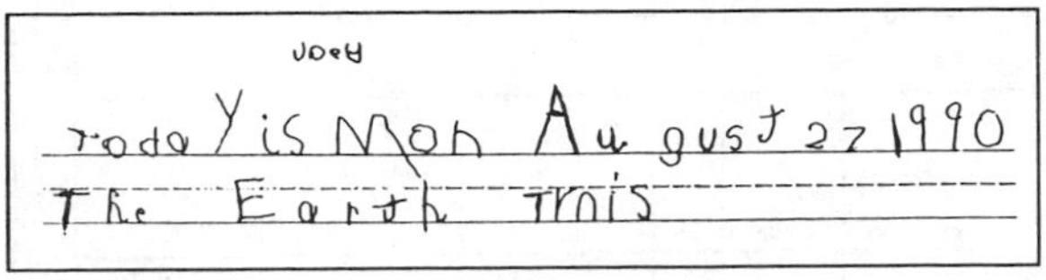

Figure 15.3. Joey's initial comment about the earth.

The following day we began afresh. We started the day in a whole group with singing from a songbook that I created; then I read a story. The amount of time allocated for language arts did not change, but I limited the choices. First we all did silent reading for fifteen minutes. Then journals. Then they all wrote in their notebooks. I wrote the schedule on the board. I did not forget P.E. that day.

In the afternoon we began a global study about the earth (pun intended). Each kid had a specific list of centers from which to choose, such as browsing a collection of atlases and geology books, creating a papier-mâché globe, reading selections from the social studies and science texts, and experimenting with flashlights and balls to gain understanding of day, night, rotation, and revolution. They could choose which center to do which day. I allowed forty-five minutes for cleanup with the hope that it would take less—it took forty-three. Oh well, we would have to work on cleanup.

We continued in this way, far more structured that previously, with our mornings being whole-class time. I began to feel comfortable pulling out small groups for guided reading or writing conferences. Soon I observed that many of the kids were ready to become a bit more independent again. Following the kids' suggestion, I began to write a few choices into our morning schedule, such as:

8:30 Silent Reading

8:45 Journals

9:00 Your Choice:

    Writing notebook

    Make a birthday card

    Write a thank-you letter

For the most part, this was successful; however, I was not satisfied. It was all pretty much whole group. Kids were not experiencing the range of possibilities that I could really provide. And it felt neither child-centered nor child-directed.

Figure 15.4. Sample daily schedule for language arts activities.

Thursday September 20 Names	8:00-8:30	8:30-8:45	8:45-9:10	9:10-9:35	9:35-10:00	10:00 to 10:20
	Morning Meeting Everybody	Journals	Independent Reading	Writing Notebook	Listening Center	Whole Group Meeting
		Journals	Independent Reading	Artistic Response to Reading	Writing Notebook	
		Guided Reading With Me	Response to Reading	Journals	Writing Notebook	
		Journals	Independent Reading	Guided Reading With Me	Writing Notebook	
		Journals	Listening Center	Read With Assistant	Writing Notebook	
		Read With Assistant	Journals	Independent Reading	Writing Notebook	
		Journals	Independent Reading	Writing Notebook	ESL With Assistant	

Early in October I implemented a new schedule. My goal was to provide for a wider range of activities, guide students in making their choices, and still have sufficient time to work with all the kids, both in small groups and individually. I made the schedules on poster boards for student display, one for each day of the week, and I made myself computer-generated copies for my own planning. (A sample schedule appears in Figure 15.4.) Everything was flexible and moveable on the posters. I used symbols such as a closed book for "reading alone," an open book for "partner reading," a clipboard for "work with the teacher," and so on. I scheduled myself to work with two or three groups a day. The groups were homogeneous based on the strategies used by the children in reading. This new structure provided opportunities for groups to use the listening center, to respond artistically or dramatically to a reading, and so on. I guided each group through these choices the first time that they were offered. Organizing this schedule was a time-consuming process, but I felt that it was worth the effort.

Sometime in January, kids began to come up to me saying things like, "I know I'm supposed to be listening to a tape right now, but I'd rather keep reading. Is that okay?" or "The chart says I'm supposed to be reading now, but I wanted to write a letter to my grandmother. May I do that instead?" Again I followed the students' lead. We had another discussion about responsibility in democracy and went back to a schedule posted on the board, with some changes:

8:30 Read Quietly [I gave up saying silently; who ever really saw second graders reading silently, anyway?]

9:00 Journals [Note the time for reading has increased]

9:10 or when you're done with your journal:

Work on a story

Read some more

Check with the teacher if you have another idea

Although I would sometimes list various things to be written or read, expectations and norms had been established, and choice in our morning time was finally coming back. In late March I was able to put the Language Arts Choices list back up. We kept a designated quiet reading and journal-writing time. The kids insisted that I deliver ten-minute and five-minute warnings before the end of Language Arts Choices time so that they could find good stopping places or come to closure. Sometimes they even insisted on foregoing P.E. so that they could have more language arts time. An hour and a half just did not seem long enough to them.

Retrospective Success

As the school days passed, I often found myself wondering, even fearing, that I was not doing enough. We seemed to get so little done each day. I saw what other whole language teachers were doing with literature study or graphing and worried about what my students were not getting on a day-to-day basis. But I shoved this fear to the back of my mind as best I could and kept on.

In January we studied water. The first day back from winter break, we brainstormed what we knew about water. I was astounded to see all the things the kids already knew. I sent home the following letter to let their parents know what we would be doing:

> Dear Room 3 Parents,
>
> We will be kicking off the new year with an intensive unit of study about *water*. While the actual study of "water" is in the Science curriculum for second grade as we learn the properties of water, the function of water to support life, and later, the role water has in our weather, our study will go beyond to integrate Social Studies as we learn about people's dependence on water, major bodies of water on the map, and islands; and Math, as we investigate measuring water, graphing water changes, and volume. We will, naturally, be doing a great deal of reading, writing, speaking and listening as we pursue our studies.
>
> As part of our study of water, our science book suggests that the children observe a small fish and document their observations. The kids will observe their fish for the month of January and write in their "science observation journals" instead of their personal journals daily. With your written permission, they may take their fish home at the end of the month.
>
> Wendy

Responding to what the kids knew, I put together a packet of activities and research guides. The unit lasted for the full month. Each kid had a mini-aquarium consisting of a plastic peanut-butter jar with a guppy, a piece of seaweed, and a snail. Instead of our usual dialogue journals, we did Fish Journals in which the kids documented their observations. Initially, Jon wrote his from the fish's point of view: "I don't like this school water!"

Every afternoon during our theme-study block of time, each kid chose what aspect of the study to pursue and whether to work alone or with friends. Some kids needed gentle guidance. A few even needed strong pushes. José regularly lost everything that he had done the day before. I was able to be the facilitator helping José find his stuff and get started, giving Jon and a few others that initial push, gently guiding the rest, and interacting with each child or small group as needed. One day I helped Isaac try to find out how squid make ink. Another day I helped someone search for information on beluga whales. Sometimes I would set out materials for experiments and invite small groups to make discoveries with me. At the end of the month, so much had happened. I summarized this in the introduction I wrote to the book that we published as part of the unit:

> We started off January learning all about water:
>
> 1. We've learned about the differences between fresh and salt water.
> 2. We've learned about the need to keep water clean.
> 3. We've observed clean and dirty water under a microscope.
> 4. We experimented with floating objects.
> 5. Each child had a guppy, and later a snail, to observe and take care of. We learned about life, birth and, unfortunately, death through our guppies. We kept journals about our fish.
> 6. The timing of freakish Tucson weather—two mornings of fog—helped us understand that water forms clouds.
>
> Together and on our own, we've read books about water and animals and plants that depend on water.
>
> All of the children have been involved in research. Their keen interest in the inhabitants of the earth's waterways helped them as they pursued those interests, coming up with and finding the answers to their own questions. The writing in this book is one result of that research—the kids' written reports. They have also created many art projects to show what they have learned. As the kids learn to ask their own questions and discover that their own ability to read and write is the key to finding all the answers, this is just a beginning.

I am so proud of that book and the process that the kids went through to produce it. I am proud of Melba, who on her own researched and wrote the following about dolphins:

> This animal is a dolphin. This animal eats fish and squid. He catches its food. He dives for them. He is this big: 6 to 9 feet. This animal lives in the sea or the ocean. This animal is the kind of animal it is a mammal. He weighs 200 to 400 pounds. This animal is special because it could talk and the other animals

can't talk and he dives. He is pretty and they communicate with each other. I'm studying about a dolphin.

I am proud of Isaac, who asked a tough question and never gave up his quest:

> My report is about the squid. It makes its own lights and it has a shell in its head. It has light organs all over its body. Below its eye is a tube that squirts out ink when intruders come. The squid is a mollusk. The squid eats fish.
>
> Ms. Hood and Ms. Folanco helped me get my information from the Compton's Dictionary of Natural Sciences and a National Geographic book.

I am proud of Russell, who kept saying that he was done after each sentence until he realized he could enter his own words in the computer and not copy by hand his drafts on the hammerhead shark:

> I found out about the hammerhead shark in a book. Babies grow inside their mother for two years instead of nine months, like people.
>
> A shark is a hammer head is mostly by the shore. The hammer head is 15 feet long. Babies are fairly dangerous same as shark hammerhead. The hammerhead is not as big as the whale shark that is 40 feet long. A hammer head's babies are born alive during a storm mostly.
>
> The hammer head can attack any other shark. It can jump out of the water and do flips and spin, a giant Squid is immune to a hammerhead.
>
> The hammer head has a flat head like a hammer but its head is longer or wider. The hammerhead has eyes on the side of his head. The hammerhead lives in the ocean and the ocean has salt in the ocean. Crabs, whales, and sharks, just about everything lives in the ocean and hammerhead.

I am equally proud of José, who finally found his stuff and painstakingly created his report on the manatee, writing down his answers to the questions that I asked as we discussed his reading:

> It swims in the sea and the ocean. Some are in a lake. It is a mammal. It's friendly. It eats plants. It has flippers.

When I wrote the introduction to the water book, I reflected not only on what we had done that month but also on everything the kids had accomplished and experienced since August. Wow! I could hardly believe how much we had done. I could not believe that I had ever worried about not getting in enough instruction. And it was only February!

From time to time throughout the school year, kids would ask to study this or that, and my stock response was, "We'll do that later." It worked well for the ones who wanted to study sharks in September. But for those who wanted to study paper construction or sewing, it did not work. As our third quarter came to a close, I realized that I would lose the kids' trust if I did not keep to my promises. But how could we ever study all the various things they wanted?

In April I posed that dilemma to the kids. My statement, "We could all choose one thing to study together, or perhaps you could each choose a topic to investigate," was met by a vigorous chant of "Vote. Vote. Vote." "Vote on what?" I asked. "That" was the reply, but as it turned out, the kids proposed a third option for which they voted overwhelmingly. They wanted to choose a variety of topics and they wanted to work in groups. That day we brainstormed topics, which ranged from sewing to electricity, World War II to basketball. I let the kids know that we would have to establish some ground rules.

When the kids left that day, I ran to Myna. "I'm taking a big gamble," I said, and I explained what I had agreed to do with the kids. I also let her know how very nervous I was about it. Myna, supportive as always, said that she thought it was wonderful, asked me to let her know if I needed anything that she could provide, and assured me she would help field any questions from concerned parents. Somewhat comforted but still wary, I wrote the following letter to the parents that evening, explaining the research project and outlining my ground rules:

Dear Room 3 Parents,

Well, here it is, the last quarter. Your kids and I have counted and, at the time of this writing, there are only 36 more days of school left!! It seems that there is so much still to do. But looking back, we've done so much already.

Today in class the kids and I quickly recapped what we've done. We shared about ourselves, studied, in depth, the earth (geology and geography), volcanoes, fossils, rocks, dinosaurs, Native Americans, our desert, water, trees, soil, trash, laws & rules, neighbors, work, New Zealand, and that was just during our afternoon time!

Every child has read dozens of books and written research reports, letters, cards, poetry, stories, charts, captions and more. Reading and writing have become one way of learning more about the world. In using reading and writing this way, we have become better readers and writers.

One major goal I've had through all our work has been to help the students become self-directed learners. What I mean by that is that the kids find a goal for learning and go about that work with little adult direction. This frees me to work with more kids more of the time. It also helps them discover that they are in control of their learning.

Most of your children are, in fact, well on their way to becoming independent learners.

The kids have asked if they can pursue a variety of topics of their choosing. They voted to work in groups. Every child will be a member of a group. The topics selected by the students range from electricity, to sewing, to jets, to basketball, and so on.

Each group will have to write a "proposal." They will have to say what they want to learn. They will record what they know already about it. They will come up with questions to ask about it. They will tell me in advance how they will find the answers to those questions. Each group will come up with a plan. In the end, each group or each child within the group will have a project to display. Each kid will have a "contract." The contract will be an agreement to follow through on the group's agreed plan and project. The proposal becomes an individual's contract when it is signed by the kid, the teacher, and the parent.

I will be sending those contracts home soon for your signature. I will need the contracts back to follow the kids' work. The contract will go home again with the final project.

I ask for your help during this time. Those kids who are working hard will be proud of that work. Ask them how their projects are going. Perhaps they may need supplies from your home or the library. Please help them get what they need.

I will insist that all children be responsible for themselves during our work time. I am letting the kids, and you, know ahead of time that if any child is not ready for this kind of responsibility, I will have to intervene and take them out of their group and they will have *very* limited choices in our classroom while others are working. If this happens with your child, *they* will let you know right away.

If you have any questions about this, please feel free to call me.

Wendy

The following day we got underway. We wound up with eight groups: WWII, jets, airplanes, electricity, paper construction, two groups on sewing, and basketball. I provided each group with a printed Project Proposal (see Figure 15.5), with spaces for filling in what they already know, what they want to know, how they are going to find out, and how they are going to inform others of what they learned. I also included specific questions about what topics they would look for in the library. After each group filled out the proposals, we prepared their contracts.

Project Proposal

YOUR NAME _____

NAMES OF THE OTHER KIDS IN YOUR GROUP

_____

_____

What are you going to study? _____

Did you write what you know about it? _____

What do you want to know about it? _____

_____

_____

_____

Is your group all asking the same question or is each kid asking a different
one? _____

_____

How are you going to find out? _____

_____

How are you going to show others what you learned? _____

_____

_____

Are there special things or books you will need for doing this project? _____

_____

List them _____

_____

How many days will you need to: Write questions? _____

Find answers? _____ Make project? _____

_____
Student Signature

_____
Teacher Signature

_____
Parent Signature

Figure 15.5. Project Proposal for students' independent group research
projects.

During the research projects, I had an instructional assistant who helped the groups that were learning about sewing. I worked intensely with many of the groups. I was most concerned about the three boys studying basketball: Micah, Noah, and Albert. I was afraid that they thought they would get to play basketball while the other kids did research. They promised me they really wanted to learn *about* basketball. I worked with them first.

What they knew consisted of team and player names. What did they want to know? Who made up the rules? Who invented the game? Who was the first coach? How were they going to find out? "Ask Micah's dad." It took some time, but we eventually broadened that list to include reading basketball cards, writing to Arizona Wildcat Coach Lute Olson, and, maybe, getting a book from the library. I think it was Noah who found a book about the history of basketball when we went to the school library. Immediately the three began to pour over it, almost forgetting to check it out.

One day I helped the boys glean information from that book. I read the table of contents and bits of the index. They choose where to look. I read most of it. They each read a bit. We found the answers to their questions and more. They were fascinated with the evolution of the basket from the original peach basket to today's net. They found it remarkable that it took ten years from the time a cloth basket was first used to the time when someone thought to open the bottom of the net. Someone used to stand on a ladder next to the basket and retrieve the ball. They took four or five days drawing their illustration of the "old fashioned" and "new fashioned" game.

That might seem like a long time. As I observed, however, I noticed that at some point each child in the class made his or her way around to where the trio was on the floor. The basketball experts explained how stupid people used to be and that it took ten years to cut the bottom off the net. They also informed everyone that basketball was invented one hundred years ago by Jim Niasmith. Those who stayed got more information.

Their final project is most impressive. One day the boys were listing all the teams that they could think of and where each team was located. Always searching for that teachable moment, I asked if they would like to make a map showing all the major basketball teams in the country. They eagerly agreed. Randomly they started to list teams and places. I asked if they knew some way we could get a complete list. "Ask Micah's dad." Any other way? They had no idea. I asked where people get information about games and scores and stuff. "The sports section!" Where could we get a newspaper? Every school has that one teacher who has everything. "Mr. Tate," the three shouted and were out the door, with no pass or note, before I could blink. They were back equally fast, with that day's sports section in hand. I did not ask if Mr. Tate even knew that they had it. But the sports section only listed places, not teams, so I read out the place-names, and the boys came up with the team names. They elected me scribe—because I could write faster.

Another day we took that list, along with an outline map of the United States, string, stars, and tape, over to our big wall map. I read the place-names to the boys, who found the names on the wall map, relocated them on the small map, and placed a star atop the location. Then we taped string from each star to a clear spot and wrote each place-name and team name. Again I was elected scribe—because I could write smaller.

We posted the results of their research in the school cafeteria—their illustration and report (see Figure 15.6) and their map (see Figure 15.7). The only problem arose when it was time to take their report down. "Who would take it home?" Noah asked me one day. I suggested that he go talk it over with the others. Albert returned in tears because Noah had announced that I had told him that he could take the project home. Leaving the assistant briefly in charge, I gathered the trio, went to the cafeteria, took down the posters, and went to the copy machine, where we reduced and reduced until it would fit on regular-size paper. All the while the boys were debating who would take the originals—until they saw the copies. I explained that I had some teacher friends that I would be seeing in the summer and suggested that maybe the boys would let me take their posters to show my friends. Reluctantly they agreed, beaming with pride.

I would be remiss if I allowed you to believe that everything in the classroom was smooth sailing once I made a few adjustments in my original plans. Not only were there occasional squalls, even frequent ones; there were even parts of my voyage to Xanadu that were missing.

I had difficulty balancing my desire to provide as many meaningful engagements with books as I could through literature study and to provide direct instruction in becoming proficient readers. I found it difficult to do literature studies when few of my students could read the material independently. I knew other primary teachers accomplished this, but, somewhat guiltily, I made a decision to focus mostly on guided reading with my small groups and used my whole-group time—sharing reading and reading to kids—for making connections with literature.

I also did not establish the math program that I had envisioned. I admit that I made the kids use the math text far more often than I was comfortable with. Much of our math time was spent with hands-on

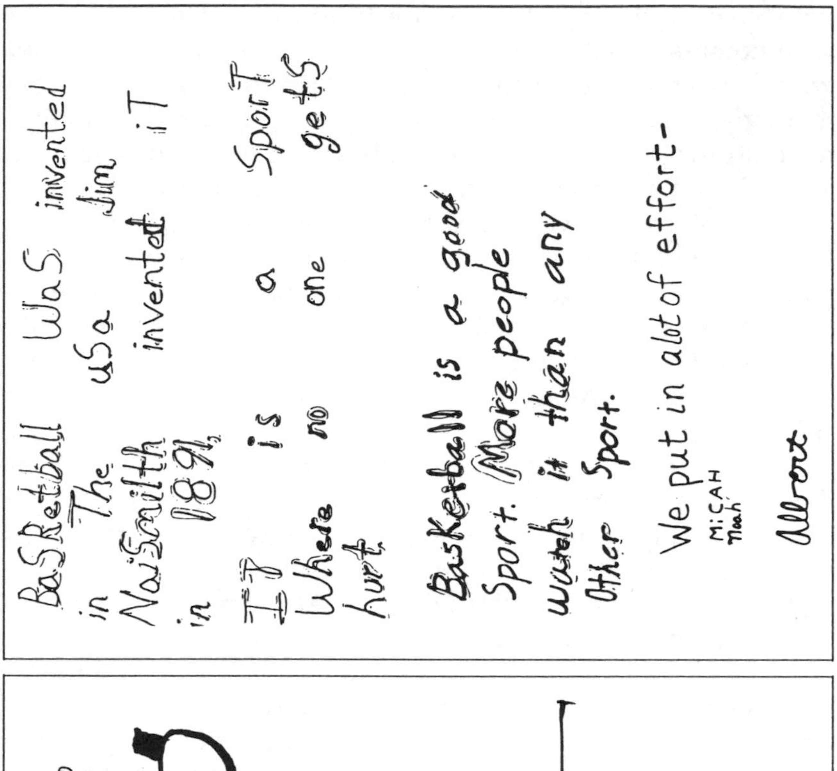

Figure 15.6. Micah, Noah, and Albert's research project on basketball.

BaSketball waS invented in The NaiSmith Jim invented iT in 1891.

IT is a Sport Where no one getS hurt.

Basketball is a good Sport. More people watch it than any Other Sport.

We put in alot of effort—

MiCAH
Noah

Albert

Passes and Balls

The old fashiond

The new fashiond

First Thay Used Peach baskets Than They Used Nets tird oT The boTTom Now Thay use nets ofwull the boTTom

The baskets have always been 10 feet high

329

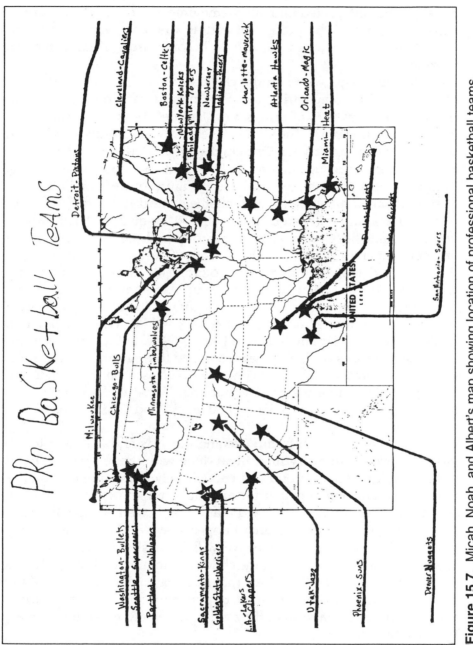

Figure 15.7. Micah, Noah, and Albert's map showing location of professional basketball teams.

materials and integrated into our theme time and our special events. I tried to emphasize the process of getting to an answer over instant correctness. I also wanted the kids to become users of mathematical language.

In February, I wrote on the chalkboard, "We have 30 kids [our enrollment had momentarily dropped] in our class. Tomorrow is Valentine's Day. If every kid brings 30 valentines, how many cards will we have in our room?" The students self-selected groups in which to work through to an answer. One child with a calculator watch immediately began pressing buttons. Others said that she was cheating. I assured them that she would have to figure out which buttons to push. She called a couple friends together, and this is what they produced: "I used my calculator. I put in 30 × 30. It equals 900. I know that was like times." Meanwhile, another group had the number 30 listed on their paper thirty times. They wrote, "We add it." Their paper demonstrated that they added by counting by tens. A third group wrote 30 + 30 = 60 = 90 = 120 and so on until they reached 900. On the flip side of the paper was written 3, 6, 9, up to 27, indicating some sort of discovery of the relationship between 3 and 30. Their explanation reads, "To do it to explain it, I added 30 30s." Most of the other groups followed processes similar to the second and third groups, but a fourth group spread out all over one corner of the classroom the small manipulative blocks that we use for counting. "We put blocks of groups and we got the answer 900. We put 30 blocks and 30 groups and that was the answer 900."

I learned so much from watching the kids and listening to the kids. But even with everything I had done with them, I still had that nagging fear that I was not doing enough to help them make connections. It did all come together for me, though. I knew it was all okay one day in March when I realized that my kids were always thinking and making the connections that I hoped they would. It was the day that I said to the class, "Today we will learn about fractions," and Russell jumped up, pointed to the child next to him, and said, "This is a whole boy. . . . " I realized then that I do not have to provide all the connections for the kids. Given the opportunity, and the experience of a whole language classroom, they will quite freely make the connections for themselves.

16 Booksharing: Teachers and Parents Reading to Deaf Children

Carolyn Ewoldt
York University, Toronto, Ontario

As part of a longitudinal study of young deaf children engaging in literacy (Ewoldt and Saulnier 1991), parents and teachers were videotaped annually as they shared books with their deaf children. The children were approximately age three at the beginning of the study and age seven at the end. Nine of the thirty children had unaided hearing losses in the severe range (71 to 90 dB), and the remaining twenty-one children had profound unaided losses of 91 dB or greater.

The seemingly simple activity of sharing a book with a deaf child or children was found to be a dynamic and complex event, involving diverse agendas and meanings. Like texts, any event has a semantic potential which is available to language users within a particular context of situation (Halliday 1973). By asking teachers and parents to be videotaped while reading to children, we set up a context of situation, made up of the *field*, the *mode*, and the *tenor*. Discussion of some of the findings from this study will follow that organizational construct.

Teachers

Little research has been directed at teacher booksharing with deaf children. We are aware of only two such studies, both conducted by Susan Mather (1987, 1989), using data from our project. Thus, this paper is not meant to be an indictment of current practice. Because of the paucity of research, teachers have not had access to information about effective booksharing. This chapter is only a beginning.

Field

In the *field* we included the teachers' agendas, goals, formats, interpretations, and selections of text. We found that teachers tended to have "scripts" in their heads from which they did not like to deviate. In the following example, the teacher has a predetermined answer to her question about what made the mittens dirty in *The Three Little Kittens:*

> *Teacher:* Jack, how did their mittens become dirty? What did they do?
>
> *Jack:* Eat the pie.
>
> *Teacher:* Linda, do you remember? How mittens become dirty?
>
> *Linda:* Wash.
>
> *Teacher:* Why wash? How become dirty? Make them dirty?
>
> *Linda:* Don't know.
>
> *Teacher:* Say, "I don't know." Say, "I don't know."
>
> *Linda:* I don't know.
>
> *Teacher:* Do you remember, Judy? How? What do? They what?
>
> *Judy:* Eat.
>
> *Teacher: (Shows picture of kittens outside in snow eating pie with mittens on.)* Okay. *Play outside.* Also pie on mittens. Right? Play outside.

[In the above example, as in all future examples, a gloss for the signs of the teacher is presented. Often the voice was used to fill in missing words, but only the language accessible to all the children, regardless of hearing loss, is presented.]

Although the children rightly answered that eating pie with mittens on would make them dirty, the teacher was reluctant to accept this answer because it did not match the answer in her "script." Note that she did deviate from her own agenda when Linda's language was deemed incorrect.

Also of interest within the field was the format of the booksharing event. The teachers in this study were encouraged to share a book as they would normally share a story with their children. All of them chose to face the children rather than gather them to their sides, even when the session involved only two children.

One teacher used a flannel board and cutouts of the story characters, which she and the children manipulated during the reading. This use of the flannel board in conjunction with the book *Three Ducks Went Wandering* by Paul Galdone (Ticknor and Fields, 1987) resulted in dissonance caused by the simultaneous creation of two texts. As Snow and Ninio (1986) point out, book events occur outside of real time. The flannel board put the action in the present, as in the following example:

> *Text:* With a snort the bull lowered his head and charged the
> ducks.
>
> *Teacher:* The bull is going to chase the ducks. *(Puts bull on flan-
> nel board.)*

A second reason for dissonance was that the story created by the flannel board resulted in plot and role reversals. For example, the ducks had already been put on the flannel board when the teacher added a fox, signing, DUCKS SEE FOX. In the book the foxes were stationary, and the ducks wandered up to the foxes. As well, the foxes saw the ducks, and not vice versa. Because the ducks were already on the flannel board, the situation became reversed.

Third, the fact that the ducks stayed in one place and the other animals came to them could have caused confusion over settings. The dangerous places that the ducks went in the story were in the same location on the flannel board as their home, the safe place.

Combining the two activities of booksharing and reenacting with the flannel board introduced other difficulties as well. Almost all the interactions initiated by the teacher in this session were related to the logistics of putting on and taking off the pictures and discussion about which child had the next turn.

Mode

With regard to *mode,* we found a variety of presentations of story information. The preferred mode was an almost verbatim rendition of the text. While none of the teachers read the text exactly as written, ten teachers read almost verbatim, including all five of the oral teachers and five of the simultaneous communication teachers.

The next most preferred mode was a full reading but in the teacher's own words. This occurred primarily because of the differences between signing and speaking, as in the following example:

> *Text:* "What! Lost your mittens, you naughty kittens: Then
> you shall have no pie."
>
> *Teacher:* Mother was mad. "Lost your mittens, you bad kit-
> ten." *(Mimes scolding.)* "No pie for you-all. No pie for you.
> Sorry." Mother was mad because the three kittens lost
> their mittens.

A deaf teacher offered two renditions of some parts of the text, signing the same page in different ways:

> *Text:* " . . . a big angry bull! "What are those three ducks doing
> in my field?" said the bull. I'll teach them a lesson!"

First reading: Look what happen! Big angry mad bull say,
  "What three ducks doing on my land? Me teach lesson."

Second reading: Bull not like ducks on its land. "Go away,
  ducks." Bull, ducks don't know; walk away. The ducks
  don't see the bull.

The deaf teacher in the above example read other parts of the text only
once but mimed the action. She easily moved back and forth between
American Sign Language (e.g., BULL, DUCKS DON'T KNOW; WALK
AWAY) and a manual code on English (e.g., THE DUCKS DON'T SEE
THE BULL).

The dissonance noted earlier with regard to the use of the flannel
board was similarly created when teachers attempted to sign and
speak simultaneously. Many examples occurred in which a teacher
mistakenly signed one word and said a different, nonsynonymous
word. An additional problem was that the teachers frequently signed
an incomplete message, filling in orally the words that were not
signed. For the children who depended almost entirely on manually
coded information, the message was often not only incomplete but
erroneous, as in the following example:

Voice: The hawk wants to fly down, grab the, the ducks, and
  bring them home for lunch.

Sign: The eagle fly down, catch one, get duck, bring home for
  lunch.

The message to the children dependent upon sign was that *the eagle
actually caught the ducks,* which is false.

Misunderstandings occurred in oral settings as well:

Teacher: Listen. How much money are they going to cost if
  they are free?

Child: Three.

Teacher: Not three. They're free. What does *free* mean?

Children: (Unintelligible.)

Teacher: Ok. Stop. I'm not saying *freeze.* I'm saying *free.*

Eye gaze as a means of involving children in the booksharing
event became an important focus of our analysis because of the work
of Susan Mather (1987, 1989). Comparing a deaf teacher and a hearing
teacher videotaped for our study, Mather found two types of eye gaze
in use—the individual gaze and the group gaze. The group eye gaze
was effectively used by deaf teachers and some hearing teachers to
involve all the children in the booksharing. Inappropriate individual

eye gaze was noted when a teacher commented, SOME OF YOU DON'T KNOW THIS STORY, and focused her gaze on one child, who responded defensively, ME KNOW, ME KNOW.

In another example, a teacher was sharing a book with two children, one of whom, Mandy, was a deaf girl in our study and the other, Mark, a differently abled deaf boy with no intelligible speech, who was not a continuing participant. In this setting, the teacher almost completely excluded Mark by focusing individual eye gaze on Mandy and using her name frequently. Even when Mark initiated comments or pointed at pictures, he received only a brief glance from the teacher, revealing an attitude that he would not understand the story or participate in the booksharing to the same extent as the other child. This, however, was not the case, for Mark actually attempted to initiate as many interactions as Mandy.

Tenor

According to Halliday (1973), the *tenor* is the role relationship between the audience and the speaker or writer. With regard to the tenor of the teacher doing the booksharing, we found a great deal of evidence for a transmission model, as described by Cummins:

> The basic premise of the transmission model is that the teacher's task is to impart knowledge or skills that she/he possesses to students who do not yet have these skills. This implies that the teacher initiates and controls the interaction, constantly orienting it towards the achievement of instructional objectives. It has been argued that a transmission model of teaching contravenes central principles of language and literacy acquisition and that a model allowing for reciprocal interaction between teachers and students represents a more appropriate alternative. (1989, 63–64)

We also found extensive use of triads (i.e., question, answer, evaluate or correct), as described by Edwards and Furlong (1978). Teachers used a variety of correction responses, such as simply telling the child, "You're wrong," providing the answer, restating the teacher's own interpretation, ignoring the child's answer, or changing the meaning of the child's message to fit the teacher's interpretation, as in the following:

> *Child:* Say water hose? (*Reading sign above fire hose.*)
>
> *Teacher:* (*Nods.*) Fire dog will help fireman hose water?
>
> *Child:* (*Nods.*)

> *Teacher:* Oh, I see . . . I think dog will help fireman, smell
> where people. People walk through, find people in fire
> building, pull out. Safe people. *(Nods; holds up book.)*

In the preceding example the child seems to accept the teacher's interpretation without contesting it. This was usually the case, although there were a few instances in which a child would hold to his or her own interpretation despite the attempts of the teacher to change it:

> *Teacher:* While he walk along, he yell, "Hat, hat for sale, 50¢ a
> hat."
>
> *Child:* 25¢.
>
> *Teacher:* Yell. Why did man yell?
>
> *Child:* 25.
>
> *Teacher:* 50¢ hat. Why yell?
>
> *Child:* 25, 25, total 50. 25, 25, add 50.
>
> *Teacher:* 25. Why say 25?
>
> *Child:* 25 and 25, add 50.
>
> *Teacher:* Did I say 25?
>
> *Child: (Unintelligible.)*
>
> *Teacher:* No. 25, 25, 50, but still not say. Hat cost 50.
>
> *Child:* Price.
>
> *Teacher:* Not say hat cost 25.

Within the tenor of the teachers' interactions with children we found many examples of missed opportunities, when the children demonstrated an interest in, or awareness of, some learning potential that the teachers did not. It might well be argued that it is difficult in the thick of interaction to pick up all the signals and react to all the cues given by children about what they are ready to learn. However, we found that even when teachers had time to study the text in advance, they often did not take advantage of a text's potential for helping children learn. One book in particular, Dick Gackenbach's *A Bag Full of Pups* (Houghton Mifflin, 1981), afforded multiple opportunities to capitalize on children's knowledge of and interest in environmental print, which appears on almost every page. For example, one full-page picture of a grocery store has the following print in the illustration: *Soda Pop 39¢ each, Soap Suds 58¢, Cheese, Fresh Eggs.* There is also a scale in the picture with the numerals 1 through 11 on it.

Of the six teachers who read this book to their children, only three ever referred to any of the print in the pictures, with all three reading the words in a cartoon bubble on one page. Only one of these teachers pointed out or read any of the other environmental print, with that teacher telling the children that one of the signs in the grocery store said *cheese*. As well, none of the teachers picked up on the children's pointing and attempts to read the environmental print. The following exchange about the *Fresh Eggs* sign occurred between two children:

> *Boy:* Egg.
>
> *Girl:* Egg.
>
> *Boy: (To another boy)* Egg.
>
> *Teacher:* He teacher?
>
> *Boy:* No.
>
> *Teacher:* Watch me, please.

Other missed opportunities had to do with intertextual tying (DeBeaugrande 1980). One teacher, having asked how many dogs were in the picture, did not react when she received the answer of 101. Another teacher did not react when a child pointed to a spinning wheel and signed, GOLD.

These examples further emphasize the teachers' inflexibility with regard to agenda and interpretation, as well as their lack of response to the children's attempts at initiation and perhaps their misunderstanding of the children's language.

Negotiation of Meaning

The negotiation of meaning involves all three components of register—field, mode, and tenor. Texts provide a semantic potential within which readers construct their own meanings. In life outside of school, this is usually a private process between reader and author. In school, this negotiation of meaning usually involves a third party—the teacher—and the negotiation of meaning becomes a negotiation of the territory within which the teacher and child construct their meanings.

In a language event in which one participant has more power than another (due to position and/or language proficiency), there is a strong possibility that the semantic potential will be restricted to or dictated by the meaning constructed by the person in power. This almost always means maximum power and control for the teacher and minimum ownership for the child, even in situations where the teacher makes every sincere effort to avoid this outcome.

With faulty and/or counterproductive messages or intentions on the part of the teacher, the teacher and child will be even less likely to discover a common ground, and the child may construct a meaning that is quite distant from the teacher's intentions or may maintain original intentions which may be outside the semantic potential. The teacher may be quite unaware that this is happening.

As a matter of fact, we suspect that the greater involvement of the children in repeated readings of the same text may be explained, at least in part, by the fact that the children had learned the teacher's agenda and were able to provide the expected responses, without necessarily adopting the teacher's interpretation.

Teachers have several responsibilities in any booksharing event:

1. To convey meaning clearly. The use of simultaneous communication or oral language often does not result in clarity of meaning or conformity to intentions for deaf children and their teachers.

2. To lay his or her ideas alongside those of the students for consideration. Teachers' ideas necessarily carry more weight by virtue of their position in the context of situation. To lay them down alongside the children's is sufficient.

3. Not to consider himself or herself "the final arbiter of what the learner should think, nor the creator of what the learner does think. The important job for the teacher is to keep trying to find out what sense the students are making" (Duckworth 1987, 133).

Parents

In support of Duckworth's statement that a teacher is not the creator of what the learner thinks, we found in the parent-child booksharing that the children conveyed messages about literacy that were never observed over the four years of the study as coming from either teachers or parents. In other words, the children had created their own views of literacy. The greater comfort of the parent-child booksharing context afforded more opportunities for observation of this phenomenon.

One message conveyed by children but not by adults was that a reader can interact directly with a text without mediation. One child demonstrated this by signing directly to the characters in the story:

Mother: Maybe bug like eat food. *(Talking about a picnic in which the ants were invading the blanket.)*

Child: Not permit. *(To characters:* Put it [food] away!)

Likewise, Maxwell (1980) reported a child saying to Little Red Riding Hood: GO HOME NOW RUN! In contrast, parents (and teachers) indicated that mediation through fingerspelling, speech, or signing was necessary or important.

Phillips and McNaughton found that both parents and children in their study emphasized the authority of text: "Both caregivers and child assumed that the process of clarification, anticipation or integration was to be checked against the narrative" (1990, 207). We found, however, that some children did challenge the authority of the text, conveying the message that text is not infallible, as in the following example:

> *Text:* Mr. Bird brought a pink worm. Mrs. Bird brought a
> green one.
>
> *Child: One* wrong.
>
> *Mother:* Green *one* mean green *worm.*

Another child indicated that a picture was wrong because the buttons on a character's shirt were in the back instead of in the front.

The following exchange occurred between a hearing mother and an oral child:

> *Child:* He [star] close his eyes.
>
> *Mother:* No, he's keeping watch. Stars stay up at night.
>
> *Child:* What if they don't have eyes?
>
> *Mother:* Well, this one does.

Thus, the parent accepted the book's authority, but the child did not. These examples belie the commonly held view that the relation between teaching and learning is direct and linear. Ferreiro and Teberosky state, "A method may help or hinder, facilitate or complicate, but not create learning. Obtaining knowledge is a result of the learner's own activity" (1982, 15).

Power struggles between parents and children occurred during booksharing and provided insights into how children learn about language and literacy. Cox says of such struggles, "Literary meaning was . . . subject to constant negotiation between competing interests. And, as such, it was marked indelibly by the tensions that emanated from those negotiations" (1990, 250).

Interestingly, it was the absence of such negotiations, or the children's thwarted attempts to negotiate in the teacher-student booksharing, that alerted us to their importance. We did not find in the context of teacher-student booksharing the "struggle of students and teachers to establish their own definitions of situations" (Waller 1932, 297, cited in Cox 1990).

We noted previously that texts provide semantic potential within which readers create their own meanings through negotiations with the author. Negotiation implies a give-and-take situation in which neither side is solely a giver or a taker. In the school settings we observed, however, children were required to be takers most of the time, and we also noted in the parent-child booksharing that parents expected that role for their children in year two of the study.

Story Reenactment

Parents have frequently reported that children for whom storybook reading is a regular occurrence in the home exhibit reading-like behavior before any evidence of conventional reading is observed. These children usually have favorite storybooks that they "read" to their stuffed animals or younger siblings, and this reading has many of the characteristics of adult reading with regard to mannerisms and intonation. The reading may so accurately reflect the print message that the child is perceived by the parents to have memorized it (Sulzby 1983).

These observations have led researchers such as Sulzby (1983) and Otto (1984) to conclude that not only are booksharing experiences with adults pleasurable and memorable for children, but that children can reveal through their re-creation of these events what they understand reading to be. Thus, we asked the children in our study to re-create those events in a procedure called story reenactment (Sulzby 1985).

Comparisons were made between the messages about literacy conveyed by the children in the story reenactment and by adults and children in parent-child booksharing and teacher-student booksharing. There were commonalities between the children's messages in the story reenactments and parent-child booksharing and the parents' messages, or between the parents' messages and the teachers' messages. However, there were only two messages that prevailed across all three contexts.

One message was that of the adult as an authority about reading. This was not the message of the first two years of the study for the children, but it was the message of the teachers from the beginning of the study and the message of many of the parents from year one or two.

The other message found in all contexts was that reading should be verbatim and error-free. Again, this was not a message that was conveyed by the children in the earlier years of the study, but it was consistently conveyed by teachers and most parents. The children showed us that meaning (intentionality) was involved from the time of their earliest engagements with reading and writing and that the form evolved slowly. This runs counter to the dominant instructional practice of attending to form rather than meaning in face-to-face and written language.

In any longitudinal study, a researcher leaves the field with the regret that the study must end, for new and important insights appear to be forthcoming. One of the regrets in this study was that we could not remain with the children long enough to know whether this search for meaning and belief in their own abilities would return or if the game of school had become once again an important outcome of their scholastic endeavors.

But even a nonparticipant audience negotiates meaning, and the very fact of the existence of a text to work on provides some opportunities for negotiation and transformation of knowledge by the child. We have a lot to learn about booksharing with deaf children, but one thing that we do know is that we must continue to do it and we must strive to do it better.

References

Cox, S. 1990. "Who the boss?" Dynamic tensions in oral storybook reading. *International Journal of Qualitative Studies in Education* 3 (3): 231–52.

Cummins, J. 1989. *Empowering minority students.* Sacramento: California Association of Bilingual Education.

DeBeaugrande, R. 1980. *Text, discourse, and process: Toward a multi-disciplinary science of texts.* Norwood, N.J.: Ablex.

Duckworth, E. 1987. *"The having of wonderful ideas" and other essays on teaching and learning.* New York: Teachers College, Columbia University.

Edwards, A., and V. Furlong. 1978. *The language of teaching: Meaning in classroom interaction.* London: Heinemann.

Ewoldt, C., and K. Saulnier. 1991. *Engaging in literacy: A longitudinal study with three to seven year old deaf participants.* Final report for Gallaudet Research Institute, Center for Studies in Education and Human Development. Toronto: York University.

Ferreiro, E., and A. Teberosky. 1982. *Literacy before schooling.* Exeter, N.H.: Heinemann.

Halliday, M. 1973. *Explorations in the functions of language.* London: Edward Arnold.

Mather, S. 1987. Eye gaze and communication in a deaf classroom. *Sign Language Studies* 54:11–30.

———. 1989. Visually oriented teaching strategies with preschool deaf children. In *Sociolinguistics and the deaf community,* ed. C. Lucas. San Diego: Academic Press.

Maxwell, M. 1980. Language acquisition in a deaf child: The interaction of sign variations, speech and print variations. Ph.D. diss., University of Arizona, Tucson.

Otto, B. 1984. Emergent reading ability and the zone of proximal development. Paper presented at Thirty-fourth National Reading Conference Symposium, St. Petersburg, Fla.

Phillips, G., and S. McNaughton. 1990. The practice of storybook reading to preschool children in mainstream New Zealand families. *Reading Research Quarterly* 25:196–212.

Snow, C., and A. Ninio. 1986. The contribution of reading books with children to their linguistic and cognitive development. In *Emergent literacy: Writing and reading,* ed. W. Teale and E. Sulzby. Norwood, N.J.: Ablex.

Sulzby, E. 1983. *Children's emergent abilities to read favorite storybooks.* Final report to the Spencer Foundation. Evanston, Ill.: Northwestern University.

———. 1985. Children's emergent reading of favorite storybooks: A developmental study. *Reading Research Quarterly* 20 (4): 458–81.

17 Written Dialogue with Young Children: Making Writing Live

Nigel Hall
Manchester Polytechnic, Manchester, England

Traditional methods of teaching writing have often reduced the activity of writing to the copying of teacher-authored texts or the creation of safe, short texts. The experience of such teaching has many consequences for young children's perceptions of the value, use, and pleasure of writing. The consequence is usually that writing is seen as having little value, having few uses, and being most definitely not pleasurable.

In the past, such methods and consequences have been seen as somewhat inevitable. However, the exciting work of the last fifteen years has demonstrated clearly that children can be authors who enjoy creating their texts and who view writing as an intrinsically worthwhile part of their everyday lives. One technique which has enormous potential for helping children see writing as a personally significant experience is interactive writing.

What is interactive writing? A working definition might be: Interactive writing is writing involving the participation of two or more friendly correspondents who exchange meaningful and purposeful texts across an extended period of time.

This dialogue can take many forms. Children can write to each other; teachers may write to children; and other adults, including parents, may act as correspondents. The exchanges could be through written conversation, dialogue journals, or letters, and the medium could be journals, mail, computer, or fax. Interactive writing, an exercise in mutuality, offers a meeting place for minds. It creates opportunities for developing special relationships between people. It can be so much more than just sending messages or letters to each other.

In recent years, there has been a substantial shift in the way the teaching and learning of literacy is viewed (for a sustained review see Hall 1987). This, in turn, is linked with a revaluation of learning to write which has focused away from ritualistic copying exercises and toward helping young children develop as authors (Hall 1989). Interactive writing has come to be seen as a powerful way of helping children develop their abilities as authors by allowing them to concentrate on meaning and purpose—in other words, on "authorship" rather than form.

Teachers and children in Manchester, England, have been exploring interactive writing for some years. In this chapter I explain some of the thinking behind what we have been doing and offer a glimpse of some of the work that has been carried out.

Principles

One thing is certain. It is not sufficient that two people write to each other. What they write must be mutually interesting; there must be a coming together in talk. Hall, Robinson, and Crawford asked: "What kind of conversation would it be if people simply talked at each other with no regard for each other? Would it even be called dialogue?" (1991, 118).

It is critical that the communication is based upon clear principles and rights. This becomes particularly important when one of the correspondents is an adult, and especially if that adult is the class teacher. I have identified certain points as fundamental to successful "coming together in talk" (Hall 1991). This "mutuality" is rendered most powerfully in interactive writing when it is developed within the following five central precepts.

1. *Mutuality is strengthened when the written exchange extends over time.* "One-off" letters or messages are not as interesting, meaningful, or motivating as extended dialogue. Of course, discrete writing activities have a place in life, but the achievement of mutuality requires real time. Participants must have the chance to get to know each other, to develop a style of exchange, and to understand the varied obligations of a sustained relationship.

2. *Mutuality is strengthened when there is a high degree of authenticity in the relationship between the writers.* Authors should engage in dialogue in which each participant has equal rights. Although some interactive writing may be between mature writers and young children, it is vital that the experienced writers do not use their competencies in a didactic way. It is not the function of any one party in a dialogic exchange to exert continual control over the dialogue. When

participants have equal rights in the dialogue, they each have the freedom to select and introduce topics, and to avoid or reject topics; together they negotiate the development of the dialogue.

3. *Mutuality is strengthened when it is the meanings of the exchange that are significant, rather than the form.* Friends do not normally correct, mark, or grade each other's letters. Friends write because they have important or interesting things to say to each other, because they want to know about each other's lives, feelings, and thoughts. Each accepts the other's letters as they are.

4. *Mutuality is strengthened when there is trust between the writers.* Friends do not seek to embarrass or humiliate each other. Dialogue between friends is private until both correspondents agree to what they write being made available to others; people who "tell all" find fewer opportunities to engage in mutual exchange.

5. *Mutuality is strengthened when children are "invited" to correspond.* The achievement through writing of an honest relationship with children is impossible if those children have been forced to take part in the exchange or are made to respond for didactic reasons rather than because they find the dialogue rewarding and intrinsically interesting.

From the children's point of view, the above principles offer them the chance to have their voices be heard, to have their thoughts be taken seriously, to have someone respond to the meanings of what they write, to avoid having their writing treated negatively, to be perceived as successful writers, and to have the chance to get to know their correspondents as people.

Most interactive writing with which we have been associated has been between teachers and children. However, we are also exploring exchanges between adults and very young children, and exchanges between children. For teachers, interactive writing offers the opportunity to know their children as people and the chance to observe the children's growth as language users.

Interactive writing can be carried out with children of all ages. We have been involved with children from the ages of three years up to eleven years. Teachers and researchers across the world have used interactive writing with all ages, including adults, deaf children, people learning second languages, and student teachers.

It is important to recognize that children do not have to be able to write perfectly or even to write at all in order to participate in interactive writing. Indeed, it could be carried out with very young children through drawings. The principles would remain the same, in particular that whatever they produce is treated as reasonable and sensible communication. This is, in effect, no different from how a parent of a one-year-old child responds to its babbling and single-word phrases as meaningful communication. We do not tell our children off for speaking like that—on the contrary, we encourage them. We invite them to be conversationalists.

Interactive Writing from the Start

In one of our Manchester studies (Price 1989), a teacher (writing in the character of a giant Ladybird) exchanged letters with a group of three- and four-year-old children. Each day, to the children's great excitement, there was a letter from the Ladybird. The children were used to thinking of themselves as writers; they had a writing center in their classroom and were encouraged to write whenever they wished. They did not hesitate when invited to reply to the Ladybird's letters, and during the six weeks of the project hundreds of letters were created for the Ladybird. Some of the letters were no more than a scribble, while some incorporated the children's dawning knowledge of letters; a few children were able to have a go at writing some words, either copying from the Ladybird's letters or working out the words for themselves. When asked to guess how old the Ladybird was, children responded in different ways (see Figures 17.1 and 17.2). And all the talk about ages and birthdays led one child to write the message shown in Figure 17.3. This last example may at first sight look like a jumble of letters, but when examined closely and split up (as in Figure 17.4), it can clearly be seen as a clever construction for a four-year-old child: "Joe, you can come to my party."

  In any conventional sense, these children were not letter writers. However, the teacher's decision to treat their responses as serious pieces of communication gave the children confidence to tackle writing, enticed them to explore writing, made them feel like writers, and helped them understand that their efforts were valued. Along the way, many of the children developed real insights about dialogic communication. Since this original study, teachers across England and the United States have used, with considerable success, the technique of writing to the children from the standpoint of a fictional character.

Figure 17.1 One child's letter to the Ladybird, estimating its age.

Figure 17.2 Another child's letter to the Ladybird, estimating its age.

Teachers as Correspondents

The most fulfilling exchanges, though, come when teachers write as themselves. This is not always easy for teachers. We are led to think of ourselves as people with status, who must keep control and who must not get too personal with children. We also develop techniques of

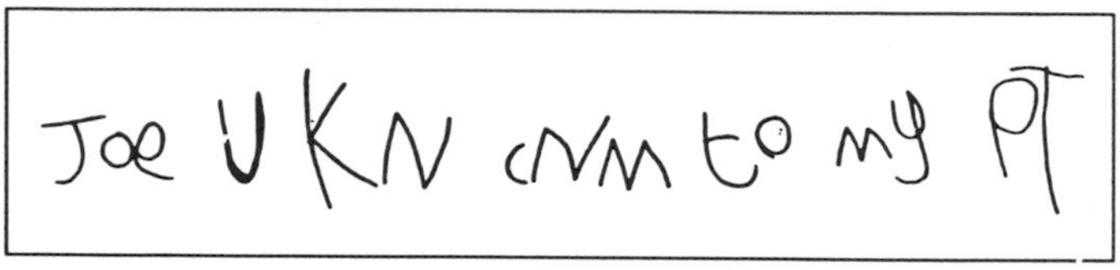

Figure 17.3 Invitation offered to the Ladybird.

Figure 17.4 Invitation offered to the Ladybird, with additional word spacing.

always asking the questions, always insisting on correctness, and always controlling dialogue within our classrooms. Just as we learn to act as teachers, so children learn to act as pupils. It is difficult for us and for the children to change this pattern.

Hall and Duffy (1987) explored the tension of this change. In their study, the teacher began to use dialogue journals with her class of five year olds. Dialogue journals are simply books in which the letters of both correspondents are written. The books pass backward and forward between the two participants, allowing each writer to view all the letters that have been written (for further details see Hall and Duffy 1987; see also Staton et al. 1988). At first, the teacher's letters consisted only of questions, and the child's replies consisted only of answers. In other words, it was a typical teacher-pupil exchange in a classroom. As a consequence, the exchanges were fairly impersonal, contained little of the child's natural voice, and lacked any sense of dynamism. Unhappy with this, the teacher eventually decided to stop asking questions and to offer some information. She simply wrote about having a friend: "I have a friend called Judy." The child's response changed straightaway: "What does she look like? Does she look nice?" (See Figure 17.5.) For the first time since the exchange had begun, she asked questions.

From then on, the exchanges became much more like one person writing to another person and less like those in a teacher-pupil relationship. The child had learned that she had rights in this exchange; she could question as well as respond. Her voice could be heard. The

```
Dear    Mrs    Duffy   wot
dose   She   Luk   like
dose   She   luk   nis

          Love   from
              Aileen
```

Figure 17.5 Student's letter to teacher.

benefits to that child and the others in the class were significant. Hall and Duffy comment:

> Aileen had discovered her voice in writing as a result of communicating to a real audience, someone who was not standing over her shoulder as she wrote, and someone whom she knew would be interested in what she wrote and would treat her words with respect. (1987, 528)

However, it was also the teacher who changed. By loosening her need to feel in control, the dialogue became richer, she learned more about what the children really could write, and she began to appreciate that it was not necessary to exert tight control over what children wrote. The teacher learned to become a correspondent.

Children as Correspondents

Our experience is that children love writing their dialogue journals. Indeed, many of them say they prefer writing these journals over other school activities. Children seem to get so much more involved and take greater responsibility when their work is taken seriously. This can be clearly seen in the next example from a dialogue journal written by five-year-old Georgina (G) interacting with her teacher (T). This journal has more the flavor of conversation than letters. The teacher wrote a sentence, then the child wrote one, and so on. This type of interactive writing was carried out by the teacher when working with a group of children. The following entries (shown in their handwritten form in Figure 17.6) are from one day.

> *T:* What a nuisance! My car would not start this morning.
>
> *G:* My daddy had to take it to the garage.
>
> *T:* Why?
>
> *G:* Because the tire wouldn't go.
>
> *T:* My tire was flat too!
>
> *G:* Did you take it to the garage?
>
> *T:* I couldn't drive it there!
>
> *G:* You could have rung up the man who gets the cars.
>
> *T:* I'll do that next time. I am worried about my dog.
>
> *G:* It could have got stolen last night.
>
> *T:* No! She was sick!
>
> *G:* Where was she sick?
>
> *T:* She was sick on the carpet.
>
> *G:* Did you have to wash it?
>
> *T:* Yes.
>
> *G:* Where did you put your dog after you had washed the carpet?
>
> *T:* I took her to the vet.
>
> *G:* What did the doctor say about her?
>
> *T:* He gave her some medicine.
>
> *G:* Was it nice medicine?
>
> *T:* I don't think she liked it much.
>
> *G:* I am worried now.

There are a number of points worth making about this dialogue. First, it was more like conversation than it was like any other genre. The topic derived from the everyday experience of both correspondents. The exchange contained twenty-two turns of about equal length. (In fact, Georgina's sentences were a little longer than the teacher's; Georgina's were, on average, 6.9 words long, and the teacher's were 5.5.) As conversation, however, it was much more like everyday conversation between two people than it was like a conversation between a child and a teacher.

In this written conversation, Georgina had equal participatory rights and could even be considered as the controller of the dialogue.

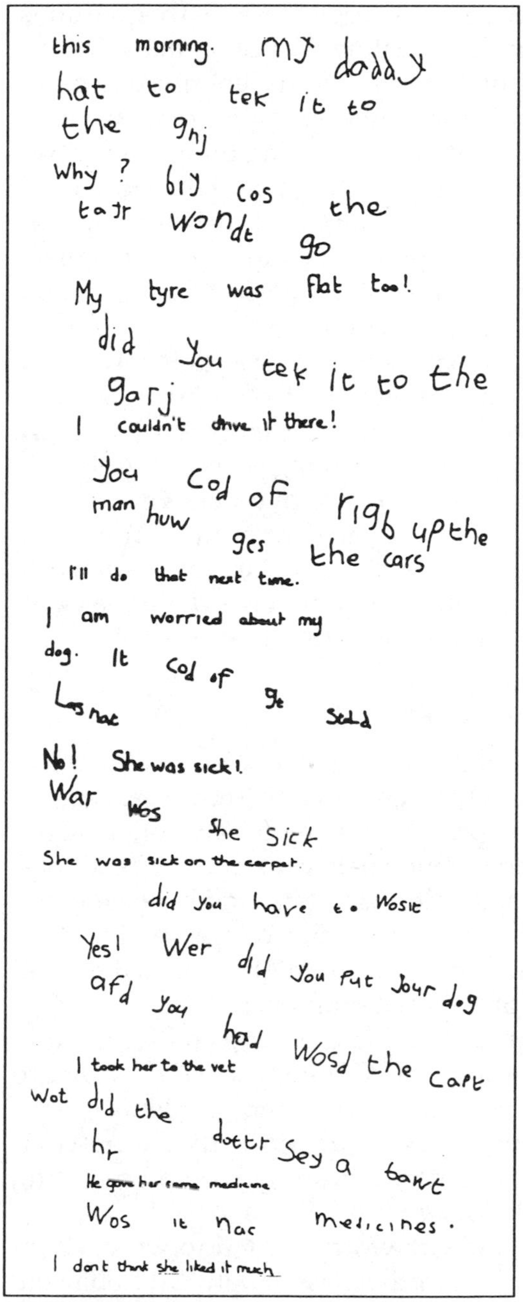

this morning. mJ daddy hat to tek it to the ghj

Why? biJ cos the tajr wondt go

My tyre was flat too!

did you tek it to the garj

I couldn't drive it there!

You cod of rigb upthe man huw ges the cars

I'll do that next time.

I am worried about my dog. It cod of ge Los nac Seld

No! She was sick!

War wos she sick

She was sick on the carpet.

did you have to wosit

Yes! Wer did you put Jour dog afd you had wosd the capt

I took her to the vet

Wot did the hr doctr sey a bout

He gove her some medicine

Wos it nac medicines.

I don't think she liked it much

Figure 17.6 Portion of one day's entries in dialogue journal between teacher and student.

The teacher asked only one question; Georgina asked six questions. The topic was the teacher's, but the direction was Georgina's.

Another side of this control was evident in Georgina's freedom to write whatever she wanted. These conversation journals were for exchanging meanings, for being authors, for having things to say. The conversation journals were not the only writing that the children did. Indeed, the journals were a relatively small part of their writing, and the other writing activities offered opportunities to explore language in more formal ways. The children understood perfectly well that the journals were for conversation, not instruction.

The final point relates to what Georgina was doing with the words that she wrote. Instead of a typical diet of copying teacher-influenced short recount or declarative sentences (such as "Last night ..." or "This is me and ..."), she was ranging across a variety of functions. She questioned and was prepared to hypothesize: "It could have got stolen last night"; she was prepared to argue: "You could have rung up the man who gets the cars"; and she was prepared to respond effectively: "I am worried now." In one day's dialogue Georgina had a rich, powerful, and demanding writing experience.

Written Interaction with Other Adults

Interactive writing is not to be found only in dialogue journals. Indeed, dialogue journals appear a relatively recent phenomenon in education. Letter writing has a much greater provenance. Yet for all that, dialogue journals have, as far as education is concerned, captured the headlines. There are now a large number of articles, chapters, and books relating to dialogue journals; there are very few studies of young children's letter writing, and most of those concern what might be called one-off letters, that is, letters that are not part of a dialogue.

In an effort to increase understanding of young children's abilities as letter writers, Hall, Robinson, and Crawford (1991) decided to see whether very young children could handle the problems of sustaining a letter-writing dialogue. Indeed, the difficulties were compounded by the fact that the children in this study would be writing to adults that they did not really know.

Two of the authors (Hall and Crawford) started to write, on an individual basis, to all the children in the class taught by Robinson. The children were at that time around five and a half years old. The two adult writers first visited the classroom for one day, working and playing with the children. Each of the children then received a letter from one of the two adults. The letter invited the child to write back.

Would the children actually reply? There was to be no compulsion to take part; no children had to reply if they did not want to. No help whatsoever was to be given to the children if they did write; they would have to complete their letters unassisted. The teacher was prepared to remind the children if necessary, but no pressure was to be put upon the children to respond. As it turned out, such encouragement was not needed. Every single one of the children wanted to write, and none of them asked for ideas or information.

The completed letters were bundled up and mailed to the adults. This was a real writing exchange. The children were separated from their correspondents by time, distance, age, and status. The letters back to the children made few concessions to their age. The adults tried to write neatly but used, as far as possible, the kinds of expressions and language that they would use with other adult correspondents.

Within two weeks all the children had written to their adult correspondents, and within another week they all received individual replies. None of the adults expected the exchange to last very long; they were well aware of the volatility in young children's interests, and the exchange was not a compulsory activity for the children. Would it last a few weeks, a few months, a year . . . ? Three years later they were still wondering! An interview with the children after two years revealed that the children still enjoyed writing and receiving the letters; they wanted to continue the correspondence and had no particular end in sight.

In a short chapter only a brief flavor of the exchanges can be given. The extracts that follow are from the letters of one child whom we will call Marie. Her first letter (see Figure 17.7 for the original) was short but effective as a letter:

> Dear Nigel
> Did you like being in my class and have you got any children
> and would you like to come to the Strawberry Fair?

In this letter she related back to my visit to the classroom, asked a personal question, and extended an invitation which implied a degree of friendship. It was a short but very reasonable first letter. As the exchanges continued, Marie's letters quickly grew longer and more involved. Marie lived on a farm, and most of the other children in her class were familiar with her lifestyle. Her correspondent offered a new audience for news and details about life on the farm. In a letter about a year after the start of the correspondence, she began by writing:

Dear Nigel didyou LAke beeIhg in myclss andhuv yougorAhi chIldren yN wudyou ltketocun rrmBr rawberryFair

Figure 17.7 Student's first letter to teacher correspondent.

Dear Nigel

Thank you for the letter and my dad has bought us five lambs and one is very cheeky and that is my sister's and one has a brown face and one did not used to drink and the fifth one has three legs and a half and Sally's is the fastest drinking and we always feed them in the morning before we go to school and we have the alarm after my mum and dad have gone on the milk round and we have the alarm being set off at seven o'clock and we have been finished before eight o'clock and we take turns in making the breakfast and it was my turn to make the breakfast and I hope it will snow a lot because I do not like school very much . . .

Marie continued this letter, reaching a total of 270 words—not bad for a six year old, but a six year old who knew she had an interested audience.

The most important point learned from studying the children's letters was that those young children, from the beginning, functioned totally efficiently and appropriately as correspondents. From their first replies, they demonstrated an ability to handle dialogue, and the relationships implicit in the dialogue, in a strategic way. They were able to adjust to the social distance and the spatial distance of exchanging letters with adults. In the first letters they demonstrated they knew that you could tell other people about yourself, that you could ask other people about themselves, that referring to a shared experience was a good way to start a written relationship, and that it was nice to express your friendship in an explicit way.

As the exchanges progressed, the children showed that they could generate novel topics, sustain topics, and, when appropriate, close topics. They did so in ways that were always friendly—well, almost. On one occasion I had been a bit slow in replying to the children. One day the following letter arrived:

Dear Nigel

Will you please get a move on with your letter. I have been waiting ages and ages for you to write me a letter. I wish you would hurry up. If you don't write soon I will never write to you again in. What is holding you up? Love David

Needless to say, the letter had its desired effect—within one day I had written back. That six year old knew how to elicit a response from an adult.

Conclusion

Young children clearly do not have to have a diet of writing experiences that are confined to copying or to stories and news recounts. A growing body of evidence reveals young children's ability to make forays into many different genres (Hall 1989; Newkirk 1989), and children who have participated in interactive writing show, so vividly, an astonishing confidence and competence in tackling issues of great complexity. The conditions that were created for them within those exchanges allowed them to demonstrate success. Those conditions included (1) being able to engage in authentic correspondence; (2) being able to pursue the correspondence over an extended period of time; (3) being able to choose to participate; (4) being given space, time, and resources within the classroom; and (5) being able to write to mature writers who were sensitive to the children's texts.

When children correspond with an adult, be it teacher or other adult, those mature writers are able to provide more extensive demonstrations simply by being correspondents, rather than as a result of deliberate instructional policy. The letters or entries written by adults "scaffold" certain aspects of the children's development. Mature writers are able to make requests which elicit different and more extensive replies than might otherwise be the case, and are able to comment in ways which expand, and sustain, ideas and themes initiated by the children. They are able to show how texts can be interrogated and are able to do this in situations which are, for the children, without threat or fear of failure.

Judith Lindfors (1990) reports how she had asked a number of adults to recall good memories of their schooling. When she analyzed these events, they tended to share four characteristics: they were events where the person was able to say "I was competent," "I was special," "I did it myself," and "My teacher treated me as a human being." For the adults, those events and those characteristics were clearly very special, very powerful, and very meaningful. All the children whose work has been included in this chapter could make similar claims about their experiences of interactive writing. In all cases what the children wrote was taken as evidence of competence; it was responded to as meaningful communication. In all cases the children were special; it was their voices that were being honestly recorded. In all cases it was the children's own decisions, words, and sentences that were important; they wrote their letters on their own; they did it themselves. And in all cases the teacher or adult correspondent responded to the children as human beings who had thoughts to be taken seriously and who wrote things that demanded recognition.

Interactive writing, when carried out in the ways described above, is the nearest thing to a magical way of encouraging children to be interested in writing. Nothing will ever work for every child, but the teachers in Manchester tell us time and time again how much the children enjoy writing, how much they write, how much they develop as writers, and how much they reveal about themselves as writers. It is not the letter the child writes that is important—it is the first reply. That reply tells children that someone has cared about what they have written, and cared enough to want to reply. That reply says that a dialogue has started, and once started, dialogues have a habit of continuing.

References

Hall, N. 1987. *The emergence of literacy.* Portsmouth, N.H.: Heinemann.

———. 1989. *Writing with reason: The emergence of authorship in young children.* Portsmouth, N.H.: Heinemann.

———. In progress. Interactive writing. In *Keeping in touch: Interactive writing with young children,* ed. N. Hall and A. Robinson.

Hall, N., and R. Duffy. 1987. Every child has a story to tell. *Language Arts* 64 (5): 523–29.

Hall, N., A. Robinson, and L. Crawford. 1991. *"Someday you will no all about it": Young writers' explorations in the world of letters.* Portsmouth, N.H.: Heinemann.

Lindfors, J. 1990. *They gonna think its a beautiful book: Composing in the kindergarten.* Stockholm: World Congress on Reading.

Newkirk, T. 1989. *More than stories: The range of children's writing.* Portsmouth, N.H.: Heinemann.

Price, J. 1989. The ladybird letters. In *Writing with reason: The emergence of authorship in young children,* ed. N. Hall, 1–13. Portsmouth, N.H.: Heinemann. London: Hodder and Stoughton.

Staton, J., R. Shuy, J. Peyton, and L. Reed. 1988. *Dialogue journal communication: Classroom, linguistic, social and cognitive views.* Norwood, N.J.: Ablex.

18 Max Beltmann: The Many Voices of Teacher Change

Rudi Engbrecht
Language Arts Consultant, Winnipeg School Division, Manitoba

What was it that made Placido Domingo, the renowned Spanish opera star, look into the distance with glazed eyes as he spoke about his role as Tosca, a role in which it was—in his words—"wonderful to be a part of the mystery of the creator of this great music," where, in the end, he could meet the "marvelous mystery of the silver chalice said to have held Christ's blood."

What was it that made the seemingly hard, at times even cruel, yet favorite professor Halstead stumble and choke as he tried to read those lines of Othello—"I loved not wisely but too well"?

Just what was this mystery?

Stephen Mitchell's introductory words in his translation of the *Tao Te Ching* (1988) by Chinese writer Lao-Tzu touch on this mystery:

> A good athlete can enter a state of body awareness in which the right stroke or right movement happens by itself, effortlessly, without any interference of the conscious will. This is a paradigm for non-action: the purest and most effective form of action. The game plays the game; the poem writes the poem; we can't tell the dancer from the dance.

Max Beltmann had always wanted to teach as these "good athletes" play, these poets write, these dancers dance. He had somehow intuited that therein lay the "marvelous mystery" that had brought glazed eyes to Domingo and tears to Halstead. But how to do it?

And as he mused during his early morning jog, distilled moments of his entire teaching life rolled before his consciousness, almost as a lifetime does when one suddenly feels one only has moments to live.

Story I: 1967 (Class Strategies)

He remembered his early years in teaching before "response learning" had come into his life, before he learned of the 1966 Dartmouth Conference. In those days he had always read papers word by word. He had always heard the voice of the student-writer, a voice that had always seemed to echo its way into his consciousness even when he had tried to hurry the reading. He had heard not only the very sound and rhythm of the student's voice speaking the writing, but also the intentions and motivations of this voice as it had prompted the writing. This compulsion to read from the student's point of view, in the very sound, feeling, and thinking of the student's voice and voices—it had been this that had taken so much time, but it had been this that had brought him so much joy. Students had always been so eager to hear his "analysis" the next day—and it had always been the next day, for he had always returned papers the day after they had been written. The students would be eager to know what he had thought of their thoughts and their expression of their thoughts. After removing student names from papers, he would use an opaque projector to project selected papers onto the huge screen in his classroom, would illustrate the rationale for the letter grades he had assigned them, and would always find something good about a paper no matter how low the mark. Even more, he would copy what he considered misworded sentences—one from each paper up to thirteen—to a photocopy master and would duplicate these sentences for class revision. And after a twenty-minute lesson on style using Strunk and White's *Elements of Style*, student pairs, trios, or quads would revise these sentences. Because no one knew whose sentence was being revised, except the writer, these classes always provided as much fun as hard work, what with sentences like "The accident happened when the right front door of a car came around the corner without signalling" and "As I backed out of my driveway, the gentleman struck me on my backside. He then went to rest in my bush with just his rear end showing."

Now, years later, he realized that he had heard the sound and the intentions of these student voices, but they were the voices of students who were writing in a voice that students use to write for the teacher and not in a voice discovering one's self. He had given them the topic and the form in which it was to be written. He had not really heard the soul of their voices, voices discovering life, literature, expression. He had forced them to fill the blanks, so to speak, to write only that five-paragraph essay. But he had not known better, given department expectation for so-called standards, given community pressure to prepare students for university, etc., etc.

And in those days it seemed students were always amazed that they were heard at all. In most classes, so their chatter went, essays were never returned the next day and often not returned for several weeks. When they were returned, there was little or no discussion and certainly no personal interviews during which marks could change. And so, Max worked—too much but always with enormous energy, enthusiasm, joy. For him, the constant appreciation that students expressed always made it worthwhile.

But often this feeling of worth was also severely tested. The pain of returning these essays to student writers brought him other kinds of voices, voices crying in the wilderness, voices expressing feelings which were not being heard. To hear a voice, as he realized now, was to take an awesome responsibility as well; for to hear a voice was also to lend it caring, and caring, he had learned, always brought as much pain as joy. Like childbirth to a mother—and a caring father—like raising children who stubbornly want their own voices when adults are least willing to grant them these voices.

Story II: 1974 (Carol)

He remembered Carol and the many like her, students who had craved discovery of a voice that needed expression.

During those early years, he was always "real tough" in marking his students' work. It was a way of enforcing his authority, a way of letting students—and parents—know that in this class it was business. No monkeying around! In the first set of in-class essays each year—always assigned and submitted on the third day of term (and marked for next day's class, of course)—less than a half-dozen papers would receive a passing grade. And so it was that after spending half a class projecting sample papers on the screen and another half having students revise those selected, "misworded" sentences, would come the interviews. Every student who had failed needed to arrange for a personal interview with Max—before school, noon hour, spares, after school, whenever. Those who admitted they had received good marks for years knowing that what they had written was the drivel produced in thirty minutes the night before submission—these were easy interviews. A few suggestions, and they were off to rewrite their work.

But those who had always worked hard and always received high marks, these were difficult. Carol had been one of these. With tears and rage, she had insisted on an interview, as he had always encouraged students to seek. Max met her in the library during his spare. She was even angrier by then. And so Max began another of those tough hours, in this case forty minutes, of an agonizing read with a student. Max would speak softly. He would tell Carol that he knew how she felt, that he had failed whole English courses, not just an essay, that he had learned that failure did not mean much unless students stopped there, that Connie had failed her first essay in his grade-eleven class some eight years ago, that she had scored an A+ in her final exam in grade twelve, and that she was now a very successful lawyer in Toronto and had even written a book. Carol continued to tear. He had asked her to talk about her paper—what did she consider its strength? She had done so. Then he would ask her to read it with him, and as she did, he would ask further—had she meant "this" or "that" or "something else." How did "this" link with "that" and so on and on. And as the reading and the questions continued, it seemed that Carol had sensed his willingness to search, to see it from her point of view, even admitting at certain points that she was more accurate than he. Carol had seemingly sensed that he had not just failed her, that he had really cared about what she had written, that he wanted her to say exactly what she had intended to say. And so, gradually, the anger and the tears had receded, the encounter had become two people in search of meaningful writing—at least as meaningful as a lit-crit five-para-graph essay could ever become. When the reading was complete, the task redefined, Carol could leave to do another partial rewrite for the next day, and Max, he could go on to another, maybe even more "difficult," interview.

He had often wondered why he had done these interviews. At the time no other English teacher in the school had spent the hours that he had with students, going over their papers. And yet intuitively he had known. He had wanted students to work at their writing, and he had not known how to instill serious work habits. He had also wanted students to do well in their examinations. He had learned that if he studied old exams, if he challenged his students to the most difficult of questions that he could find there, if he failed them in the first weeks of the term, then he had that captive audience that always scored unusually high in end-of-term examinations. And so he had done it, even though it had brought pain, agony, and tears, and had required of him a love and a patience that teachers had not usually shown.

Story III: 1976 (David)

He remembered how much David, a very talented grade-twelve student, had hated the works of Margaret Laurence, whom Max idealized, a writer who had given light to the experience of woman and her struggle with identity on the Canadian prairies, identity as female in a world where women had mainly been relegated a minor role. David had given Max the "gears," had told him that Laurence was a bigot who used men, that she must have been a slut because her female characters always pursued sex, and, worst of all, that she did not know how to "spin a story," what with all the "flashback stuff." Max remembers always listening—intently, encouraging David to read another of Laurence's Manawaka novels, asking questions like "What is it in people that makes them gravitate obsessively toward sex? Is it similar to that which has them gravitate toward food? Are the two different?" David would debate, as he could so well do, having been declared top debater in Western Canada earlier that year. But somehow David could not enter with any empathy the character world of Margaret Laurence. His defiance was so acute that classmates isolated him, ostracized him, not because they disagreed with him about Margaret Laurence necessarily, but because he was so often aggressive, occasionally abrasive. Did he give a sweet damn? Not on your life. "Screw them," he had told Max.

Max continued to listen, to let David feel that David's questions were important, that here was reason for search. And search David did. At the end of the unit Max showed the National Film Board film about Margaret Laurence. In this forty-minute film, Laurence talks of her life, the nature of loneliness, the need for serious writing to be moral though not moralizing, the need to speak honestly about what we feel, the need to struggle for what we think important, and the need for what is important to have moral dimension. As the film ended and Max again moved to the front of the room, all was unusually silent. Head down, David slowly got up from his desk and walked to the front of the room. He had tears in his eyes. He came to a stop before Max and extended his right hand. Max looked at David, somewhat dumbfounded, and bewilderingly extended his own right hand. After momentary suspension, the hands met. "You must always show this film when you study the works of Margaret Laurence," said David. "I have read four of Laurence's Manawaka novels [the only student to have done so], and after this reading and after watching this film, I will never be the same again." Max was moved; his eyes, too, became a

little smooth. Thirty-seven classmates were stunned to silence—
David? Not David? David doesn't weep. But David had wept, and
Max had sort of wept with him. And then the bell had rung.

Now, years later, Max wondered how this had happened. What
had made the difference to David? It had not been easy not to give
David a piece of his mind, to give David what his baseball buddies
would have termed "a bit of hell." Even five years earlier he would
have "stuck it" to David, debated him into submission. But seemingly
because he had not, David had responded with feeling, not merely
debate. In 1976 Max had intuited his response; now, in the 1990s, it
seemed that he could intellectualize somewhat about it. Had it been
because he loved David for his capacity to debate in formal debates?
Or because he sensed that debate was easy for David, but that compassion was not? Was it because his wife had gone through such serious,
manic-like depression for five years, years in which he had gone
months on three hours of sleep a night, and that through this ordeal he
had learned that the making of meaning was messy business, took
time, had no formula? Had he somehow learned what had escaped
him for most of his life—that to be human was to grant others the right
to be human, the right to make mistakes, the right to hurt him without
his retaliation? Above all, had he learned the courage to love others
simply because they were human beings rather than because they did
him favors?

Story IV: 1978 (Provincial Curriculum Committee)

Max had been asked to join the provincial committee for curriculum
review of the English Language Arts program. Little did he know that
this would be a very stormy time for him, the teacher into whose
classes students cheated at guidance offices in order to obtain entry,
the teacher to whom parents constantly expressed their appreciation;
the teacher in whom the school administration had placed so much
confidence.

The early curriculum meetings were amiable enough. But it
soon became evident that he was facing agendas that he had not
anticipated. He was expected to read the work of people like John
Dixon and Leslie Stratta, like James Moffett and Louise Rosenblatt.
Sure he had always read CCTE, NCTE, and IRA journals. These had
helped him change little things—an assignment here, a technique
there. These researchers, however, were asking him to change his
whole way of seeing, of teaching, of learning. He did not want to

believe what he read. How could he change a way of teaching that had brought him so much success?

And so, curriculum committee meetings brought conflict. The consultants made their case for response learning; he made his case for the way he taught—he was not sure what it was, but it worked, he thought. They had the theory, the ideas; he thought that he had the strategies. It just did not make sense to him that writing was not narrative, descriptive, expository, that it was to be all those, depending on audience, purpose, style, structure. Sure, audience was important— with a letter, that is; but in high school they did not write letters. They wrote essays. These kids had to survive at university. And to write, students needed to know their grammar before they could express themselves properly. "They needed the word to know the world," he kept saying. And group work! He had always used groups, had used them for fourteen years, you know, assigning one topic to each group and then they reported. He had used groups but did not consider them very successful. Kids were always bored with the many poor presentations. The stronger students carried the weaker ones, the former always resentful that this happened. And so he resisted the theory and its possible influence on his classroom—at least, he realized now, the way in which he had understood the theory.

For eighteen months he made his case, but it became increasingly more difficult. The theoreticians were gaining ground. He was getting angrier and angrier. Finally, he resigned from the committee. He just would not be pressured. His success at school continued. Why should he cater to those who did not work in the heat of the classroom? So there, he thought. To hell with them and their theories. Let them try to fend in the classroom, every day, rain or shine, through those tough days when teachers feel ill but come to meet their students nevertheless. Let them try it, he had thought. Meantime, he would do his thing; they could do theirs.

Years later, he wondered about those times, wondered how the change to adopt their ways had come about. He remembered one experience in particular that had changed his teaching life.

Story V: 1983 (Research)

They had decided to make it a reputable research piece. They would use a control group and an experimental group. He would orchestrate the latter. They would use the same material, in this case poems, allow the same time for study, use pretests and posttests, and use two independent readers for final evaluation—one a former high school teacher; the other, a university English teacher. The results were shocking. The experimental group scored 17 percent higher than the control group. He could not argue with this. His compassion to see things from perspectives other than his own now came to haunt him. He had to listen—both to the research and to other voices within himself. The scoring curves of both pretest and posttest readers had been identical. In short, the theory that he had defied during his stint on the curriculum committee had now been put to practice, and in this practice it had made mockery of the way in which he had usually taught—he at the front of the room, students doing what he expected of them.

He wanted to believe that it was an aberration. But as he read and as he talked with students about their experiences, he realized that he needed to make changes if he wanted to fulfill his dream of becoming the best teacher possible. And so he read more and more—Britton, Rosen, Dixon, Moffett, Rosenblatt, Emig, and others. He talked with his students. He remembered Sheryl, who had come to his class from another school where she had never written anything longer than a few sentences to answer questions on works of literature; who thought all this essay writing was her fate in life; who had hated the experimental group because she had insisted that she had not learned anything, what with no teacher to tell her what was right about an interpretation, about an essay, about the way to think; who had agreed after the third class to stay in her group only to please the teacher whom she had come to respect so much. This was clear enough. But the puzzle. Why had she scored one out of five in the pretest and five out of five in the posttest? When he had asked her this, she had shrugged her shoulders and muttered, "I don't know. All we did was read, talk, and write."

Max had also been confused. Three years later in a shopping mall a young woman had come toward him in a hurried walk, with a big smile. He had not immediately recognize her. "I'm Sheryl," she had said enthusiastically. "Sheryl. The student who didn't like the research we did. Remember? Well, for a year now I have wanted to tell you something. I still have those poems. Occasionally I pull them from a file in my room and reread them. For old time's sake. I learned to love poetry that year, and today I read a lot of poetry, have even started writing it. It was a great time. How are you?"

During the three years between Sheryl as student and this shopping mall encounter, much had changed in his classroom. But the change was only very gradual. He could not risk his reputation with sudden changes. He knew that he was regarded as a great teacher, and though he wanted to be the best teacher he could be and felt that he needed to change drastically to get there, he needed to maintain, or at least feel he needed to maintain, control, a control where he made the decisions about what students learned, a control that gave him, and he thought his students, a kind of assurance that all would be well come exam time and, later, university time.

Story VI: 1984 (Personal Effect of Research)

He remembered how, during the latter part of the first semester in 1984, he had adopted a totally student-centered model of classroom management. A risky trial, he had thought. He had not felt well for the last two months of that semester, and he suspected all this student-centered stuff was partly to blame. Just the pressure of it. He had lost his love for teaching. He really did not want to go to school. This made him feel even worse, for during the years before this research and this shift to this student-centered stuff, he had always looked forward eagerly to the mornings, especially Monday mornings. His unwellness was evident in his "jogging." His legs no longer seemed to have the life that they once had. It was a difficult time. The semester had come to an end, and his students had done remarkably well in end-of-term examinations—with all this group-work stuff he had tried to beat the old exam game by having students write mini-essays, pieces of correct "filling in the blanks," each day during the last three weeks before exams instead of the journal which asked them to explore. They had certainly filled in the blanks well. But he did not seem to care—not much, anyhow.

But then he had noticed something peculiar. The new semester had begun. He had suddenly felt life again. He had enjoyed the first three days of the new semester immensely. His running had become fun again. His legs once more felt energetic. Great, he had thought. It was just winter blues . . . for the last two months! However, within a week of the new semester, he had fallen back into depression. What is this? he had thought, as he ran sluggishly, just as sluggishly as he had run for several months before the end of the first semester. He had began to trace his life over the last months. What had he done that might have contributed to these feelings? He had made only one change, he thought. He had taught a student-centered model during the last two months of semester one, returned to his old style—to lay down the law of the land, so to speak—for the first three days with his new classes in semester two, and had returned now to that student-centered model. Was that possibly it? he had thought. How could he again feel worthwhile? Should he go back to his old style? He would. With one class. As he did, he once more felt that energy surge. But after a few days, these students asked whether they could return to that other way in which they could take some control of their learning. He had agreed. Same depression set in. Now he knew. It was this damn student-centered stuff which was bringing him depression. But he could not very well return to his old ways now, especially now that students were requesting more control and, even more especially, now that they had done better than ever at these very traditional, lit-crit, debate kinds of end-of-term examinations.

Later that year at graduation he had received the final blow to his old ways. For years female students had wanted to have at least one dance with him at the Grad Dance. He loved dancing and danced well. He was on the dance floor as he was in the classroom—center stage, skilled, and peacock-proud. The students had loved his wit and had loved his dance, and he had loved them the more for feeling so. This year, however, no such attention came his way. Female students would talk with him, even eagerly, meet his wife, introduce their boyfriends if he did not know them, wish him well. But they had not asked him to dance. He had been puzzled. Why not? he had thought. Had he aged sufficiently in one year that these young female students had suddenly considered him old? And then, his winter experience with depression came to mind. He had similar feelings now—you know, that almost depression-like feeling? Female students obviously respected him. Why else would they have come to talk? He could only conclude that the classroom had made this change. He was no longer center stage, so it made perfect sense to him that he would not be center stage on the dance floor. He had come to realize as never before that learning how to teach meant learning how to live.

Story VII: 1987 (Teachers as Artists)

Now, years later, he mused that great teachers, like great actors, could only function in two ways—either they immersed themselves totally in the life of their students, just as novice or struggling actors might immerse themselves totally in the character roles they played, *or* they distanced themselves from their students, just as the "great" and experienced actors distance themselves from their roles, at once feeling the intensity of their characterization, their art, their creation, while at the same time remaining aloof and letting the art take its own shape. To become the artist in the classroom meant letting students explore their way through the chaos of experience in literature and in life, and through this exploration reach some kind of sense making; it meant letting students take risks, letting them fail often, letting them find their own ways to meaning; it meant that he prepared the "contexts," the possibilities for students to create their own courses, their own tracking systems, their own evaluations.

First he needed to let go more, to let himself feel that he was still serving as teacher even though he now only learned with his students; he talked *with* them, not *at* them; he wrote with them, read with them, thought with them. The attempts to do this had earlier brought him depression. Now these depressions did not occur. Not only had the depressions lifted, but he had acquired a joy for life that he had never known before. It now delighted him when students searched for their centers as they planned their programs, chose their partners, agreed on evaluation procedures. It had begun to delight him that students used their learning to make social statements, such as researched briefs sent to car insurance companies, followed with an interview of a company director; that they influenced the direction of a committee on several heritage homes, on zoning bylaws, and so on. It delighted them when they made choices about their reading, when a group of seven grade-eleven females read adolescent fiction dealing with incest and rape and then used their reading logs, journals, and discussions to help free several of them who lived in the worlds that this literature explored. As he began to see the effect of a way of learning rather than his earlier way of teaching, a way in which students remained at the center and remained responsible for learning, it was then that he noted a peace coming over him he had never known before.

He had thought of this, this mystery with a life force that he could feel but could not understand. He needed an image to structure this experience. He had found it in the cup. His cup had always been full—full of caring, full of excitement, full of deeply rooted commitment and sense of "this is right," a sense of the deep mystery that is learning, that is life. Now, however, he realized that cups came in different sizes; that the cup was now much larger than it had been twenty-five, fifteen, ten, even five years ago; that, in fact, his cup now seemed not only larger but also flexible and expanding daily.

And so he had learned to use groups in such a way that students thought them important. Gone was the boredom that they had inspired during the early years. Groups were now dynamic, collaborative attempts to read text, text in the truest sense, in the sense where readers examined their silences, the multiple nuances of words, and the form into which words were shaped, text in the Rosenblatt sense where words were "the printed signs in their capacity to serve as symbols," (1978, 12) where "the magic . . . of language is the fact that it must be internalized by each individual human being" (20), where students can find a personal voice for themselves and for their relationships with others and their environment. Groups now used their own silences to think rather than to fidget, to meet the mystery within and beyond themselves.

Story VIII: 1989 (Teacher Shapes Context)

More and more he learned the sense to become involved at the level of process rather than with merely product or content. He had learned to respond to a student like Kathy in an advanced placement class, Kathy who had asked—during a study of Margaret Laurence's *The Diviners*—what he thought about Morag having an affair with Dan, the artist, and Dan bringing his lover home to meet his wife, Bridie. During his peacock years Max would have been only too happy to have given his opinion, to have given it without thinking much. Now he thought before he spoke. He allowed himself silence to think. Students allowed him this silence, too. And after some many seconds of reflection, he spoke. "Think of the assumptions inherent in this act," he began. "Further. What would be the assumptions if Dan had failed to have Morag meet Bridie yet had continued the affair? Or if he had told Bridie that he was having the affair before he brought Morag to meet her? In short, what set of feelings, behaviors, customs, would be set in motion in each case?"

This, of course, led to renewed and vigorous discussion. He could now listen with patience and with interest, and instead of interjecting with opinions as he once would have done, he could now summarize what students had said, ask them further questions, open-ended ones, questions which made them feel that he really wanted to know their thoughts. They would continue to talk eagerly. He had learned to feel good about this. At times he even wondered what the late Halstead would have said could he have been present.

It reminded him of Billie, a grade-ten aboriginal student from northern Manitoba. Billie had always come late, had written no more than three lines in any journal entry, would never read much, would not talk with his peers. However, when Max became enthused with the work of John Dixon, Leslie Strata, and Harold Rosen and their ways of reading student stories, he adapted the spirit of their ways. After three months of journal entries, he asked all students in Billie's class to choose three of their own entries. He asked their groups of five to help each other choose one of these three to develop. Billie was encouraged to develop his three-line comment of how in grade nine he had shot the dog of his much-hated teacher. Ten days later, with a system where students served as readers and editors, Billie's story was three and one-half pages. Billie's emotional struggle is illustrated by a portion of his paper:

> The dog was a nice dog. He was a big dog. He was like a strong husky. His eyes looked like he would like to hunt. I would like to have took this dog to go hunting. He liked me too. He would come close and wag his tail hitting my legs as he wagged it. But I had to kill him. I knew my teacher who owned him wouldn't let me hunt with him anyway. So I let him follow me into the woods two miles from the village and I took my gun and shot him. It was hard. I cried a little too. He had big eyes and when he saw what I was going to do they got funny looking but he didn't have time to run because I shot him quick. I still think about it today and I get sad. But I would have to shoot him again because I couldn't stand the teacher.

Max reflected on this experience, how students had been so eager to write during these ten days, eager to read each other's work and make suggestions.

And then there was Easton, the black nineteen-year-old, 6'3", level-04 student from Jamaica. He was the basketball star, but he would not attend classes—except English, that is. He attended religiously, and on the last days of June, when other students had long left the school, he was there, whole afternoons, completing his life story, some of which went like this:

> Living on the street is not a pretty thing to do the bigger guys gave me drugs to use sometimes it is too strong for me. They look at me and laugh. Doing that for a very long time I get used to it. Then they taught me to use a gun. Practicing with the gun I feel like a cop. It drew me deeper in the street. Then they show me how to be a pimp. Lots of girls making money for us. We wear the most expensive clothes sleep most of the days and go out at nights. The gang committed lots of robbery crime beat up lots of people. On the street every one become afraid of us if anyone saw anyone of us they ran away. Some ran and cried. I used to sell drugs everyday and night making lots of money for the gang members and myself. I didn't sell to anyone under 18

years of age because the gang was against that. I used to drive a car with no licence no insurance no plates. Then the police heard that something bad was going on in the village with a group of guys who wanted to live an easy life. . . . We began running. We all live in a cave which only a few people know about . . . we all stayed in the cave for three months. We had to feed on mangoes wild pigs goats and birds after about a couple of weeks I came home for one day to my grandmother. She told me to stay and go to Canada with my mother. . . . I slept under the bed for eight nights until my plane ticket arrived . . . I took off and the rest of the gang keep running from police. I will never run again because I give up badness I knew that it is life and death. I have already faced enough that I could almost lost my life. I don't want to run again because when you are running you cannot stay at one place and so many bad things happen.

Max reflected on the urgency that he had noted in Easton's desire to do this life writing, the eagerness with which he had always wanted Max to read what he had written. Amazing, thought Max, amazing for a student in a program for slow and nonlearners, for a student with such minimal language skills. He remembered the principal looking at Easton's work and saying, "believe me, this is the only class he attends, and when I see that he has written anything, I'm amazed. That he has written these ten pages on computer stuns me." Max was convinced that it had happened because Easton had planned his own course.

And then there were the students from the Far East. These five had been isolated from the twenty-three Caucasians. One day Max had decided to have these Asian students teach the Caucasians ten or more Chinese words needed to arrange a date. For most it had been arduous. However, not only had it been fun, but in succeeding days and months these five melded into friendships with the twenty-three.

As Max reflected on his many classroom experiences, it came to him that he had once believed that knowing the word came first. Now in the silences of his students—as they had probed and explored—he wondered if it were not the inverse; namely, that reading the world preceded reading the word.

Story IX: 1990 (Improvisation and Storytelling)

Max could not remain static though. He needed to do something more with his classes. And he did. He went on to develop skills in improvisation drama. He had always enjoyed drama, but he had never been able to use it as an integral part of each class, as a part that allowed another way into text, experience, life, understanding, as a way of playing in role, as a kind of conscious, persona-voice play, as a means to discovery of a personal voice. And so he had developed contexts for student improvement in their exploration of Othello, contexts that asked the questions about Othello's behavior. Max asked if to allow hurt rather than jealousy would not have brought Othello more happiness; he asked what it meant to feel that there was only one person, Desdemona, who kept him from "chaos come again"; he asked what it meant when we love someone but feel that we cannot express our love.

And further, he had learned the use of storytelling as an alternative and/or supplement to improvisation drama. Students had told stories in their own voices as well as in chosen voices. They told stories of experiences which were humorous, sad, frustrating, dangerous; they had told stories, taking the role of a child, a doctor, an athlete. Debriefing discussions of these stories had allowed students to explore literature, life, and their own voices in these experiences in which they deliberately become the voices of others.

In short, he had found better ways to become deeply involved with his students once more, involved with them and their experiences as intimately as he had been before this "response stuff" had brought these changes. However, now he had become more like the artist who could be deeply involved without being immersed, the artist who could let the game play the game, the poem write the poem, the dancer become the dance.

This evolution, this simultaneous distancing and intimacy with learning and with students, brought him new ways of evaluation of oracy and reading and writing. Students designed many of their own evaluation procedures. Then, when they had evaluated their group discussion skills, they would often discuss these with peers even before discussing them with Max. When they evaluated their writing, they wrestled with voice—audience, purpose, style, structure. Max had become just another reader. Students felt free to choose a student suggestion rather than his. The classroom was always a buzz of activity. When visitors came to the door to see Max, they would often leave, thinking he was not there. But he was there—it was just that he might have been talking or listening to a student in a corner of the room or kneeling at a desk or standing in the middle of a group. His place was now not at the front of the room but wherever he was needed. It was a great time.

Story X: 988 (Difficult Times)

Oh, there had always been the difficult times. A university professor and his wife had made it known that the B mark that their son Tim had received in the grade-ten midterm was the fault of the method, for previously Tim had always scored A's. They had proceeded to challenge Max. When he had provided theory research to support his student-centered focus, they had discarded it as a minority point of view. It remained an icy standoff. For two weeks he had slept little. However, later that year the parents had come to express regret for their critical behavior, to express their appreciation that Tim had done more work in English during this one semester than he had ever done before. Why had they found need to make it an encounter rather than a dialogue? he had wondered. It had been a horrible time. Could he have survived this calculated, cold attack earlier in his career? He could only guess.

On another occasion, some influential grade-twelve students had decided that this emphasis on voice in reading, writing, and storytelling was okay for some of the time, but that formal, in-class, five-paragraph essays should be written every week to prepare them for university. That they wrote daily journals on their responses to reading, writing, and oracy did not seem to count. Nor did the daily mini-essays during the last three weeks of the term; nor the one major class essay assignment; nor their research paper. That most had chosen to write novellas rather than research papers did not cross their minds at this point. During such times, other students, even parents, came to his defense, as always. Once after having slept little for three nights, he received an encouraging note from the parents of one student. It read:

> Our son tells us that some students want you to revert to a teacher-centered classroom. We hope you will keep your courage, continue to insist students become responsible for their learning. We know that Jesse has become a very different student and person since he came to your classroom.

Story XI: October 1990 (Max Leaves to Be a Consultant)

The seven school days between the announcement of his leaving and his actual leaving could best be described by Elisabeth Kubler-Ross and her seven stages of grieving. He had known it would be hard to leave, but he had not realized that it would be this hard.

In one grade-twelve class, Becky, a track star constantly at wrestle with suicide, had delivered a speech in place of the story that she was to tell to begin the class. A part of it went as follows:

> The most important things are the hardest to say. . . . It is difficult to describe what you mean to us, and when we try it comes out differently than how we wanted it. . . . A lot of teachers told me that I will never amount to anything. Well . . . isn't that encouraging. But one teacher actually told me I could be anything I wanted to be—if I put my mind to it. He said I could even be a writer. Now I know I wasn't born with a talent like Stephen King or anything. But I was able to write when I worked hard and especially when I was inspired. It wasn't until last year, however, that I was able to be creative on paper and actually enjoy it. The person who turned it all around . . . was the legendary . . . Max. . . . The only comfort is that he will teach teachers his effective ways, his brilliant methods, and maybe, just maybe . . . if it's possible . . . he'll teach teachers . . . to be in their own unique way . . . just like him. . . . "I am leaving" . . . those three words sounded like a thud and double locking of a tomb door. Our tomb door . . . the time we did have with you . . . we will cherish, brief as it was. Thank you for the greatest gift of all. . . . The gift of hope. . . . The knowledge to realize . . . I can be something. And the courage and strength to actually do it.

The class had voted to make this tribute a class tribute. And Max, he had spent the night at his computer, writing a response. Borrowing from Stephen Mitchell and *Tao Te Ching* (1988), he wrote: "A good athlete can enter a state of body awareness in which the right stroke or right movement happens by itself, effortlessly, without any interference of the conscious will." Max continued:

> It is this state of being that we must strive for. Before we can reach this state, we must, just as the athlete must, train our bodies, our minds, our hearts; train them to act, to think, to feel in ways that are true to each moment we live. The body must feel the pain which comes when muscles develop, when new skills thread the complex circuits of the brain. In those moments when body says, "no more," we must ask of it—"just a little more." When the mind wants not to ask another question, wants only to rest with what is, in that moment, we must ask of it—"just a little more." And, when the heart aches with the sorrow of loss, when it is discouraged, unwilling to live even now—let alone tomorrow—when such discouragement wants only cessation and not living, then and especially then, we must ask of it—"just a little more," just a little more of that love that encourages, that says to us "we must ALL help that it can be

done," the love that accepts the hurts we feel others impose on us as expression of their imperfection, their being still cloaked with foible, not yet ONE with the essence that binds humankind into a bond where we all become brothers and other, become each other's keepers, become ONE in Spirit. "It is this wonderful state of being in which we lose ourselves to find ourselves. . . . "

As Max had written this reply, he had wondered if he were really the student-centered teacher/learner that he had thought he had become. Was Becky expressing merely an appreciation? Or was it a dependence? He could not find answers.

Story XII: October 1990 (Max as Consultant)

Now, as a consultant, Max had wondered how he could work with teachers as he had finally learned to work with students.

The first months had been spent largely in the office trying to catch up on work not done during September when the position had been vacant. He had missed the classroom so very much. He had been lonely, depressed. How, in this madhouse office and this skirting around to schools, could he ever feel the love that he had always felt he and his students had given each other? He had become so disoriented that in the simple process of putting mail in a neighbor's mailbox he had slipped and fallen so forcibly to the cement step that it had taken seven stitches to close the head wound. Ironically, these were the only neighbors who had carpeted their steps. It had been a lonely time.

Gradually, very gradually, months later, he sensed change. The administration of one school had asked him to help Teresa teach English more effectively. They would arrange a half-day inservice for Teresa and some of her colleagues. Teresa needed to know how to plan thematic units. He had agreed. When he had arrived that afternoon, three cheerful female teachers entered the room—ten minutes late. He had already thought that this might well be difficult for him. They had sat in desks in a close circle. He had known that he was suspect simply because he was male. This had been one of the most difficult parts of his job so far. Each time he had met females for the first time, he could feel their mistrust for him. How better to respond than by listening, he had always thought and done, listening very carefully but without seeming nosy. But this time, however, he had to say something. He asked them to give him some background about themselves and their work in the classroom. What started as largely small talk quickly became significant talk, talk about philosophy, strategy, and teacher feeling and behavior.

He had said very little during the two hours, had only entered the discussion at the level of process, as he had always done during his later years with students—bringing together statements that they had made but had not pursued. He had been able to share some insights at strategic points, but really his comments were only reinforcement of what one of the three had usually already said or implied. He had, however, earned considerable trust from them. That, he had felt, had been most important. And so for the first time as a consultant, he had felt a glimmer of the excitement that he had experienced in the classroom.

Toward the end of the year things had changed quickly. He had walked into the school in which this discussion with the three female teachers had occurred months earlier. In the hall near the entrance, he had met Teresa, this teacher he was to have helped. When she saw him she hurried toward him, enthusiastically took his right hand in both of hers, and said, "I've been waiting to see you—how are you—can you come to my class—I don't know what to do for the last three weeks of term—these students don't want to do anything and I don't know what to do." Teresa and Max had agreed to do a three-week writing unit and to begin with the writing of poetry. Teresa had been skeptical. Her students were, after all, lower-level grade tens, poor attenders, lethargic, not interested, at least not in school. She had suggested that they try something with the "better" class of the three, and that Max teach several classes in a kind of model teaching role. Only one problem—they would not see this "better" class for four days, a bit late with only three weeks left till end of term. Max had agreed, nevertheless, but a day later he had called saying they needed to do it sooner. Too few days left in the term. When he had suggested the class the next day, she had expressed reservation. "It's a bad class, that one. They'll never write poetry." "Well," he had answered, "if you don't mind me failing, we'll do it with them." "No, I don't mind," she had answered, "I fail with them all the time. It will be nothing new."

Max had known he was now on the block. But then that was how he had lived his whole life. Always on the block of his own expectations and the expectations of others. For the rest of the day he had planned feverishly. He had planned his "model lessons," had planned the unit that Teresa could use after he left. He had planned every detail. Since these were the leather-jacketed, the unwashed, the tough eggs, he would wear jeans and a coarse-textured gray shirt—

sleeves rolled halfway to the elbow and two buttons open at the chest. He would have his overheads ready for snappy use, his sheets of poems handy for quick distribution. When the day came, Teresa was delighted that he had come. Enthusiastically she had helped him set the room—desks in a circle, sheets and overheads in strategic places. "How shall I introduce you?" she had asked. "Oh, just something short—like 'he works for the school division and he loves young people,'" he had answered.

As students walked into class as only these types could—a trio laughing hilariously over what seemed to be the latest joke, a pair glancing almost with ridicule at this visitor—he had taken his pose, slouched to the left with his left arm over the filing cabinet beside the door. When he had sensed some males mocking him, he had looked their way and responded half in jest, "You guys makin' fun of me?" with a half-smirk on his face, his eyes sending messages of forked meaning. They had all laughed, wholeheartedly, as if to break the ice. When Teresa had introduced him as someone who worked with the school division, some smart character asked if he was a bus driver. Max interrupted with, "Yeah, you guys ever driven a bus?" More laughter. This time a more relaxed, stronger laughter. Max had taken control, had told them that "we" wanted to take a look at poetry, read some, write some. Groans! He started by telling them that poetry was life, a way of saying a lot in just a few words, like a telephone conversation if we heard only one of its speakers. "What, poetry like a one-way telephone conversation?" a mouthy character at the back chuckled? Here was his chance. He improvised two brief one-way scenarios to illustrate that language use leaves much to the imagination:

1. Fearful son after smashing his father's car (father at the other end of line—not heard)
2. Son talks tough to a friend about the same event (jock friend at other end of line—not heard)

Then he proceeded to read a poem. "Who is talking here? What is happening?" he had asked. The baseball guys immediately recognized it was the catcher. "Is it a fake or a real voice? Why is he talking this way? Do we hear any other voices here besides the voice of the catcher?" Just as they began to talk, he interrupted and placed a second poem on the overhead—nothing needed saying. They had loved it. He had read several more poems, student-written ones.

The ice had been broken. They had loved him. And as usual, he had loved them. He had asked them to list five memories of their childhood. He had illustrated with his own memories of growing up on a farm—how he had been spanked at age five for smearing gun grease on the old shed door, all the gun grease that his father had bought for a whole year of farming; how his father had arranged with the farm hands to tease six-year-old Max to smoke four cigarettes and a cigar after he had been caught smoking cigarette butts rolled in catalogue paper while sitting in the outhouse. They had loved it.

The students listed their own memories. Max, too, listed his memories—more memories—for several minutes. Then he walked about them, helping, encouraging—a slap on the back of big Jim, a wink at slinky looking Todd, a warm smile for shy Nathan and for a very reticent Wanda. Meanwhile, he had insisted that Teresa, the regular classroom teacher, write with the students, become part of the process. Five minutes later he asked them to share their memories. Some had only two, some had seven; some memories brought laughter, some silence. But memories they had. Max then read a poem that he had written about one of his own memories. He had asked them to listen carefully because writers write about their own experiences, but in doing so they add stuff that did not actually happen. Writers imagine, Max had stated emphatically. They change experiences to blend into their own voice. And so Max read his poem aloud (shown in Figure 18.1).

After the reading, he had asked questions. "What was the real experience here? What was invented? What was the lie? Why do writers tell lies?" After some eager talk, he had asked them to take one of their experiences and to write a poem, to write in the voice that they had chosen to do the talking in the poem—to indicate to the reader how the voice might have felt by using line spacings, punctuation or its absence, words, rhythms, sounds, anything they wished to use; importantly, they were to change their experience to suit the voice of their speaker. As they had begun to write, Max had quickly written part of his own new poem; then he had again walked about the room. Everyone had tried. Max showed his own effort to those who could not get started. Later all but two students had read their poems. Wanda had seen his hurried effort and had proceeded to write about her night out on the streets. And Teresa, the teacher, had read a wonderful piece about her talk with her mother hours before going on her first date at sixteen. She had read it with flair. Max had noticed how these students had appreciated her effort. When the bell had rung, they scrunched up the papers on which they had written their poems. "No, no," Max had said rather loudly, "these you will save and show me when I come

```
                            6 yrs. old
        Frightened          (he put Dad's expensive gun grease on the
                                 old tractor-shed door
        Hiding.             (behind the old shed
                                 in the weeds, among old tires
        "Come here!"        (standing by the house
                                 waving left hand
                                 cedar shingle in the right
        He whimpered,
            slowly crept from the weeds trudged toward his Dad
                trudged toward his Dad
                    (wished he hadn't smeared
                        the door
                            with gun grease.

                Dad's expensive gun grease!
        "Don't you know I can't buy another can of gun grease!
        Don't you know that?"

                He nodded.
                    Feeling real bad now
                        (Dad not able to buy more gun grease
                        He hadn't thought about anything then
                            when he smeared it on the shed door
        "Pull your pants down!
            Bend over!"

                He felt the sting of the cedar shingle
                    His bum stung—
                        Once
                            Twice
                                Three times
                    . . . and a final time.

        "Git your pants on!
            Into the garden
                to pull the weeds!"

                He, crying bitterly, now,
                    making his way to the garden
                        to pull the weeds,
                    looking back just once
                        (to see his Dad,
                            head bent . . . forward . . .
                                . . . crying??? . . . too??? . . .
```

Figure 18.1. Max's poem about an incident in his childhood.

back at end of term." Slowly, but rather pleased, they had unscrunched their pieces of paper.

After they had left, Teresa was in glee. "You know," Max remembered telling her, "I bet you could do this yourself now." "I think I could too," she had answered enthusiastically, her voice higher, her hands clasped, her body riding on tiptoes.

Two weeks later, Max had arrived at her classroom just as the students had left for lunch. Teresa had been delighted. "I can't tell you how much fun we have had. And look how much they have written," she bubbled as she showed him their writing folders. "Would you have time to work with me all of next year?" she had asked. Max had felt better than he had ever felt as a consultant. Maybe consultant work was not so bad after all.

Five weeks later, after exams had been written, he had done a three-hour session with an entire English department on the nature of voice in reading, writing, listening, and talking. He had followed a similar approach. They had all brought a piece that they or their students had written. The discussion generated by these teachers about these writings illustrated all the concepts that he had wanted to share—that literature was less about themes and character sketches and more about voice and about voices, about discovering personal voices—the voices that these teachers had recognized in the writings that they had brought and those that they had recognized as they talked and shared. They had internalized their learning as they had explored these voices. Finally, with half an hour to go, he had been asked to tell them what he had prepared for them. Again, as he would have done in his classroom, he summarized the significant statements that these teachers had made, illustrated how they had touched on so many crucial points about voice and voices. When he had raised what might have seemed a new dimension, he would link it to some statement that they had made during the morning of talk.

When the session had come to a stop at lunch, their enthusiasm spoke the worlds of language that Max so much wanted to hear—language where their own experiences, and the words that they used to describe and shape these experiences, became meaning.

With these and other sessions during the latter part of his first year as consultant, he had begun to feel again the excitement that he had so repeatedly felt in his classroom. To help others gain confidence had always been his goal, and as they had gained it, unusual things had always happened. He saw that these teachers had left with a reassurance that they "could do it." And so he believed as firmly as ever that people had to feel confident before they could change. He knew that this had always been the case with him.

Epilogue

And as Max wondered if he was coming closer to the nonaction of the dancer becoming the dance, further words of Stephen Mitchell echoed their way through his consciousness: "Nothing is done because the doer has wholeheartedly vanished into the deed; the fuel has been completely transformed into the flame. This nothing is, in fact, everything."

Was this the mystery of which Placido Domingo had spoken, the mystery that had brought tears to the eyes of Professor Halstead? Max so wanted to reach this "nothing," this "everything," this "mystery" where the learning that is teaching would always remain freeing, exciting, and wonderfully mysterious.

References

Mitchell, S., trans. 1988. *Tao Te Ching: A new English version.* By Lao-Tzu. New York: Harper and Row.

Rosenblatt, L. 1978. *The reader, the text, the poem: The transactional theory of the literary work.* Carbondale: Southern Illinois University Press.

Editors

Alan D. Flurkey most recently taught first grade in the Phoenix area, where he has also taught fourth-, fifth-, and sixth-grade learning-disabled students and upper elementary grade students in a Communications Disorders self-contained program. He has presented at local, statewide, and national conferences on the topics of reading and learning disabilities. He is vice-president of the board of directors of the Center for Establishing Dialogue in Teaching and Learning, a nonprofit support organization serving teacher support groups in the Phoenix area. He is currently a doctoral student at the University of Arizona in the Program in Language and Literacy, where he is involved in reading research. He and his wife, Jane, co-chaired the second annual Whole Language Umbrella Conference.

Richard J. Meyer taught elementary school in New York State for sixteen years prior to earning his doctorate at the University of Arizona in Tucson. He has taught in inner-city, suburban, and rural schools. He is presently an assistant professor at the University of Nebraska–Lincoln, where he teaches graduate courses in literacy and literacy assessment, teaches undergraduate courses in literacy strategies, and supervises student teachers. He coauthored an article with Ken Goodman in a New York journal for principals and is also a contributor to *The Whole Language Catalog Supplement on Authentic Assessment.*

Contributors

Ethel Buchanan is a freelance language arts consultant and former elementary language arts consultant with the Winnipeg, Manitoba, School Division. She is past president and honorary life member of the Reading Council of Greater Winnipeg, and founder, past president, and honorary life member of the Child-Centered, Experience-Based Learning (C.E.L.) Group. She is editor of *For the Love of Reading,* author of *Spelling for Whole Language Classrooms,* and coauthor of *Reading, Writing and Caring* and *Where Butterflies Go.*

David B. Doake is professor in the Faculty of Management and Education, Acadia University, Wolfville, Nova Scotia. Beginning with a one-room school in New Zealand in 1945, he has taught in elementary and junior high schools, and for the past thirty years he has been involved in teacher education in New Zealand and Canada. His particular interest is in literacy development, and since 1977 he has been part of the whole language movement in North America. He has presented papers at conferences in Europe, Australia, the United States, New Zealand, Jordan, and in every province in Canada. He has numerous publications and videotapes on reading and whole language, including his forthcoming book, *Changing the Assumptions for Literacy Learning: A Revolution in Progress; Reading Begins at Birth;* and *Reading-like Behavior: Its Role in Learning to Read.*

Carole Edelsky is professor at Arizona State University. She received her Ph.D. from the University of New Mexico in 1974 and has since published research and essays on such topics as conversational analysis, gender and language, first- and second-language acquisition, literacy and literacy learning, bilingual education, and whole language. She has conducted workshops with teachers throughout the United States and Canada, working for several years with single schools interested in shifting to a whole language theoretical perspective. She is coauthor, with Bess Altwerger and Barbara Flores, of *Whole Language: What's the Difference?* and author of *With Literacy and Justice for All: Essays in Rethinking the Social in Language and Education.* She is currently researching the classroom interaction in an exceptional whole language classroom.

Rudi Engbrecht is presently English language arts consultant at the secondary level for the Winnipeg School Division in Manitoba. He taught high school from 1964 to 1990 and was president of the Canadian Council of Teachers of English, NCTE's sister organization, from 1988 to 1990. He has served on many provincial curriculum committees and is presently a member of the NCTE Standing Committee on Testing and Evaluation.

Carolyn Ewoldt is professor in the Faculty of Education at York University, Toronto, Ontario, where she teaches in the graduate program in Language and Literacy and the inservice program in Preparation of Teachers of Deaf and Hard of Hearing Students. She is author of *Speaking of Writing . . .* and is currently finishing two books based on seventeen years of research in deafness and literacy.

David Freeman and **Yvonne (Bonnie) Freeman** codirect the Language Development Program at Fresno Pacific College in Fresno, California, where he also directs the Secondary Education Program and she directs the Bilingual Education Program. Both are interested in whole language for second-language learners. In addition to staff development with school districts across the country, they present regularly at national and state conferences, including TESOL, NABE, NCTE, and IRA meetings. They have published articles jointly and separately on the topics of literacy, linguistics, bilingual education, and second-language learning in professional journals and books. They are coauthors of *Whole Language for Second Language Learners*.

Mary Kenner Glover cofounded Awakening Seed School in Tempe, Arizona, in 1977 as alternative education for her two young daughters. She is currrently director of the school and a teacher in a first/second-grade classroom; she has taught preschool through third grade since founding the school. She completed her M.A. in Elementary Education at Arizona State University in 1988. She is author of *Charlie's Ticket to Literacy* and *Two Years: A Teacher's Memoir,* and coauthor of *Not on Your Own: The Power of Learning Together.* She lives with her husband and two daughters in Tempe, where she also is an educational consultant, poet, and artist.

Yetta M. Goodman is Regents Professor of Education at the University of Arizona, Tucson. She is a member of the Department of Language, Reading and Culture in the College of Education, where she teaches courses concerned with language development, miscue analysis, and literacy processes and where she conducts research in early literacy development, the composing processes, and retrospective miscue analysis. Her research touches the lives of a range of populations of learners, demonstrating her interest in multicultural education. She is a well-known speaker and advocate for whole language—for children and for teachers.

Nigel Hall is Senior Lecturer in Education in the School of Education at Manchester Polytechnic in Manchester, England. He is author or coauthor of a number of books for teachers: *The Emergence of Literacy; "Some Day You Will No All about Me": Young Children's Explorations in the World of Letters; Literacy in Action;* and *Play in the Primary Curriculum;* as well as a number of books for young children. He lectures extensively all over the world and has served on the editorial board of *Language Arts and Reading.*

Wendy Hood has taught fifth grade, preschool, and Chapter 1 bilingual kindergarten in the Tucson, Arizona, area. She recently moved to a second-grade classroom, where she continues to learn and teach in a reading/writing whole language classroom. She has presented extensively at local, state, and national conferences and is well known for her child-centered focus. She has coedited two books with Ken and Yetta Goodman, *The Whole Language Evaluation Book* and *Organizing for Whole Language,* and has also contributed to *The Whole Language Catalog* and *The Whole Language Catalog Supplement on Authentic Assessment.*

Sarah Hudelson is a former elementary school teacher who worked in migrant and bilingual education programs in southern Texas and Detroit, Michigan. Since completing a Ph.D. from the University of Texas at Austin in 1975, she has been involved in bilingual/second-language teacher education in Texas, Arizona, and Florida. She currently teaches in the College of Education at Arizona State University, where her research interests focus on bilingual children's written language development. She has published in such journals as *The Reading Teacher, Language Arts, TESOL Quarterly,* and *NABE Journal* and is coeditor, with Judith Wells Lindfors, of *Delicate Balances: Collaborative Research in Language Education* (NCTE, 1993). She is a member of the board of directors of the Center for Establishing Dialogue in Teaching and Learning.

Judith Wells Lindfors is professor of Curriculum and Instruction at the University of Texas at Austin in the area of Language and Literacy Studies. Her special interest is in language acquisition, both first language and English as a Second Language. She has taught second grade in Massachusetts and Illinois, secondary English in Kenya, and adult ESL in California; she has worked with inservice teachers of children from many different backgrounds, including Hispanic American, Native American, Zulu, and Czechoslovakian. She is author of *Children's Language and Learning,* in which she makes connections between children's ways of developing and using language and the classroom environments that teachers provide, and is coeditor, with Sarah Hudelson, of *Delicate Balances: Collaborative Research in Language Education* (NCTE, 1993).

Norma Mickelson is a professor in the Faculty of Education at the University of Victoria in Victoria, British Columbia. She has a Ph.D. from the University of Washington, an M.A. from the University of Victoria, and a B.Ed. from the University of British Columbia (Victoria College). She was a teacher and supervisor of instruction before coming to the University of Victoria in 1968. In 1972, she was an I.R.A. Dissertation-of-the-Year Award winner. She is the author of many articles, monographs, and book chapters on literacy and on assessment and evaluation and is coauthor of *Evaluating Literacy: A Perspective for Change.* She is internationally known for her inservice work with teachers and administrators.

Adrian Peetoom has been involved in educational publishing for thirty years, as sales representative, manager, editor, author, and speaker. He is currently Director of Research and Development for Scholastic Canada in Chatham, Ontario. He has always worried more about the lasting effects of materials on learners than on making and selling "pretty packages." One of his recent pleasures has been time spent in the third-grade classroom where his oldest daughter is a whole language teacher.

Irene Alicia Serna teaches curriculum and instruction courses in Early Childhood and Bilingual Education at Arizona State University. Her research focuses on biliteracy development of young children. She taught for eight years in bilingual early childhood programs at Stanford University and the University of New Mexico.

Patrick Shannon is professor at Pennsylvania State University. He teaches one morning a week at the State College Friends' School and is author of *Broken Promises: Reading Instruction in Twentieth-Century America* and *The Struggle to Continue: Progressive Reading Instruction in the United States*, editor of *Becoming Political*, and coauthor of *Report Card on Basal Readers*. Currently he is working on two books: *Developing Democratic Voices*, a discussion of the what, why, and how of critical literacy in elementary schools, and *At Risk No More*, a study of literacy use and learning in the American labor, civil rights, and women's movements.

Kathy G. Short has focused her inquiry and teaching on children's literature and on reading and writing as authoring processes. She teaches graduate courses in children's literature at the University of Arizona in the Department of Language, Reading and Culture. She has worked extensively with teachers in their efforts to develop curricula that actively involve students in using reading and writing to learn. Much of her work has centered around integrating children's literature into the curriculum and literature circles. She is coauthor of *Creating Classrooms for Authors; Talking about Books: Creating Literate Classrooms;* and *Creating Curriculum: Teachers and Students as a Community of Learners.*

Dorothy Watson became the first president of the Whole Language Umbrella in 1989. She is a member of and receives personal and professional encouragement from her local support group, the Mid-Missouri TAWL. She spends a great deal of time talking with, and learning from, teachers, preservice teachers, and kids. She is a faculty member at the University of Missouri–Columbia.

Constance Weaver is professor of English at Western Michigan University in Kalamazoo, where she teaches courses on the reading and writing process and a whole language approach to literacy and learning. She has recently served as director of the NCTE Commission on Reading. Her major publications include *Understanding Whole Language: From Principles to Practice; Reading Process and Practice: From Socio-Psycholinguistics.to Whole Language;* and *Grammar for Teachers: Perspectives and*

Definitions (NCTE, 1979). She is a contributor to a debate in print, *Two Reactions to the Report Card on Basal Readers,* and coeditor, with Linda Henke, of *Supporting Whole Language: Stories of Teacher and Institutional Change.* She currently is coauthoring *Growing into Whole Language: An Odyssey in Theme Exploration* and is editing a collection of essays dealing with alternative approaches to educating students with attention-deficit disorders.